Management and Leadership – A Guide for Clinical Professionals

Sanjay Patole
Editor

Management and Leadership – A Guide for Clinical Professionals

 Springer

Editor
Sanjay Patole
Department of Neonatal Paediatrics
KEM Hospital for Women
Perth
West Australia
Australia

ISBN 978-3-319-11525-2   ISBN 978-3-319-11526-9 (eBook)
DOI 10.1007/978-3-319-11526-9
Springer Cham Heidelberg New York Dordrecht London

Library of Congress Control Number: 2014955167

Springer is part of Springer Science+Business Media (www.springer.com)

Foreword

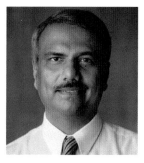 Management and leadership skills are critical for developing a successful and productive career, and achieving organisational goals. Irrespective of our designation, and knowingly or unknowingly, every day at work we play the role of a colleague, teacher, mentor, supervisor, manager, or a leader while dealing with the clients. Formal training in essential management and leadership skills is therefore an important issue for both, the employee and the employer. Unfortunately, it is often ignored or not provided enough attention in many organisations, especially those providing health care services.

Some of the most experienced authors from around the world have come together to provide an understanding of management and leadership skills that are essential for staff in a health care organisation, in a simple and clear fashion in this book. I am grateful to them for their valuable contributions, the quality of which reflects their expertise in various aspects of management as clinicians, supervisors, and managers. Without their help it would have been impossible to complete a book such as this in a remarkably short time.

The topics covered in this book range from preparing for an interview, the art of negotiation and handling difficult behaviour, to clinical leadership, evidence based management, and managing grief and its consequences at the workplace. I hope that with its simple and practical approach this book will be useful for all clinical and non-clinical staff working in a health care organisation irrespective of their faculty, position, and stage in career in developing the essential management and leadership skills. I would like to take this opportunity to thank Springer, their publishing editor Thijs van Vlijmen, and publishing assistant Sara Germans-Huisman for their encouragement and support in getting this unique book published. We hope that it will help readers in becoming successful consultants, managers, supervisors, and leaders at workplace.

Contents

Contributors

Sachin Amin Division of Neonatology, University of Illinois at Chicago, Chicago, IL, USA

Neonatal Intensive Care Unit, Children's Hospital of University of Illinois, Chicago, USA

Robert Anderson Department of Pastoral Care Services, Women & Newborn Health Service, King Edward Hospital for Women, City of Perth, WA, Australia

Child & Adolescent Health Service, Princess Margaret Hospital for Children, Perth, WA, Australia

Haribalakrishna Balasubramanian Department of Neonatal Paediatrics, King Edward Memorial Hospital for Women, Perth, WA, Australia

Rose Boucaut School of Health Sciences (Physiotherapy), University of South Australia, Adelaide, SA, Australia

Denise Bowen Mediation & Legal Support Services, Women & Newborn Health Service, KEM Hospital for Women, City of Perth, WA, Australia

Paul Byrne Stollery Children's Hospital, John Dossetor Health Ethics Centre, University of Alberta, Edmonton, AB, Canada

Catherine Campbell Neonatal Clinical Care Unit, King Edward Memorial Hospital, Western Australia

UWA Centre for Neonatal Research and Education, School of Paediatrics and Child Health, University of Western Australia, Western Australia

John Clark Department of Health, Institute of Health Leadership, East Perth, WA, Australia

The King's Fund, London, UK

University of Warwick Medical School, Coventry, UK

Marie-Louise Collins Department of Pastoral Care Services, Women & Newborn Health Service, King Edward Hospital for Women & Child & Adolescent Health, Service Princess Margaret Hospital for Children Perth, WA, Australia

Child & Adolescent Health Service, Princess Margaret Hospital for Children, Perth, WA, Australia

Paul Craven Neonatal Intensive Care Unit, John Hunter Children's Hospital, Newcastle, NSW, Australia

Matt Green BPP University School of Health, Abingdon, Oxfordshire, UK

Christopher Griffin Department of Maternal and Fetal Medicine, King Edward Memorial Hospital for Women, City of Perth, WA, Australia

School of Women's and Infants' Health, the University of Western Australia

Lucky Jain Department of Pediatrics, Emory University School of Medicine, Atlanta, GA, USA

Fiona Lake University of Western Australia School of Medicine and Pharmacology, Crawley, WA, Australia

Harry Perkins Institute of Medical Research, QEII Medical Centre, Nedlands, WA, Australia

Brendan Leier Stollery Children's Hospitals & Mazankowski Alberta Heart Institute, John Dossetor Health Ethics Centre, University of Alberta, Edmonton, Canada

Ravi Madhavan Katz Graduate School of Business, University of Pittsburgh, Pittsburgh, PA, USA

Olachi J. Mezu-Ndubuisi Departments of Pediatrics and Ophthalmology, School of Medicine and Public Health, University of Wisconsin, Madison, WI, USA

Brendan Paul Murphy Cork University Maternity Hospital, Cork, Ireland

Department of Paediatrics and Child Health, University College Cork, Cork, Ireland

Rajkishore Nayak School of Fashion and Textiles, RMIT University, Melbourne, Australia

Ajay Niranjan Department of Neurosurgery, University of Pittsburgh, Pittsburgh, USA

Rajiv Padhye School of Fashion and Textiles, RMIT University, Melbourne, Australia

Sanjay Patole Centre for Neonatal Research and Education, University of Western Australia, Perth, Australia

Department of Neonatal Paediatrics, King Edward Memorial Hospital for Women, Perth, WA, Australia

Aarti Raghavan Division of Neonatology, Department of Pediatrics Children's Hospital University of Illinois, University of Illinois Hospital and Health Sciences System, Chicago, IL, USA

Corinne Reid School of Psychology and Exercise Science, Murdoch University, Perth, WA, Australia

Paul Rothmore Discipline of Public Health, School of Population Health, University of Adelaide, Adelaide, SA, Australia

Bronwyn Shumack Clinical Excellence Commission, Sydney, NSW, Australia

Sarah Sloan Women and Newborn Service, King Edward Memorial Hospital for Women, Subiaco, WA, Australia

Deepika Wagh Department of Neonatal Paediatrics, King Edward Memorial Hospital for Women, Subiaco, WA, Australia

Princess Margaret Hospital, Perth, WA, Australia

Lijing Wang School of Fashion and Textiles, RMIT University, Melbourne, Australia

Chapter 1
Succeeding in Your Consultant Interview

Matt Green

There is a great deal of truth in the old adage: 'If you fail to prepare, you are preparing to fail'. This is especially true for securing your Consultant post. With a thorough understanding of the interview process and taking sufficient time to prepare, you will give yourself the best possible chance of succeeding

Abstract Whilst most doctors invest considerable time, energy and money into progressing their career from an academic point of view, few invest the same into securing their Consultant post. Despite possessing exemplary clinical, patient and interpersonal skills together with being held in high regard by their peers, many shortlisted candidates still fall down at the crucial Consultant Interview hurdle. When interviewing for Consultant posts, panels are looking for individuals who are aware of the challenges facing their particular field, have the potential to become accomplished leaders and are therefore worth investing in.

With thorough preparation, a clear understanding of the type of individuals the panel are looking for and a good grasp of the person specification, your Consultant Interview is something that you should view as an enjoyable experience. Remember when you are called to interview you have earned the right to be there. It is your opportunity to demonstrate your passion for your chosen specialty, outline what contributions you can make to the department and ultimately define why you should be offered the position over other candidates.

The key to succeeding in your Consultant Interview is preparation, preparation, preparation. If you are fortunate enough to be shortlisted and you turn up on the day of the interview ill prepared then you are destined to fall short. This chapter will explore the various stages you will need to work through to successfully secure your first choice Consultant post.

M. Green (✉)
BPP University School of Health, McTimoney House, Kimber Road, Abingdon, Oxfordshire, OX14 1BZ, UK
e-mail: mattgreen@bpp.com

© Springer International Publishing Switzerland 2015
S. Patole (ed.), *Management and Leadership – A Guide for Clinical Professionals,*
DOI 10.1007/978-3-319-11526-9_1

Keywords CV · Curriculum vitae · Application form · Person specification · Job description · Pre-interview visit · PIV · Interview · Confidence · Leadership · Psychometric testing · Mock interview · Communication skills · Team work · Clinical audit · Rapport · Clinical governance · Management · Advisory appointments committee · Risk management · Ethics and law · Complaint handling · Service innovation and improvement

Key Points

1. Invest the time to ensure that a particular opportunity is right for you, including undertaking a Pre-Shortlisting Visit
2. Gain sight of the Person Specification/Job Description for the vacancy at the earliest opportunity
3. Tailor your application to the particular opportunity in question
4. Ensure you make the most of your Pre-Interview Visit and remember you never get a second chance to make a first impression
5. Seek opportunities to practice your interview technique with senior colleagues and peers through mock interviews
6. Never leave the interview without correcting a glaring error

The first question that you must ask yourself before embarking on your journey to secure your Consultant post is 'Do I feel ready to undertake a Consultant post'? [1]

Clearly you will require the necessary paperwork to enable you to work at Consultant level together with the clinical skills required. However you must be realistic with yourself in terms of acknowledging whether you possess the non-clinical skills required of an effective Consultant which often separate candidates at interview when clinical skills are similar [2, 3].

Some of the skills required to succeed as a Consultant include [4, 5].

- Leadership
- Team working
- Problem solving & analytical approach
- Emotional intelligence
- Self-reflection
- Personal effectiveness and time management
- Ability to be flexible
- Current opinion and ethical challenges

Pre-Application Research & Pre-Shortlisting Visit

Research prior to application will make or break your application. The next step therefore is to research advertised Consultant posts and begin to identify whether they are suitable for you and whether you are suitable for them. It is important to note that if you are successful in the selection process you could very well spend the majority of your working career in that particular organisation.

Questions you should begin to ask yourself at this stage, and then can develop further through a Pre-Shortlisting Visit if you wish to progress with the application, are:

- Do I meet the criteria (generally essential & desired) required for the post?
- Are there any shortfalls in my experience I need to address?
- Can I see myself working in this organisation?
- Do the clinical priorities of the organisation fit in with my interests?
- Does the role provide desired opportunities in non-clinical areas such as teaching or research?
- What are the career progression opportunities available?
- Do I like the surrounding area to live in?
- Are there implications on my family I need to consider?

Sources of information you should seek to review are:

- The Job advert and the Person Specification
- The Organisation's Website and Intranet
- Care Strategy
- Annual Reports
- Informal discussions with members of staff during a Pre-Shortlisting Visit
- Regional and National Health Authority Websites

A Pre-Shortlisting Visit is when an individual who is interested in an advertised Consultant Post visits the department in a relatively informal manor with the sole aim of determining whether they feel they should apply for the post. It is important to remember that you never get a second chance to make a first impression. So even though informal those you speak to may be canvassed for opinion at the latter stages of the process. If you have made a bad first impression it is only going to count against you. In many ways you should view your interactions with the organisation as though you are a rising politician mounting a Public Relation campaign [6]. The more favourable impressions you make the better.

These visits take place prior to the advert for the post closing, so individuals have therefore not applied for the position. This is not the opportunity to canvas all of those likely to be on the panel but rather to speak to a select handful of people to determine whether the post is right for you.

Your questioning at this stage should be restricted to topics specific to you such as queries around the person specification, working logistics and the wider area. Those you should seek to speak with are the Clinical Director, the Directorate General Manager/Operations Lead, and a handful of Consultants and other staff working in the department.

Once you have identified opportunities that meet your career aspirations you are ready to submit your application.

The Application

After determining that a particular opportunity is right for you the next step in successfully securing your Consultant position is to become shortlisted. And the sooner you begin planning your application strategy the better. The first thing you need to do is to review the Person Specification or equivalent at the earliest opportunity, for example for a similar role advertised the previous year. This will allow you to see what the application process involves and the attributes that are being sought. Is it CV based or is an application form used?

If performed well ahead, this exercise can guide your personal development plan to ensure that, when the time comes to apply, you have as much of the required experience as possible and are in a strong position. Remember multiple people will be reviewing your application and you need to make it as easy for them as possible to pick out the salient points. Ensuring your application cross references the Person Specification as much as possible is key to achieving this. You must also ensure accuracy and consistency between your application form, CV and potentially any online profiles you may have such as LinkedIn.

If not required for the application itself you will need to distribute copies of your CV as part of the Pre-Interview visit. You should always tailor your CV to a particular opportunity, rather than using the same version repeatedly [7]. For example, if you are applying for a position where the Person Specification makes reference to significant weighting on say, teaching experience, you must ensure this is presented prominently in your CV. This can be achieved by listing your teaching experience towards the front of your CV, making reference to this in your professional statement on the first page and generally tailoring each section to put a teaching spin on it [8].

You can structure your CV along the following headings:

- Personal details
- Career statement
- Education and qualifications
- Career history
- Clinical skills and experience
- Management and leadership experience
- Development courses and conferences attended
- Research experience
- Clinical audit
- Presentations and publications
- Teaching experience
- Information technology skills
- Personal interests
- Referees

It is important not to embellish or include anything in your application that you are not prepared to expand on at the interview. The interview panel will have sight of your CV (and application form if needed) prior to the day and anything contained within are fair game for the panel to explore. A dim view will be taken if it comes to light that you have fabricated any facts.

In terms of the format and layout of your CV, consistency is the watchword here:

- The length should be as long as it needs to be but be mindful to keep the content short and succinct
- Use a strong font e.g. Ariel
- Font size—14 for headings, 10 for body text
- Follow a consistent format of layout
- Present information in chronological order
- Avoid solid blocks of text; use of bullet points

If you are unsuccessful in your application it is important that you ask for feedback. Identifying any areas for development will be helpful for future applications.

Pre-Interview Visit

If you are successful in being shortlisted for interview the next stage in the process is to arrange a more formal visit to the department, namely a Pre-Interview Visit (PIV).

The aim of the PIV is to:

- To demonstrate a genuine interest for the role rather than to simply canvass individuals
- Familiarise yourself with some of the individuals who will be interviewing you
- Understand the issues and challenges faced by the department
- Speak to other staff members to collect intelligence that will inform your approach to the interview itself

You should dress smartly as you would if attending the actual interview. More information on what to wear is detailed on page 10. Print lots of copies of your CV for you to take with you to hand to those you meet.

Who You Should See

Your interview itself will inevitably be a panel format with the individuals present commonly referred to as the Advisory Appointments Committee (AAC). When notified of being shortlisted you will be informed of the individuals comprising the AAC and be given the opportunity to contact some of them to arrange to meet them as part of your PIV. Failure to make contact with certain members of the AAC prior to the interview itself will reflect incredibly poorly on you. Members of the AAC to meet during your PIV can include the following (but be sure to follow the invitation guidance):

- Chief Executive Officer
- Medical Director
- Clinical Director
- Lead Clinician

The AAC comprises other members which you should not attempt to canvas as part of the PIV. These include the Chairman, the Royal College Representative and the University representative. If you do approach these individuals then you risk having your application thrown out. As mentioned previously it is important that you view this process as a Public Relations exercise where the primary aim is to create the right impression with as many people from the organisation as possible.

So do not limit yourself to only speaking to those on the AAC when conducting your PIV. You will be surprised just how many comments from other staff members get back to the AAC following a potential candidate's Pre-Interview Visit. Other members of staff to seek an audience with could include:

- Directorate General Manager
- Departmental Nursing Lead (Matron)
- Other Executive Directors e.g. Finance, Nursing, HR, Quality & Improvement, Corporate Development, Service Innovation and Improvement, Environment
- Departmental staff e.g. Consultants, Nurses.
- Other Departmental Leads e.g. If your in Paediatrics you should consider seeing the Obstetric Lead

Through engaging as many people as possible during your visit you will portray an all inclusive team working approach. When meeting with individuals it is important to convey an understanding of the importance of a strategic approach to moving the department forward. Your conversations can lay a solid foundation on which to build on during the interview and it is inevitable that your conversations will be reported back to and discussed between members of the AAC prior to the actual interview. You should also be mindful of departments that are located on split sites. If this is the case then it is important that you visit both sites to engage with all staff. During conversations set out to ensure you convey the following:

- Your reasons for wishing to apply for the post
- What you will bring to the post
- Acknowledgement of the challenges faced by the department
- That you wish to play a key role in 'strategic problem solving' within the department to move it forward.

General Questions to Seek Clarity On

Together with any outstanding questions about the logistics of the role it is important to gather as much knowledge as possible to appreciate the full picture of the department and the wider organisation.

- Discuss the role in greater detail to address any areas you are still unsure of?
- Confirm that the reasons that attracted you to apply for the position in the first place are still the case?
- Confirm what the expectations of the post are?
- Confirm the special interests of each of the members of the AAC?
- Whether there is an internal candidate?
- Strengths and weaknesses of the department and the wider organisation?
- Current departmental goals?
- Revenue generating priorities?
- Cost cutting areas?
- Patient experience priorities?
- Efficiency drivers?

Questions Specific to Individual Staff

Questions specific to individuals that seek to clarify key issues facing the department and the wider organisation include:

Member of staff	Information to clarify
Chief Executive Officer	Future direction and any sensitive topics for the trust
Medical Director	Perennial Managerial problems with regard to the Department and the wider organisation
Clinical Director	Clinical Shortfalls of the department
Lead Clinician	What the departments clinical interests are
Departmental Staff inc Doctors, Nurses, Physiotherapists, Ward Clerks, Technicians etc	What could be done differently, better, opportunities for improvement
Directorate General Manager	What the non-clinical perception of the directorate is and the interface between management and clinicians
Departmental Matron	Issues faced by nursing staff
Executive Directors	Strategic and topical issues

(Ghosh and Green [1])

Psychometric Testing

The use of psychometric testing is becoming more common in the Consultant Interview process. Although they may be used at the application stage they are more likely to be incorporated into the PIV for which you will be made aware of if this is the case. The aim of psychometric testing is to identify desired behavioural and personality characteristics for the role and you should never attempt to second guess the answers. Skills and traits that will be tested for are leadership, assertiveness, team working, propensity to stress and anxiety.

The Interview

Preparation Prior to the Day

There are a number of things that you should consider upon receiving the good news of being called to interview:

- Portfolio preparation
- Interview practice
- Presentation
- Right frame of mind and improving your confidence
- Dress code

Portfolio Preparation

Depending on the opportunity in question, together with the guidance you receive in your invitation to interview, you may be required to prepare a portfolio of evidence to bring with you to interview. The aim of the portfolio is to present your experience to date in greater detail for the panel to review if they so wish. The structure of the portfolio will be dictated to you but commonly these follow the same order as your CV. Again first impressions are key here so ensure that your portfolio is presented in a professional manner.

Interview Practice

The importance of interview practice should never be underestimated. The more time and effort you invest in practicing your interview technique the better. The time to make mistakes is in the safe environment of a mock interview and not on the actual day! The aim here is not to resemble an automaton regurgitating answers word for word but rather to come across during the actual interview as relaxed and composed. Together with practicing with peers you should attempt to participate in as many mock interviews with senior colleagues (at a very minimum this should be three). Constructive feedback on both the content and substance of your responses should be sought together with any feedback on your body language.

Presentation

Being asked to perform a presentation as part of the interview process is becoming increasingly common and could form part of the interview itself or be performed on a separate day. You could be informed of the topic in your invitation to interview or provided with the topic on the day of the interview itself. Either way it is important that you identify why you are being asked to present on a particular topic and take the appropriate steps to ensure you follow the guidance and address the topic being asked. You will receive clear guidance on expectations regarding duration and what audiovisual equipment you will have available. As with practicing your interview technique it is vitally important that you gain plenty of presentation practice prior to the day to ensure that your performance is polished.

When performing your presentation employ the IMS approach:

- *I*ntroduction – begin by outlining what you will cover
- *M*ain body of the presentation
- *S*ummary and conclusions

For example a topic could include 'Prepare a 15-minute presentation on how you would improve the department if XXX funds were made available to you'

Right Frame of Mind and Improving Your Confidence

The right frame of mind will directly influence your performance on the day. Ensure you have an early night the evening before and are clear on the timings of the day and directions. Aim to arrive early as there is nothing worse than arriving late and flustered on such an important day of your professional career. Upon arriving go for a walk, read your notes. You know what works for you—ensure you do it!

Your level of confidence will stem from the amount of time and effort you have invested in preparing for the day. The more prepared you are the more calm you will feel. If you do suffer from nerves on the day do research techniques that can be employed on the day to calm yourself such as positive visualisation, anchoring and 'Top 50' achievement lists.

Dress Code & Building Rapport

How you dress is not your opportunity to make a particular statement. This should be left to the responses you give. You should dress smartly, professionally and conservatively to ensure the focus of the interview is upon your answers and the rapport that you build with the interview panel. Inappropriate clothing, club ties, jewellery and strong aftershave/perfume/cooking smells should be avoided.

How you come across in the interview will be dictated by more than just the answers you provide. What if everyone on the day has the same clinical skills, qualifications and experience? How do you ensure that you stand out for the right reasons?

If everyone on the day does indeed have the same clinical skills, qualifications and experience how you present yourself in terms of dress, communication and enthusiasm is what will make the difference. According to the research by Mehrabian when communicating words account for 7%, tone of voice accounts for 38%, and body language accounts for 55% of the impact it has on the audience [9].

Remember the panel are looking for an individual that will 'fit in' with the department. It is therefore important to build a positive rapport with every member of the panel. Steps you can take to achieve this are:

- Posture—be mindful of your seating posture and overuse of hand gestures
- Eye contact—engage all members of the panel when providing your answers
- Speech—avoid monotone answers and to not speak too quickly. Ensure your responses are neither too long nor too short.
- Smile
- Avoid being controversial in your answers
- Be positive
- Don't rush your answers (repeat the question out loud to give you time to compose your response if need be)

Questions You Will Encounter

Upon entering the interview room you will encounter questions on a whole variety of topics. It can be helpful to understand that the questions can be grouped into four broad categories [10]:

- **Questions of fact**—require an expression of your working knowledge of your speciality and any current hot topics and are usually used as warm up questions e.g. 'Can you tell me the annual government budget for treating XXX?'
- **Questions of reflection**—reflective attributes are key to continued success and will be appraised in the interview. These can be grouped into distinct subsets including application/role, speciality, personal qualities, and closer scrutiny. e.g. 'What do you dislike about this specialty?'

- **Questions of opinion**—require a balanced expression of the positives and negatives in response to a particular question together with a measured conclusion. There are no right or wrong answers to these but they do require a viewpoint being drawn.

e.g. 'What is your opinion on the new approach of XXX for treating the condition XXX?'

- **Questions of scenario**—require the problem to be identified and when responding to questions of this type it is helpful to begin by framing the situation i.e. 'I believe this is a case of unethical behaviour from a colleague'. Solutions commonly require a patient safety or service improvement focus.

e.g. 'You are on a night shift when you stumble across a fellow Consultant viewing child pornography, what would you do?'

Structuring Your Responses

An effective approach to composing high quality responses is to follow the **NEURO** approach as described [11]:

- *New*—Have you already mentioned a particular scenario/topic in a previous response or are you striving to introduce as many different examples of your diverse experience and/or understanding of a particular area into the interview? The broader a picture that you paint of your experience the better.
- *Example*—Is the particular scenario/topic you intend to use relevant to the question you are being asked? Begin your responses by briefly setting the scene and putting your response in context.
- *Unique*—Is your response unique in terms of helping you to stand out over your rival applications? The higher and rarer the achievement the better you will fare with the interview panel.
- *Role*—What was your role in the response given? For example leading a particular project or initiative is obviously a much stronger example than playing a small part in it. Does your description of the role you played address what is being asked in the question? Does your answer focus on what you achieved and not what others did? Do not try to pass off someone else's achievement as your own.
- *Outcome*—What did you achieve? How is it special? What did you learn from the experience? How has it informed your decision to follow your chosen specialty? How has it made you a better doctor?

Key Concepts

When you are asked a question it is important to determine in your mind why you are being asked the question and into what context it fits in with the below (awkward ending).

- **Non-Clinical Skills**—your clinical skills should be a given. Focus your responses on demonstrating an awareness of leadership, the organisational structure, business planning, financial considerations, complaint handling and ethical considerations.
- **Standards**—have a clear understanding of the relevant standards to your speciality. These can be national standards through to speciality specific standards together with local standards. Virtually all questions will be linked to standards in some way or another and therefore a comprehensive working knowledge of these in relation to your speciality are paramount.
- **Questioning**—understand that a number of different questions can be asked to ascertain the same thing e.g. strengths, weaknesses, leadership competencies
- **Opinion**—have an opinion but don't be too opinionated! The interview is not the forum to be overly controversial. Striking a balance between demonstrating a sound professional opinion but at the same time giving the impression you can fit into a team is key.
- **Specialty**—always strive to relate your answers to your specialty and the interviewing organisation.
- **Hot topics**—know what local and national hot topics are likely to come up in the interview and ensure that you are fully conversant in them in terms of governance, quality and safety and how they reflect on your specialty and the wider healthcare landscape

The Political Landscape

In preparation for your interview it is important to have a clear understanding of the political landscape in the form of the National as well as regional Health Governing bodies and the organisation's Boards and divisional/directorate structures, functions and responsibilities.

Questions You May be Asked—For Use in Mock Interviews

Below are a series of questions that you may come up against in your interview and you can use as part of your mock interview practice with colleagues.

Questions of fact	1. 'What year did you complete your membership exams'?
	2. 'When was the XXX standards document published?'
	3. 'How long did it take you to complete XX?'
	4. 'How many beds are currently in our organisation?'
	5. 'What services does your current employer provide?'
	6. 'Who is your current Medical Director/Chief Executive? What is their background?'
	7. 'How did you hear about this opportunity?'
	8. 'Where did you complete your training?'
	9. 'How long have you been applying for positions?'
	10 'Are there any areas of competence that you still require further development in?'

Questions of Reflection

Your application	1. 'So why do you want to join our organisation?'
	2. 'What do you feel you will be able to contribute to our department?'
	3. 'What do you think will be your biggest challenge in the role?'
	4. 'What will be your biggest contribution to the department?'
	5. 'Why did you apply for this post?'
	6. 'I see from your CV that you worked with XX at XX, what was that like?'
	7. 'I see from your employment history that you moved from XX to YY in 20XX, why was that?'
	8. 'I see from your CV XX, why did you do that?'
	9. 'What will you do if you are not offered this post?'
	10. 'How many research publications do you have?'

Your Specialty	1. 'Where do you see the future of your specialty in 5/10/15-years?'
	2. 'Tell us about a recent advancement in your specialty that you feel could be of benefit to our department?'
	3. 'What are the challenges facing modern day doctors in our specialty?'
	4. 'How would you persuade/dissuade a colleague to follow a career in this chosen speciality'
	5. 'What do you think about the latest development XX in our chosen specialty?'
	6. 'What areas of our speciality do you dislike?'
	7. 'If you could make one improvement to our specialty what would it be?'
	8. 'If you could have your time again what changes would you make to your career?'
	9. 'What steps have you taken to ensure that this is the right career move for you?'
	10. 'How do you intend to keep abreast with new developments in our speciality'
Personal Qualities	1. 'Why should we offer you the role over your rival candidates?'
	2. 'What are your strengths?'
	3. 'What are your weaknesses?'
	4. 'What will you bring to the post?'
	5. 'How would you describe yourself in three words?'
	6. 'Where would you like to be in 5/10/15 years times?'
	7. 'How would your colleagues describe you?'
	8. 'How have you learned from your mistakes in the past?'
	9. 'Tell us about an obstacle you have encountered in your career? How did you overcome it?'
	10. 'What patient feedback would we see for you?'
Additional questions	1. 'How do you maintain your work life balance?'
	2. 'Tell us about your life away from medicine?'
	3. 'How do you unwind after a stressful day at work?'
	4. 'How do you cope with stress?'
	5. 'Why do you think doctors suffer from stress?'
	6. 'What are the key leadership skills required of doctors?'
	7. 'Do all doctors need to be leaders?'
	8. 'Are you a leader or a follower?'
	9. 'What attracts you to teaching/research/management?'
	10. 'What experience do you have in the planning, preparation and execution of a business case?'

Questions of Opinion	1. 'What do you think the Government's key priorities should be with regards to this specialty?'
	2. What is the role of the national body XX? Do you think they are doing a good job?
	3. Do you think appraisal works?
	4. 'Do you think clinical audit works?'
	5. 'Should practicing doctors spend less time on research and more time on seeing the patient?'

Questions of Scenario

Service Innovation and Improvement	1. 'The organisation has made available funds of XXXXX to you. What would you spend the money on within the department?'
	2. 'Upon starting your role in the department it is identified that budget cuts of 10 % need to be sought—what steps would you take to identify where these cuts can be made?'
	3. 'Six months into your post you attend a conference that highlights some positives advancements in your speciality—what steps will you take to transfer this new best practice back into the workplace?'
	4. 'You are approached by a medical devices company who showcase a device that believe will enhance patient outcomes, what do you do?'
Complaints & Risk Assessment	1. 'How do you deal with a patient complaint?'
	2. 'How would you approach a complaint that has been made by a patient's family towards one of the junior doctors in your team?'
	3. 'A complaint has been made by a patient towards one of the senior nursing staff's rude manner, what steps will you take to address this?'
	4. 'Upon commencing in your new role it becomes apparent that complaints in the department are at an all time high and you are asked to implement measures to address this, talk us through how you will go about this?'
Poor Performance	1. 'You stumble upon a Consultant colleague viewing pornography in the staff room on his laptop what do you do?'
	2. 'One of the junior doctors in your team is persistently arriving late/leaving early on their shift, what steps will you take?'
	3. 'You suspect one of the junior doctors has been drinking whilst on shift, they smell of alcohol, what do you do?'
	4. 'A member of your team is constantly being rude and obnoxious to colleagues, how will you address this?'

Ethics and Law	1. 'A female patient in her mid-forties who has been under your care for the past 6-months has provided you with a gift in the form of a very expensive watch, what do you do?'
	2. 'A seemingly competent elderly female in her seventies persistently keeps withdrawing her consent to treatment that will vastly enhance her quality of life, what steps do you take to address this?'
	3. 'You come on shift and it becomes immediately apparent that a 29-year-old male has received a blood thinning agent that could be life threatening, how do you deal with this?'
	4. 'It has become clear that ongoing treatment for a terminally ill patient will no longer provide any clinical benefits. How will you approach this with the patient and their family?'

Ending the Interview—Questions for You to Ask

At the end of the interview when asked if you have any questions ensure you choose your words carefully. It is perfectly acceptable to say that you have covered all the questions you had during your Pre-Interview visit and would like to thank everyone for the opportunity of being invited for Interview.

Never, ever, raise questions about how much you will be paid, holiday allocation etc. Also never leave an interview feeling that you should have corrected an answer—obviously you can't go back and correct all of the answers you have given but if there is one question that you wish you had provided an alternative answer then do so!

And Finally….

I would like to take this opportunity to wish you the best of luck with securing your first choice post and all the best for the future!

References

1. Ghosh R, Green M (2012) Succeeding in your consultant interview: how to stand out for the right reasons. BMJ Car 15 Feb:6–7
2. Green M, Gell L (2012) Effective medical leadership for consultants: personal qualities and working with others. BMJ Car Nov 14:3–4
3. Green M, Gell L (2012) Effective medical leadership for consultants: managing services, improving services & setting direction. BMJ Car Nov 28:6–7
4. Christie S, Green M (2012) How to improve your time management skills. BMJ Car Feb 22:6–7
5. Spurgeon P, Klaber B, Green M (2012) Becoming a better medical leader. BMJ Car Jan 31:6–7
6. Opaneye O (2013) Becoming a consultant: how to succeed at interview. BMJ Car 4 Apr:7
7. Green M (2011) Preparing the perfect medical CV. BMJ Car 1 Sept:67–68
8. Green M (2010) Preparing winning CVs and application forms. BMJ Car 15 Sept:8–9
9. Mehrabian, A (1971) Silent messages (1st ed). Wadsworth, Belmont
10. Ghosh R (2012) Succeeding in your consultant interview (2nd ed). BPP Learning Media, London
11. Green M (2011) Shining through at a specialty training interview. BMJ Car 27 Sept: 102–103

Further Reading

12. Ghosh R (2012) Succeeding in your consultant interview (2nd ed). BPP Learning Media
13. Spurgeon P, Klaber B (2011) Medical leadership: a practical guide for tutors and trainees. BPP Learning Media

Chapter 2
Clinical Leadership and Engagement: No Longer an Optional Extra

John Clark

> *...the quality of clinical leadership always underpins the difference between exceptional and adequate or pedestrian clinical services which in aggregate determine overall effectiveness, safety and reputation*
>
> —(Sir Bruce Keogh, NHS, UK) [1]

Abstract Effective clinical leadership and engagement are increasingly being recognised as important contributors to the delivery of high standards of clinical care and organisational performance. This chapter argues that it is no longer acceptable for a doctor just to be a clinical expert. Other competences, including appropriate management and leadership skills, should be integral elements of practice and thus need to be included as part of selection of medical students and doctors at all levels as well as incorporated within education and training.

This chapter outlines some of the key management and leadership competences all doctors at every level should attain. It also provides some advice on how best these might be realised during postgraduate training.

Whilst all doctors as practitioners require a basic tool-kit of management and leadership competences others, who decide to move into positional leadership roles, will potentially need some more advanced ones.

However, engaging doctors in the running, planning and improvement of services, in conjunction with other clinical and non-clinical managers and leaders, is critical to the delivery of high quality care. This chapter will discuss what good clinical engagement can look like and offers advice on how doctors can help create service and organisational cultures where patient-care is genuinely the number one priority.

J. Clark (✉)
Department of Health, Institute of Health Leadership, Level 2B, 189 Royal Street, East Perth, WA 6004, Australia
e-mail: john.m.clark@health.wa.gov.au

The King's Fund, London, UK

University of Warwick Medical School, Coventry, UK

© Springer International Publishing Switzerland 2015
S. Patole (ed.), *Management and Leadership – A Guide for Clinical Professionals,*
DOI 10.1007/978-3-319-11526-9_2

Key Points

- With increasing emphasis on clinical leadership and engagement, doctors are expected to not only be clinical experts but also have management and leadership skills
- Working collaboratively not only in the clinical domain but also in management and leadership leads to more effective outcomes
- The terms leadership and management are often used interchangeably but there are important differences. Leaders ask themselves "where are we going" whereas managers tend to ask "how do we get there?"
- The five domains of the medical leadership competency framework include demonstrating personal qualities, working with others, managing and improving services, and setting direction. However delivering highest quality services to patients, service users, carers and the public is at its heart.
- Engagement of clinicians as a 'shareholder' in the running, development and improvement of their specialty or service should not be an optional extra. It should be central to their role as a good doctor.

Keywords Medical leadership · Clinical leadership · Physician leadership · Medical engagement · Staff engagement · Medical leadership competences · Leadership development

Health organisations are putting increasing emphasis on clinical leadership and engagement for the delivery of the highest quality of care. This chapter seeks to demonstrate that to be a good doctor in the twenty first century requires good management and leadership ability as well as clinical expertise. Once a doctor is appointed to a consultant or GP position they ipso facto become leaders in their specialty, service or hospital not necessarily in a formal leadership role but as professionals who are expected to give a lead. Some doctors once appointed as consultants take on positional roles (part or full-time) e.g. Head of Department, Director of Education, Clinical Director or Director of Clinical Services at some stage but all doctors at every level in their practitioner roles need to practice good management and leadership. It should not be an optional extra.

The desire for greater medical leadership and engagement within healthcare organisations needs to be understood within what organisational theorists call professional bureaucracies [1]. In such organisations, front line staff have considerable control over the content of the work they do by virtue of their training and specialist knowledge. Executives, and particularly non-clinical executives, will often have considerable difficulty directing those that they feel should be under their control often leading to minimal impact or indeed downright resistance. In essence, this means that clinical staff and particularly doctors can have greater influence than the hierarchy might initially suggest. This can, of course, be both positive and negative and highlights the importance of effective leadership and engagement at all levels and recognition that clinicians and managers working closely together to enhance clinical services should be the goal.

Doctors have been involved in the running of health services, locally, nationally and internationally since the pioneers who initiated and organised health services many centuries ago. What is new is the emerging evidence of the relationship between the extent to which doctors are engaged in the planning, prioritization, shaping and improvement of services and the wider performance of that service and organisation, including clinical outcomes and quality of care [1].

What is Clinical Management and Leadership?

Later in this chapter the range of management and leadership competences that all doctors and indeed all clinical professionals should practice will be explored and how they might be acquired and when? But what do we mean by management and leadership?

A quick review of any airport bookstall will confirm that there are probably more books and texts on management and leadership than any other subject. There are thousands of definitions and descriptions and numerous serious and less-serious authors offering their particular nuance. One of the most quoted definitions is perhaps from John Kotter [2] who differentiates between management processes that are concerned with planning, budgeting, organising, staffing, controlling and problem-solving and leadership processes that involve establishing direction, aligning people, motivating and inspiring.

The King's Fund, an independent charity ('Think Tank') that works to improve health and health care in England, has undertaken considerable research and published widely on health management and leadership, particularly clinical. Their website (www.kingsfund.org.uk) offers some rich material that should be of interest to readers of this book. In their Commission [3], The Fund defines leadership as the art of motivating a group of people to achieve a common goal. This demands a mix of analytical and personal skills in order to set out a clear vision of the future and defining a strategy to get there. This requires good communication skills and ensuring the appropriate skills are assembled to achieve it.

As the Commission also highlighted, leadership requires considerable management skills to get any job or change implemented and confirms that leadership in healthcare is needed from the executive team or board to the ward and should involve clinicians as well as managers.

There is perhaps some perceived sense of differential status between being called a medical administrator, manager or leader. Some may argue that a medical administrator or manager is more about maintaining the status quo whereas a medical leader conjures up a vision of a heroic leader driving change. It is perhaps no coincidence that more doctors appear to be willing to get involved in leadership if it is about leading service improvements and with the title of physician or medical leader.

Over the past decade, there has been a steady growth of designated medical leadership roles. Initially, many of these were seen as roles to represent medical colleagues in the senior executive governance arrangements. This often meant a sense of doctors taking it in turns to assume the role, generally reluctantly. Over time, as

Table 2.1 Characteristics of management and leadership. (Bolman and Deal [6])

Aspect	Management	Leadership
Style	Transactional	Transformational
Power base	Authoritarian	Charismatic
Perspective	Short-term	Long-term
Response	Reactive	Proactive
Environment	Stability	Change
Objectives	Managing workload	Leading people
Requirements	Subordinates	Followers
Motivates through	Offering incentives	Inspiration
Needs	Objectives	Vision
Administration	Plans details	Sets direction
Decision-making	Makes decisions	Facilitates change
Desires	Results	Achievement
Risk management	Risk avoidance	Risk taking
Controls	Makes rules	Breaks rules
Conflict management	Avoidance	Uses
Opportunism	Same direction	New direction
Outcomes	Takes credit	Gives credit
Blame management	Attributes blame	Takes blame
Concerned with	Being right	What is right
Motivation	Financial	Desire excellence
Achievement	Meets targets	Finds new targets

demands for greater improvements in quality, efficiency and resolving inappropriate variations have increased, so doctors have increasingly been extorted to move from representational to executive roles.

As Griffiths et al [4] comment, the terms *leadership and management* are often used interchangeably but note there are important differences i.e. managers work within a system to maintain or meet goals and direction through effective use of resources. They contrast this with leaders who set the vision and direction and motivate others to achieve the goals. Put simply, leaders ask themselves "where are we going" whereas managers tend to ask "how do we get there?"

Long [5] refers to the work of Bolman and Deal [6] which reaffirms that leading and managing are distinct but both are important. They provide a really useful taxonomy of the characteristics of management and leadership as outlined in Table 2.1.

Exercise

You might want to consider the characteristics of management and leadership in the table above and use it to self-assess and also perhaps to assess a manager and a leader you know well in your organisation.

Understanding that there is no single universal and evidence-based set of characteristics that define an effective leader is often hard for doctors with scientific leanings to understand. It means that individuals with different qualities can contribute very effectively as leaders but in different ways, depending on their own personal sets of strengths and weaknesses.

Shared leadership is becoming more and more prevalent in health organisations. The days of the heroic leader are perhaps becoming history. As healthcare becomes ever more dependent on multi-disciplinary working so it is becoming increasingly recognised that working collaboratively not only in the clinical domain but also in management and leadership leads to more effective outcomes. Evidence shows that shared leadership often involving at specialty level the Clinical Head of Department, Nurse Unit Manager and Business Manager can create the climate for innovation and improvement. In some of the top performing hospitals in the USA, the Board hold the duality of the medical leader and business manager at specialty or directorate level jointly accountable for performance; joint rewards for good performance and joint penalties for poor performance.

Alimo-Metcalfe and Franks [7] argue that the new focus for leadership is on how to increase employee engagement with the aim to increase not only the performance of the organisation but also the satisfaction of its employees. This notion of greater engagement will be explored later in this chapter.

What Management and Leadership Competences Do ALL Doctors Need?

You will be very familiar with competency frameworks throughout your medical education, training and practice. Until fairly recently, few frameworks explicitly included management and leadership competences although historically some have been incorporated within, for example, professionalism, personal or professional development, communication skills and teamwork. More recently, some student-selected modules have offered management and leadership outside the core curriculum.

The UK, Denmark and Canada have perhaps led the way in seeking to develop a common and recognised management and leadership framework for all doctors. Other countries, including Australia, through the Royal Australasian College of Medical Administrators (RACMA), have developed excellent management and leadership frameworks for doctors moving into positional leadership roles but it is my contention that doctors at all levels should attain a core set of management and leadership competences to be a good doctor.

The Royal College of Physicians and Surgeons of Canada developed the CanMEDS Roles Framework and associated competences. CanMEDS is not a medical management and leadership group of competences. It offers a high level of description and implies a range of underlying sub-sets of competences in terms of how these would actually be achieved in practice through the application of specific skills and knowledge to particular situations. It, in effect, describes what is expected of a good doctor i.e. in addition to being a medical expert, a doctor should be a:

- Professional
- Communicator
- Collaborator
- Manager
- Health Advocate
- Scholar

This CanMEDS network is now informing many other frameworks around the world. The original framework (2005) and later iterations can be accessed at www.royalcollege.ca.

In response to various scandals of poor care being delivered in NHS hospitals (UK), the medical profession was put under pressure during the first decade of this century to take a more active role in the management, leadership and improvement of health services. This led to the development of a Medical Leadership Competency Framework (MLCF) jointly by the Academy of Medical Royal Colleges (AoMRC) and the NHS Institute for Innovation and Improvement (NHS Institute) [8] in 2008. It has subsequently been refined but the MLCF describes the leadership competences doctors need to become more actively in the planning, delivery and transformation of health services as a normal part of their role as doctors.

The purpose of the MLCF is to provide the medical professional, regulatory, educational and service bodies and individual doctors with a description of the core management and leadership competences expected of all doctors as they graduate from medical school, progress though postgraduate education and training and become consultants or GPs. Although some of the competences might have previously been implicit in medical education and training, the MLCF provides a consistent and explicit framework that should apply to all medical school curricula, postgraduate education and college standards. The whole concept of the MLCF is based on the concept of shared or distributed leadership where leadership is not just the province of those in positional roles but where there is a shared responsibility for the success of the service or hospital.

The General Medical Council (GMC) in the UK has provided some very powerful messages about the importance of medical leadership. *Tomorrow's Doctors* [9] specifies expected outcomes and standards of undergraduate medical education including the need for doctors to have a commitment to improving healthcare and providing leadership. This view has been reinforced in the GMC paper *Leadership and Management for all doctors* [10] which stresses the importance of all doctors at all levels providing leadership and vision as well as contributing to improvements in the quality of service. The GMC's *Good Medical Practice* [11] is even more specific offering some key ethical guidelines with reference to professional and personal responsibilities of doctors as leaders. These include working with colleagues, communication, teamwork and service improvement along with many other competences.

There are five domains of the MLCF (Fig. 2.1) but delivering services to patients, service users, carers and the public is at the heart. The premise is that EVERY

Fig. 2.1 Medical leadership competency framework image. (The Medical Leadership Competency Framework and associated graphics are © NHS Leadership Academy and Academy of Medical Royal Colleges, 2010. All rights reserved)

doctor should be competent in each domain to deliver appropriate, safe and effective services.

Each of the five high level domains is divided into four elements and each of these is further divided into four competency outcomes (Table 2.2).

Whatever stage you are in your career as a doctor, the MLCF should apply to you. As Spurgeon and Klaber [12] confirm, the MLCF was designed to be relevant to doctors at all levels; undergraduate, postgraduate and the first revalidation following award of Certificate of Specialist Training. It provides a progressive statement of the relevant management and leadership competences that need to be acquired over time. For example, it would not be appropriate for a medical student to be required to demonstrate ability in *Setting Direction* upon graduation but *working within teams* would clearly be important.

The figure below (Fig. 2.2) offers a general sense of which particular competences should be acquired at different stages of career.

Exercise

Undertake a self-assessment of your management and leadership competences by accessing the following MLCF website: www.leadershipacademy.nhs.uk/discover/leadership-framework/

List those where you have identified development needs and consider how you might best meet them.

Table 2.2 The medical leadership competency framework domains

Domain	Elements
Demonstrating personal qualities	Developing self-awareness
	Managing yourself
	Continuing personal development
	Acting with integrity
Working with others	Developing networks
	Building and maintaining relationships
	Encouraging contribution
	Working within teams
Managing services	Planning
	Managing resources
	Managing people
	Managing performance
Improving services	Ensuring patient safety
	Critically evaluating
	Encouraging improvement and innovation
	Facilitating transformation
Setting direction	Identifying the contexts for change
	Applying knowledge and evidence
	Making decisions
	Evaluating impact

More recently Health Workforce Australia (HWA) has developed Health LEADS Australia: the Australian health leadership framework. It focuses on the capabilities required to deal with contemporary Australian health issues and builds on validated international work. It has five areas for focus:

- (L)eads self
- (E)ngages others
- (A)chieves outcomes
- (D)rives innovation
- (S)hapes systems

The framework is being developed and has the potential to inform future curricula for medical and indeed all clinical professionals. It can be accessed at www.hwa. gov.au

Management and Leadership Training and Development

An increasing number of health organisations and medical colleges are now offering management and leadership training and development. Some Departments of Health and Health Services in Australia, particularly Western Australia and Vic-

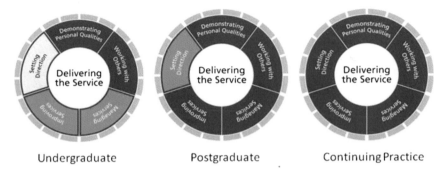

Undergraduate   Postgraduate   Continuing Practice

Fig. 2.2 The Medical Leadership Competency Framework and associated graphics are © NHS Leadership Academy and Academy of Medical Royal Colleges, 2010. All rights reserved

toria, have schemes where junior doctors are encouraged to take time out of their specialty training to undertake a service improvement project and to learn more about management and leadership that is relevant to their stage of career. Some very impressive initiatives have been implemented and a new cadre of doctors keen to be engaged in shaping the future modus operandi for delivering care is being created.

Other enlightened health systems, hospitals and health services are recognising that management and leadership training and development should be offered to all new consultants and well before some may take on positional leadership roles. The days of remedial management and leadership development for Clinical Heads of Departments etc should be past but there is still some way to go.

Historically, a few doctors have opted to study for a Masters in Business Administration or Management but there is now some increasing interest in studying for a postgraduate program in medical or clinical leadership focused on specific local issues i.e. theory applied to the context of the participant's workplace. Such programs can be just for medical leaders e.g. Clinical Heads of Department or perhaps the clinical department leadership team studying and working together to solve local issues.

Some of the best performing hospitals and services internationally are typified by sustained investment in management and leadership. Some of the development programs are uni-disciplinary, particularly for postgraduate trainee doctors and new consultants. Others reflect the multi-disciplinary nature of healthcare delivery and are included within a suite of development programmes for all senior managers and leaders. Learning about management and leadership with others particularly around real local issues helps create the culture of mutual respect and partnership working.

Most hospitals and health services have someone with responsibility for management and leadership development and this person should be delighted to discuss your interest and development needs. Securing greater engagement of doctors, as 'shareholders', in the running and shaping of services and hospitals is increasingly being seen as critical to the enhancement of quality, safety and effectiveness and the reduction of inappropriate clinical variation.

The past few decades have seen the growth of a general management culture generally supported by some limited medical leadership with perhaps too many doctors seeing themselves as 'stakeholders'. High performing hospitals internationally tend to be typified by cultures where doctors and managers work closely together to achieve the common goals of high quality care and value and where all doctors feel highly engaged.

Medical Engagement: No Longer an Optional Extra

As Spurgeon et al. [13] suggest, engagement has become a popular, much used term supplanting more traditional concepts such as job satisfaction and motivation. Feeney and Tiernan [14] provide a very useful overview of the literature on the emergence and development of the concept of engagement.

MacLeod and Clarke [15] offer an excellent review of staff engagement across a range of sectors and identify more than fifty definitions of employee engagement. They conclude that there is no universal definition but that there is strong relationship between the extent of engagement and performance.

Guthrie [16] argues that medical engagement should be one of the top priorities for chief executives. He argues that at a structural level (creating appropriate facilitative arrangements) and a personal level (one-to-one communication) it is possible for executives and managers to build up levels of physician engagement. Toto [17] using Gallup survey data, demonstrates that engaged physicians can have a direct impact on the financial performance of hospitals in the USA.

West and Dawson [18], in a paper commissioned by The King's Fund, reported that engagement is linked to a range of individual and organisational outcome measures including staff absenteeism and turnover, patient satisfaction and mortality and safety measures including infection rates. They concluded that the more engaged staff members are, the better the outcomes for patients and the organisation generally.

Involving doctors in leadership roles in the UK has been an explicit aim since the Griffiths Report into the NHS management was published in 1983. Dickinson et al. [19] refer to the consequences of doctors not being involved in leadership by citing the highly publicised The Francis Inquiry Report [20] into the failings of care at The Mid-Staffordshire Hospitals (UK) highlighting that most doctors felt disengaged and undervalued. This report concludes that much more needs to be done to support.

The Institute for Healthcare Improvement (IHI) in the United States has developed a framework for how organisations can improve medical engagement. Given the evidence supporting the importance of engagement and working with some of the highest performing hospitals in the USA, the IHL have developed a framework for engaging physicians in quality and safety. This framework includes:

- discovering common purpose, such as improving outcomes and efficiency
- reframing values to make doctors partners in, not customers of, the organisation, and promoting individual responsibility for quality
- fine-tuning engagement to reach different types of staff—identifying and encouraging champions, education leaders, developing project management skills and working with laggards

- using improvement methods such as performance data in a way which encourages buy-in rather than resistance
- making it easy for doctors to do the right thing for patients
- supporting clinical leaders all the way to the board
- involving doctors from the beginning—working with leaders and early adopters, choosing messages and messengers carefully, making doctor involvement visible, communicating candidly and often, and valuing doctors' input by giving management time to them

Full details of the IHI Paper *Engaging physicians in quality and safety* can be found at www.IHI.org

In the UK, a medical engagement scale was developed as part of the joint Enhancing Engagement in Medical Leadership project between the Academy of Medical Royal Colleges and the NHS Institute of Innovation and Improvement that also developed the Medical Leadership Competency Framework (MLCF) already referred to earlier in this chapter.

Spurgeon et al. [13] advise that the Medical Engagement Scale (MES) was developed on the conceptual premise that medical engagement is critical to implementing the radical changes and improvements sought by the NHS (UK) and that medical engagement cannot be understood from consideration of the individual employee alone. They contend that it is not sufficient for an individual doctor to express a desire to be engaged but that the organisation must create the conditions, opportunities and processes whereby such individuals are encouraged and supported. They define engagement as 'the active and positive contribution of doctors within their normal working roles to maintaining and enhancing the performance of the organisation which itself recognises this commitment in supporting and encouraging high quality care'.

The Index of Medical Engagement has three meta-scales: working in an open culture; having purpose and direction; and feeling valued and empowered. Data from over 70 hospitals has now been collected from hospitals in the UK which shows a strong association between medical engagement and performance as measured by the independent health care regulator. Data is also now being collected from a number of Australian and New Zealand hospitals and the MES is being extended to use in a number of other countries.

Another King's Fund Report [21] confirms further evidence of the benefits of medical engagement in referring to a study undertaken by McKinsey and the Centre for Economic Performance at the London School of Economics [22]. Their work examined the performance of around 1300 hospitals across Europe and the USA. Overall they found that hospitals that are well managed produce higher quality patient care and improved productivity, including significantly lower mortality rates and better financial performance.

A really good example of the application of the IHI model for medical engagement can be found at the McLeod Regional Medical Center in South Carolina. Here, doctors engage with each other to drive learning, quality and professional satisfaction. The study by Gosfield and Reinertsen [23] of how McLeod Regional Medical Center used medical engagement to secure major quality advances highlights how visitors 'marvel at the enthusiastic, effective leadership of McLeod's doctors in quality, safety and value initiatives—without any significant financial incentives'. McLeod's techniques for engaging doctors include:

- asking doctors to lead improvement—the mantra is 'physician-led, data-driven and evidence-based'
- asking doctors what they want to work on—McLeod initiates about 12 major improvement efforts each year, based on doctors' recommendations
- making it easy for doctors to lead and participate—McLeod provides good support staff for improvement and does not waste doctors' time
- recognising doctors who lead, including the opportunity to present to the board
- supporting medical leaders when obstructed by difficult colleagues
- providing development opportunities—McLeod helps doctors learn about quality, safety and human factors

The evidence from different studies only serves to reinforce the importance of both clinical leadership and engagement. To some extent taking on positional leadership roles could be seen as optional. Some clinicians just do not possess the inclination or have the ability to undertake such roles but engagement as a 'shareholder' in the running, development and improvement of your specialty or service should not be an optional extra. It should be central to your role as a good doctor.

Exercise

In what ways might you contribute more effectively to the management, leadership and improvement of your service? List ways in which you could become more of a 'shareholder'?

As mentioned previously, good engagement is achieved where there is a desire by both clinicians and the organisation to work together and to maximise the contribution the former can make to enhancing quality, outcomes and overall performance. So, what typifies highly performing and medically engaged hospitals? The evidence from the studies above suggests that some of the following are features and should provide some ideas as to how you can make an even bigger difference to the patients and communities you care about.

Structure

- are doctors seen as key contributors to decision-making and encouraged to assume leadership roles?
- are sufficient doctors (both full-time and part-time) involved in the top executive teams and boards as well as at the specialty or service level?
- are doctors encouraged to take the lead on important initiatives within the hospital e.g. ICT, Quality and Safety, Governance, Service Improvement etc?

Process

- are management, leadership and service improvement interests and competencies assessed when making appointments?
- are they also genuinely discussed and incorporated within appraisals?
- is positive encouragement given to new specialists (and indeed others) to acquire management and leadership competencies through either uni- or multi-disciplinary training and development programs?
- do non-clinical managers and leaders work in partnership at all levels with clinicians?
- do clinicians with potential for management and leadership roles get identified and supported?
- do clinicians help create cultures where quality and safety are paramount and where they take the lead in identifying new standards and ensure that unacceptable variations are challenged?
- are junior doctors given every encouragement to acquire management and leadership competencies, particularly around service improvement?

Outputs

- does your specialty and hospital compare very favourably against similar services in terms of clinical outcomes, patient experience, quality, safety and value?
- is your service the one of choice by patients and other stakeholders?

Summary

Reviews of hospitals or services where poor clinical performance has been made public all highlight failings in clinical leadership and engagement. More needless harm is done to patients through poor management and leadership than by clinical incompetence. Clinicians are in the best position to know when systems and processes are dangerous or just sub-optimal.

The challenge for clinicians today is to take responsibility for identifying such failings and to assist with improvements. This requires all clinicians to accept that they have leadership roles as practitioners and to actively engage in driving changes that enhance clinical outcomes and value. Health systems and organisations equally need to create cultures where more doctors are motivated and rewarded to assume leadership roles. However, as Braithwaite et al. [24] warn, medical leadership is not something that can be quickly brought about through a change in structure or by just exhorting clinical and managerial colleagues to change.

The evidence of the relationship between good clinical leadership and engagement means that it is no longer an optional extra. It is, as Sir Bruce Keogh indicates in the quote at the start of this chapter, central to the delivery of the very highest quality of care.

References

1. Spurgeon P, Clark J, Ham C (2011) Medical leadership: from the dark side to centre stage. Radcliffe Publishing, London
2. Kotter J (1996) Leading change. Harvard Business School, Boston
3. The King's Fund (2011) The future of leadership and management in the NHS: no more heroes. The King's Fund, London (Also available www.kingsfund.org.uk)
4. Griffiths D (2010) Clinical leadership—the what, why and how in clinical leadership: bridging the divide. In Stanton E, Lemer C, Mountford J (eds). Quay Books, London
5. Long A (2011) Leadership and management in ABC of clinical leadership. In Swanwick T, McKimm J. Blackwell Publishing, Oxford
6. Bolman L, Deal T (1997) Reframing organization: artistry, choice and leadership. Jossey-Bass, San Francisco
7. Alimo-Metcalfe B, Franks M (2011) Gender and leadership in ABC of clinical leadership. In Swanwick T, McKimm J. Blackwell Publishing, Oxford
8. NHS Institute for Innovation and Improvement and Academy of Medical Royal Colleges (2010) Medical leadership competency framework, 3rd edn. NHS Institute for Innovation and Improvement, Coventry
9. General Medical Council (2009) Tomorrow's doctors. General Medical Council, London
10. General Medical Council (2012) Leadership and management for all doctors. General Medical Council, London
11. General Medical Council (2013) Good medical practice. General Medical Practice, London
12. Spurgeon P, Klaber B (2011) Medical leadership: a practical guide for tutors and trainees. BPP Learning Media, London
13. Spurgeon P, Mazelan P, Barwell F (2011) Medical engagement: a crucial underpinning to organizational performance. Health Serv Manage Res 24:114–120
14. Feeney Y, Tierman J (2006) Employment engagement: an overview of the literature on the proposed antithesis to burnout. Ir J Psychol 27:130–141
15. MacLeod D, Clarke N (2009) Engaging for success: enhancing performance through employee engagement. Department for Business Innovation and Skills, London
16. Guthrie M (2005) Engaging physicians in performance improvement. Am J Med Qual 10:235–238
17. Toto D (2005) What the doctor ordered: the best hospitals create emotional bonds with their physicians. http://gmi/gallup.com/content/18361/what-the-Doctor-Ordered.aspx. Accessed 27 May 2011
18. West M, Dawson J Employee engagement and NHS performance. http://www.kingsfund.org.uk/sites/files/kf/employee-engagement-nhs-performance-west-dawson-leadership-review2012-paper.pdf. Accessed on 27 March 2014
19. Dickinson H, Ham C, Snelling I, Spurgeon P Medical leadership arrangements in English healthcare organisations: Findings from a national survey and case studies of NHS trusts. http://hsm.sagepub.com/content/early/2014/03/10/0951484814525598. Accessed 12 March 2014
20. Francis R (2013) Report of the Mid Staffordshire NHS Foundation Trust Public Enquiry. London. The Stationery Office
21. The King's Fund (2012) Leadership and engagement for improvement in the NHS: Together we can. The King's Fund, London (Also available at www.kingsfund.org.uk)
22. Dorgan S, Layton D, Bloom N, Homkes R, Sadun R, Van Reenen J (2010) Management in healthcare; Why good practice really matters. McKinsey and Co and Centre for Economic Performance, London
23. Gosfield A, Reinertsen J Achieving Clinical Integration with Highly Engaged Physicians. www.providence.org/holycross/MedicalStaffServices/Documents/. Accessed 17 Apr 2012
24. Braithwaite WM (2005) Rethinking clinical organisational structures: an attitude survey of doctors, nurses and allied health staff in clinical directorates. J Health Serv Res Policy 10:10–17

Chapter 3
The Art of Negotiation, Handling Difficult Behaviour, and Facing the Media

Lucky Jain, Sanjay Patole and Sarah Sloan

Let us never negotiate out of fear. But let us never fear to negotiate
—John F. Kennedy

Abstract Mastering the art of negotiation and handling difficult behaviours is essential for a happy and productive work life. Managers, supervisors, and consultants in most of the health care organisations often find it difficult to acquire these skills as there is little formal education. Most learn these skills by a trial and error method while struggling through the daily work load. As one rises in work place hierarchy there is always a possibility of being called upon to respond to media enquiries by providing information or taking part in media appearances. The types of such enquiries may be related directly to clinical work or the health service in general.

Handling media is stressful even for the most experienced staff. Prior training is essential for responsible handling of media otherwise potentially one could risk the reputation of the institution. This chapter focuses on ways to become a successful negotiator without making the process too complicated, and provides tips for handling difficult behaviours and facing the media.

L. Jain (✉)
Department of Pediatrics, Emory University School of Medicine, Uppergate Drive, Atlanta, GA 30322, USA
e-mail: ljain@emory.edu

S. Patole
Centre for Neonatal Research and Education, University of Western Australia, Perth, Australia

Department of Neonatal Paediatrics, King Edward Memorial Hospital for Women, Perth, WA, Australia

S. Sloan
Women and Newborn Service, King Edward Memorial Hospital for Women, Subiaco, WA, Australia

© Springer International Publishing Switzerland 2015
S. Patole (ed.), *Management and Leadership – A Guide for Clinical Professionals,*
DOI 10.1007/978-3-319-11526-9_3

Keywords Negotiation · Bargaining · Harvard negotiation · Principles · Emotions · Styles · Failure · BATNA · Difficult behaviours · Difficult interactions · Personality · Volcano · Sniper · Chronic complainer · Stars · Sliders · Negativist · Know it all · Super-agreeable · Management · Strategies · Radio · TV · Social media · Print · Dos and Don'ts

Key Messages

- Successful negotiation requires adequate advance planning, preparation, and patience
- The most important step is to remove emotion from the process of negotiation; this requires separating people from the problem
- Knowing the "Best Alternative To a Negotiated Agreement" (BATNA) is an important step towards protecting our self from getting into an agreement that we will regret later on
- When dealing with difficult behaviour remember that you can control only your emotions and responses and not of the other person; it is about them and not you
- Patience, compassion, and active listening help in dealing with difficult behaviours, but setting boundaries, and showing the way you wish to be respected is important
- Be well prepared, and 'cool, calm and collected' when facing media as a spokesperson and never provide personal opinion, even if asked

The Art of Negotiation

Why Negotiate?

In their introduction to "*Getting to Yes*", a landmark publication [1] about the art of negotiation, authors begin with a profound statement: "*Like it or not, you are a negotiator: Negotiation is a fact of life*". Indeed, we are constantly negotiating. We do it with varying degrees of success, often oblivious of the act itself. We negotiate with our peers [2], patients, families [3], colleagues, hospital administrators, spouse, children, pets; the list goes on! We negotiate our compensation [4] and our clinical responsibilities. We negotiate the number of weekends we work. A successful negotiation requires adequate advance planning, preparation, and patience.

Yet, few have mastered the art of negotiation. The process often becomes unduly complex and unruly, mixing people with the problem, and positions with interests. There is little formal education and we all stumble and fumble as we make it through negotiations big and small. Little do we know how we have missed opportunities to create bigger/better options and more win-win situations. This chapter focuses on ways to become a successful negotiator without making the process too cumbersome or complicated.

Table 3.1 Elements of principled negotiation

People	Separate the people from the problem
Interests	Focus not on positions but on interests
Options	Create multiple possible options which address mutual interests
Criteria	Objective standards guide the negotiated agreement, not opinions

The Art and Science of Negotiation

Negotiation can be viewed as a strategy for resolving a conflict [2]. Indeed, if there weren't any conflict, there wouldn't be much to negotiate. In a successful negotiation, all parties win. Perhaps the foremost lesson in the art of negotiations is to avoid bargaining over positions, even though that is what everyone focuses on, and that is what our minds are trained to do. The downside of focusing on positions is that we tend to lock ourselves into certain outcomes of options making it hard to settle the issue when the other party disagrees. As we argue to defend our "position", we start believing in it as the only option, and before we know, our ego locks in its horns as well. The overall approach using positions is highly inefficient as it takes forever to come to an agreement; it also threatens relationships because it involves a test of wills, a win or lose format that has a sizeable risk of leaving one party bruised and hurt. A common assumption is that one can avoid this outcome by embracing "soft" rather than "hard" bargaining techniques, but being Mr. Nice often forces one to yield to a less desirable compromise.

So what is the alternative? The *Harvard Negotiation Project* which forms the basis of the book *Getting to Yes* [1], developed an alternative to positional bargaining. In "principled" negotiation, one negotiates on the merits, eliminating some of the negatives we discussed earlier that are much too commonly encountered in positional bargaining.

As one can tell from Table 3.1, the approach to principled negotiation is quite different from the one we saw in positional bargaining. The *first step*, and perhaps the most important one, is to remove emotion from the process; this requires separating people from the problem [5]. It matters not how much we may personally like or dislike the other party, and how much we may want to crush them in this round; successful negotiation requires objectivity and focus on merits. One has to proceed with the negotiation even in the absence of trust. The goal is an outcome that both parties like.

The *second* principle requires focusing on interests, not on the bottom line. People often become impatient and somewhat fixated on the bottom line: "I will not pay more than this"! This invites the other party to think: "I will not sell it at less than this, take it or leave it". The result is a stalemate. This type of undesirable outcome also requires a focus on the style of negotiation (Table 3.2). Not everyone is aware of their own style of negotiating and their inherent tendency to veer towards a particular (often less desirable) tactic when the situation gets tough.

Table 3.2 Five basic styles of negotiators (adapted from Hill MJ and DeCherney AH [2])

Negotiating Style	Description
Accommodating	Emphasize relationship, see views of the other side
Avoiding	Avoid conflict if at all possible
Competing	See conflict as a win-lose scenario
Collaborating	Create problem solvers
Compromising	Emphasize what is fair and equitable

Next, one needs to think of options that are not one sided; winning options are ones that all parties can live with. The final agreement should use objective criteria to reach an agreement that holds to independent scrutiny and reason, and should not under duress or undue pressure from either side.

Know Your BATNA

What if a negotiation fails? Do you leave the job offer on the table? What if the last car on the lot that you like is sold? Or your best friend turns her back on you and walks away? And finally, what if the other party is more powerful? The biggest problem a negotiator faces is when all efforts to reach a mutually agreeable option fail. Experts feel that it is critical that we proactively work towards a finding an alternative to the perceived ideal/desired outcome. This is called the BATNA (Best Alternative To a Negotiated Agreement). It is an important step towards protecting oneself from getting into an agreement that we will regret later on. Having a BATNA does two things: first, it helps steer us towards a reasonably good option when the preferred option is simply not achievable because of the leverage the other party has; second, it allows us to objectively compare options. In the medical profession, this often requires finding more than one positions. It also requires knowledge of what a typical work week looks like for one's subspecialty at a comparable institution (call, attending time, weekends etc.).

Information about salaries is often available from organizations that collect such information using annual surveys. In the US, the Association for Academic Medical Colleges (AAMC) publishes an annual report [6] on medical school salaries. The report presents total compensation attributable to teaching, patient care, and research for nearly 100,000 full-time faculty at 140 medical schools. Similar information about compensation is also published by Medical Group Management Association (MGMA) which tracks salaries for both academic physicians as well as those in private practice. These data help us determine what we are worth. If the training we have is rare and the market need outstrips supply, we clearly are in a better bargaining position [7]. If the employer has a pressing need with an open position they have to fill, one can ask for more.

Once one has access to accurate information, decisions become relatively easier. In the business world, we can use this information to decide on our break-even point. In financial terms, this is the lowest salary or cheapest price we will accept in the deal. In non-financial terms, this is the "worst-case scenario" you we willing to accept before walking away from the negotiation.

There are, of course, many other good resources available to the interested reader who may be want to learn more about conflict resolution and negotiation [2, 5, 8]. It is never too late to become a good negotiator!

How to Handle Difficult Behaviours

Stress is an inevitable part of our work life. The level of work related stress differs according to the type of work, the position held, and importantly our ability to cope with it. With the passage of time we often realise that it is not the work per se, but the people with difficult behaviours at work that tire us out. As pointed out by Dr Griffin in this book, there is a reasonable chance that we will see more of our work colleagues in our life than other people outside of the work environment. The ability to recognise and deal with difficult behaviour is therefore one of the most important skills required to assure a peaceful and productive work life. So how do we recognise a difficult behaviour? Here are few clues based on our emotional responses to difficult behaviours/interactions at work:

1. *Every time I face this person, I get stressed*: This is perhaps the commonest response indicative of a difficult behaviour by a colleague at work.
2. *I get stressed just by thinking that I have to meet this person*: Once you start getting anxious and stressed just by the thought of an impending meeting with a person, or worse, start finding excuses to postpone or cancel it, it is time to realise that things have worsened to an extent that an intervention is required.
3. *I am not myself when I meet this person; I always come back after meeting this person, thinking about things that I should have said*: These feelings confirm that something is not right. They indicate that the person's behavioural pattern is not allowing you to express yourself properly. Meetings, interactions with this person are mostly a one way affair.
4. *I have had enough of this person; I just feel like walking away*: Such an extreme response indicates that an intervention is urgently required to address the underlying issues because the price one may end up paying professionally by taking such a step could be very high.

Are There Any Difficult Personality Types?

Sherman [9] describes four characteristic difficult personalities as follows:

1. **The Volcano**: This is an intimidating, arrogant, and extremely aggressive person, who behaves like an adult having a temper tantrum, and will not mind making a scene in public. Widell and Pitts describe people with such behaviour as "Sherman

tanks" because you feel like you have been run over by a Sherman tank after facing their outburst [10]. They make a very informative comment on why their overtly explosive, aggressive behaviour is often difficult to spot as a pattern. They suggest that this is because these people might not always behave this way. Their behaviour emerges only when their internal stress reaches a level they can't tolerate, and it is easy to dismiss this behaviour- as "Oh, that is him/her" [10].

2. **The Sniper**: These are people who are highly skilled in passive-aggressive behaviour. Sherman decries them as mean spirited people who work to sabotage their leaders and colleagues. Widell and Pitts point out that a sniper prefers to remain hidden and not take responsibility for his/her actions or the consequences, and that sniping can take the form of gossip, rumour –mongering, and making behind-the-scene derogatory remarks [10].

3. **The Chronic Complainer**: These are whiny people who find faults in every situation, and accuse/blame others for the problems. Sherman describes them as people who see it as their responsibility to complain to set things right, and rarely provide solutions to the problem [9].

4. **The Clam**: These people are described as those who are disengaged, unresponsive. They avoid answering direct questions, and don't participate as a team member [9].

Widell and Pitts have described other traits to recognise difficult behaviour [10]. These include the "**Super-agreeable**" who agrees with everything, the "**Negativist**" who sees only the bad side in everything, the "**Know it all**", and the "**Staller**" who undermines attempts to reach a decision by procrastination [2]. Suzi Welch adds "**Stars**" and "**Sliders**" to the list [11]. Stars are the important staff members who add value to the institution. Without their results, the organization can not survive. Welch points out that some Stars can develop into real bullies realising that they are untouchable [11]. Fetzer describes such a Star as a highly recognized lone wolf, about whom you cannot do much since the brilliance the person is an accepted part of the organizational culture [12]. Sliders are former Stars, resting on their laurels and undermining their teams with apathy, their unspoken excuse is "I have proven my worth around here; I don't need to scramble anymore" [11].

Why is it Stressful to Deal with Difficult People?

Bill Tiffan states that the fear of escalating the situation, the uncertainty about how best to handle the situation, and the discomfort with conflict, are the three commonest reasons we find it hard to handle difficult behaviour [13]. He points out that the fear of escalating the situation is closely tied to the uncertainty about how to best handle the situation [13]. Conflict resolution is a skill that is not easy to acquire. It is therefore not surprising that the fear of conflict is one of the commonest reasons for the stress in handling difficult behaviour.

Managing Difficult Behaviour

The literature is full of 'tips' for handling difficult people, and difficult behaviours. At first glance most of them seem to be based on common sense. However on close inspection one realises that many of the suggested responses/actions are not easy to adopt because each one of us has a different personality and a different way of thinking and responding to difficult situations, difficult conversations based on our inherent nature and life experiences. Here are some general strategies [14–28] that are useful in handling difficult behaviour:

1. *Remember that you can control only your emotions and responses and not of the other person.* It is easy to get carried away by the emotions and react, but this will only worsen the situation as a hurried and emotional response will almost always be inappropriate, and worsen the situation.

2. *Try to separate the behaviour in question from the person.* This is easier said than done as what one sees is a 'person' manifesting the bad behaviour, and in an emotionally charged situation it is difficult to separate the person from the behaviour. A conscious effort is required to do so. Visualising our response to a difficult behaviour is a good way to train our mind during peace time.

3. *Stay calm, listen with compassion, and acknowledge the emotions of the person in as few words as possible.* Even the most upset people run out of steam very quickly once they know that they are being listened to. They are bound to get more agitated if they feel they are being ignored. It is important to show genuine and not fake compassion.

4. *Let the person speak without interruption. Try to find out if there is some truth in what is being said.* It is easy to forget that even the most agitated, and seemingly out of control person may be trying to convey an element of truth.

5. *Hold your ground, set boundaries that should not be crossed, and show the way you wish to be treated.*

6. *Be aware of strategies for managing anger and aggression.* Supervisors and managers need to assure that all employees have been trained in handling anger, and aggression at workplace. [29] The important thing is not to aggravate the situation and protect yourself, and people around you. If possible, let the professionals handle it.

7. *Try and differentiate whether you are dealing with just a difficult behaviour or a seasoned bully.* Differentiating a person with difficult behaviour from a bully is a difficult task unless there is a clear and documented pattern of recurrent bad behaviour directed towards you. Note down the event and witnesses if any. Documentation of a pattern is useful in standing up to a bully while safeguarding yourself. Without witnesses, it often becomes a "your word against mine" situation. Moreover bullies are experts in bullying under the disguise of "constructive criticism" which "you failed to take in the right context". Recognition of not only the valid part, if any, of the criticism but the way it was provided is important for the staff handling the issue. A detailed discussion on bullying at workplace is beyond the scope of this section. However it is important to know

that bullying and other acts of hostility can range from being yelled at in front of others, subject to accusations related to errors made by others, and gossiping, to being humiliated in front of others, and subjected to nonverbal remarks such as stares, glares, and negative facial remarks [30]. It is the responsibility of the supervisors and managers to educate themselves and their staff on the topics of bullying and hostility, and work with human resources and organizational leadership to develop a culture of zero tolerance to such behaviour [30].

8. *Get help, talk to a colleague who knows you well.* Seniors who may have handled such situations can help. Employee assistance program is always an option to get expert help while assuring confidentiality.

9. *Reflection*: After a difficult interaction think over the reasons why it may have occurred, your response, whether you could have handled it better, and last but not the least, whether you could have prevented it. Think over the probability of resolution if you escalate the matter, and the associated cost.

10. *Walking away* with an untarnished reputation is the last resort if you have tried your best to resolve the issue and feel that there is too much to lose by escalating the matter to a higher level. Unfortunate as it is, the burden of proof often lies with the victim rather than the aggressor.

11. *Don't burn your bridges.* In most difficult situations, after the emotional surge is over, a candid talk away from workplace often helps in understanding each other. Try to forgive. Remember

The weak can never forgive. Forgiveness is the attribute of the strong
—*Mahatma Gandhi*

In summary, it is important to appreciate that everyone, including you, is difficult at times. We can not change everyone and there is no need to change everyone. People are difficult to deal with because our normal way of dealing with them has failed [18]. Few strategies that may help in dealing with specific difficult behaviours are summarised in Table 3.3 [10, 11, 19]. It is important to know that what works for someone else may not work for you. Improvisation of strategies may be necessary as a difficult behaviour may not fit into a typical pattern. As said

With some people, the only way to win is to refuse to play
—(Source unknown)

Facing the Media

Media Do's and Don'ts

Being an experienced or senior member of staff at your workplace means you can be called upon to respond to media enquiries by providing media information or taking part in media appearances. The types of enquiries you get may be related directly to your clinical work or the health service in general. Usually it will relate directly to your clinical work but unavailability of other staff or spokespeople or a

Table 3.3 Strategies for dealing with specific difficult behaviours

1. *Volcano/Tank*: Pick your battles carefully. Confronting them is difficult as almost always these will be seniors with more expertise so you are unlikely to win. If you are too upset avoid confrontation and ask for a meeting later to think over your strategy. They expect you to crumble but do stand up using the "I" strategy (i.e. "*I disagree with you*"). Once they know you can stand up to them they tend to get friendly [10, 11, 19]
2. *Sniper*: Bring them out in the open and disarm them. Do not ignore or laugh off their remarks. Refuse to be attacked indirectly. Ask blunt questions such as "*I heard you don't like the new plan have you got a better one that you would like to share?*" Do not give them power by seeking advice [9–11, 19]
3. *Chronic complainer*: Listen actively; check facts; acknowledge the problem and solve it quickly to stop the complaint cycle. Don't listen to them on behalf of others; offer to talk to them and the source of the complaint together; set limits; use them as problem solvers [10, 11, 19]
4. *Clam*: Keep eye contact invite a response and wait patiently. Use open questions (e.g. "*What do you think?*"). Be attentive if they respond; let them know that their input is valuable. Give them time if they don't respond but be persistent (e.g. "*Let us discuss this tomorrow*") [10, 11, 19]
5. *Super-agreeable*: These trusted pleasers will commit to any task to please you so help them in setting realistic goals. They will not openly talk about problems they see so watch out for their hints in the form of humour and sarcasm. Try to establish genuine personal connections. Let them know that you are truly interested in their feedback [10, 11, 19]
6. *Negativist*: These regular devil's advocates may have something right to say so no harm in listening to them to explore all possible negatives; there is nothing to lose [10, 11, 19]
7. *Know it all Stars Sliders*: When dealing with these in house experts make sure you know exactly what you are talking about; do not disturb and listen attentively to convey that their input is valued. Never patronise or ignore them; positive disagreement is preferable than confrontation. Acknowledging their expertise keeps them on your side. Shift them to a different task if their expertise is frustrating the team [10, 11, 19]
8. *Staller*: Encourage them to speak. Listen to them carefully for indirect words hesitation or omissions that may indicate problem areas. If you help them develop a positive image they find it easy to speak up [10, 11, 19]
9. *Passive-aggressive colleague*: Be clear about what is expected from them; don't accept poor performance; be open and avoid being defensive; challenge distortions or half-truths [22, 31]

crisis situation may mean you will need to comment on broader issues relating to the health service. Media enquiries can come through at any time and most health services have a media liaison person on-call 24 h a day, seven days a week. Media coverage is important when it comes to health as it can be used to promote health messages, create awareness and immediately inform the community of health or health service issues which could impact them.

When it comes to handling media the best advice is; if you don't want it published or broadcast, don't say it or write it.

All media activities should be directed through your health service's Public Relations (PR) department. Your PR department can translate medical terms, research notes and statistical information into language suitable for the intended audience. PR can also identify the most newsworthy aspects of the information you intend sharing with the media and cut out superfluous information, increasing the likelihood of your research or comments getting published.

As part of your medical role you may be asked to act as a spokesperson in your area of expertise, which can include live or pre-recorded television and radio interviews. Many organisations offer media training, which is a valuable tool for helping you engage with journalists and appropriately handle difficult media situations.

Media can have both a positive and negative impact on your organisation, your decision to, and how you respond can determine this.

Refusing to comment on contentious issues can have a negative impact and a "no comment" response implies you don't want to answer because accusations are true. The same can be said of taking too long to respond and missing the journalist's deadline so the story is published without the health service having the opportunity to defend accusations or add their version of events.

If responding to a contentious issue, less is more; only provide a short, accurate answer to the question asked and no further information. If the issue has negatively impacted a patient or staff member it is respectful to show empathy to the person but without forgoing patient confidentiality obligations.

During an interview, if a question is asked that you cannot or do not want to answer you should politely decline, e.g. "I'm unable to comment on that" or "I am speaking on behalf of the health organisation so I cannot give my personal opinion."

Print Media

Print media can have a long or short deadline; the journalist may give you a week or so for a feature article or a couple of hours for tomorrow's newspaper or online article. In either case, the quicker you respond the better the chance of being published.

Formulate a response in language suitable for your audience; i.e. simple language for local newspapers, medical terminology for medical journals.

Most stories for print media will be derived from a media release or prewritten information formulated by your PR department, provided to the news outlet or by direct request from the news outlet.

If you have a story you really want told such as ground-breaking research or awards won by yourself or a colleague, it helps immensely to have images to accompany the story to give it a better chance of prominent publishing. Many news stories can rely solely on having an impressive accompanying image. From an editor's perspective, the top stories aren't those which are most newsworthy but those with the best pictures.

Radio

Radio is considered the most immediate form of media. Radio interviews will often have a short lead time and the journalist will want to speak to you within a few hours of requesting the interview.

Radio interviews may be live or pre-recorded. If possible, request examples of the questions the journalist wants to ask so you can think about your responses and write down some speaking notes. Your interview should sound natural and unrehearsed.

Radio host are usually very experienced and skilled so will help the interview tick along nicely without 'dead air' or silence. They may also pull out an unexpected question, unrelated to the agreed topic. If this happens it's OK to laugh it off and politely decline to answer or recommend saving the question for 'another time and place'.

Television

Your personal presentation will be a direct reflection of the organisation you are employed by so should always be professional, neat and correspond with the duties you are employed to undertake.

If speaking live, which usually only happens in a crisis situation, try to stay calm and visualise a few bullet point topics you need to speak about–you can learn more tips on this by undergoing media training. If you stumble over your words just correct yourself and keep going as you would if you were talking to a friend.

Pre-recorded television can often require an hour of filming for a two minute news story. You may be asked to walk down a corridor multiple times, shuffle papers on a desk or type on a keyboard for visual illustration. It may seem pointless but it makes for better television. Offer some ideas to the camera team and journalist if you think they could work for your story e.g. if you are talking about research and have access to specific equipment or a lab relevant to the story, offer it up to be filmed.

Social Media

The explosion of social media as a news tool means your comments can be published by anyone, anywhere, in a matter of seconds and because of this, it is pertinent to assume anything you say in the public domain could be published. Be careful about what you say about your work place in front of members of the public. This also goes for your own use of social media, uploading photographs or commenting about the specifics of your work or workplace is not advisable.

Summary

Remember, you are acting as a spokesperson for your organisation and should never provide your personal opinion, even if asked. Be 'cool, calm and collected'; when all is said and done the media outlets have control over what is shown and what gets edited so make sure you only give them what you want published or broadcast.

References

1. Fisher R, Ury R, Patton P (2011) Getting to yes, 3rd edn. Penguin books, New York, p xxvii
2. Hill MJ, DeCherney AH (2013) Negotiation for physicians. Semin Reprod Med 31:215–218
3. Larson HJ (2013) Negotiating vaccine acceptance in an era of reluctance. Hum Vaccin Immunother 9:1779–1181
4. Linney BJ (1996) Negotiate the salary you want. Physician Exec 22:12–17
5. Hake S, Shah T (2011) Negotiation skills for clinical research professionals. Perspect Clin Res 2:105–108
6. Association of American Medical Colleges (2014) Report on medical school faculty salaries, 2012–2013. Washington DC
7. Shell RG (2006) Bargaining for advantage, 2nd edn. Penguin Books, New York
8. Marcus JM (2011) Renegotiating health care: resolving conflict to build collaboration, 2nd edn. Jossey-Bass, San Francisco
9. Sherman RO (2014) Dealing with difficult people. Am Nurse Today 9:61–62
10. Widell J, Pitts CA (1990) Coping with problem personalities. Nursing 20:102–106
11. Wiese KT (2003) Bombers, complainers and clams, oh my! Dealing with difficult people. Prairie Rose 72(1):18–24
12. Fetzer J (2004) Dealing with those on "the dark side"—difficult and worse people. Anal Bioanal Chem 380:727–728
13. Tiffan B (2009) Dealing with difficult people. Physician Exec 35:86–89
14. Zanni GR, Wick JY (2011) Dealing with those difficult coworkers. Consult Pharm 26:672–678
15. Westwood C (2010) Managing difficult behaviour. Nurs Manag (Harrow) 17:20–21
16. Roman LM (2007) Finding the words. How to handle difficult conversations. RN 70:34–38
17. Hinchey P (2006) Attitude—the essential element of quality outcomes. Nurs N Z 12:2
18. Salazar J. (2004) Dealing with difficult people. Mich Nurse Aug:13
19. Wiese KT (2003) Bombers, complainers and clams, oh my! Dealing with difficult people. Prairie Rose 72:18–24
20. Jameson C (2001) Handling difficult people and difficult situations. Cranio 19:214–218
21. Keenan-Hayes S (2001) Dealing with difficult people. Can Oper Room Nurs J 19:21–25
22. Whitaker C (2000) Dealing with difficult behavior. Nursing 30:82–83
23. Medland JJ (1994) Dealing with difficult people. Nurs Dyn 3(3):6–7, 9–11
24. Cooper R (1993) Dealing effectively with difficult people. Nursing 23:97–98, 100–102
25. Widell J, Pitts CA (1990) Coping with problem personalities. Nursing 20:102–106
26. Baum N (2009) Dealing with difficult patients. J Med Pract Manage 25:33–36
27. Frings CS (2003) Dealing with a difficult supervisor. MLO Med Lab Obs 35:32–33
28. Peters JA (2003) The devil in the doctor. How to cope with problem physicians. MGMA Connex 3(2):50–53, 1
29. Neff L. (1995) Positive responses to difficult behavior. J Post Anesth Nurs 10:332–335
30. Cohen S. (2014) From sheep to lion: confronting workplace bullying. Nurs Manage 45:9–11
31. Whitaker C. (2000) Dealing with difficult behavior. Nursing 30(6):82–83

Chapter 4
Handling Complaints, Meetings, and Presentations

Haribalakrishna Balasubramanian and Sanjay Patole

> *...God created the world in six days. On the seventh day, he rested. On the eighth day, he started getting complaints. And it hasn't stopped since*
> —James Scott Bell

Abstract Being responsible for handling complaints, meetings, and presentations is a part and parcel of work life, especially as one rises higher up in the workforce hierarchy. Effective complaint management is important in order to deliver high quality services to the satisfaction of the consumers/clients while maintaining the accreditation standards and credentialing criteria, using clinical and performance indicators. Understanding the essentials of complaint management is therefore important for advanced trainees, as well as supervisors and managers in any workplace. Health care organisations strive for quality improvement in clinical care and management. Besides clinical skills, the health care staff needs managerial skills to coordinate with various staff for a range of processes including human resource management, research activities, networking, and education. Meetings are usually the starting point for all these processes. Effective meetings and effective presentations are thus crucial to achieve the organisation's goal. This chapter reviews the essentials of how to handle complaints, meetings, and presentations at workplace.

Keywords Management · Steps · Organisational structure · Dispute · Resolution · Agenda · Information · Problem solving · Decision making · Educational · Planning for · Ground rules · Brainstorming · Round robin · Fish bon diagram · Multi-voting · Straw poll · PowerPoint · Oral · Posters · Font size and colur · Tables · Graph · Bullet points · Engaging the audience

S. Patole (✉)
Centre for Neonatal Research and Education,
University of Western Australia, Perth, WA, Australia
e-mail: sanjay.patole@health.wa.gov.au

H. Balasubramanian · S. Patole
Department of Neonatal Paediatrics, King Edward Memorial Hospital for Women,
374 Bagot Road, Subiaco, Perth, WA 6008, Australia

© Springer International Publishing Switzerland 2015
S. Patole (ed.), *Management and Leadership – A Guide for Clinical Professionals*,
DOI 10.1007/978-3-319-11526-9_4

Key Points

- If approached, any front line staff can accept complaints; and forward to the appropriate authority in the organisation for assessment and response
- Poor communication by the staff is the most common cause for complaints
- Prevention of complaints by open disclosure, effective communication and transparency in delivering health care services should be the primary goal
- Meetings should not be considered as casual events; well planned agenda, directed discussion and good time management are essential for productive meetings
- There is no substitute for subject knowledge and practice for an effective presentation; advice from seniors is always valuable

Handling Complaints

A complaint can be defined as an expression of dissatisfaction with treatment, care, conduct, behaviour. Considering the complex and stressful nature of the work involved, it is inevitable that health care staff will sooner or later face complaints at the workplace. Effective complaint management system is considered a mandatory requirement for hospital accreditation in many countries. [2] Given the stigma associated with complaining in hospitals, the incidence of complaints in hospitals is probably underestimated. The complaints could be from the patient or the employees. Complaints from patients and their relatives are of a more serious nature. It is important to know as to why patients complain. Wilson et al. from Australia [3] reported that 17 % of hospital admissions experienced adverse events and 4 % resulted in deaths. 51 % of the adverse events were preventable. Different large scale surveys [4, 5] have revealed that the patient's expectation out of complaining was to prevent recurrence of such incidents (90 %) and change practices of health care organisations. Only a minority (9 %) were interested in financial compensation. Complaints usually relate to clinical incidents, adverse events, dissatisfaction with care provided, wait times, bills, poor communication, and poor handling of complaints. Poor communication from medical staff is the most common reason for complaint [6]. It is not the incident, but poor communication from the clinician post incident, that provokes patients to complain. It has been reported that approximately 2/3rd of patients were dissatisfied with handling of complaints in hospital [7]. Complaint handling in hospitals is not uniform throughout the world. The principles and steps of complaint management in developed countries have been elaborated.

Table 4.1 Requisites for effective complaint management

National interest
Effective Leadership [1]
Organisation structure (independent personnel and committee)
Record maintenance, complaint database and electronic information systems
Standardisation of complaint handling strategies
Quality improvement surveys
Training on communication and information dissemination

Principles in Complaint Management

Health care in US and Australia has transitioned from patient care services to customer or consumer care [8]. Clinicians have transformed to health care providers. Hospitals are responsible for patient's health as well as satisfaction. Clinical governance is an important concept of health care delivery in Australia. The office of safety and quality in Health Care in Western Australia has defined clinical governance as "a systematic and integrated approach to assurance and review of clinical responsibility and accountability that improves quality and safety resulting in optimal patient outcomes. The long term goal of clinical governance can be achieved by continuous education, vigilance, and audits of health care processes, quality assurance, ethical and evidence based practice, maintaining accreditation standards and credentialing criteria, using clinical and performance indicators [9]. Effective complaint management is essential to meet this goal. The requisites for effective complaint management at hospitals are shown in Table 4.1 [8, 10].

Patients should be informed how to make a complaint, and to whom. Written, verbal, telephonic complaints should be accepted.

Details of complaint management process should be available in hospital handbooks, websites and posters. All hospital staff are required to register the complaint if approached. Sixty five percent of all complaints are first reported to front line staff [11].

Steps in Complaint Management

1. Acknowledge the complainant; Update the complainant about the process and time frames.
2. Document time, date, hospital no, provider no, relevant addresses, witnesses name -maintain for records.
3. Register the complaint with the institutional database and clinical governance unit. Complaint notification form and clinical incident form to be filled as appropriate (written or electronic).
4. Assess the severity of the complaint for appropriate management strategy and referral.

Table 4.2 Alternate dispute resolution strategies

Negotiation: Both complainant and accused mutually decide on resolving dispute
Conciliation: Complainant and accused resolve the dispute in presence of a facilitator
Mediation: Facilitator actively influences resolution of dispute
Arbitrarisation: The facilitator makes the decision
Mini trial: Jury of senior officers, representing both the disputing parties, decide on the dispute
Summary jury trial: Jury of lawyers representing both the disputed parties, argue in the presence of an independent jury. The decision here is nonbinding

5. Ensure fairness of procedure, communication, and outcome.
6. Investigation of the complaint.
7. Outcome- explanation/apology, health care policy changes, training and monitoring of health staff, fee exemption, disciplinary action, no action.

Complaint Handling- Organisational Structure

Who Registers Complaints?

Complaints from patients can be accepted by the front line staff (doctors, nurses, technicians, pharmacists) and assessed by the complaint committee or complaint manager. Complaint from an employee is notified to the immediate supervisor, line manager, human resources or the occupational safety and health representative

How to Handle Complaints?

The informal procedure: The complaint manager will not investigate or refer, but mediate or assist the employee in the resolution. To avoid the time and money spent on legal course, Alternate dispute resolution (ADR) systems have emerged to address patient complaints in an informal way [12]. The various ADR strategies are enumerated in Table 4.2.

A formal process is used if the issue cannot be resolved informally or if the employee chooses it. Here, manager will investigate, interrogate and resolve the dispute.

Who Handles Complaints?

1. **Health Care Personnel:** In a survey of literature from US, UK, Australia, NZ and Singapore, patient complaints in most hospitals were initially handled by social workers [13]. Complaints regarding staff behaviour were handled by the public relations unit (PRU). However, the priority for PRU was organisation

reputation over complainant satisfaction. Complaints about clinical incidents involving doctors or nurses were handled by the Line Manager. Complaints involving medical malpractice were referred to Medical disputes team.

2. **Complaints committee**: This is a committee formed by independent professionals in a hospital or region and occasionally board members and designed to address non legal complaints from patients [14]. The committee acts a mediator between the patient and the professional. It advises the patient about the outcome of the complaint and the corrective measures taken. The primary goal is to restore patient satisfaction and trust in the health care system. The committee lacks discretionary powers and can only advice the professionals. If the complaint is unresolved, serious, complex, involving multiple staff or departments, the committee refers it to the line manager and senior complaints officer and then to the board of executives.

3. **Statutory disciplinary system or Registration board:** This addresses patient's complaints that require legal proceedings. The primary purpose of the board is to inspect and regulate quality of clinical care and professional conduct in hospitals. The board is empowered to issue warnings, suspension, work prohibition and cancellation of licenses of the professional.

4. **External agencies:** For unresolved patient complaints at the level of the hospital Board or serious complaints (criminal, corruption charges against medical practitioner), liaison with the Medical council or Registration Board, Civil Court, Police, Coroner is required. Government Ombudsman services are available in many countries for dispute resolution of general public. In UK, Australia and New Zealand, the State Health Service Commissioner specifically addresses complaints of patients and hospital employees. [15, 16] In New Zealand, The Health and Disability Commissioner is responsible in upholding the rights of a patient-right to respect, right to information, right to complain [17]. Fairwork Ombudsman is an independent agency of Australian Government to investigate complaints of all commonwealth employees including health care staff.

In summary, complaints in health care settings are very common. Poor communication by the staff is the most common cause for complaints. Every health care organisation should have a strategy and team to manage complaints. Prevention of complaints by open disclosure, effective communication and transparency in delivering health care services should be the primary goal.

Handling Meetings

Health care organisations today strive for quality improvement in clinical care. Besides, clinical skills, the professional needs managerial skills to coordinate with medical and management staff, ensure safety of patients and employees, manage complaints, allocate resources, organise research activities, network with professionals, and educate staff and students. Meetings are usually the starting point for all these processes. The Oxford Dictionary defines meeting as 'An assembly of people for a particular purpose, especially for formal discussion'. The importance of planning and conduct of meetings in the context of health care organisation is discussed and few tips are provided to make them effective.

1) Is the meeting needed?

The first step is to question if a meeting is really needed. Most meetings are poorly planned, time consuming, and are organised in short notice. It is a collaboration of heterogeneous group of thinkers or planners. Face to face meetings are becoming less popular, given the various modalities of information exchange. However, for taking major decisions and disseminating information quickly and confidentially, face to face meetings will be indispensable.

2) Type of meetings

Meetings are generally classified into 3 types—(1) Information meetings (2) Problem solving or decision making meetings (3) Education meetings.

Lectures and conferences are examples of education meetings. Most of the departmental or staff meetings in health care settings are held for making decisions. Informational meeting differs from the former in that the decision is already made prior to the meeting. Decision making meetings can be further classified as parliamentary, hierarchical, and facilitated [18].

- Parliamentary meetings are dictated by Robert's Rules of Order for debating, decision making, addressing other members, and disagreeing with other speakers. Some executive level meetings are conducted in this manner. Decisions that achieve majority by voting get accepted.
- Hierarchical meetings follow an individual centred approach, where the chair person gives information and takes the decision on behalf of the members. Members have more freedom to express their opinions.
- Facilitated meetings have a group approach, where every member in the meeting equally contributes to arriving at a decision that is finally upheld. The decision is made by consensus, where every member of the group is amicably convinced to either adopt or support a particular decision at the end of the meeting. Since all members are stake holders of the decision, no one loses (win–win situation). Consensus decisions, though time consuming, are the most effective decisions for implementation [19]. The chair person or facilitator is the key person in these meetings.

Most of the meetings have characteristics of both hierarchical and facilitated type.

3) Planning for meetings

3.1) Main agenda: The subject matter of the meeting is divided into various components which are described in order in the agenda. The time and person allotted to discuss each of the components is also listed in the agenda. An agenda format is represented in Table 4.3. The agenda, reading material/reminders must be sent much in advance to make the meeting productive. Consent agenda is a subset of the main agenda. It is a group of informational, self explanatory and non controversial items in the agenda, which do not require much discussion in the meeting. This is a tool to streamline meetings and direct members solely to issues that need discussion [20].

Table 4.3 Agenda format

Name of the hospital	
Department	
	Venue
	Date
	Time
Topic of discussion	
Chair	
Members	
Guests	
Sponsor	
Apologies	

3.2) Participants

Meetings generally comprise of key decision makers, persons with analytical skills, managerial skills, persons to whom assignments will be allocated, sponsors, resource allocators, minutes recorder, and time keeper. Occasionally, a scribe would be required to express ideas on a board or flip chart. The chairperson is in charge of moderating the discussion. Not every meeting would need all these participants. Participation by no more than 15 people is usually required for effective interaction. The members are required to declare conflict of interest (COI) before the meeting in relation to any item on the agenda. Depending upon the nature of the conflict, the chair can allow the member to participate after registering the conflict, restrict his role in the meeting, or recruit another member in his position. In extreme situations, the member can be removed from the meeting/organisation and can be ordered to relinquish from the COI.

3.3) Venue and time

The venue should be easy to locate, calm, comfortable, and preferably sound proof. It should support optimised use of lighting and devices for projections, animations, videos, etc. Round table with chair arrangements is preferred if there are less than 15 members and all are required to interact. Theatre style chair arrangements is suited for a group over 20 people [21]. Name cards are required, if it is a formal meeting of important stake holders. Facilities for housekeeping and trouble shooting should be in place. Departmental staff meetings are preferably scheduled during lunch time, when hospital staff members are free of clinical commitments. Meetings on weekends, public holidays and Friday afternoons are best avoided to ensure attendance [21].

4) The ground rules for successful and productive meetings [22] and **responsibilities of the chairperson** are covered in Tables 4.4 and 4.5.

Table 4.4 Ground rules for successful meetings

Start and end on time
Avoid briefing late comers
Mobile phones in meeting mode
No smoking
Breaks after every 45 min
Coffee and refreshments during long meetings
Speak one at a time
Avoid personal criticism and private conversations
Respect everyone's ideas
Avoid repetition and irrelevant discussion

Table 4.5 Responsibilities of the chairperson

Prepare the agenda
Select and invite the participants, organise venue date and time
Collect background information and review previous meetings
Introduce the participants
Set ground rules and time limits
Facilitate discussion, and consensus decision
Assignment of tasks with deadlines
Summarise and evaluate the meeting

5.1) Handling speakers

- **Incessant speakers**: The chairperson can hint the speaker to stop by making gestures (turning around, looking disinterested, having side conversations), asking to summarise thoughts, promptly thanking for input, or by asking another speaker to comment on his/her opinion. At times, active interruption is needed.
- **Passive participants**: Subtle cues like frequent eye contact, asking questions that will yield a yes-no answer (e.g. do you share the same opinion?), and complimenting the comments are likely to engage them in discussion. Breaking into smaller groups for discussion usually helps in shedding the inhibitions [23].
- **Disruptive speakers**: The chairperson should announce a break, ask speakers to put their comments to paper, privately counsel the speakers, and make escape statements (e.g. can we have this discussion later?)

5.2) Active listening includes non verbal responses (smiling, nodding) and verbal responses (compliments) to acknowledge the speaker's idea. [24] This positively reinforces the speaker. Active neutrality (listening most of the time and asking few, but relevant questions) also has similar effect [25].

5.3) Confrontation

The preferred ways of confronting speakers to clarify the message include open ended questions (e.g. "Can you explain your point with an example?"), and paraphrasing ("Is that what you are trying to say?")

5.4) Handling antagonism

Partly agreeing with the opposing speaker without giving up one's stand on the issue (fogging), asking another member's view point and assertiveness while talking can control antagonism [26].

5.5) Handling mundane discussions

Coffee breaks can be a respite from mundane discussions. Visual presentations, videos, question answer sessions and tasteful humour can raise the spirit of meetings.

5.6) Body language

It is essential that speakers deliver the message effectively. Leaning forward and placing forearms on the table shows keenness in conversation. Facial expressions and gestures convey different moods of the speaker. Standing while talking, placing hands on hips, maintaining direct eye contact and referring colleagues by their first name demonstrates authority [25] Smiling most of the time could reflect nervousness and be interpreted as weakness.

- **Speech:** Clear short sentences without hidden messages, avoiding words of probability (e.g. may be) make meetings effective. Speaking loudly and fast paced can be intimidating.
- **Positioning:** During an informal meeting with colleagues of the same department, sitting amongst the speakers is preferred. During a formal meeting for major decision, the chairperson should take centre stage.

6) Decision making tools

Some meetings use problem solving or decision making tools to improve objectivity of the decisions taken.

6.1) Brainstorming: The chair poses an issue and the members are asked to spontaneously respond with as many ideas or solutions possible. Piggybacking and overlapping of ideas are acceptable [27, 28].

6.2) Round robin: This is a regulated variant of brain storming session, wherein each member adds an idea in turns. Ideas are well conceived and less repetitive, and equal participation is ensured [18].

6.3) Fishbone diagram: This is a schematic representation of a problem in the form of a fish. The problem is represented as the head of the fish and the components like resources, manpower, and equipment are the fins. It can explain priorities in solving problems. [29]

6.4) Straw poll: It is a nonbinding vote cast to make trivial decisions or to confirm more obvious decisions

6.5) Multi-voting: This is the process of narrowing down the list of ideas obtained in a brain storming session. Multiple votes are cast on selected ideas and thus, ideas are rank ordered. The narrow list can be further subjected to multi-voting to facilitate decision making [30].

7) Minutes of the meeting

This is an official and at times the only unbiased report of closed door meetings. Minutes are integral to ensure fair conduct of meetings. Protocols should be generated to allow consistent reporting of the minutes at all meetings. The minutes have to be circulated to other participants for approval and finally signed by the chairperson. The chair decides whether non participants can access the minutes. They cannot be deleted without checking the organisation policies.

8) Conclusion of meeting

The meeting has to close with the chair person's evaluation of the success in terms of agenda management, active participation, task assignment and goal achievement. Some ideas that were not addressed in the meeting due to lack of time or relevance should be listed. This is called the 'Parking Lot' list of issues, to be considered in future meetings. The chairperson could hold back some members after the meeting for discussion on confidential or controversial matters, agenda of future meetings.

In summary, meetings should not be considered as casual events. If so, the necessity of such meetings should be evaluated. Well planned agenda, directed discussion and good time management are essential for productive meetings. Documentation of minutes is as important as the meeting.

Handling Presentations

PowerPoint presentation has become the rule for conference presentations worldwide. It gives an agenda to didactic talks. Since their inception in 1987, Power-Points are installed in at least 1 billion computers and 350 presentations happen every second all over the world. [31] Lowenthal [32] in his literature review stated there are 300 million users of PowerPoint worldwide and 30 million presentations happen every day. With the rising popularity of online education, PowerPoint has transformed from being an aid to becoming a replacement of oral presentations. Ability to project images along with text is the main reason for the wider use. With every version, it is becoming increasingly easy to customise the PowerPoint to the context of the presentation. We discuss the principles and basic requisites of a PowerPoint to keep the audience engaged and evidence related to multimedia learning. Discussing the exhaustive features of PowerPoint is beyond the scope of this article.

PowerPoint presentations are ubiquitous, hence it is difficult to standardise PowerPoint models for universal use. Evidence on PowerPoint practises is intuitive. Research indicates that PowerPoint is preferred as a teaching modality among the student community, but does not improve academic performance [33–35].

Mayer in 2009 [36] described multimedia as a combination of 2 forms of presentation material- words and pictures. He further postulated 5 principles to enhance multimedia based learning (Table 4.6).

There is evidence to suggest that music integrated with the visual and verbal input could sustain attention and improve retention [37]. However, we remind the thin line between music and noise.

Table 4.6 Principles of multimedia based learning

Coherence: Content unrelated to the presentation should be excluded
Redundancy: Reading out directly from the slide should be avoided
Signalling: Key content to be summarised as short phrases
Spatial contiguity: Images and corresponding text to be juxtaposed to each other
Temporal contiguity: Image projection and narration should occur simultaneously

Two other important principles are: (1) Retroactive inhibition- As the details of description increases, the learning and retention is reduced. (2) Grammatical parallelism- every line in the slide should have the same grammatical structure. An example is given below.

Improper structure	Proper structure
Benefits of probiotics in preterm infants	**Benefits of probiotics in preterm infants**
• Reduced incidence of death	• Reduced incidence of death
• Reduced incidence of NEC	• Reduced incidence of NEC
• Reach full enteral feeds earlier	• Reduced time to full enteral feeds

Basic Features of PowerPoint

Colour

Colour scheme of the PowerPoint is expected to convey the theme of the presentation. The colour of the text should contrast and complement the background. Bradshaw showed that high contrast colours increase learning [38]. High contrast colours on a white or light blue background are preferred. It is recommended to avoid using primary colours (red, blue, yellow) for both text and background [39]. Colour constancy should be maintained through the presentation. Patterned backgrounds and gradation of background intensity within the same slide are best avoided. Colour discrepancy between monitor screens and lighting at the venue of presentation should be considered while planning colours.Light background and dark text is preferred for well lit room. Dark background with light text is preferred for dimly lit room [40].

Font Type

Serif fonts are conventionally used for the printed page in textbooks and journals [41]. The serif (meaning stroke in German) is the stylish small tail added to the edge of an alphabet. Examples—Times New Roman, Courier New, Palatino, Verdana, Georgia.

Sans serif font is recommended for PowerPoint and poster to facilitate viewing from a distance [42]. Sans serif font has a simpler structure (without the tail at the end of a letter) and includes Arial, Helvetica, Geneva, Comic Sans MS, and Century Gothic.

Serif font	Sans Serif font
Power Point	Power Point

Mackiewicz [43] reported that Gill Sans, Souvenir, and similar fonts enhance readability. Lowercase type styles are associated with improved reader comprehension [44].

Font Size

Holzl [45] described appropriate font size based on size of the presentation room.

No of seats	Heading font size	Main text font size
>200	42	36
50–200	36	28
<50	32	24

For departmental conference presentations, font size of at least 24 for core message and 32 for the title is preferred.

Tables and Graphs

A two-column table should generally have four or fewer rows. [46] For a three-column table, the maximum number of rows should be three. Line charts are used to depict trends over time. Bar charts are used to display specific point values. When X axis uses a continuous scale, bar charts are to be used instead of line charts.

Mahar in 2009 [47] showed that use of custom animation increases cognitive overload and affects student performance and is best suited to depict step by step problem solving method.

Tips for preparing PowerPoint and prerequisites for effective PowerPoint Presentation are listed in Tables 4.7 and 4.8.

PowerPoint presentations are not free of criticism. It has been considered as a virtual secretary to poor public speakers. Avid public speakers reckon that the attention of the audience could get diverted from the presenter [49]. It could reduce reasoning, analysis and interaction among the audience. The fact that a PowerPoint presentation can be downloaded and looked up later could make learning process lethargic.

Table 4.7 Tips for preparing PowerPoint presentations

Use sans serif font
Font size 20 or greater
Minimum of two different fonts to be used, one for title and one for body of the text
Not more than 8 lines should appear in a slide [2]
Short phrases should be used instead of full sentences.
Overuse of uppercases, italics and bold typefaces has to be avoided.
Text should be aligned away from margins
Use of bullet points in PowerPoints improve retention [48]
Use of institutional logo or template creates an impression
Presentation pace of 1–2 slides per minute is appropriate

Table 4.8 Prerequisites for effective PowerPoint presentation

Viewing the PowerPoint before the presentation is essential to avoid surprises and embarrassments
Formal rehearsal of the presentation will give a clue to expected questions and also help in timing the presentation
Ensure compatibility with the operating system at the venue of the presentation
Convert into a read only PowerPoint to avoid copyright misuse
Providing handout of the PowerPoint prior to the presentation can improve comprehension

Steps to Effective Oral Presentations

- Start preparation 6–8 weeks before the conference [50].
- Never overshoot the allotted time for presentation.
- Content of the presentation should cater to the audience. Exquisite detailing would be required while addressing group of experts, but not a multidisciplinary audience.

Engaging the Audience

- Choosing a relevant, hot topic or even a controversial topic arouses curiosity.
- Narration interspersed with examples, illustrations, real life scenarios, relevant stories or jokes can keep audience engaged
- Encouraging the audience to interact during the talk
- Oral presentation should be complemented by an effective PowerPoint.
- Presentation should not last beyond 30 min. A survey among medical students showed that the level of concentration drops after 15 min of lecture [51].
- Slide time (time per slide) should be no more than 3 min

Table 4.9 Tips for handling question answer sessions

Clear, short and succinct answers (one liners) are preferred over vague explanations
Admitting of not knowing the answer is always appreciated
Deliberate avoidance of explanation during the presentation can be used as a tactic to trigger some questions that the speaker had expected
Diverting questions to experts in the audience or to panel members are well accepted escape strategies that can be employed
Acknowledging and appreciating genuine questions is important

Body Language

- Calm and relaxed demeanour, adequate rest and light refreshment prior to the presentation ensure effective delivery of the content. Confidence of having monopolised the topic is essential to overcome stage anxiety.
- Constantly gazing the projection screen, swaying away from the microphone, making breath sounds audible are markers of nervousness. Eye contact with the audience is essential, but should not be restricted to selected few members of the audience.
- Pace, clarity and loudness are the three elements of speech that need to synchronise with each other.

Tips for handling the question answer session are given in Table 4.9

At the end of the day, it is the responsibility of the audience to maintain the sanctity of the session, and not use it as a vehicle for marketing or networking.

Poster Presentations

Poster presentation is usually the first milestone in the career of a researcher. For most researchers, poster presentations have been the precursor to journal manuscripts and oral presentations.

Technicalities of Poster Presentation

According to Hess et al. [52], more than 30 % of the posters in conferences fail to make an impression; they lose out on technical aspects rather than content. Most common reason was excessive description. Organisation guidelines regarding size, dimensions, background, font, templates, adhesives, interfaces to fit in the presentation boards should be meticulously followed. Posters have been classically designed on paper but fabric posters are preferred for easy maintenance and transport. Microsoft PowerPoint is preferably used to customise the poster. The most commonly used font type is Arial and font size is 24. Recommendations for font size are tabulated below [53].

Table 4.10 Tips for poster presentation

Succinct, yet self-explanatory description is the basic requirement
Restricting the information is essential
Novelty and creativity in projecting ideas make a poster stand out
Appropriate use of tables, graphs and images is preferred
Abbreviations are best avoided

Main title	100 points	At least 4 cm high
Subheading	50 points	1.5–2 cm high
Body Text	25 points	0.5–1 cm high

The main purpose is to make the text clearly legible up to 1.5 m (6 feet) and reading distance. Headings should be clearly seen at 10 ft reading distance [54]. Margin of 0.75 inches on all sides is preferred for symmetry and to allow for trimming the poster to fit the board. Most institutions have medical illustrations or professional graphics department that can print/arrange to print the poster. Velcro hook and loop or Velcro dots are the preferred adhesives, as they cause less damage to the poster and the presentation board. Poster tubes should be used to transport the poster in good condition.

Tips for poster presentation are given in Table 4.10

It is important to note that both art and science are blended to create an effective poster, and the triumph of a poster is in getting it published.

References

1. Mintzberg H (2002) Managing care and cure—up and down, in and out. Health Serv Manage Res 15:193–206
2. Van Der Wal G, Lens P (1995) Handling complaints in hospitals. Health Policy 31(1):17–27
3. Wilson RM, Runciman WB, Gibberd RW, Harrison BT, Newby L, Hamilton JD (1995) The quality in Australian health care study. Med J Aust 163:458–471
4. Bark P, Vincent C, Jones A, Savory J (1994) Clinical complaints: a means of improving quality of care. QHC 3:123–132
5. Vincent C, Young M, Phillips (1994) A Why do people sue doctors? A study of patients and relatives taking legal action. Lancet 343:1609–1613
6. Gallagher TH, Waterman AD, Ebers AG, Fraser VJ, Levinson W (2003) Patients' and physicians' attitudes regarding the disclosure of medical errors. JAMA 289:1001–1007
7. Daniel AE, Burn RJ, Horarik S (1999) Patients' complaints about medical practice. Med J Aust 170:598–602
8. Bendall-Lyon D, Powers TL (2001) The role of complaint management in the service recovery process. Jt Comm J Qual Improv 27:278–286
9. Braithwaite J, Travaglia JF (2008) An overview of clinical governance policies, practices and initiatives. Aust Health Rev 32:10–22
10. Hsieh SY (2009) Factors hampering the use of patient complaints to improve quality: an exploratory study. Int J Nurs Pract 15:534–542
11. Tax SS, Brown S (1998) Recovery and learning from service failure. Sloan Manage Rev 40:75–88
12. Rotarius TM, Liberman A, Osterman KC, Putnam P (1999) Alternative dispute resolution programs in health care: a study of organizational utilization. Health Care Superv 17:63–71
13. Hsieh SY (2012) An exploratory study of complaints handling and nature. Int J Nurs Pract 18:471–480
14. Friele RD, Kruikemeier S, Rademakers JJ, Coppen R (2013) Comparing the outcome of two different procedures to handle complaints from a patient's perspective. J Forensic Leg Med 20:290–295
15. Veneau L, Chariot P (2013) How do hospitals handle patients complaints? An overview from the Paris area. J Forensic Leg Med 20:242–247
16. Allsop J,Mulcahy L (1996) Regulating medical work: formal and informal controls. Open University Press, Buckingham
17. Dew K, Roorda M (2001) Institutional innovation and the handling of health complaints in New Zealand: an assessment. Health policy 57:27–44 (Amsterdam, Netherlands)
18. Garon JE (2002) Facilitating meetings. Clin Leadersh Manag Rev 16:215–223
19. Ogborn SE (1994) Running effective meetings, running effective groups. Health Care Superv 13:69–77
20. Harolds J (2011) Planning and conducting meetings effectively, part I: planning a meeting. Clin Nucl Med 36:1106–1108
21. Haynes ME (1990) How to conduct quality meetings. Clin Lab Manage Rev Offic Publ 4:29–36
22. Hawkins C (2008) Make meetings matter. Franklin Lakes, NJ: Career Press
23. Harolds JA (2012) Planning and conducting meetings effectively, part III: keeping meetings on track. Clin Nucl Med 37:164–165
24. Bone D (1988) The business of listening. Menlo Park: Crisp Publications Inc.
25. Umiker W (1990) How to generate power in meetings. Health Care Superv 9:33–38
26. Salzman J (1987) How to get results with people. Boulder, Colo: Career Track Publishers
27. Haynes ME (1988) Effective meeting skills. Menlo Park: Crisp Publications Inc.
28. Lippincott (1999) Meetings: do's, don'ts and donuts: the complete handbook for successful meetings. 2nd ed. Pittsburgh: Lighthouse Point Press

29. Rees F (1998) The facilitator excellence handbook. San Francisco: Pfeiffer
30. Kelsey D, Blumb P (1997) Great meetings: how to facilitate like a Pro. Portland, ME: Hanson Park Press
31. Stein K (2006) The do's and don'ts of PowerPoint presentations. J Am Diet Assoc 106:1745–1748
32. Lowenthal PR (2009) Improving the design of PowerPoint presentations. The CU online handbook. Teach differently: Create and collaborate. Raleigh, NC: LuLu Enterprises: pp 61–66
33. Hastings M, Attila S (2000) Using IT in the undergraduate classroom: should we replace the blackboard with PowerPoint ? Computers & Education 35:175–187
34. Levasseur DG, Sawyer JK (2006) Pedagogy meets PowerPoint: A research review of the effects of computer-generated slides in the classroom. Rev Commun 6:101–123
35. Berk RA (2011) Research on PowerPoint: from basic features to multimedia. Int J Technol Teach Learn 7(1):24–35
36. Mayer RE (2009) Multimedia learning, 2nd edn. Cambridge University Press, NY
37. Berk RA (2008) Music and music technology in college teaching: classical to hip hop across the curriculum. Int J Technol Teach Learn 4(1):45–67
38. Bradshaw AC (2003) Effects of presentation interference in learning with visuals. J Vis Lit 23:41–68
39. Collins J (2004) Education techniques for lifelong learning: making a PowerPoint presentation. Radiographics 24:1177–1183
40. Kosslyn SM, Kievit RA, Russell AG, Shephard JM (2012) PowerPoint ® presentation flaws and failures: a psychological analysis. Front Psychol 3:230
41. Crosby J (1994) Twelve tips for effective electronic presentation. Med Teach 16:3–8
42. Vetter R, Ward. C, Shapiro S (1995) Using color and text in multimedia projections. IEEE Multimed 2:46–54
43. Mackiewicz J (2007) Audience perceptions of fonts in projected PowerPoint text slides. Tech Commun 54(3):295–306
44. Hartley J (1986) Designing instructional text. Kogan, London
45. Holzl J (1997) Twelve tips for effective PowerPoint presentations for the technologically challenged. Med Teach 19:175–179
46. Garson A Jr (1999) Meeting improvement: a guide to preparation of "slides" for presentation, J Am Coll Cardiol 34:886–889
47. Mahar S, Yaylacicegi U, Janicki T (2009) The dark side of custom animation. Int J Innov Learn 6(6):581–592
48. Katt JM, Murdock J, Butler J, Pryor B (2008) Establishing best practices for the use of PowerPoint™ as a presentation aid. Hum Commun 11:189–196
49. Taylor D (2007) Opinion: death by PowerPoint. Dev Med Child Neurol 49:395
50. Hammerton F (1999) Successful presentations. Prim Health Care 9:24–27
51. Stuart J, Rutherford RJ (1978) Medical student concentration during lectures. Lancet 2:514–516
52. Hess GR, Tosney KW, Liegel LH (2009) Creating effective poster presentations: AMEE Guide no. 40. Med Teach 31:319–321
53. Hardicre J, Devitt P, Coad J (2007) Ten steps to successful poster presentation. Br J Nurs 16:398–401
54. Wood GJ, Morrison RS (2011) Writing abstracts and developing posters for national meetings. J Palliat Med 14:353–359

Chapter 5
Performance Appraisal and Assessment

Paul Craven

> *Don t lower your expectations to meet your performance. Raise your level of performance to meet your expectations. Expect the best of yourself, and then do what is necessary to make it a reality*
> —Ralph Marston

Abstract The training of students and clinicians is enhanced by accurate appraisal and assessment, with improved outcomes not only for the trainee but the trainer and the system in which they work.

Understanding that throughout our lives we continue to learn and this forms part of a cycle whereby we continually establish goals we wish to achieve. In clinical work, these goals may be knowledge, skills, communication or attitudes is important. To ensure a trainee has achieved goals, set by both trainee and trainer together, the processes of appraisal and assessment are applied. Appraisal provides an ongoing review of a trainee's current performance as well as highlighting future learning requirements. An assessment on the other hand, is a more formal process of ensuring the trainee meets set requirements ensuring clinicians are competent. Finally evaluating any learning episode, allows the trainee to feedback about the trainers abilities, hopefully enhancing future learning opportunities in our education, training and work institutes.

In this review we will highlight the importance of both appraisal and assessment and how, although often used interchangeably, these terms have very different meanings, with very different outcomes for both trainee and trainer.

Keywords Learning · Cycle · Goals · Teaching · Knowledge · Skill · Communication · Attitude · Appraisal · Assessment · Evaluation · Feedback · Trainee · Trainer · Formative · Summative · Constructive · Criterion · Competent · Performance

---

P. Craven (✉)
Neonatal Intensive Care Unit, John Hunter Children's Hospital,
Newcastle, NSW 2310, Australia
e-mail: Paul.Craven@hnehealth.nsw.gov.au

© Springer International Publishing Switzerland 2015
S. Patole (ed.), *Management and Leadership – A Guide for Clinical Professionals,*
DOI 10.1007/978-3-319-11526-9_5

Key Points

1. Appraisal is the key to ensure optimal learning and is a confidential understanding between the trainee/student/employee and trainer/teacher/employer regarding the trainees' current performance and future learning goals
2. Assessment is the key to ensure the trainee/student/employee achieves a suitable standard in their practice. This should be transparent and fair
3. Both appraisal and assessment are pivotal to the learning cycle
4. Evaluation is often used interchangeably with appraisal or assessment but is actually a judgement made by the trainee/employee/student about the trainer/employer/teacher
5. An assessment can be used for an appraisal but an appraisal cannot be used for an assessment, as this may bias the assessment. Ideally an appraisal and an assessment should be done by two different people

Most clinicians either in training or already in clinical practice have no doubt been through some sort of performance review, whether to review current practice, set goals for future development, set educational requirements or review their achievements and be accredited for a training period or pass an exam.

Whereas some trainees see performance review as a useful, systematic opportunity to enhance their education or develop their careers, others see it as a mere formality of a once in a year sit down with the boss.

A properly orchestrated performance review can be very powerful allowing for a systematic approach to coaching and professional development whereas a negative review may be detrimental to both trainee and trainer and may actually violate an employee's rights [1].

Assessment, Appraisal and Evaluation are terms often used in performance review. They are often used interchangeably during educational or clinical training and within the clinical workforce. These terms, however are very different and should thus be used effectively, as they have extremely different meanings to both trainee and trainer.

Throughout this chapter, I will use the word trainee to talk about a student or employee and trainer to talk about a teacher or employer, unless stated otherwise.

Despite specific meanings to each term, many forms and processes are wrongly labelled and described and can sometimes be detrimental to both trainee and trainer.

Essentially appraisal is the key to ensure optimal learning and goal achievement, whereas assessment is essential to ensure we achieve a set standard either in training or at work, and thus allows us to progress.

Appraisal and assessment, although being used interchangeably are used in a host of different settings. They can be used to formalise the process of individuals undergoing a review of knowledge, skills, attitudes or communication, especially in an educational or work related forum. Other terms such as work performance or performance review are often used and the term evaluation may be used to review the process or effectiveness of training either in a work related or educational setting, sometimes altering curriculum design or training schedules [2].

To commence any understanding of this complex subject, a more detailed definition of each term and how they are relevant to our training and work is imperative

Definition of an Appraisal

An appraisal is a confidential, honest and non-intimidating review of a trainee's current education/work performance, involving constructive feedback, and an opportunity to identify future learning or work related goals. It focuses on educational or developmental goals and relies on a two way interaction between trainee and trainer. A good appraisal will identify strengths in a trainee and areas where a trainee may need to concentrate on improvement. Appraisal forms a continuous process throughout one's life and can stimulate ongoing learning and skill acquisition [3].

In a clinical setting an appraisal forms part of a supervisor review process and often involves self-reflection of the trainee as to their own strength's and perceived weaknesses.

Definition of an Assessment

An Assessment is the judgement of a trainee's performance, by many trainers. It determines whether the trainee has reached the standard deemed necessary to progress further, whether that is with study or work.

It should be objective in nature and based on clearly defined external criteria, which should be known to both trainee and trainer, at the start of the training period. It generally counts towards the progress of the individual by demonstrating their learning and skill acquisition and stimulates ongoing learning and education.

An assessment should be an integral part of the learning and teaching cycle of all students and workers

An assessment can either be formative (developmental) or summative (judgemental) and should be detailed, accurate and constructive [3].

Feedback may or may not occur during an assessment and the outcome is often the ranking or grading of an individual, depending on whether it is a criterion based or a norm-referenced assessment [2]. Methods commonly used for assessment in clinical settings are:

- Exams
- MCQ
- Training reports/Supervisors reports

An assessment can be useful and meaningful to both trainee and trainer, stimulating both learning for the trainee and reflection on teaching and supervision for the trainer.

Although the terms are often used interchangeably, they do have very specific meanings and should be used appropriately. An assessment can be used for an appraisal, but an appraisal should never be used for an assessment. This will be explained below [4].

Use of Assessment and Appraisal

Both assessment and appraisal involve the judgement of an individual or trainee by numerous individuals. Both assessment and appraisal may involve a formal process of "feedback" and both may involve a degree of self-reflection.

Although closely intertwined in meaning, an assessment can be used for an individual's appraisal, but an appraisal should not be used for an assessment. The appraisal identifies current progress and is a confidential process which highlights both areas of strength and areas of improvement. If an appraisal was used for an assessment then the trainer may focus on the areas of relative weakness and bias the overall outcome of an assessment. Preferably the appraisal process should be performed by a different person to the final (summative) assessment process. In reality it is often the same person, but one needs to remain vigilant of the potential for bias in this.

In the clinical setting where trainees are often supervised by the same person doing an appraisal and an assessment, ensuring that the assessment is fair, not biased and has external input from other people involved in an individual's training is essential. Having set "external" criteria to base the assessment on and having the input of many individuals will reduce any inherent bias, from concentrating on areas of identified weakness in an individual's training.

Definition of an Evaluation

Often used interchangeably with the terms assessment and appraisal is the term evaluation. The true meaning of this term however is an assessment of the trainer as undertaken by the trainee. In clinical training, evaluation of the teaching or training opportunity is what is evaluated and is a very important process to ensure we are and remain effective trainers and educators. Ensuring we review the feedback

Table 5.1 Comparison and contrast of appraisal and assessment [3, 4]

Assessment	Appraisal
1. A judgement by many people of an individual's performance based on external criteria, generally at the end of a training period and may rank or pass/fail and individual	1. A judgement based by many people on an individual's current performance and identifies future learning and developmental needs
2. Involves many people's judgement	2. Involves many peoples judgement
3. Counts towards their progress	3. Identifies future learning needs and stimulates future learning
4. Generally ranks people or grades them or allows a pass/fail to be awarded	4. Generally does not rank people, but identifies areas of strength and weakness
5. Should be objective	5. May be more subjective and could be biased
6. Often exam based	6. Often consensus based
7. Must be transparent and fair	7. May be biased depending on the experience of both trainee and trainer
8. Involves feedback	8. Involves feedback between trainee and trainer

given in the evaluation process is important; trainer's should reflect on this and alter future training or educational experiences to address highlighted issues (Table 5.1).

Background to Appraisal

Appraisals are essential to ensure trainees progress through learning and skill acquisition and they are an ongoing process looking at mainly education and developmental needs. An appraisal looks at current performance as well as future personal and training requirements

Appraisals are a two way process benefitting both the individual being appraised and the organisation in which they work or study.

Every member of a clinical or work team should be appraised on a regular basis by their line manager (trainer). This should be done at the right time, by the right person, in the right place and include relevant and accurate information.

A well-constructed appraisal at the right time will allow the management and monitoring of standards, it will allow an agreement on objective's or goals to be met and a review of those that had previously been agreed to. An appraisal should motivate trainees and create a behaviour which aligns with both an individual's needs and the organisations values and it should foster a positive relationship between the trainee and trainer or organisation.

Appraisals should be a positive experience, benefitting both appraiser (trainer) and appraisee (trainee), they are often however daunting and dreaded by people, who may avoid them and thus conduct them in a poor fashion.

Introducing an effective appraisal process into a clinical team whereby the line manager (trainer) meets each trainee on a regular basis will however help to break down some of these fears [5].

A clinical appraisal often focuses on clinical knowledge, skill and communication, but really should go beyond this to include personal self-development, career aims, hopes and dreams and common interests [6]. This will immediately put both trainer and trainee at ease, which reduces the stress and uncertainty of the appraisal. Such an all-encompassing appraisal has been reported as a "whole person" developmental appraisal. At no time should such an in depth appraisal discriminate based on age, gender, sexual orientation, race, religion or disability [5].

Such a "whole person" appraisal seeks to help the person to grow in whatever direction they want, not just to identify relevant work skills and knowledge. A whole person approach builds positive attitudes, advancement, and motivation and also develops many new skills that are relevant to working productively and effectively within an organisation. In health care, a holistic approach to an appraisal would lead to a review of knowledge, skill, communication, attitude as well as personal goals that an individual clinician wishes to achieve in not only their career but life as a whole.

An appraisal can be instigated by either the trainee or the trainer.

A good appraisal has the ability to achieve and contribute to many important areas of an individual's education and training. These include [5]:

1. Knowledge, skills and communication
2. Short, medium and long term performance
3. Clarifying and redefining objectives with training
4. Future learning needs analysis
5. Career and succession planning
6. Team roles and team building
7. Personal strengths and direction
8. Counselling and feedback
9. Values/Aims and strategies of an organisation

An appraisal is an excellent way to ensure a face to face meeting occurs, in a world where this is getting harder to do. There are many ways to perform an appraisal and there are multiple systems and processes in place to ensure it is held effectively. Some people like traditional appraisal forms based on objectives identified during ones training whereas others advocate for a 360° feedback form. Any type of appraisal can be effective if performed correctly and done by both someone who understands the process and someone who is used to being appraised.

To ensure a successful appraisal is performed there are certain key issues to focus on [4]:

1. Ensure both the appraiser (trainer) and appraisee (trainee) understand the process of appraisal and that both understand what areas are going to be looked at during an appraisal. These goals or objectives of what are being appraised are generally elicited during the first meeting between trainer and trainee and often form part of an orientation period. Both trainer and trainee should have input into what these objectives should be. Appraisals should be a positive experience, but should none the less provide help if required and identify solutions to identified problems.
2. Both the trainer and trainee should be prepared for the appraisal, have notes, evidence and anything pertaining to performance and achievement available.
3. Allow the trainee to bring their organisations self-appraisal form, which is approved by the training or employing organisation, to the meeting. This forms a good starting point for appraisal
4. Think about "whole-person" appraisal as outlined above as this is appealing and inspiring to trainees
5. Choose a time when both the trainer and trainee will not be disturbed
6. Choose a place that is suitable to talk quietly and not be distracted.
7. Have the meeting space set up in a fashion that is non-threatening, room layout can have a huge influence on the atmosphere and mood of an appraisal. A relaxed environment is most conducive to effective appraisal
8. Set up regular times to meet, especially at the start of a training term, mid-way and at the end, so as to avoid the "negative cascade" at the end of the term. A more regular meeting allows familiarity and better information gathering, which can identify problems early and nurture improvement through an agreed training plan.
9. Identify a person who is going to be the appraiser and ensure their availability during the training period.
10. Have an informal introduction at the start of training to relax the trainee and discuss expectations of the training site or work place, as well as the trainee's expectations.
11. Ask the trainee "how do you feel things are going" at the start of the session both to relax them and to allow self-reflection. Most people in training or in work have great insight into what is going well and what can be improved. Self-appraisal is a very powerful tool but be wary that many people start with negatives, this may need managing to ensure a focus initially on positive attributes, before addressing identified areas of improvement.
12. Once a plan of action for improvement has been agreed, then decide on a course of action to achieve such objectives. Agree on an effective solution to each area discussed. Such help may include additional education, courses, bedside teaching, simulated learning and additional training time
13. To finish an appraisal it is always best to summarise the agreed objectives and finish on a positive note
14. If an area to improve has been identified agree on an action plan of how to address such an issue. When identifying areas to improve and a way to achieve this outcome, use the "SMARTER" rule [5–7]

a. Be Specific
b. Make it measurable
c. Agree on the area to improve
d. Be Realistic
e. Have a Time frame for improvement
f. Make it Enjoyable
g. Record your conversation

To ensure effective appraisals occur each time, people may use many of the appraisal forms generated; these must match the agreed objectives set out at the beginning of the training period between trainee and trainer.

It is always gratifying to appraise the whole person. To watch someone develop skills beyond those basics required of a training position or job is most satisfying but you will only realise someone's full potential by having that discussion around whole of person objectives, which often go beyond basic goals outlined on specific forms.

A popular choice of appraisal, to ensure feedback occurs from many people, has been the 360° appraisal process. This tool does not replace the one to one feedback process, but augments it and can be used as a stand-alone tool in appraisal. A 360° appraisal involves getting feedback from people whose views are considered helpful, relevant and un-biased. As part of the same process the trainee should self-appraise using the same 360° form? As many responses will be received for the same question by a multitude of different people, thought must be given to the weight of each reply and thought must be given regarding how to summarise such results to make them effective and make them able to be used to stimulate further development or learning.

As an appraisal is a confidential process that identifies both areas of strength and relative weakness, it should not be used for the summative or "final assessment as there may be an inherent bias to focus on identified weaknesses and as such may under value the actual learning or contribution of an individual.

A formal assessment is different to the appraisal process, outlined above and is the process of ensuring that an individual has achieved a standard that has been set, usually by an external agency and ensures that someone has achieved a standard of learning or of work achievement. An assessment will often allow a trainee to progress in their studies or in their career

Background to Assessment [2]

An assessment is an integral component of learning and teaching and refers to all processes employed by trainers to make academic judgements about the achievement of a student or a worker over a period of time. To make an accurate assessment often many people are involved in providing feedback, this is assimilated and interpreted and this feedback/information is then fed-back in a formal process to the student or employee. To ensure that assessments are accurate they must be based on pre-defined learning/work objectives and both student/trainee and assessor must have a common understanding on what they are assessing and being assessed. Following an assessment there is often a progression in either study or career. To set goals both the trainee and trainer must have input in deciding what goals or objectives should be assessed.

An assessment has a number of key purposes which can equate to either study or work development:

- They guide learning or development
- They inform an individual as to their progress
- They inform staff as to the progress of a student or employee
- They provide meaningful data that is often used to pass or fail, grade, rank or help a person progress in their study or work

Assessment provides evidence that things are basically working well and is a process, to see if someone is competent to perform a task or has achieved a set standard, usually based on set external criteria. In the clinical setting as a student, if successful, it allows them to pass from one academic year to the next and in the clinical work setting, If successful, it allows for the completion of one clinical term and progress to the next clinical term, or to progress from one job to another job, having been competent in the care of patients.

Competence is roughly described as the ability to perform a task. In medical terms, the Royal College of Obstetrics and Gynaecologists has broken competence down into five key criteria [8]

1. The doctor or medical practitioner must be adequately qualified for the job he or she is doing
2. They must be up to date with advances in their field
3. They must be an accurate diagnostician
4. They must have an appropriate technical ability
5. They must have proficient communication and interpersonal skills.

To ensure that competence is thus met, the assessment tool must be able to reliably and transparently measure all five outcomes listed above.

Assessment tools must therefore be [8]

1. Transparent
2. Accurate
3. Reliable
4. Interpretable
5. Implementable in a timeframe

In the clinical field the overall idea of an assessment must be to improve the quality of medical practitioners in the workforce, maintain their competence and must be an early warning system to us should someone fail to meet acceptable criteria.

An assessment is a two way process between the trainee/employee and the trainer/employer and should support future development and learning. It highlights their progression to date over a set period of time, as agreed between trainee and trainer at the start of the learning cycle. During an assessment there should be a formal feedback process which should be detailed and constructive. It should be timely and not only does an assessment provide information for a trainee it also provides it for the trainer or employer on which to base their judgement for ongoing employment, training or education. An assessment will generally allow a trainee to progress in training or career choice [3].

Often when we assess an individual we base it on a predefined set of agreed criteria. There are instances where we look at pre specified criteria, without reference to the achievement of others. This, criterion based assessment, would be typical of a career assessment whereas an education assessment would often base assessment on ranking with peers and colleagues [2].

Having a criterion based assessment allows the trainee/student to have clearer expectations, have more control to achieve these criteria, be more satisfied than being ranked against colleagues and allows the assessor and those being assessed to have and share a common language. Thus in a criterion based assessment all could theoretically pass or all could fail, whereas in a ranking system, there is often a certain percentage pass rate and failure rate.

The phenology around assessment is quite expansive, some of the commonly used terms may be

1. Criterion referenced
2. Competency based
3. Norm referenced assessment
4. Formative assessment
5. Summative assessment

A criterion referenced assessment is a process of assessment of learning based on pre-specified qualities, without reference to the achievement of others. For each criterion there is generally a pass or fail mark.

A competency based assessment is one whereby both criterion and performance are judged to ensure a trainee has achieved a specified skill. Often with a competency based assessment someone would be declared as either competent or not, however some institutions or workplaces are now rating trainees as being ranked from basic to highly skilled.

Naturally the extent of training and level of exposure to such skills would influence the overall competence and it would be important to set pre-defined definitions of what it means to be competent at each level of training.

Norm-referenced assessment is one whereby the assessment depends on the ranking within a group, which is the normal group. In clinical training this could be our university year of clinical attachment group. Thus depending on the cohort, a trainee may be awarded a higher or lower grade based on the position in the group, independent of the actual score/mark achieved.

A formative assessment is one which provides the opportunity for a trainee to determine whether they have reached the required standard in a "trial run", thus allowing time and opportunity to work on areas of weakness

Finally a summative assessment is the final result and counts towards the trainee's progress.

Overall an assessment judges achievement to progress in one's training and may be seen as a final stage of the learning pathways, whereas an appraisal is an ongoing process looking at current achievements and future needs.

Summary

Despite the interchangeable nature of the terms, appraisal, assessment and evaluation, their use is for different purposes.

The terms relate to an imperative part of the learning cycle whether used in an educational, work related or developmental scenario.

The learning cycle involves the initial establishment of goals, by both trainee and trainer, so that both know exactly what is expected of them, either as a trainee or a trainer. This can occur in settings such as education, work or training.

As part of the learning cycle the trainee learns/performs and hopefully achieves the set goals permanently. The trainer should have regular meetings to ensure current goals are achieved and future goals are set as well as a performing a final assessment to ensure the trainee achieves a standard that both trainee and trainer agreed was fair at the commencement of the training period.

In medicine, appraisal and assessment are used extensively in our training both as an undergraduate student and postgraduate trainee. As a student we are well versed with assessment, often performed as part of an examination process allowing us to move from 1 year to the next. As a junior trainee we become versed more with appraisal, setting career goals and then being assessed to progress from one training year to the next or from one term to the next.

Although we focus on the assessment of knowledge, skill and communication, if we consider the patients emphasis on what they expect of clinicians it is confidence, empathy, humanity, personality, respect and thoroughness. Altering the goals or objectives to ensure we appraise and assess both the classic context of knowledge and skill as well as the patient centred aspects of care, will allow a global measure of value and should capture most if not all of the diverse elements of desired clinical performance [9].

74   P. Craven

References

1. Clark JR (2013) Performance reviews: a saving grace or the devil? Air Med J 32:115–117
2. University of Tasmania (2011) Good assessment practice. Revisited edition. http://www.teaching-learning.utas.edu.au/assessment/moderating-teacher-judgments - Guidelines for good assessment practice - revised edition 2011
3. Lake FR, Ryan G (2005) Teaching on the run tips. Assessment and appraisal. Med J Aust 182:580–581
4. Lake FR. Teaching on the run: assessment and appraisal: pre course preparation package. Edcent, Faculty of Medicine and Dentistry University of Western Australia, Version 0105
5. Businessball.com. Performance Appraisals. Performance appraisals, performance evaluation and assessment of job skills, personality and behaviour, tips for 360° feedback, 360° appraisals, skill-set assessment and training needs analysis tips and tools
6. Somaseker K, Shankar J, Conway KP, Foster ME, Lewis MH (2003) (28 January 2014) Assessment of basic surgical trainees: can we do more? Postgrad Med J 79(931):289–291. http://www.ncbi.nlm.nih.gov/pubmed/12782777
7. Bacal and Associates (2006) What are SMART goals? Performance management Help Centre
8. Report of an RCOG Working Party Bridging the Gap between Assessment and Appraisal. The Royal College of Obstetricians and Gynaecologists. December 2006
9. Berenson RA, Kaye DR (2014) Grading a physicians value-the misapplication of performance measurement. N Engl J Med 369:2079–2081

Chapter 6
Quality Improvement

Brendan Paul Murphy

Quality is everybody's responsibility
—W. Edwards Deming

Abstract Increasing patient demands and expectations, an ever expanding complexity of healthcare needs and dwindling resources mean that an understanding and incorporation of quality improvement into daily practice has become essential for all healthcare professionals. Clinicians, managers and information technology analytical professionals each have quite different areas of expertise and at times speak very different languages. These diverse groups must learn to work together, communicate effectively, analyse structures and processes, manage change and evaluate outcomes to bring about meaningful sustainable improvements in healthcare delivery.

In this chapter we discuss the introduction of quality improvement techniques into the modern healthcare setting, outline some basic quality improvement principles and terminology and introduce some tools that can be used by healthcare teams on their local quality improvement journey.

Keywords Quality Improvement (QI) · Key performance indicator (KPI) · Control chart · Dashboard · Case-mix · Risk adjustment · Benchmarking · Process · Outcome · Data · Measurement · Clinical value compass · Plan-Do-Study-Act (PDSA) cycle · Leadership

B. P. Murphy (✉)
Cork University Maternity Hospital, HSE South, Wilton, Cork, Ireland
e-mail: brendanpaul.murphy@hse.ie

Department of Paediatrics and Child Health, University College Cork, Cork, Ireland

Key Messages

- Quality Improvement (QI) is a continuous structured process involving all members of the healthcare team to bring about change to optimise patient outcomes, improve healthcare system performance and enhance professional development.
- Healthcare delivery systems are complex dynamic environments in a constant state of flux. The key to identifying beneficial change is measurement.
- To determine whether a change leads to an improvement, QI teams must test it in the real work setting—by planning it, trying it, observing the results, and acting on what is learned.
- QI team members across clinical, managerial and information technology professions need to work together communicating effectively, to analyse, interpret and evaluate clinical, functional, satisfaction and cost outcomes to achieve sustainable healthcare improvements.

Stakeholders, quality improvement, key performance indicators, toolkits, dashboards—all terms with differing degrees of relevance and importance to the many members of today's diverse healthcare team—medical, nursing and allied clinical and non-clinical health professionals contributing to the patient journey through our healthcare system. To move on from good intentions and aspirations about improving quality of care, we must move beyond our own areas of comfort and expertise and examine care processes, cooperating across professional disciplines at local, regional and national level in a continuous attempt to improve what we do and how we do it. In this chapter we aim to demystify quality improvement (QI) tools and language.

Much of today's QI methods were developed in industry in the 1940s and 1950s in Japan pioneered there by the US experts W Edwards Deming, Joseph Juran and Armand Feigenbaum and the Japanese expert Kaoru Ishikawa [1]. Each of these QI pioneers recognised the contribution of each individual worker to their organisations goals, the importance of empowering all staff and encouraging each and every individual to take responsibility for quality improvement, every member of staff needing to continually improve what they do.

In the late 1980's, in the U.S. the National Demonstration Project on Quality Improvement in Health Care (NDP) was launched to explore the application of modern quality improvement methods to health care. "Improving Health Care Quality" courses were added to the Harvard School of Public Health curriculum and in the late 1980's the NDP launched its first national forum which became incorporated into a National Forum on Quality Improvement in Health Care [2]. The Institute for Healthcare Improvement (IHI) was founded around this time by Dr Don Berwick and colleagues in Boston who were committed to adapting these same principles for use in healthcare [3–5]. Over the past 25 years, IHI have collaborated nationally in the US and internationally, in UK with the NHS and the National Institute for Clinical Excellence (NICE) and with several other European health institutions as well as promoting QI methods throughout the developing world. In collaboration with the British Medical Journal, the Quality and Safety in Healthcare Journal was launched in 2002.

Definition and Dimensions of Quality

Quality: the following definition, from the US Institute of Medicine (IOM), is often used:

"Quality is the degree to which health services for individuals and populations increase the likelihood of desired health outcomes and are consistent with current professional knowledge" [6].

The IOM has identified six dimensions of healthcare quality. These state that healthcare must be:

- safe—avoiding harm to patients from care that is intended to help them
- effective—providing service to patients based on evidence and which produce a clear benefit
- patient-centred—establishing a partnership with patients to ensure care respects their needs and preferences
- timely—reducing waits and sometimes harmful delays
- efficient—avoiding waste
- equitable—providing care that doesn't vary in quality because of a patient's characteristics

Essentially QI in healthcare can be translated as providing a structured approach, or method, that focuses on changing how we provide care, with the patient at the centre of what we do, to deliver a better outcome for the patient while aiming to achieve better performance in the healthcare system and ideally making this system a better place for all involved.

The IHI has adapted these six dimensions of quality into a 'no needless' framework, [7, 8] which aspires to promote:

- no needless deaths
- no needless pain or suffering
- no helplessness in those served or serving
- no unwanted waiting
- no waste
- no one left out.

To help in achieving these improvement aims, in its blueprint for QI in healthcare in the twenty-first century the IOM formulated a set of ten simple rules, or general principles, to inform efforts to redesign the health system [6]. These rules are:

1. Care is based on continuous healing relationships.
2. Care is customized according to patient needs and values.
3. The patient is the source of control.
4. Knowledge is shared and information flows freely.
5. Decision making is evidence-based.
6. Safety is a system property.
7. Transparency is necessary.
8. Needs are anticipated.
9. Waste is continuously decreased.
10. Cooperation among clinicians is a priority.

It is all very well to have such grand aspirations to make things "better", it is another matter entirely try and put this into practice and demonstrate objectively in a quantifiable manner that improvement is happening across patient outcomes in our healthcare system.

Measurement of Quality

All improvement requires change, but not all change results in improvement [9]. The key to identifying beneficial change is measurement. The major components of measurement include: (1) determining and defining key indicators; (2) collecting an appropriate amount of data; and (3) analysing and interpreting these data [10]. Individual measurements from any process will exhibit variation. Measurement data from healthcare processes display natural variation which can be modelled using a variety of statistical distributions. Distinguishing between natural "common cause" variation and significant "special cause" variation is key both to knowing how to proceed with improvement and whether or not a change has resulted in real improvement. Shewhart developed a relatively simple statistical tool—the control chart (Fig. 6.1) to aid in distinguishing between common and special cause variation [11]. A control chart consists of two parts: (1) a series of measurements plotted in time order, and (2) the control chart "template" which consists of three horizontal lines called the centre line (typically, the mean), the upper control limit (UCL), and the lower control limit (LCL). Where to draw the UCL and LCL is important in control chart construction. Shewhart and others recommend control limits set at ± 3 standard deviations for detecting meaningful changes in process performance while achieving a rational balance between two types of risks. If the limits are set too narrow there is a high risk of a "type I error"—mistakenly inferring special cause variation exists when, in fact, a predictable extreme value is being observed which is expected periodically from common cause variation. On the other hand, if the limits are set too wide there is a high risk of a "type II error" analogous to a false negative laboratory test. Control charts can help QI teams to decide on the correct improvement strategy—whether to search for special causes (if the process is out of control) or to work on more fundamental process improvements and redesign

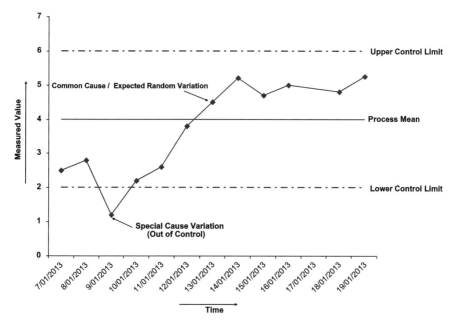

Fig. 6.1 Control chart. (Courtesy: Damber Shrestha, Department of Neonatal Paediatrics, KEM Hospital for Women, Perth)

(if the process is in control). The charts can also be used as a simple monitoring aid to assure that improvements are sustained over time [12].

Clinical Value Compass

The Clinical Value Compass framework (Fig. 6.2) places patients both as individuals and as a patient population at the centre of what we measure. It has us examine not just the traditional clinical outcomes such as mortality and key morbidities that we are familiar with, but expands our measures to include those measures that matter to patients and their families in terms of functional outcome, satisfaction and costs to include assessment of the value of our service [13]. Value can be considered as a measure of quality defined by the outcomes (clinical/functional/satisfaction) measured as a function of cost for same over a defined period of time. The strength of the Clinical Value Compass is that it encourages us to look at outcomes in all directions—clinical outcomes of interest to medical/nursing professionals, functional and satisfaction outcomes that may matter more to patients and their families (especially in the medium to longer term) and to healthcare managers who will wish to measure cost in addition to the other domains to ensure value within the healthcare system.

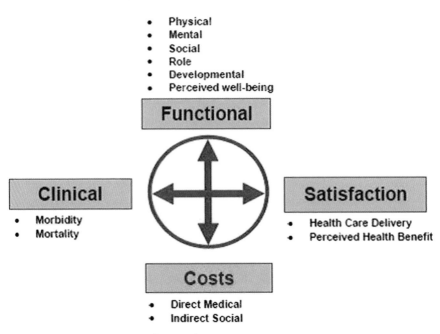

Fig. 6.2 Clinical value compass framework

In terms of driving changes and improvement, we need to measure our outcome data to quantify how patients are doing across key clinical, functional, satisfaction and cost domains. Many of our own personal drivers towards improvement include firstly comparing our current outcomes against our previous results to see if we are getting better or worse than before—time trend analyses e.g. process control charts (Fig. 6.1) and secondly comparing our own service and patient outcomes against our peers and colleagues i.e. benchmarking our outcomes against others or indeed wider international reference standards.

In discussing measurement of processes and outcomes within healthcare, it is important to be clear about the language and definitions used, particularly given the diversity of the modern healthcare multidisciplinary team. Any system can be simply defined as being composed of multiple parts working together for a common purpose or goal. A healthcare system can then be defined as the organisation of people, institutions, and resources to deliver healthcare services to meet the health needs of target populations. Within healthcare systems, process can be defined as a series of connected steps or actions to achieve an outcome. Performance measurement is the use of both process and outcome measures to understand the healthcare systems organizational performance and effect positive change to improve care [14]. A key performance indicator (KPI) is any quantifiable measure that is tied to organizational goals, used to evaluate performance over a designated time period. It is used to determine whether the practice, hospital, or other accountable organization is meeting predefined targets [15]. Many healthcare systems use dashboards which are performance monitoring systems that provide data on structure, process, and outcome variables [16]. A dashboard within a healthcare setting typically includes:

a. reports on a selection of performance indicators (feedback);
b. comparison of performance to established ideal levels (benchmarking);
c. alerts when performance is sub-optimal to trigger action (warning or signal).

Similar to the dashboard in our car, an organizational dashboard provides a visual display of how various components or systems within the organization are functioning.

Appropriate benchmarks are necessary to determine how performance compares against desired goals and objectives and against others. Benchmarking is that process through which best practice is identified and continuous quality improvement pursued through comparison and sharing [17]. However, for comparisons to be fair and valid because centres may vary with respect to their population case-mix, risk adjustment is essential to making fair comparisons. The term "case-mix" reflects the fact that, within a patient population, individual patients may have a range of risks, and that the aggregate outcome reflects the aggregate risks [18]. Risk adjustment is the process of sorting patients in each comparison group into different levels of risk and then making comparisons separately for each level. The aim of adjustment is to permit fair comparisons between groups.

"Common cause" and "special cause" variation is seen in every area of medical practice. Potential sources for variation seen in both interventions and outcomes include case-mix, chance and differences in quality or effectiveness of care. When benchmarking outcomes, if differences due to case-mix and chance can be minimised through risk adjustment, then the residual variation may provide useful information about the quality of care provided.

Benchmarking and risk adjustment requires strict definition of each specific outcome. Each risk factor is measured and weighted accordingly. Severity of illness scores attempt to measure illness severity and assist in adjusting for case mix between populations. For example, the main illness severity scores in use in neonatal medicine are CRIB [19] (Clinical Risk Index for Babies) and SNAPPE-II (Score for Neonatal Acute Physiology—Perinatal Extension II) [20]. Like illness severity scores in adult critical care medicine, both these scores rely on physiology-based items from bedside vital signs and laboratory tests to quantify illness severity. Each scores derangements from physiological norms, the greater the derangement from physiological norm, the greater the likelihood of adverse outcome with a composite severity score derived from weighted sum of derangement across all organ systems. Combining these physiology derangements with other risk factors including birthweight, gestational age, low Apgar scores and the presence or absence of severe congenital abnormalities an illness severity score with an overall risk of mortality is generated. A recognised disadvantage of both CRIB and SNAPPE-II scores is that they rely on physiological variables measured after admission to the neonatal intensive care unit (NICU). Because these variables may be influenced by the treatments provided after admission to the NICU, the scores are not independent of the effectiveness or quality of care provided [21].

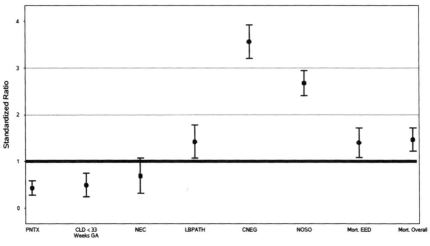

Fig. 6.3 Standardised Mortality and Morbidity Ratios (SMR). (Annual Quality Management Report. Burlington, VT: Vermont Oxford Network, 2012)

Within Perinatal-Neonatal medicine, the Vermont Oxford Network (VON) was established in 1988 as a non-profit voluntary collaboration of health care professionals dedicated to improving the quality and safety of medical care for newborn infants and their families [22]. It now comprises over 950 Neonatal Units around the world. VON facilitates benchmarking and comparison by utilising strictly defined data definitions within clearly defined patient populations within the network and case-mix risk adjustment. To adjust for risk VON uses a multivariable risk adjustment model designed to capture important factors related to patient risk [22]. The model is used to calculate an expected number of cases for each specific outcome of interest based on the case mix seen at each hospital. Measures of interest can then be created for each hospital. One such measure is the ratio of the number of observed to expected cases (O/E), called the standardized mortality or morbidity ratio (SMR-Fig. 6.3). This measure and its confidence intervals are corrected or shrunken using methods that recognize that some of the observed variation is random noise caused by chance. The shrunken values are more stable estimates because they are adjusted for imprecise estimates and filter random variation. This VON Risk Adjustment model has performed as well as the SNAPPE-II score in a study of more than 10,000 infants [23, 24].

The standardised mortality/morbidity ratio (SMR) is the ratio of observed to predicted mortality/morbidities at each centre i.e. SMR = Observed Mortality/Morbidity Rate/Predicted Mortality/Morbidity Rate. The SMR indicates whether a centre has more or fewer deaths than would be expected based on the characteristics of infants treated at this centre. If the upper bound of the SMR is less than 1, this indicates that the centre has significantly fewer deaths than expected. If the lower bound of the SMR is greater than 1, this indicates that the centre has significantly

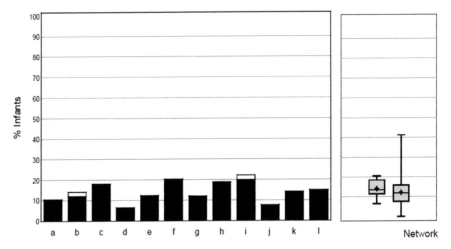

Fig. 6.4 Mortality Bar Chart with Box-Plot and Whiskers. (Annual Group Report. Burlington, VT: Vermont Oxford Network, 2012)

more deaths than expected. If the lower and upper bounds of the SMR include 1; this indicates that number of deaths expected is not significantly different from the number of deaths observed, based on the characteristics of infants treated.

A graphical representation of several standardised morbidity ratios for clinical morbidities (pneumothoraxes, chronic lung disease, necrotising enterocolitis, bacterial infections, mortality) as reported by VON to participating centres as key clinical performance indicators for a neonatal unit is shown in Fig. 6.3.

Comparison and Benchmarking of Several Centres

Comparison and benchmarking of several centres (perhaps regional networks or national collaborations) can be represented by a combination of bar charts and box-plot and whiskers. In Fig. 6.4, mortality (or any other key performance indicator) can be represented as two charts placed side by side. The left chart provides bars with the data for the individual centres within a regional or national collaborative group while the right side provides information about the overall distribution in the form of one or two boxplots. A boxplot is a graphical representation of the distribution of a set of observations. It resembles a rectangular box with a pair of whiskers extending from its ends. The "whiskers" represent the extremes of the data (minimum and maximum), while the box represents the central portion of the distribution. The top edge of the box represents the 75th percentile of the distribution and the bottom edge of the box represents the 25th percentile of the distribution. By definition, 25 % of the centres have event proportions at or below the 25th percentile (the bottom edge) and 25 % have event proportions at or above the 75th percentile (the top edge). The remaining 50 % within the box represents the middle

The Model for Improvement

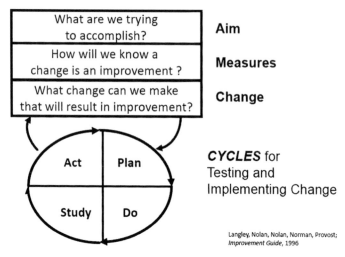

Fig. 6.5 Plan-Do-Study-Act Cycle

50% (from the 25th to the 75th percentiles) of the hospital proportions for each group. The line across the middle of the box represents the median (50th percentile). Half of the centres lie at or below this line and the other half lie above it. Finally, the cross represents the mean value of all of the hospitals.

Even when a comparison is appropriately risk-adjusted, there are important cautions about interpretation, including the source of the reference (benchmark) population, sample size, and biases from incomplete risk adjustment [18].

Plan-Do-Study-Act Cycle

The Plan-Do-Study-Act (PDSA) cycle (Fig. 6.5) is part of the IHI Model for Improvement, for accelerating quality improvement [25]. Once a team has set an aim, established its membership, and developed measures to determine whether a change leads to an improvement, the next step is to test a change in the real work setting. The PDSA cycle is shorthand for testing a change—by planning it, trying it, observing the results, and acting on what is learned [26]. This is the scientific method, used for action-oriented learning.

Pareto Principle—the 80/20 rule—named after economist Vilfredo Pareto, states that, for many phenomena, 20% of invested input is responsible for 80% of the results obtained. The point of the Pareto principle is to *recognize that most things in life are not distributed evenly*. In focussing on quality improvement in healthcare settings, we should allocate time, resources and effort based on those issues that are drivers of important patient outcomes, that are readily quantifiable

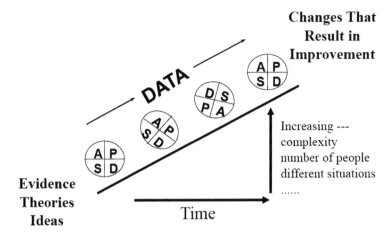

Fig. 6.6 Repeated use of the 'Plan-Do-Study-Act' cycle

and most importantly, are somewhat controlled by clinician behaviour and thus are relatively modifiable for improvement to be possible. Furthermore, we should not try and change everything at once—recognising indeed that not all changes lead to improvement, but rather recognise that repeated small changes and evaluations can lead to significant improvement in care over time (Fig. 6.6).

As QI collaboratives were developing national and internationally, since 1995, within Perinatal–Neonatal medicine VON have sponsored a series of intensive QI collaboratives in which multidisciplinary teams of healthcare professionals and families work together under the guidance of expert faculty to identify, test, and implement potentially better practices designed to improve the quality of neonatal care [27]. In these internet based international collaboratives, participants are encouraged to develop four key habits for improvement which are the basis of each collaborative (Fig. 6.7). These key habits emphasize:

- Change
- Collaborative learning
- Evidence based practice
- Systems thinking.

An example of a key clinical performance indicator that has been used by many NICU's within these collaboratives to initiate quality improvement efforts has been targeted reductions in central line associated bloodstream infections [28–34]. This SMART objective (*S*pecific, *M*easurable, *A*chievable, *R*ealistic, and *T*imed) through well recognised and validated interventions including hand hygiene and care bundles for central line placement and care, is a patient centred KPI with demonstrable improvement across all four domains of the value compass—*clinical* reduction in morbidity, improvement in *functional* outcome related to association between infection and cerebral white matter injury with impact on longer term neurodevelopmental outcome, parental *satisfaction*, particularly if infant establishes

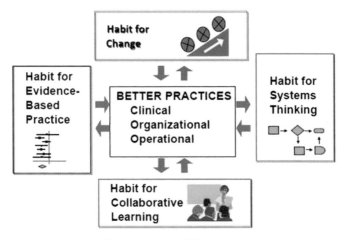

Fig. 6.7 The four key habits of the Vermont Oxford Network

feeds sooner and reduction in length of clinical inpatient stay with impact on overall patient *costs*.

Future Directions

At a national level, there are many external influences that can be used to promote improvements in quality. These include professional requirements e.g. evidence of continuing professional development, centralised government initiatives across primary and secondary care and economic drivers such as "money following the patient".

At a local level, to put data-collection and benchmarking into action, emphasis must shift from simple clinical audit and data collection towards a quality improvement approach. Instead of an endpoint in themselves, data should be seen as a resource that can show that a change is needed and that an improvement has been made. Quality improvement projects usually focus on the actual process of care at a local level. Involvement of patients/families and all members of multidisciplinary healthcare team allows for identification of specific local problems, rather than concentrating on high level outcomes laid down from higher management or national regulatory authorities trying to enforce change from a 'command and control'/top down model. The intrinsically local efforts used by effective quality improvement projects allow more targeted solutions to be developed. Local ownership of the solution should enhance the sustainability of any change project [35].

Improved information technology and clinical data management systems can make data collection for measurement easier, but with rapid expansions evolving in health information technology, we run the risk of moving from insufficient data based on manual paper derived data for QI towards data overload. For IT and electronic patient records to be properly harnessed for QI, we must ensure that data be accurate, timely, relevant (to the questions being asked), directed (at the right people), analysed appropriately and visualised in a way that makes sense to all members of the QI team [36, 37]. In the field of Neonatal Medicine in the UK, collaboration between the National Neonatal Audit Programme and the newly established Neonatal Data Analysis Unit has created the National Neonatal Database, whose collection and secure storage is greatly facilitated by electronic data capture across greater than 96 % of all neonatal units in the UK utilising a uniform technical platform (Badger.net). This National Neonatal Database is available for local regional and national projects, supporting healthcare commissioning, service development, quality improvement and neonatal research [38].

Summary

In God we trust, all others must bring data. W. Edwards Deming

Data is the foundation upon which all quality improvement is built. It is used to describe how well any healthcare system is working. Data separates what is thought to be happening from what is really happening. As outlined previously, all improvement requires change, but not all change results in improvement. Measurement and accurate data establishes whether changes lead to improvement and helps ensure that any achieved improvements are sustained as well as permitting benchmarking of performance locally, regionally and nationally.

QI teams that monitor and improve both resources (inputs) and activities carried out (processes) together will be most successful in improving quality of care (outputs/outcomes). Assessing what is done (what care is provided), and how it is done (when, where, and by whom care is delivered) together in a collaborative manner, utilising the knowledge, skills, experience and perspectives of all the different individuals within the team leads to the best and most sustained improvements [39].

True transformation in care requires not just data in real time but also clinical leadership, engaging the skills and enthusiasm of all members of the multidisciplinary team at the frontline of service delivery, involving families and especially engaging senior medical staff as partners for change. The Medical Leadership Competency Framework now incorporated into the online NHS Leadership Academy which has been adopted by all the medical royal colleges highlights that "improving services" is a fundamental part of clinical leadership [40].

Against the background of increasing demands and dwindling resources, complex healthcare systems need professionals and leaders across clinical, managerial and supporting IT disciplines who have the expertise and commitment to continually improve the quality of service they provide. QI is now a core component of our daily work. In modern healthcare delivery, it is not enough simply to turn up and do the day job and go home again. To make sustained QI integral to care, flexible, practical, clinically relevant and adaptable measures are required so that it is easy and non-threatening; a voluntary process that harnesses the intrinsic motivation to make things better for patients that brings the healthcare team to work each day.

References

1. James BC, Savitz LA (2011) How Intermountain trimmed health care costs through robust quality improvement efforts. Health Aff (Millwood) 30:1185–1191
2. Scrivens E (1997) Putting continuous quality improvement into accreditation: improving approaches to quality assessment. Qual Health Care 6:212–218
3. Improvement IoH (2014). http://www.ihi.org/about/pages/default.aspx. Accessed 19 July 2014
4. Jones FG (1990) Continuous quality improvement (CQI): solution to QA shortcomings? J S C Med Assoc 86:593–596
5. Berwick DM (1989) Continuous improvement as an ideal in health care. N Engl J Med 320:53–56
6. Medicine Io (2001) Crossing the quality chasm: a new health system for the 21st Century America CoQoHi (ed). National Academy Press, Washington DC
7. Berwick DM, Godfrey A, Roessner J (1990) Curing health care: new strategies for quality improvement. Jossey-Bass, San Francisco
8. Berwick D (1990) Escape fire: designs for the future of health care. Jossey-Bass, Hoboken
9. Berwick DM (1996) Harvesting knowledge from improvement. JAMA 275:877–878
10. Benneyan JC, Lloyd RC, Plsek PE. Statistical process control as a tool for research and healthcare improvement. Qual Saf Health Care 12:458–464
11. Miyake D (2010) Balanced scorecard measurement and control charting theory. Boston. http://www.ascendantsmg.com/blog/index.cfm/2010/11/20/Balanced-Scorecard-Measurement–Control-Charting-Theory. Accessed 30 June 2014
12. Campbell M, Fitzpatrick R, Haines A, Kinmonth AL, Sandercock P, Spiegelhalter D et al (2000) Framework for design and evaluation of complex interventions to improve health. BMJ 321:694–696
13. Nelson EC, Mohr JJ, Batalden PB, Plume SK (1996) Improving health care, Part 1: the clinical value compass. Jt Comm J Qual Improv 22:243–258
14. Nadzam DM, Nelson M (1997) The benefits of continuous performance measurement. Nurs Clin North Am 32:543–559
15. Gruber S (2012) Is it a metric or a Key Performance Indicator(KPI)? Healthcare Analytics [serial on the Internet]. 2014. http://healthcareanalytics.info/2012/02/is-it-a-metric-or-a-key-performance-indicator-kpi./#.Uw0LtWJ_uSp. Accessed 25 Feb 2014
16. Sprague AE, Dunn SI, Fell DB, Harrold J, Walker MC, Kelly S et al (2013) Measuring quality in maternal-newborn care: developing a clinical dashboard. J Obstet Gynaecol Can 35:29–38
17. Murphy BP, Armstrong K, Ryan CA, Jenkins JG (2010) Benchmarking care for very low birthweight infants in Ireland and Northern Ireland. Arch Dis Child Fetal Neonatal Ed 95:F30–35
18. Richardson D, Tarnow-Mordi WO, Lee SK (1999) Risk adjustment for quality improvement. Pediatrics 103:255–265
19. (1993) The CRIB (clinical risk index for babies) score: a tool for assessing initial neonatal risk and comparing performance of neonatal intensive care units. The International Neonatal Network. Lancet 342:193–198
20. Richardson DK, Corcoran JD, Escobar GJ, Lee SK (2001) SNAP-II and SNAPPE-II: simplified newborn illness severity and mortality risk scores. J Pediatr 138:92–100
21. De Felice C, Del Vecchio A, Latini G (2005) Evaluating illness severity for very low birth weight infants: CRIB or CRIB-II? J Matern Fetal Neonatal Med 17:257–260
22. Horbar JD (1999) The Vermont Oxford Network: evidence-based quality improvement for neonatology. Pediatrics 103:350–359
23. Zupancic JAF, Richardson DK, Horbar JD, Carpenter JH, Lee SK, Escobar GJ et al (2007) Revalidation of the Score for Neonatal Acute Physiology in the Vermont Oxford Network. Pediatrics 119:e156–e163

24. Gagliardi L, Bellu R (2007) Score for Neonatal Acute Physiology (SNAP) or Vermont Oxford risk-adjustment model for very low birth weight infants? Pediatrics 119:1246–1247; (author reply 7)
25. Horbar JD, Plsek PE, Leahy K (2003) NIC/Q 2000: establishing habits for improvement in neonatal intensive care units. Pediatrics 111:e397–e410
26. Ellsbury DL, Ursprung R (2010) A primer on quality improvement methodology in neonatology. Clin Perinatol 37:87–99
27. Horbar JD, Rogowski J, Plsek PE, Delmore P, Edwards WH, Hocker J et al (2001) Collaborative quality improvement for neonatal intensive care. NIC/Q Project Investigators of the Vermont Oxford Network. Pediatrics 107:14–22
28. Huskins WC (2012) Quality improvement interventions to prevent healthcare-associated infections in neonates and children. Curr Opin Pediatr 24:103–112
29. Kilbride HW, Wirtschafter DD, Powers RJ, Sheehan MB (2003) Implementation of evidence-based potentially better practices to decrease nosocomial infections. Pediatrics 111:e519–e533
30. Wirtschafter DD, Powers RJ, Pettit JS, Lee HC, Boscardin WJ, Ahmad Subeh M et al (2011) Nosocomial infection reduction in VLBW infants with a statewide quality-improvement model. Pediatrics 127:419–426
31. Wirtschafter DD, Pettit J, Kurtin P, Dalsey M, Chance K, Morrow HW et al (2010) A statewide quality improvement collaborative to reduce neonatal central line-associated bloodstream infections. J Perinatol 30:170–181
32. Payne NR, Barry J, Berg W, Brasel DE, Hagen EA, Matthews D et al (2012) Sustained reduction in neonatal nosocomial infections through quality improvement efforts. Pediatrics 129:e165–e173
33. Gill AW, Keil AD, Jones C, Aydon L, Biggs S (2011) Tracking neonatal nosocomial infection: the continuous quality improvement cycle. J Hosp Infect 78:20–25
34. Bizzarro MJ, Sabo B, Noonan M, Bonfiglio MP, Northrup V, Diefenbach K (2010) A quality improvement initiative to reduce central line-associated bloodstream infections in a neonatal intensive care unit. Infect Control Hosp Epidemiol 31:241–248
35. Narine L, Persaud DD. (2003) Gaining and maintaining commitment to large-scale change in healthcare organizations. Health Serv Manage Res 16:179–187
36. Strome TL (2013) Healthcare analytics for quality and performance improvement. Wiley, Hoboken
37. Spitzer AR, Ellsbury DL, Handler D, Clark RH (2010) The pediatrix babysteps data warehouse and the pediatrix qualitysteps improvement project system–tools for "meaningful use" in continuous quality improvement. Clin Perinatol 37:49–70
38. Spencer A, Modi N (2013) National neonatal data to support specialist care and improve infant outcomes. Arch Dis Child Fetal Neonatal Ed 98:F175–F180
39. Services USDoHH HRSA clinical quality and performance measures supplemental technical assistance (2011). http://www.hrsa.gov/quality/toolbox/methodology/qualityimprovement/index.html. Accessed 27 March 2014
40. Colleges AoMR (May 2009) Medical leadership competency framework. http://www.leadershipacademy.nhs.uk/discover/leadership-framework/. Accessed 25 Feb 2014

Chapter 7
Risk Management

Bronwyn Shumack

A ship in harbor is safe, but that is not what ships are built for
From Salt from My Attic
—by JA Shedd

Abstract Doctors are highly skilled at managing patients' clinical risks and consider these as part of everyday care. Many have also participated in clinical quality improvement processes, again aimed at reducing clinical risk. Yet when it comes to system level risk management, involvement by medical practitioners is much lower, and valuable insights can be missed. This chapter provides a practical example of a significant clinical risk in contemporary medicine and shows how formal risk management approaches can assist in reducing the risk of undetected patient deterioration due to alarm fatigue. It guides the reader through the core elements of risk management as described in the Australiana and New Zealand Standard, highlighting the importance of considering the context, through to identifying, applying and monitoring appropriate solutions.

Keywords Alarm fatigue · Analysis · Assess · Communication · Context · Evaluation · Governance · Hazard · Human factors · Identification · Improvement · Monitoring · Patient · Risk · Safety · Solutions · System · Team · Treatment

B. Shumack (✉)
Clinical Excellence Commission, Level 13, 227 Elizabeth Street,
Sydney, NSW 2000, Australia
e-mail: bronwyn.shumack@health.nsw.gov.au

© Springer International Publishing Switzerland 2015
S. Patole (ed.), *Management and Leadership – A Guide for Clinical Professionals,*
DOI 10.1007/978-3-319-11526-9_7

Key Points

- Medical clinicians already have many risk management skills embedded in their clinical practice, even if they don't recognise this
- Risk management frameworks assist in prioritising risks, and help to differentiate between hazards which may have no impact in a particular setting, and those which do (risks)
- Formal risk management approaches are applicable to frontline health care and provide a structured approach to dealing with risks to patient safety
- Health care delivery is about people working with other people to help patients. All risks and approaches to manage these must be considered in context and must therefore must also consider human factors
- The only way in which sustainable effective improvements to the safety and quality of care can be made is by clinical staff, management and support services all working together to identify and manage risk.

For most clinicians, mention of risk management usually conjures up images of graphs prepared by specialised staff dissociated from the clinical frontline, for the purposes of committee discussions, unfavourable comparison with imposed benchmarks or worse still, the threat of legal claims. It is not perceived to be part of daily clinical practice. Yet most clinicians consider risks whenever they prescribe treatment for their patients. They inherently quantify and stratify these before determining whether to accept that risk or attempt to mitigate it. For example, the decision to withhold or reverse the effects of anticoagulants if a patient with a known cardiac history requires surgery involves a risk management approach. Organisations which adopt procedural guidelines to ensure this component of care is considered for each patient are demonstrating the same risk management strategy on a broader scale. They are aiming to reduce the effects of uncertainty (unknown/uncontrolled coagulopathy) on the objective of patient safety and best possible clinical outcomes.

Quantifying the overall level of risk associated with health care is the subject of ongoing debate [1, 2]. Amalberti describes that while there has been a lot of work "on identifying and reducing preventable events[and] important changes have already been made to the accident and incident reporting system, and the associated techniques of analysis, the upper limit of harm prevention is unclear". The risk of dying during health care may be as high as 1:1,000, compared with 1:1,000,000 in commercial aviation [3]. Attempts have also been made to quantify the cost of risks to patient safety, but this is not easy. Etchells et al were only able to identify evidence of improvements for five conditions/protocols, three of which related to healthcare associated infections [4].

This chapter aims to describe the principles and processes of risk management as it occurs in the public health organisational context and the similarities to management of clinical risk at the patient bedside.

What is Meant by Risk?

The Australian and New Zealand Risk Management Standard AS NZS ISO 31000-2009 Risk Management—Principles and Guidelines defines risk as *the effect of uncertainty on objectives*. Risk Management is defined as the architecture (principles, framework and process) to control risks effectively. Managing risk refers to applying that architecture to a particular risk [5].

Risk Management

Most risk management models are designed to assist the user in considering all relevant sources of information and contributors to risk within their organisation, such as incident reporting systems, patient complaints, audits and comparison with expected standards. As Vincent tells us, simply counting the number of reported incidents by type does little to inform us about the underlying risks within our systems [6]. We need to identify underlying causes for incidents, so that risks can be addressed at the most basic level. We need to understand the narrative [6]. The same applies to risk management.

Amalberti and Hourlier advise that "the risk run by patients [receiving acute health care] remains hard to assess" [7], primarily because the risks don't occur in isolation. For example the patient may have inherent risk factors (comorbidities) as well as the presenting problem and the risks associated with its treatment. There is also a continual trade-off between throughput and safety [8] in order to meet demand; conditions under which Williams states that staff are more likely to make errors or take short cuts in order to get the job done [9].

Principles of Risk Management

Risk management is about addressing uncertainty. It is a structured approach, intended to assist teams and organisations in achieving their goals, maintaining health and safety of all stakeholders, and the organisation's values and integrity. In the health context, it needs to be applied to patient and staff safety, as well as the structures and processes of the health care services provided by the organisation. To do this effectively, it must use the best available information, be embedded in organisational processes and used in decision-making processes at all levels of the organisation in a structured and timely way. Management decisions must be informed by frontline staff because they have intimate knowledge about risks and their impact. The processes by which decisions are made must be logical and transparent, so that the best solutions are implemented.

As with incident management, risk management must be tailored to the context of the organisation. It must consider the human and cultural factors associated with each risk and how each may influence the strategies proposed to manage these. Risk management approaches should be proactive, to prevent harm or loss occurring, rather than just trying to prevent recurrence. Effective risk management needs to be dynamic, responsive to changes that occur in every health care setting over time. The general quality improvement cycle approach is just as applicable to risk management as it is to specific clinical projects.

Frameworks and Policies

Under the Australian and New Zealand Risk Management Standard ISO31000-2009 (10), organisations are expected to establish a framework for risk management, not just in relation to clinical or corporate incidents, but "enterprise-wide" [10]. Achieving this relies on engagement of those who have the authority, ability and will to set up and maintain the core elements of the framework. As Margaret Mead would tell us, this is best done by "a small group of … committed people" [11] with good leadership, and it involves:

• Defining and understanding the context (internal and external)
• Establishing governance, including allocation of resources and policy
• Communication, engagement and integration of the framework with existing systems
• Ongoing monitoring, review and improvement of the framework [10]

As discussed earlier, risk management should be embedded in all processes, policies and management practices. Communication and consultation must be ongoing, beginning with provision of mechanisms for input to identify and document risks (including incident and trigger reporting, patient feedback systems, audits, measurement against relevant standards). There should be no constraint or punishment associated with the reporting of risks. The core processes for identifying risks must include consideration of the internal and external contexts, and the risks associated with each, robust risk assessment processes (including identification, analysis, evaluation), treatment of the risk, followed by monitoring and review of the effect of risk treatment and any ongoing threat [10].

Considerations When Applying Risk Management Processes

"Most accidents are attributed to human error, but in almost all cases the human error was a direct result of poor design" [12]. James Reason, well known for his work on organisational accidents and human error, describes different types of risks requiring different responses. In his terms, latent risks are the conditions under which a worker operates [13, 14]. The more complex the task or organisation, the greater the likelihood that these will be imperfect or unstable, setting us up to make errors

[15]. We may fail to do something we intended to because we had to "work around" a barrier or make do with what was available. We may experience cognitive overload due to the amount of information presented to us, or be distracted by a noisy or busy environment, competing priorities or our own intruding thoughts.

The most effective risk management frameworks are those which recognise human factors, both strengths and weaknesses, "hazard and hero" [13]. The definition used by the Clinical Excellence Commission, NSW is derived from the Society for Human Factors and Ergonomics and the work of Canadian Professor Jan Davies. Human factors is about people's abilities, characteristics and limitations, their work environments, equipment interfaces, tasks, and their relationships with others [16].

In other high risk industries human factors have been recognised and managed in more structured ways. This does not always sit well with clinicians' perceptions of self-autonomy, intelligence and problem-solving abilities, the very qualities on which their careers are founded [3]. There are fundamental differences between the safety context in health care and most other industries, so even though the core components are the same, they need to be tailored to fit [17].

The findings of the public inquiry into the issues in the Mid Staffordshire NHS Foundation Trust, UK [18] show how the lack of leadership and management engagement with clinicians contributed to the breakdown of safe and effective care. This highlights the importance of ongoing efforts at all levels of the organisation in risk management.

Applying Risk Management Processes

Alarms in medical devices are intended to be a patient safety feature. The number of medical devices with alarms and the frequency with which they sound—up to 1200 times a day in a single ward [19]—is now recognised as a hazard. Alarm fatigue is a type of human error that occurs when a practitioner is desensitized to alarms and alerts [20–25]. A contemporary clinical hazard, the widespread use of medical devices with inbuilt alarms, is used to demonstrate how a risk management approach at organisational level could reduce the risk of harm for the patient, family, the staff involved, and the organisation.

The traditional corporate approach of regular audit or review processes, such as SWOT (strengths, weaknesses, opportunities and threats) analyses to identify hazards and risks are very beneficial in handling such issues. It is more common, however, for clinical risk management activities to stem from triggers, such as incident reports, investigation findings, review of literature or staff concerns. In this case, issues with alarms not sounding, not being heard or the frustration of false alarms may have been notified in the hospital's incident or complaint reporting system. Staff may also have heard about the issue from external sources. The Emergency Care Research Institute (ECRI) in the United States has been raising awareness about this issue for several years [26, 27]. It rated medical device alarms as the number one hazard for 2013, up from second place in 2011. Another US agency involved with health care quality and safety, produced a similar alert in April 2013 [28] as did the

Institute for Healthcare Improvement [29]. Numerous articles warning of problems with medical device alarms including alarm fatigue among staff, and the associated risk to patient safety have been published in the past ten years. The flow-on effects of responding to false alarms also warrants consideration, because the interruption itself may result in components care being missed. An Australian study found that 18 % of tasks interrupted in an emergency department were never completed [30], posing further risk to patient safety.

There are clearly both extrinsic and intrinsic reasons to investigate the level of risk posed by this identified hazard. While it is a hospital-wide risk, it would be best to assess it initially by looking in depth at a single unit in the hospital where monitors are used frequently, e.g., an intensive care unit.

Understanding the Context

External Context First the team should consider the external context for this unit, remembering that risks may stem from legislative, operational, financial or resource frameworks in which health care organisations operate. These influences are often beyond the control of the organisation, but may have direct consequences on health service, such as nurse-to-patient ratios and medical training resources.

There is no standardisation of medical alarm tones. Suppliers continue to develop products with features based on their experience and market research to make them competitive rather than compatible with other manufacturers' products. Public health services are therefore likely to have contracts in place which enable purchase of medical devices intended for the same purpose from different suppliers, each with their own specific alarms tones or devices with the same alarm tones and different functions. Edgworthy's [25] research in other industries, about the way in which different tones are perceived, indicates that some alarms are easily ignored.

Another contextual layer to consider is how advances in the management of clinical conditions, introduction of new devices, and promotions by media can influence clinician practice and preferences. There are few organisational constraints to the adoption of new ideas, unless there is a significant cost or dissent among clinicians. This is very different from other high risk industries where there is a more structured organisational assessment before adopting any new practice. The length of time between significant changes in "best practice" is also much faster in health than other industries—about 5.5 years, compared with 10-year cycles in aviation [31]. This presents a risk management challenge often not considered the same way budgets, overarching policies, legislation and other perceived constraints might be. For example, when the Between the Flags Program [32] and related policy [33] were introduced in NSW in 2010–2011, it prescribed the rate and type of monitoring required and focussed attention on monitoring devices. The risks associated with increasing the number of alarms in the ward environment received little attention in the face of compelling evidence for increasing and responding to physiological monitoring. More recently, the Australian Commission on Safety and Quality in Health Care introduced the National Safety and Quality Health Service

Standards. To comply with Standard 9, Recognising and Responding to Clinical Deterioration in Acute Health Care [34], health services must have systems in place to quickly recognise clinical deterioration—another strong incentive for physiological monitors to be a standard component of care.

Local Context This is best understood through consultation with frontline staff and managers. This will give information about the influences on "how we do things here", and the cultural components which drive health care delivery more than is generally recognised. Assessment includes observing staff working under "normal" conditions, undertaking all necessary tasks. This provides information about what actually happens, including workarounds and shortcuts, rather than what people believe or report that they do. It begins the communication process which must continue throughout the risk management process. For this example, the team can assess aspects such as: How many devices with alarms are in use? Are alarm sounds audible where they need to be (signal-to-noise ratio)? Are staff able to distinguish between the different device alarms? Do staff change alarms settings according to their own preferences, or because other staff do?

The team needs to ensure that issues identified from review of external and local context, and from literature search and incident reporting are also assessed. For example: Is there a culture of turning alarm tones down or off? They could observe the actual time staff spent in patient rooms, the time taken to respond to different alarms, and if there are any other sounds on the ward e.g., patient call bells, which may have similar tones. This needs to be done in a respectful and objective way, with open communication, so that a learning culture is conveyed, rather than a punitive one.

There is another vital source of information often overlooked in incident investigations and risk management—patients. They cast fresh eyes on our processes, as do their families and carers who may spend all day on the ward and can provide great insights. Again respect and sensitivity are required. If the task being assessed is not a common occurrence, then the risk management team may consider conducting a simulated exercise in a comparable clinical area, perhaps using a high fidelity mannequin. Both observation and simulation provide great opportunity to assess what actually happens, and whether suggested solutions will work.

Assessing the Risk

There are three core components to risk assessment, once the hazard and the context have been established. The risk must be identified, i.e., does the hazard present a risk in the situation where it exists, given the external and internal context. If it does, the next step is to analyse the risk, i.e., determine what could happen if nothing was done about the risk and how serious the consequences might be. The risk then needs to be evaluated, so that decisions can be made in regard to whether or not it needs to be managed, and if so, how this will be done.

Risk Identification

In this example, the team needs to decide from the information gathered, if alarms pose a risk to patient safety. Is there evidence of alarm fatigue, poor signal-to-noise ratio or practices which negate the benefits of necessary alarms? Could patients suffer harm as a result? When the answer is yes, there is a risk identified.

Risk Analysis

The team considers their findings against the relevant risk rating scale to determine the (1) likely consequences of the risk, i.e., the amount of harm to the patient, (2) likelihood of this harm occurring (based on the probability of it actually happening and the frequency with which this might occur—a two-component assessment of likelihood).

Most risk management policies in Australia have associated risk assessment matrices, which are generally "traffic light" coloured and prescribe the type and urgency of response required, for example, the Matrix associated with the NSW Health Policy [35]. In our example, the risk of harm to patients due to failure to detect or respond to an alarm would be classified as major or even catastrophic (i.e. one or more patients could die or suffer significant harm as a result). The final rating would depend on the likelihood determined.

Risk Evaluation

Without eliminating all monitors with alarms, the risk of alarm fatigue cannot be eliminated. The hospital will need to decide whether to accept this risk, i.e., do nothing, or to do something to reduce it—either by reducing the likelihood of occurrence or mitigating the consequences. Under a risk management framework, organisations may choose to accept a certain level of risk, especially if the assessment is that it has minimal consequence or is unlikely to recur. They can then direct resources and effort towards more serious or frequent risks. It is seldom possible for health care services to eliminate risks altogether. As Amalberti et al. report [3], public health providers cannot shut the door to patients.

The Risk Management Standard [10] recommends that organisations maintain a Risk Register and build review of this into their risk management framework. Most jurisdictions require that public health organisations have governance committees in place to regularly review recorded risks and oversee progress of remediation activities.

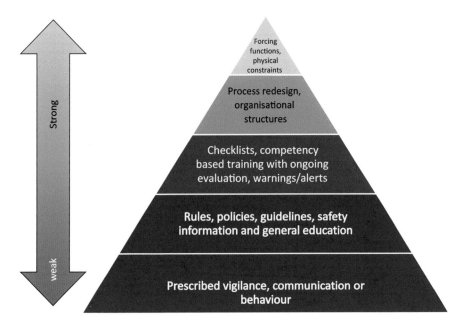

Fig. 7.1 Strength of risk management controls in health care. (Courtesy of the clinical excellence commission, NSW)

Risk Management

Once the risk has been described, the context in which it exists and must be managed is understood, and its severity has been ranked, the risk management team must decide how exactly it is to be managed ("treated"). This is a consultative and cyclical process which includes an understanding of what can and can't be changed.

Most efforts in health care improvement focus on process change, considering we rely on the actions of people to deliver care to patients. Knowing that we work with well-intentioned people, we expect that everything will be safer if we work together to maintain awareness of risks. We need to learn from other high risk industries, where human factors are considered a core element of the context and solution. Reviewing the hierarchy of controls in many safety systems is helpful, and in fact similar to the principles for managing risks. The aim is to consider options from the top of the pyramid first, as these have been shown to be more robust and reliable in preventing human error, as shown in Fig. 7.1.

Engineering solutions are not always applicable in health care, but are the most robust and should be considered more often than they actually are. For example, following an incident where a patient received a ten-fold dose due to a syringe driver programming error, the supplier worked with NSW Health staff to reprogram these devices across the state. This is a much stronger solution than adding a sticker to warn other staff (what happens when it wears off or is no longer novel?) or educating the current staff in the local area (what happens when they move on or are backfilled by agency staff? What about other areas with the same risk?).

Another common response in health care is policy or guideline development and general education. These are considered fairly weak, but are often the only option, and if done concurrently, consistently, with reinforcement and monitoring, can result in cultural and behavioural changes required.

We also need to consider the side effects. As Reason says, "don't cause the next adverse event while trying to prevent the last one [recurring]" [14]. Amalberti similarly advises us to identify potential side effects whenever we make changes to processes, and to measure these. He warns us not to fall for "the Tuesday paradigm", meaning don't design solutions which will only work in optimal conditions, when the full range of personnel and expertise is available. Sixty per cent of acute health care in Australia occurs after normal business hours or on weekends, so we need to build solutions to fit these conditions.

In the alarm fatigue example, how can the organisation manage this risk and maintain the benefits of patient monitoring? What solutions are realistic? We need to consider what is being done by National or jurisdictional bodies, by the Colleges, and check how other similar services are tackling the problem. The Joint Commission declared medical device alarm management as a patient safety goal for 2014 [36], and listed specific governance and risk management activities to reduce this risk to patients. Many of these can be applied locally and should be considered for this example. As Richard Know stated after visiting the Boston Medical Centre "it may be that less technology can actually be more effective" [19].

Monitoring the Effectiveness of the Solutions Applied

Once solutions are identified, the organisation needs to ensure their implementation and effectiveness is monitored at all appropriate levels across the hospital, and they are modified if indicated. This is likely to include structured audits, reviews and improvement cycles.

A worked example of all the stages utilised to manage this risk are shown in Table 7.1.

Applying Risk Management Principles to Clinical Care Decisions

The worked example describes an organisational approach to a hospital-wide risk. However, as mentioned earlier, many of the clinical practices and decision-making processes used daily by the clinicians are actually risk management. They may have been built from previous formal risk management processes, application of learning from other services or sources, or from discussions between clinicians or with

Table 7.1 Health care risk management example

Risk Management Component	Activities required	Medical Device Alarm example	
Establish the Context			
Team gathers and reviews the relevant information. The risk components are defined, so that changes made can be evaluated against these.			
External context	Establish the broader influences on the hospital which influence what the hospital is required or expected to do.	Bring together information about National, jurisdictional, parent organisation & professional bodies' perspectives in relation use of medical monitoring devices which have inbuilt alarms.	
Internal context	Establish the local requirements and influences – how we do things here	Bring together information about the local context, including clinician preferences, in relation to need for and use of medical monitoring devices which have inbuilt alarms.	
Risk Assessment			
Risk identification	Identify risks or determine if known risk applies in this setting	Determine if the use of monitoring devices has or is likely to cause alarm fatigue (known risk) and poses a risk for patient safety at this hospital.	
Risk analysis	Determine the likely causes and impacts of the risk and rate it	Describe the risk componets. Use the relevant Risk Rating Scale to determine the level of risk in the hospital	
Risk evaluation	Determine whether the risk will be accepted or treated and decide how to tackle the problem	Follow the prescribed process so that the risk associated with alarm fatigue in the hospital can be considered by the peak risk management committee and/or team.	
Risk treatment			
Risk treatment	Develop a detailed plan and work with staff to address risk components	Decide what strategies will be used to reduce alarm fatigue and work with staff to trial and implement these. Adapt or reject until workable strategies are in place. This may include defining processes and authority for changing alarms settings, removing monitors.	Consult and communicate
Risk monitoring			
Risk monitoring	Use the criteria agreed when establishing the context and articulating the risk to monitor and report on the effect of changes made	Decide which changes to monitor alarm usage will be measured and work out realistic ways to do this, e.g., audit tool. Defi will be assessed should it be required to introduce them. Track via the hospital's risk register or committee processes	

patients. "Steal shamelessly, but implement wisely", as context and ownership can make or break safe practice.

Many embedded clinical risk management practices promote communication about risks at the point of care delivery. The considerations are the same as in the formal processes described above: Establish the context (what do we know about the patient's current condition(s) and what does the health care community know about treating this?); Assess the risks (do they apply to this patient, if so, to what extent and what could happen next, as a consequence? The latter is also referred to as situational awareness [37]; Evaluate the risk (Should we accept the risk and proceed—or do we need to consider managing what might happen?); treat the risk (what are we going to do to reduce the risk or mitigate its harmful consequences?) Monitor the risk (Care planning would include recommendations about monitoring for any sequelae which the risk treatment did not address or may have caused). Discussing the outcome for patients in team or morbidity and mortality meetings or less formal contexts enables review and sharing of learning and continues the risk management cycle.

The aggregated learning from the application of these processes has resulted in many of the clinical structures and processes which clinicians are expected to follow. Decision support tools, protocols, guidelines and checklists have all evolved from management of identified clinical risks. For example, surgical safety checklists [38] and formal "rounding" [39] are intended to ensure staff consider the known risks for every patient and together determine how these will be managed. They also emphasise patient engagement as a vital risk management strategy. Similarly, clinical care bundles are built from information gathered about individual patient's risks and outcomes during death reviews, incident investigations and clinical audits. They build from the individual case to recommend how care should be delivered so that patient have the best possible outcome. Utilising bundles removes the need for clinicians to reconsider every risk each time they prescribe similar treatment, for example, applying the FASTHUG bundle [40] when managing ventilated patients. Considering the complexity of health care risks described by Amalberti [3], this is an important risk management strategy which allows clinicians to focus on other components of care.

In summary risk management is all about standardising the best possible care, by supporting and steering clinicians along the right pathways, for they are health care's greatest strength and our greatest hazard. Risk management is a core element of clinical practice and fits easily within the skill set of clinicians. Without their involvement, real change cannot occur. Safety, quality and risk management activities are pointless if they only occur in a domain removed from clinical care. This is not rocket science, but it does require a little time, optimistic problem solving and a commitment to a just, learning culture. This is another example of the importance of a team approach to health care. The bringing together of great minds, with a range of insights and practical knowledge is the best risk reduction strategy known to health care.

Whether the risk management cycle is part of proactive service review, or occurs in response to risks identified during incident investigations (such as root cause analysis), this tool can give us a free lesson and opportunity to prevent patient harm. Risk management utilises the most powerful element in health care—its frontline staff and managers, who are the only ones who can really improve the safety and quality of everyday care. Engaging in risk management activities and initiating them by speaking up for safety (ref) are essential elements of health care in the twenty-first century.

References

1. Wilson R, Runciman W, Gibberd R et al (1995) The quality in Australian health care study. Med J Aust 163:458–471
2. IOM (1999) To err is human: building a safer health system. Institute of Medicine, Washington
3. Amalberti R, Auroy Y, Berwick D, Barach P (2005) Five system barriers to achieving ultrasafe health care. Ann Intern Med 142:756–764
4. Etchells E, Koo M, Daneman N et al (2012) Comparative economic analyses of patient safety improvement strategies in acute care: a systematic review. BMJ Qual Saf 21(6):448–456
5. StandardsAustralia (2009) AS NZS ISO 3100-2009 risk management principles and guidelines. SAI International
6. Vincent C (2007) Editorial—incident reporting and patient safety. BMJ 334:51
7. Amalberti R, Hourlier S (2011) Human error reduction strategies in health care. In: Carayon P (ed) Handbook of human factors and ergonomics in health care and patient safety. CRC Press, US
8. Amalberti R (2006) Optimum system safety and optimum system resilience: agonist or antagonists concepts? In: Hollnagel E, Woods D, Levison N (eds) Resilience engineering: concepts and precepts. Ashgate, Avebury, pp 238–256
9. Williams JC (1988) A data-based method for assessing and reducing human error to improve operational performance. IEE Fourth Conference on Human Factors in Power Plants, Monterey, 6–9 June 1988
10. StandardsAustralia (2009) AS/NZS ISO 31000:2009 Risk management—principles and guidelines. SAI Global
11. Mead M. "Never doubt that a small group of thoughtful, committed people can change the world. Indeed, it is the only thing that ever has." 1901–1978
12. Norman D (1988) The design of everyday things. Basic Books, New York
13. Reason J (2008) The human contribution. Ashgate, Surrey
14. Reason J (1997) Managing the risks of organizational accidents. Ashgate, Surrey
15. Rasmussen J (1982) Human errors: a taxonomy for describing human malfunction in industrial installations. J Occup Accid 4:311–333
16. Ergonomics SfHFa (2013) Human factors definitions. http://www.hfes.org/Web/EducationalResources/HFEdefinitionsmain. html. Accessed Mar 2012
17. Grote G (2012) Safety management in different high-risk domains—all the same? Saf Sci 50:1983–1992
18. Francis R (2013) Report of the Mid Staffordshire NHS Foundation Trust Public Inquiry. The Staionary Office, London
19. Knox R (2014) Silencing many hospital alarms leads to better health care. Health news from NPR
20. Bell L (2010) Monitor alarm fatigue. Am J Crit Care 19:38
21. Hannibal G (2011) Monitor alarms and alarm fatigue. AACN Adv Crit Care 22(4):418–420
22. Sendelbach S (2012) Alarm fatigue. Nurs Clin North Am 47:375–382
23. Bell L (2010) Monitor alarm fatigue. Am J Crit Care 19(1):38
24. Mitka M (2013) Joint commission warns of alarm fatigue. JAMA 309:2315
25. Edgworthy J (2012) Medical audible alarms: a review. J Am Med Inform Assoc 20:584–589
26. ECRIInsitute (2013) Top ten health technology hazards. ECRI, 2012 November 2012. Report for 2013
27. ECRIInstitute (2007) The hazards of alarm overload. URL: www.ecri.org/Products/Pages/Hazards ofAlarmOverload.aspx. Accessed 9 Jan 2014
28. TheJointCommission (2013) Sentinel event alert: medical device alarm safety in hospitals
29. IHI (2013) The leader's role in medical device safety. Reprinted from Healthcare Executive May/June 2013
30. Westbrook J (2010) The impact of interruptions on clinical task completion. Qual Saf Health Care 19(4):284–289

31. Dixon-Woods M, Amalberti R, Goodman S, Bergman B, Glasziou P (2011) Problems and promises of innovation: why healthcare needs to rethink its love/hate relationship with the new. BMJ Qual Saf 20:i47–i51
32. CEC (2010) Between the flags program: keeping patients safe. http://www.cec.health.nsw.gov.au/programs/between-the-flags. Accessed 3 Jan 2014
33. NSWHealth (2013) PD2013_049 recognition and management of patients who are clinically deteriorating (replaces PD 2011_077) (CEC (ed)). NSW Health, Sydney
34. ASCQHC (2011) National safety and quality health service standards. Australian Commission on Safety and Quality in Health Care, Sydney
35. NSWHealth (2009) Risk management—enterprise-wide policy and framework—NSW health (Management CGaR (ed)). NSWHealth, Sydney
36. TheJointCommission. The Joint Commission Perspectives. The Joint Commission announces 2014 patient safety goal2013
37. Singh H, Giardina TD, Petersen LA, Smith MW, Paul LW, Dismukes K et al (2012) Exploring situational awareness in diagnostic errors in primary care. BMJ Qual Saf 21:30–38
38. Pysyk C, Davies J (2013) Using the surgical safety checklist. Acta Anaesthesiol Scand 57:135–137
39. Reinertsen J (2010) Institute for healthcare improvement: rounding to influence. Healthc Exec 25(5):72–75
40. Vincent J (2005) Give your patient a fast hug (at least) once a day. Crit Care Med 33:1225–1230

Chapter 8
Root Cause Analysis

Aarti Raghavan

Getting to the bottom of an event
—Author Unknown

Abstract Root cause analysis (RCA) is a retrospective method of analyzing sentinel events and errors aimed at identification of the "root cause" of the problem. The RCA process should be initiated upon identification of a sentinel event, and typically includes the formation of a team of key stakeholders, investigation of the situation and collection of data on the process, identification of possible causes, development and presentation of recommendations, and the implementation of "tests of change" for the new process. Studies confirm that adoption of the RCA process can lead to a cultural shift in the institution, moving from individual blame to identification of systemic errors, and the development of policies for patient safety and eventually, a reduction in the frequency of occurrence of the sentinel event in question. Appropriate application of the RCA process requires stringent use of the methodology, in-depth analysis of the situation and possible causes, and an experienced team. Hindsight bias and bias towards one possible cause of an event could seriously hamper the outcome of an RCA, resulting in changes in practice with limited benefit and potential harm including misallocation of resources. On the other hand, a well-conducted RCA can provide significant value addition to various quantitative measures of quality of care.

Keywords Root-cause analysis · Quality improvement · Sentinel errors · Error reporting · Pareto charts · Run charts · Control charts · Fishbone diagram

A. Raghavan (✉)
Division of Neonatology, Department of Pediatrics Children's Hospital University of Illinois, University of Illinois Hospital and Health Sciences System, 840 S Wood Street, MC 856, Chicago, IL 60612, USA
e-mail: araghav1@uic.edu

© Springer International Publishing Switzerland 2015
S. Patole (ed.), *Management and Leadership – A Guide for Clinical Professionals,*
DOI 10.1007/978-3-319-11526-9_8

Key Points

- Root Cause Analysis (RCA) is a systematic method of analyzing a problem or non-conformance in a non-confrontational manner, to get to the "root cause" of the problem.
- To be beneficial, rigorous methods should be employed in conducting an RCA.
- Multiple studies show that the strength of an RCA lies in introducing culture change and identifying areas of improvement.
- RCAs can be limited by hindsight bias, inexperienced leadership in RCA methodology and limited investigation.
- RCA is an excellent tool to supplement quantitative methods, to facilitate generation of new hypotheses regarding process failures, and to evaluate events not easily studied by quantitative methods.

Informal attempts at quality improvement in healthcare can be traced back to the mid nineteenth century when Florence Nightingale first identified the correlation between poor hospital sanitation and surgical site infections in soldiers wounded in the Crimean War [1, 2]. In the United States, attempts were being made at this time to improve the quality of medical education by establishment of the American Medical Education Act to regulate the training of medical personnel. Based on the Council of Medical Education's recommendations, the American Medical Association consolidated the training structure, increased the duration of study, and standardized the admission processes leading to 75–80 % of medical personnel undergoing internship from 10–11 % during the American Revolution [3, 4]. While such informal efforts at improvement continued throughout the nineteenth and early twentieth century, formal quality improvement methods emerged mainly after World War II [5].

In early 1920s, Walter Shewhart, Edward Deming, and Joseph Juran introduced a structured quality improvement process that was centered on streamlining the workflow and data-driven decision-making [6]. However, despite rapid acceptance in industry, the healthcare sector was slower to adopt these concepts [7–10]. By mid twentieth century, the Joint Commission included the methods of change recommended by Shewhart, Deming and Juran, including organizational leadership for change, data collection and statistical analysis, decision making, and standardized methodology for quality improvement [5]. From this time on, medicine depended heavily on quantitative approaches for quality improvement and reduction in errors. The US Food and Drug Administration (FDA) was one of the first organizations to develop made formal recommendations for blood transfusions that were based on analysis of data collected from all over the country on the most common types of errors since the mid-1970s [11, 12]. The Institute of Medicine's sentinel reports in 1999 and 2001 again highlighted the high and unacceptable frequency of errors in the healthcare system. The reports entitled "To Err is Human: Building a Safer Health System" and "Crossing the Quality Chasm: A new Health system for the twenty-first Century" highlighted the failure of healthcare systems to provide safe and consistent care, which was resulting in a large number of preventable deaths [13, 14].

Root Cause Analysis in Medicine—Origin and Significance

Root cause analysis (RCA), a retrospective method of error analysis, has its origins in industrial processes and is widely used in investigation of industrial accidents [15–17]. Developed by Sakichi Toyoda, the founder of Toyota, this method was first used during the development of Toyota's manufacturing process in 1958. It was introduced to health care in the 1990s by Ishida Baigan at the US Department of Veteran affairs and Richard Croteau at the Joint Commission. Many experts have championed its use in the investigation of sentinel events in medicine [18–22].

In medicine, human errors are often classified into two major categories: (1) Active error, which occur when human factors interface with a system; and (2) Latent errors, which occur due to failures in system design [15, 23, 24]. RCA is used to identify latent errors underlying a sentinel event and provides a structured, process-focused framework to analyze an event [19, 20]. The fundamental basis of the process is to direct the user towards systemic issues that need to be identified and addressed, instead of trying to identify an individual to blame [19, 25, 26]. Systematic application of RCA may uncover common root causes that link a larger collection of accidents that may appear unrelated otherwise. Since 1997, the Joint Commission on the Accreditation of Healthcare Organizations (JCAHO) has required the use of RCA in investigation of sentinel events in accredited hospitals [27].

Definition

A root cause is a specific underlying reason that may explain the occurrence of a problem or a sentinel event, which is defined by the Joint Commission. Typically, a root cause is a situation, which when identified and altered can lead to a different outcome. Root Cause Analysis (RCA) is a systematic method of analyzing a problem or non-conformance in a non-confrontational manner in order to get to the "root cause" of the problem. Simply put, this means identifying why a problem occurred and then repeatedly asking why until the fundamental aspects which caused the system to fail are identified. Findings of an RCA are, by law, confidential in the United States.

The purpose of an RCA is to identify root causes in a system, eliminate the cause by identifying solutions, and prevent the problem from recurring. Investigation of a problem should therefore have inherent obvious benefit which should be clear to the group prior to beginning analysis. The investigators' goal in RCA should be to identify specific underlying causes. The more specific the findings, the easier it is to find solutions. This is critical since poor identification of root causes could result in significant loss of man hours and other resources wasted on fixing symptoms rather than actual issues. All stake holders in the outcome, as well as participants, who were involved in the problem, should be actively involved in the RCA, since the fundamental reason for lack of implementation/ system failure could lie with the barriers faced by the end user. It is also imperative for the leaders of the RCA to remain open-minded and focused on identifying system-based problems rather than individual issues of performance. For instance, if a nurse failed to chart the administration of a medication in the electronic medical record, the goal should be to identify barriers to charting rather than individual chastising of non-performance.

Major Steps

Step 1: Identification of a Sentinel Event

The Joint Commission defines a sentinel event as "an unexpected occurrence involving death or serious physical or psychological injury or the risk thereof" and requires every hospital to develop its own definition of a sentinel event and participate in voluntary reporting of the same [26, 27]. RCA is a time consuming process with far reaching consequences, and therefore, it is important to identify at the outset the events that constitute a sentinel event. Whereas some events are clearly regarded as sentinel events (such as avoidable death or disability), others might be institution-specific depending on systems and outcome-related issues of institutional relevance (for instance, a new case of severe retinopathy of prematurity in an institution that has recently adopted new guidelines to define the range in which oxygen saturations should be targeted).

Step 2: Assembling a Team

The RCA process should be led by an individual with training and experience with this process. Although the specific composition of an RCA team may vary between one institution *vs.* another, certain common principles must be observed. At a minimum, the team should include system leaders who can authorize a change in system, individuals with clinical/ technical expertise, day-to-day leaders/champions who can lead the group through the process, and all individuals who "touch" the process being studied in any way [28, 29]. The team should be multidisciplinary involving all frontline staff who are familiar with the process as well as the system being investigated. Although every member of the team does not need to participate in every aspect of the RCA process, the team members should be trained in RCA methodology to avoid inherent bias [30, 31].

Step 3: Verification of the Situation and Data Collection

In this step, the team should focus on understanding the circumstances of the event that occurred. This involves collection of data through structured interviews, review of documents and medical charts, and/or direct observation. Usually, this is the most time-consuming piece of an RCA. Data gathering must be comprehensive and detailed.

Step 4: Charting of Causal Factors, Diagrammatic Depiction of the Process, and Documentation of the Exact Sequence of Events

Causal-factor charting provides investigators with a tool to collect, organize, and analyze data and helps identify gaps in knowledge. A diagrammatic depiction of the process shows the sequence of events leading up to the final outcome. Preparation of this diagram should begin when information is being collected about the event, and the diagram should help drive the direction of data-gathering. Once all the data have been gathered, the diagram should provide the investigators with a list of all the factors that may have contributed to the occurrence of the event, thereby laying the groundwork for identification of solutions. In this process, multiple causative factors can often be identified. If a single factor is identified, attempts must be made to confirm that the process of data collection was comprehensive.

Charting of causal factors and the sequence of events is a key step in the RCA process. A number of formats could be used for the diagrammatic depiction of these events:

Brainstorming Maps In brainstorming sessions, all members of the team present ideas without initial judgment or *a priori* analysis of feasibility or validity. Ideas are often presented in a "round-robin" fashion using a visual format such as a white board or a flip chart. The initial focus of the discussion is quantity and not quality of ideas, and no positive or negative feedback is allowed during these discussions. After all the ideas have been exhausted, a short break is encouraged to allow ideas to "incubate." When the group reconvenes, the pros and cons of each idea are openly discussed and the best options are distilled.

Brainstorming is most useful when a group with wide experience or different roles in a process is brought together to come up with solutions to frequently-encountered problems. This method encourages individual participation, enhances team spirit and encourages "thinking outside the box". It encourages creative thinking and the development of novel, yet simple solutions (Fig. 8.1).

Fishbone/ Ishikawa Diagram Fishbone, or a "cause and effect" diagram, is a graphical representation of a given situation. The process involves a systematic analysis resulting in identification of all possible causes. The fishbone begins with a skeletal diagram demonstrating the direction of the process, where the end result or "effect" is represented with a word with a box drawn around it and an arrow pointing towards it. Possible causes are identified and categorized (such as people, material, methods, environment, etc.), and the group then brainstorms situation-specific causes under each category (Fig. 8.2). Categories may vary depending on the circumstances [32].

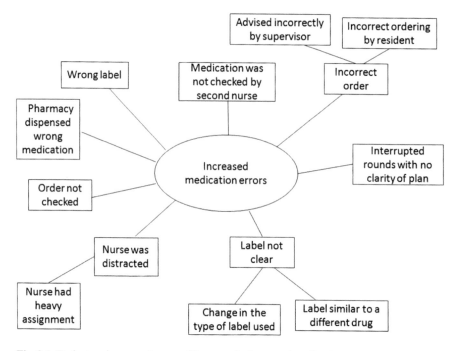

Fig. 8.1 Brainstorming regarding possible cause for increased medication errors

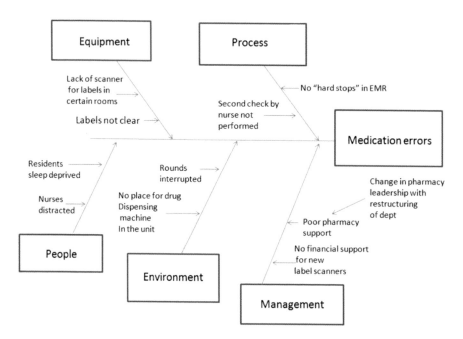

Fig. 8.2 Fishbone Diagram showing potential cause for medication errors

Pareto Chart The pareto chart is based on the '80/20 principle,' which stems from a belief that 80 % of solutions are found in 20 % of causes. A pareto chart combines bar and line graphs, where the bars represent occurrence of each cause and the line graph represents occurrence of cumulative totals. This method helps isolate common causes that lead to a particular event and draws the attention of the group to the "vital few" rather than the "trivial many" causes leading to an event. Solutions can then be formulated to specifically target these important causes, leading to better utilization of resources and reduction in waste—a key component of quality improvement [33, 34].

Performance Matrix This method involves a process of categorization of potential causes into one of four categories which are represented by a graph where the X-axis represents the frequency of events and the Y-axis represents the seriousness of the event. Causes are categorized into one of four categories and then plotted on this graph. Unimportant (rarely root causes), serious but seldom (often root causes due to impact of a single event), frequent but harmless (may not be a significant root cause based on single impact, but gains impact due to frequency of occurrence), high frequency high seriousness (most important group for RCA due to high impact and frequency of occurrence).This method allows investigators to identify areas with maximum impact [35].

Scatter A scatter plot is a mathematical diagram where two variables in a given set of data are depicted using Cartesian coordinates. In these graph, the cause is plotted on the X-axis, whereas the effect is plotted on the Y-axis. As an example, to analyze compliance with a central line maintenance bundle, the use of the bundle/patient may be plotted on the X-axis and CLABSI events/patient on the Y-axis. If lower compliance with the central line bundle were to coincide with greater number of events, it would cause and effect (Fig. 8.3).

Flowchart A flow chart is a diagram representing a sequence of occurrences leading up to a final event. This method allows the team to identify contributing factors, whether direct or indirect [29].

Shewhart/Control Charts A control chart is a graphical representation of an event in comparison to the upper and lower limits of acceptable norms, which are represented by continuous lines).In this format, the occurrence of events within the range between the upper and lower control limits may be considered acceptable. This format is best used to monitor compliance with a prescribed behavior, for example, the use of a maintenance bundle for central catheters to reduce CLABSIs in an intensive-care setting [8, 9].

Histogram A histogram is a bar graph representation of data. In the RCA process, histograms are often more useful than tables because these provide a visual, easy-to-understand tool to understand the frequency of various occurrences. This format may allow the investigator to identify major causes and the solutions that most likely to be effective. Interestingly, the patterns on a histogram may also demonstrate different issues. For example, a comb-like distribution demonstrates too many categories without enough numbers in each, indicating that there may be a common underly-

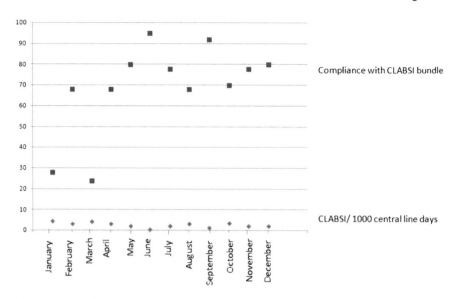

Fig. 8.3 Scatter diagram showing compliance with central line-associated blood stream infection (CLABSI) care bundle and incidence of CLABSI

ing cause behind multiple sub-categories. In contrast, a curve demonstrates a trend towards single-factor dominance, whereas a single peak indicates the presence of a single over-riding cause contributing to the occurrence of the event (Fig. 8.4) [36].

Run Chart A run chart is an illustration of certain measures plotted against time with annotations of ongoing changes in a system. Such an illustration can help in identification of variations and trends in events, and if followed prospectively, could identify a cause- effect relationship between changes in the system and outcomes (Fig. 8.5) [37].

Causal Tree A causal tree is also a diagrammatic representation of why an event occurred. In this format, the event is placed at the top of the diagram and potential causes are placed under it until all possible causes are explored. A comprehensive approach would be to ask the question "why" five times to ensure the thoroughness of investigation. Each time the question "why" is asked, it forms a new layer in the causal tree [38]. The number 5 is arbitrary, but highlights the need for extensive questioning into the process.

This method of investigations is simple and ensures exhaustive exploration of potential causes. This method also encourages analysis even in "near-miss" events, which are represented to the side of the "event". This allows the identification of systemic strengths and helps operational leadership to identify areas that need to be protected at the time of budget cuts (Fig. 8.6).

Once the entire sequence of events has been charted out, the investigators are now well-placed to identify the "causal factors". Although the group is usually focused on the most obvious and the single most-important factor at this stage, there is a need to exercise caution about not missing other contributors.

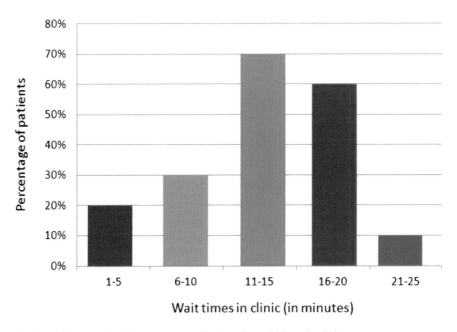

Fig. 8.4 Histogram showing percentage of patients by wait times in clinic

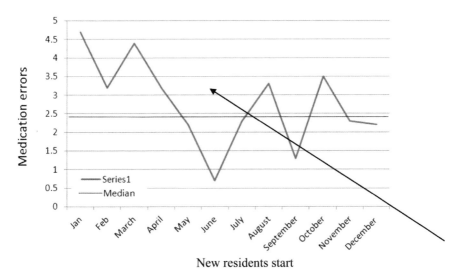

Fig. 8.5 Run chart depicting occurrence of medication errors per month

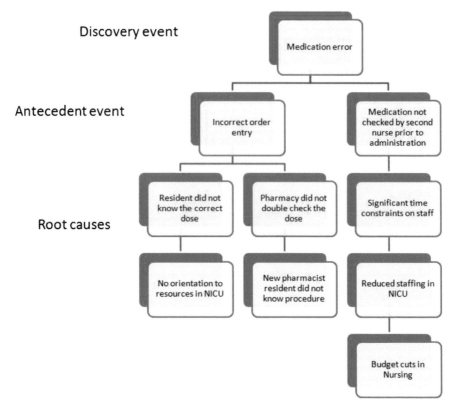

Fig. 8.6 Causal Tree demonstrating investigation of medical errors

Step 5: Identification of the Root Cause

Once all the causal factors have been identified, the investigators then begin the process of RCA using the root cause map. This map structures the reasoning process and helps highlight the major causes. This is a key step in the process, since a limited approach at this stage could result in pursuit of the wrong cause behind a sentinel event.

Step 6: Recommendations and Implementation of Change

The goal of the RCA is to identify system-based problems and make recommendations regarding solutions that will prevent a sentinel event from occurring again [19]. Often, the leaders involved in RCA are not the operational leaders, and therefore, are not directly responsible for implementing the changes. At this stage, the involvement of the operational leadership is critical to ensure efficiency in the process.

Where to Aim Recommendations The findings from an RCA should be brought to the attention of the highest level of management involved in the process. There should also be a forum for periodic and ongoing review of the sentinel events and the implementation of changes where such issues can be discussed periodically. Finally, for the RCA process to accomplish its logical goals, all stakeholders need to be in consensus about the risk posed by the sentinel event(s), the quality of evidence, and the strength of the recommendations.

Step 7: Presentation of Results

Root-cause summary tables are perhaps the most comprehensive way to report findings from a root cause analysis. These tables are typically comprised of three columns: the first column represents a description of the causal factor with adequate background information to allow an uninitiated reader to understand the significance of the causal factor. The second column represents the piece of the root-cause map involved in the causal factor, and the third column presents recommendations to address that specific causal factors. This three-column method of reporting is simple, and yet ensures that all the identified causal factors are addressed. While final reporting tools depend largely on the administrative needs of each hospital, this method includes all information that is typically required in a final report and could be used as a tool by the QI group, to prepare the final report on a given sentinel event.

Step 8: "Tests of Change"

Before implementing a change, the leadership should consider one or more pilot tests to identify any unforeseen difficulties that could limit its acceptance by the end-users. If the recommendations need to be revised, there may be a need for repeat pilot testing prior to widespread implementation.

Barriers to an Effective RCA

Since methodology is critical to a high quality RCA, the process should be led by an individual with experience and training. An RCA can be flawed if undue emphasis is placed on a single finding, ignoring other possible cause. Exhaustive analysis of all possible root causes is essential for this tool to be effective. Additionally, undue emphasis should not be placed on a "single" cause for error and efforts should be made to find common factors across investigations [16, 21].

Evidence of Effectiveness of Method

Several studies show that the effectiveness of RCA is dependent on the implement- ers' knowledge of the process, and that there is a need for training healthcare pro- fessionals in this technique. A study conducted in England showed that training healthcare professionals in the RCA process led to a significant increase in the num- ber of individuals taking on leadership roles in the process and a reduction in diffi- culties reported during the process [39]. Studies also confirm the utility of RCAs in shifting institutional culture from individual blame to the identification of systemic errors [40]. A study in Texas demonstrated a significant reduction in in self-reported adverse drug events following the implementation of a blame-free RCA process. This led to changes in organizational leadership and the development of policies to promote patient safety. Other organizations that adopted active surveillance systems experienced an increase in error reporting in a blame-free environment, eventually leading to a reduction in the frequency of various sentinel events [18].

Despite significant evidence to support the value of RCA in institutional culture change, very few studies have rigorously measured the efficacy of this method in promoting change in practice. The authors of the Texas study reported that the RCA process resulted in improvements in medication ordering and distribution, includ- ing placement of "hard stops that reduced medical errors [18].A study from the Veterans administration hospitals showed that the recommendations from an RCA were implemented in their entirety in 61–68 % instances, and were only partially implemented in 20 %. The he outcomes from these changes were not reported [41– 43]. Similar limitations were noted in a different healthcare system, where an event reporting system for blood transfusions was implemented [44]. At another study at the Veterans administration hospitals, RCA identified the most frequent causes for falls in the community setting and showed that even though several changes were implemented, the only one that actually improved outcome was modification of the patient's environment [45]. A review of 23 articles describing the RCA process by Percarpio et al. highlights improvement in patient safety following implementa- tion of RCAs, but also draws attention to the difficulty in developing improvement strategies by this method because of the lack of a sound quantitative analytical framework [46].

Limitations of Root Cause Analysis

RCA can have major methodological limitations. The RCA process may not always provide a complete and efficient analysis or effectively-implemented solutions for complex problems. While the difficulties of hindsight bias are well-recognized in RCA [15, 47, 48], other limitations may originate from individual variation on the depth with which the causes are probed and influenced by ongoing concerns of the moment [48, 49]. Since the occurrence of accidents is extremely unpredictable, it is impossible to know if the root cause established by the analysis is the cause of the accident [31]. RCAs are time-consuming and labor intensive, requiring approximately 20–90 h per event [50]. Despite legitimate concerns about the role of RCA in medical error reduction, the *Joint Commission on Accreditation of Healthcare Organizations* (*JCAHO*) in the United States now requires that RCA be widely used to, to supplement quantitative methods for the analysis of sentinel events [27], to facilitate generation of new hypotheses regarding process failures, and to evaluate events not easily studied by quantitative methods (for example, those that occur rarely and for which data is not being collected during the quality improvement process [51]. The credibility of the RCA lies in its qualitative process, and could provide a significant value addition to quantitative measures [52, 53].

Potential for Harm

A flawed/ inadequate RCA could result in implementation of an unnecessary new system that may not eradicate the original sentinel event because the true root cause was never identified. Additionally, the implementation of increasing complex and expensive systems that are themselves fraught with the risk of error may increase costs with limited effectiveness [15, 48]. Poorly conducted RCAs could result in ineffective system changes and leading to poor staff morale, and the harm caused by pursuit of incorrect root causes would offset by the costs of not conducting them at all.

Costs and Implementation

The costs involved in RCA have not been reported in the literature. However, considering that the process is labor-intensive and time-consuming, the costs are likely to be significant. If performed inaccurately, the correction action plan emanating from the RCA is also likely to add to the costs. In any institution, the culture of individual blame and medico-legal concerns are most likely to limit the implementation of this process [26, 46], and the importance of administrative support for blame-free RCA cannot be over-emphasized [30]. Other studies comment on the receptiveness of staff to blame-free investigation in the name of quality improvement, with one health system reporting a 10-fold increase in reporting [39, 47].

When not to Pursue an RCA

Sentinel events involving unintentional harm, physical abuse of any form, substance abuse by employees or criminal acts should not be evaluated by RCA. In the event that such a situation is identified, the RCA process should be halted and the event should be reported to hospital leadership for further action.

Table 8.1 Major steps of an RCA

Step 1: Identify a sentinel event
Step 2: Assemble a team consisting of all individuals who touch the process and include operational and executive leadership
Step 3: Verify the situation and collect data on the process leading up to the event
Step 4: Chart causal factors and develop a diagrammatic depiction of the exact sequence of events and the process using brainstorming maps, fishbone diagrams, pareto charts etc
Step 5: Identify the root cause by using the "5 why" method
Step 6: Develop recommendations for change in process and implementation of change
Step 7: Present results to stake holders
Step 8: Perform "Tests of Change"

Summary

The findings of a well conducted RCA can provide excellent qualitative support to conventional quantitative measures of quality improvement. However the value of an RCA is heavily dependent on the leader's expertise in its methodology, the rigor with which the methods are implemented, the depth of analysis conducted and involvement of the entire team in developing new processes (Table 8.1). It is imperative to conduct an RCA within this framework, to prevent incorrect identification of system problems leading to misallocation of resources and potential harm with unnecessary new processes. Proper use of an RCA encourages a shift in institutional culture from individual blame to identifying opportunities for system improvement and promoting a culture of patient safety.

Acknowledgements The author would like to thank Dr. Akhil Maheshwari for his guidance and support with this chapter.

References

1. Kalisch PA, Kalisch B (2004) The advance of American nursing (4th Ed.). Lippincott Williams & Wilkins, Philadelphia
2. Henry B, Woods S, Nagelkerk J (1992) Nightingale's perspective of nursing administration. Sogo Kango 27:16–26
3. Starr P (1982) The social transformation of American medicine. Basic Books 39–124, Cambridge, Massachusetts, USA
4. Buchbinder SB, Shanks NH (2007) Introduction to health care management. Jones and Bartlett, Sudbury
5. Chassin MR, O'Kane ME (2010) History of the quality improvement movement. In: American Academy of Pediatrics (ed) Toward improving the outcome of pregnancy III. March of Dimes, White Plains
6. Luce JM, Bindman AB, Lee PR (1994) A brief history of health care quality assessment and Improvement in the United States. West J Med 160:263–268
7. Kolsar P (1993) The relevance of research of statistical process control to the total quality movement. J Eng Technol Manag 10:317–338
8. Shewhart W (1931) Economic control of quality of manufactured product. Van Nostrand, New York
9. Shewhart W (1939) Statistical method from the viewpoint of quality control. The Graduate School of the Department of Agriculture, Washington, DC
10. Juran J (1986) The quality trilogy: A universal approach to managing for quality. Presented at: ASQC 40th annual quality congress in Anaheim, California, 20 May
11. Sazama K (1996) Current good manufacturing practices for transfusion medicine. Transfus Med Rev 10:286–295
12. Food and Drug Administration (1997) Biological products; reporting of errors and accidents in manufacturing. Fed Regist 62:49642–49648
13. Institute of Medicine (1999) To err is human: building a safer health system. National Academy Press, Washington, DC
14. Institute of Medicine (2001) Crossing the quality chasm: A new health system for the 21st century. National Academy Press, Washington, DC
15. Reason JT (1990) Human error. Cambridge University Press, New York
16. Reason J (1990) Human error. Cambridge University Press, Cambridge
17. Carroll JS (1998) Organizational learning activities in high-hazard industries: the logics underlying self-analysis. J Manage Stud 35:699–717
18. Battles JB, Kaplan HS, Van der Schaaf TW, Shea CE (1998) The attributes of medical event reporting systems: experience with a prototype medical event-reporting system for transfusion medicine. Arch Pathol Lab Med 122:231–238
19. Eagle CJ, Davies JM, Reason J (1992) Accident analysis of large-scale technological disasters applied to an anaesthetic complication. Can J Anaesth 39:118–122
20. Vincent C, Ennis M, Audley RJ (1993) Medical accidents. Oxford University Press, New York
21. Iedema RA, Jorm C, Long D, Braithwaite J, Travaglia J, Westbrook M (2006) Turning the medical gaze in upon itself: root cause analysis and the investigation of clinical error. Soc Sci Med 62:1605–1615
22. Bagian JP, Lee C, Gosbee J, et al (2001) Developing and deploying a patient safety program in a large health care delivery system: you can't fix what you don't know about. Jt Comm J Qual Improv 27:522–532
23. Reason JT (1997) Managing the risks of organizational accidents. Ashgate Publishing, Farnham
24. Reason J (2000) Human error: models and management. BMJ 320:768–770
25. Leape LL (1994) Error in medicine. JAMA 272:1851–1857

26. Berman S (1998) Identifying and addressing sentinel events: an Interview with Richard Cro-
    teau. Jt Comm J Qual Impro 24:426–434
27. Joint Commission on the accreditation of healthcare organizations. Sentinel event policy and
    procedures. http://www.JCAHO.org/sentinel/se_pp.html. Accessed 10 March 2014
28. Damschroder LJ, Banaszak-Holl J, Kowalski CP, et al (2009) The role of the champion in
    infection prevention: results from a multisite qualitative study. Qual Saf Health Care 18:434–
    440
29. Ellsbury D L, Ursprung R (2000) A primer on quality improvement methodology in neona-
    tology. Clin Perinatol 37:87–99
30. Rex JH, Turnbull JE, Allen SJ, Vande Voorde K, Luther K (2000) Systematic root cause anal-
    ysis of adverse drug events in a tertiary referral hospital. Jt Comm J Qual Improv 26:563–575
31. Runciman WB, Sellen A, Webb RK, Williamson JA, Currie M, Morgan C, et al (1993) The
    Australian incident monitoring study. Errors, incidents and accidents in anaesthetic practice.
    Anaesth Intensive Care 21:506–519
32. Ishikawa K (1985) What is total quality control? The Japanese way. Prentice Hall, Engle-
    wood Cliffs
33. Langley G, Nolan K, Nolan T, et al (2009) The improvement guide: a practical approach to
    enhancing organizational performance. Jossey-Bass, San Francisco
34. Nelson EC, Batalden PB, Godfrey MM (2007) Quality by design: a clinical Microsystems
    approach. Jossey-Bass, San Francisco
35. Hubbard D (2007) How to Measure Anything: Finding the Value of Intangibles in Business.
    Wiley, Hoboken
36. http://www.ihi.org/knowledge/Pages/Tools/Histogram.aspx. Accessed on 10 March 2014
37. Perla RJ, Provost LP, Murray SK (2011) The run chart: a simple analytical tool for learning
    variation in healthcare processes. BMJ Qual Saf 20:46–51
38. Williams PM (2001) Techniques for root cause analysis. BUMC Proc 14:154–157
39. Bowie P, Skinner J, de Wet C (2013) Training health care professionals in root cause analysis:
    a cross-sectional study of post-training experiences, benefits and attitudes. BMC Health Serv
    Res 13:50
40. Bagian JP, Gosbee J, Lee CZ, Williams L, McKnight SD, Mannos DM (2002) The veterans
    affairs root cause analysis system in action. Jt Comm J Qual Improv 28:531–545
41. Braithwaite J, Westbrook MT, Mallock NA, Travaglia JF, Iedema RA (2006) Experiences of
    health professionals who conducted root cause analyses after undergoing a safety improve-
    ment program. Qual Saf Health Care 15:393–399
42. Mills PD, Neily J, Luan D, Osborne A, Howard K (2006) Actions and implementation strate-
    gies to reduce suicidal events in the veterans health administration. Jt Comm J Qual Patient
    Saf 32:130–141
43. Mills PD, Neily J, Luan D, Stalhandske E, Weeks WB (2005) Using aggregate root cause
    analysis to reduce falls. Jt Comm J Qual Patient Saf 31:21–31
44. Kaplan HS, Battles JB, Van der Schaaf TW, Shea CE, Mercer SQ (1998) Identification and
    classification of the causes of events in transfusion medicine. Transfusion 38:1071–1081
45. Lee A, Mills PD, Neily J (2012) Using root cause analysis to reduce falls with injury in com-
    munity settings. Jt Comm J Qual Patient Saf 38:366–374
46. Percarpio KB, Watts BV, Weeks WB (2008) The effectiveness of root cause analysis: what
    does the literature tell us? Jt Comm J Qual Patient Saf 34:391–398
47. Caplan RA, Posner KL, Cheney FW (1991) Effect of outcome on physician judgments of
    appropriateness of care. JAMA 265:1957–1960
48. Perrow C (1999) Normal accidents: living with high-risk technologies with a new afterword
    and a postscript on the Y2K problem. Princeton University Press, Princeton
49. Rasmussen J (1990) Human error and the problem of causality in analysis of accidents. Phi-
    los Trans R Soc Lond B Biol Sci 327:449–460
50. Wu AW, Lipshutz AKM, Pronovost PJ (1990) Effectiveness and efficiency of root cause
    analysis in medicine. JAMA 299:685–687

51. Pope C, Mays N (1995) Reaching the parts other methods cannot reach: an introduction to qualitative methods in health and health services research. BMJ 311:42–45
52. Giacomini MK, Cook DJ (2000) Users' guides to the medical literature: XXIII. Qualitativeresearch in health care A. Are the results of the study valid? Evidence-based medicine working group. JAMA 284:357–362
53. Giacomini MK, Cook DJ (2000) Users' guides to the medical literature: XXIII. Qualitative research in health care B. What are the results and how do they help me care for my patients? Evidence-based medicine working group. JAMA 284:478–482

Chapter 9
Occupational Health and Safety

Paul Rothmore and Rose Boucaut

Safety doesn't happen by accident
—Author Unknown

Abstract The management of Occupational Health and Safety (OHS) within the healthcare environment is challenging. Workers are exposed to a complex array of hazards and risks and the outcomes can range from minor illness and injury to catastrophic events including death. Worker health and safety is often seen as secondary to the provision of patient care but these two priorities are not mutually exclusive and safe work practices and environments are beneficial to all. The management of OHS in this environment requires an understanding of legal obligations, the application of a systematic approach to the identification of hazards and the management of risks, and ongoing consultation with staff. While prevention is an overriding principle, managers also play a key role in the outcomes of workplace injury and illness. Early reporting and a supportive and accommodating return-to-work environment can have a significant effect on injury and illness outcomes. In this already challenging environment technological changes will pose even greater demands on managers. Emerging fields such as nanotechnology, while providing therapeutic and diagnostic benefits in patient care, expose workers to new set of OHS risks. However, the overarching principles for their management remain unchanged.

Keywords Health and safety · Hazards · Risks · Musculoskeletal disorders · Workplace violence · Biohazards · Workplace stress · Injury management · Safety culture · Governance · Nanotechnology · Psychosocial hazards · Physical hazards · Chemical hazards · Biomechanical hazards

P. Rothmore (✉)
Discipline of Public Health, School of Population Health,
University of Adelaide, Adelaide, SA, Australia
e-mail: paul.rothmore@adelaide.edu.au

R. Boucaut
School of Health Sciences (Physiotherapy), University of South Australia,
Adelaide, SA, Australia

© Springer International Publishing Switzerland 2015
S. Patole (ed.), *Management and Leadership – A Guide for Clinical Professionals,*
DOI 10.1007/978-3-319-11526-9_9

123

Key Points

- Hospitals are complex and demanding work environments which pose significant OHS challenges
- Managers play a key role in both the prevention and management of workplace injury and illness
- The identification of hazards and the management of risks requires a systematic approach
- Worker safety and patient safety are of equal importance and are not mutually exclusive

Hospitals are inherently complex and demanding working environments and pose significant Occupational Health and Safety (OHS) challenges. Internationally, the healthcare industry employs more than 59 million people, each of whom are exposed to variety of hazards on a daily basis [1]. Exposure outcomes can range from minor illness and injury to catastrophic events including death [2]. These workers need protection from workplace hazards yet due to the nature of the industry worker health and safety is often viewed as secondary to patient care. However, the protection of worker health can improve patient care. Many of the hazards faced by workers also affect patients (e.g. infection transmission, stress from understaffing). The ongoing health of the workforce is also of critical importance given the global shortage of healthcare workers. These factors have led to the development of specific national strategies to address a number of concerns including the prevention of musculoskeletal disorders, contact dermatitis, biological exposures and mental health issues [3–5].

OHS is more than general compliance with organisational policies and procedures and the suitability and comfort of our own, immediate, work environment. It deals with all aspects of health and safety within the workplace and involves the identification and management of hazards which may result in illness or injury risk to all those within the hospital environment. This includes all staff, patients, visitors and volunteers. The challenge for healthcare managers is to enable staff to deliver the required services within the hospital environment to the best of their ability while simultaneously balancing the dual priorities of staff and patient safety.

Governance of OHS

The primary approach to the management of health and safety by governments in developed countries is the enactment of legislation and regulations supported by the regular inspection of workplaces to ensure compliance [6]. While sound in principle, there has been a gradual shift from an environment of over-regulation, where control strategies for each hazard are described and mandated, to one where each organisation is responsible for the identification of hazards and the development of control strategies within an overarching framework. As an example, in Australia this approach is referred to as the legislative framework which incorporates Acts, Regulations, Codes of Practice, Standards and Guidance Material.

Acts are laws passed by parliament. They establish the legal framework with which all workplaces must comply. Their aim is to ensure that, so far as reasonably practicable, people within working environments do not suffer from injury or illness.

Regulations outline how the general obligations of the Act will be applied in the workplace. While these include the overall governance of health and safety they also prescribe the management of specific hazards (including manual handling tasks and hazardous chemicals). In common with the relevant Act, compliance with Regulations is mandatory.

Codes of Practice provide practical guidelines for achieving the standards required under the Act and Regulations. In most circumstances they are not mandatory. While they provide a suggested approach an alternative means of controlling a hazard may be used providing it is at least as effective as that outlined in the relevant Code.

Australian Standards and other Guidance Materials provide practical advice and guidance for controlling workplace hazards and risks in specific industries and under specific circumstances. They are not mandatory.

Under this framework there are specific obligations on organisations to provide a healthy and safe workplace. For certain high risk hazards (asbestos, hazardous chemicals etc.) control mechanisms are mandated. While in many circumstances the means of control is discretionary the identification of hazards is mandatory.

Hazards and Risks

An understanding of the dual concepts of hazards and risks, and how they differ, are critical. A *hazard* exists when something has the *potential* to cause harm. A *risk* exists when people may be *exposed* to that hazard [7]. For example an X-ray machine is a hazard—it has the potential to expose staff to ionizing radiation. However, a risk only exists when it is in use. The identification of hazards and an evaluation of the level of risk they pose are critical components in the development of strategies to adequately manage OHS risks in the hospital.

Identifying Hazards

Hospital staff are employed in a diversity of occupations including but not limited to: the healthcare team, administration, maintenance, housekeeping, catering, security and gardening. Each of these occupations has its own hazards and risks. The nature of hazards encountered by hospital employees include:

- Biomechanical
- Physical
- Biological
- Chemical
- Psychosocial

The first step in the development of a control strategy is the identification of hazards, the jobs in which they occur and the staff who may be exposed. A structured approach that incorporates the collation and interpretation of information from a variety of disparate sources—known as data triangulation—can assist. In this process information from three distinct sources are combined to improve the level of confidence in the findings.

1. Injury, incident and hazard records—These can provide indicators as to the location of hazards and the occupational groups affected. They can also provide important information on upward trends which could indicate that controls are ineffective or new hazards are emerging [2]. It is important to recognise though that such records are often incomplete. This is due to the known chronic under-reporting of adverse events in the healthcare sector [8].
2. Staff consultation—Workers frequently have a good understanding of hazards associated with their work. Consultation with staff, either through formal or informal discussion, can frequently identify hazards which have not been previously identified or reported.
3. Direct observation—Regular walk-through inspections of the work environment, and the actions of the people operating within them, are invaluable. They provide an insight into the *actual* rather than *predicted* (*or expected*) behaviour of people within the environment. Checklists can be a useful tool to focus direct observations and when completed provide a record of inspections undertaken.

For examples of these hazards, health outcomes and control strategies see Table 9.1.

Assessing Risk

When hazards have been identified an assessment of the possible outcomes following exposure, and the likelihood of it happening, needs to be undertaken. This is known as a risk assessment. The nature of the risk assessment will depend on the type of hazard, information relevant to the hazard and the available resources [7] This process should assist in determining the severity of the risk, the effectiveness of any existing control measures, the actions which should be taken, and the level of urgency.

Table 9.1 Common OHS risks in hospitals, possible outcomes and examples of control measures

Hazard	Potential outcome	Possible controls
Biomechanical		
Manual tasks involving patients and materials	Musculoskeletal injury	Patient handling equipment (e.g. lifters), powered bed movers for travel between wards
		Height adjustable equipment (e.g. beds/barouches)
		Use of trolleys
		Purchasing strategies—safe and user-friendly design
		Adequate lighting and space
		Regular equipment maintenance
		Training
		Team lifting
Wet, slippery floors	Traumatic injury, slip, fall	Appropriate flooring surfaces
		Regular cleaning/signs
		Appropriate footwear
Physical		
Ionizing radiation	Cancer, reproductive effects	Shielding
		Restricted area access
		Equipment maintenance
Physical assault	Traumatic injury	Workplace design
		Systems to screen patients and visitors from staff
		Alarm systems
		Adequate staffing levels
		Video surveillance
		Training
		Security staff
	Post-traumatic stress	Counselling post-event
Biological		
Needle stick injury (exposure to patient body fluid—e.g. blood)	Transmission of blood-borne virus e.g. Hepatitis	Eliminate unnecessary use of sharps
		Eliminate needle re-sheathing
		Safe needle disposal systems
		Staff vaccination
		Staff training in technique and about post exposure management
		Personal protective equipment

Table 9.1 (continued)

Hazard	Potential outcome	Possible controls
Chemical		
Latex gloves	Contact dermatitis	Provide latex free gloves
Hazardous substances	Cleaning	Single-use items
		Alternative methods of cleaning, e.g. ultrasound
		Substitute with less hazardous chemical alternative
Psychosocial		
Work stress	Distress	Code of respectful conduct for all staff
	Sleep disorders	
	Gastrointestinal disorders	Supportive management
		Workload demands matched to staff capacity
		Clarify work expectations to reduce role ambiguity
		Adequate staffing
		Stress management programs
		Training

Controlling Risk

Once hazards have been identified and risk assessed the next step is the develop-ment of control strategies. A hierarchical approach provides a range of options for controlling risk. These range from the most to the least preferred [9] As a general principle, the higher the level of assessed risk (death or serious injury) the higher up the hierarchy the control strategy should be (elimination or substitution). In de-scending order the preferences are:

- Elimination—Removal of the hazard and its associated risk
- Substitution—Where elimination is not possible the hazard is substituted for a less-hazardous option
- Engineering—Where elimination or substitution are not possible engineering controls designed to reduce the level of risk are provided (such as the provision of mechanical devices)
- Administrative Controls—These include the development of policies and safe operating procedures, staff education and training
- Personal Protective Equipment—This is the least preferred option and requires worker compliance

Note: where elimination is not possible controls are often used in combination—for example a noisy workplace may introduce engineering (noise dampening), admin-istrative (job rotation) and PPE controls (hearing protection).

Table 9.2 Control strategies for the manual handling task of moving patients from bed to barouche[a]

Control method	Question	Brainstorm thoughts
Elimination	Can we eliminate (manually) moving patients from bed to barouche?	This task cannot be eliminated but the method can be improved (i.e. redesign task)
Engineering	What equipment could assist?	Assistive devices such as lifting devices, Hovermatts, slide boards and slide sheets may assist. These devices will reduce the load on staff
		The beds are height adjustable so can be set to an appropriate height to facilitate the transfer
Administration	Are there policies to guide staff?	No lift/no injury policy
	What training might be needed?	Train staff in use of new equipment, safe systems of work and problem solving
Personal protective equipment	Is there any appropriate PPE available?	PPE considerations are not appropriate

[a] A range of controls are considered in a brainstorming process and are listed in order of the hierarchy of control

Manual handling tasks associated with patient care are an integral part, and a high risk aspect, of healthcare; they often result in musculoskeletal disorders. An example of a hazardous task is transferring a patient (who is unable to assist) from a bed to a barouche. Table 9.2 illustrates the use of the control hierarchy in the development of strategies to manage this task safely.

Evaluating and Reviewing Outcomes

An evaluation of control measures determines whether they are effective in controlling the risk. It also ensures that their introduction has not created an unforeseen outcome—e.g. the introduction of a new risk in another work unit. Reviewing risk controls is an ongoing process. Any change to the work environment, such as the purchase of new equipment or the identification of new hazards, generally requires a review of existing control measures.

Safety Culture

The safety culture of an organisation is an important concept. It has been defined as "the product of individual and group values, attitudes, perceptions, competencies and patterns of behaviour that determine the commitment to, and the style and proficiency of, an organisation's health and safety management system" [10]. It is more than the existence of a health and safety system and reflects the everyday context within which hospital staff work.

Senior staff and managers set the tone of the safety culture at the workplace and have a key role in safety promotion. Their activities reveal their beliefs about safety more strongly than their words, thus employees can determine managers' attitudes to safety and follow their lead. While there may be an overall organisational safety culture, workgroups within an organisation may have their own discrete culture [11]. Some teams foster a collaborative and reporting culture. Others foster a blame culture. There is a correlation between poor (negative) safety culture and work injury [11]. Organisations with a positive safety culture are characterised by communications founded on mutual trust, by shared perceptions of the importance of safety and by confidence in the efficacy of preventive measures [10].

A positive safety leader will work proactively to promote safety, consult with staff, encourage the reporting of hazards and facilitate the implementation of controls. However, this frequently relies on the provision of adequate resources and staffing levels.

Musculoskeletal Disorders

The most prevalent of occupational risks in healthcare is the moving and handling of patients and equipment and the adoption of sustained or static postures. Injuries related to these activities result in musculoskeletal disorders—predominantly in the lower back. These are among the most frequent and costly of work-related injuries [12] and have been the focus of numerous interventions and reviews. Despite consistent evidence that technique training in isolation has little to no effect on injury rates this remains the most commonly used intervention [13–15]. Where evidence for its effectiveness does exist it is as part of a multi-component intervention including exercise [16] and risk assessment programs [14].

Reasons for the ineffectiveness of training may be related to the inadequacy of the techniques taught or to the inability of the training to change ingrained behaviours [15]. Other reasons may also be due to the failure of such training programs to address the non-physical factors such as work organization and job satisfaction [17] which have been linked with both the severity and prevalence of back pain [18–21].

Psychosocial Risk Factors and Workplace Stress

Psychosocial risk factors and workplace stress are among the most difficult OHS issues to manage in the workplace. They can arise when work is poorly designed and organised and when workplace management is lacking. Examples of psychosocial risk factors include environments where workloads are excessive; there is lack of role clarity; communication is poor; support from colleagues and supervisors is absent, and when workers can exert little control over their work. Workers experience stress when they are unable to cope with work demands and pressures which do not match their knowledge and abilities [22]. Workers who are stressed may be less productive, less safe at work and take increased periods of sick leave [22]. They may also suffer serious physical conditions such as heart disease, gastro-intestinal disorders, increased blood pressure and musculoskeletal disorders (including low back pain) [22]. Managers can play a key role in the prevention of workplace stress by considering factors related to the organisation of work. This includes matching job requirements with staff abilities, clear communication of expectations, providing work variety and providing increased control over work in the provision of flexible work arrangements and regular consultation.

Workplace Violence

Workplace violence (WPV) is a widespread occupational health and safety issue experienced in many industries including healthcare. WPV refers to "any incident in which a person is abused, threatened or assaulted in circumstances relating to their work" [23]. "It includes physical and psychological violence, which often overlap. Terms frequently used are assault, attack, abuse, bullying/mobbing, sexual/racial harassment, threat" [24].

There is difficulty determining the full extent of WPV [25] although the International Labour Organisation (ILO) reports that almost 25 % of workplace violence occurs in the healthcare sector [23]. Healthcare workers may be particularly vulnerable for several reasons: staff gender, with nurses a particularly high risk group [26]; a culture of commitment to patient care taking priority over staff safety; patients in pain and distress and the related anguish experienced by visitors; and understaffing which can stretch/strain staff capacity to deal with the emotional and physical burden of work.

There are four categories of WPV [25]. These relate to: criminal intent (e.g. robbery), customer (e.g. patients), worker on worker (e.g. bullying) and personal relationship (e.g. domestic violence).

Managers can influence the prevention of WPV. Fostering a respectful and supportive culture within the department provides a sound basis for prevention together with consideration of the work environment (e.g. lighting, furniture), training (e.g. learning de-escalation techniques) and work organisation (e.g. reduction of waiting times).

Biological Hazards

Biological hazards are prevalent in hospitals and a key risk for all staff. They can be transmitted from patients to staff through contact with body fluids and waste products. Routes of exposure include skin, mouth and mucous membranes. Managers should ensure staff are trained, are up to date with recommended immunisations, and are familiar with standard operating procedures including the wearing of personal protective equipment as required [27].

Sharps injuries are a common way in which biological hazards are spread, both among clinical and non-clinical staff. Sharps safety devices (engineering controls) have been shown to reduce injuries [28]. Organisational factors may also influence the number of sharps injuries staff experience. Needle stick injury has been found to be more prevalent in workplaces with poor safety culture or low staffing levels [29–31].

Injury Management

The collection of injury data is an important aid to injury prevention. As part of their OHS management system, hospitals have an injury reporting system with which both managers and employees need to be familiar. The reporting system is used to track incidents, illnesses and injuries, hazards and near miss events.

Safe work is influential in the general health and wellbeing of the working population [32]. Once a person is injured or becomes ill, injury/illness management becomes vital and the manager plays a key role in this process [33]. Recent evidence indicates that some important factors influence a successful return to work. These often lie beyond management of the injury/illness itself [34]. Early recognition of psychosocial factors that may adversely affect recovery is critical. These factors include the beliefs and attitudes of the worker about their condition and their perceptions of the workplace.

The provision of suitable duties to either allow injured workers to remain at work or to return them to work as soon as possible are key factors. This may require some modification to their usual hours and duties. Managers play a key role, as part of a rehabilitation team, in the identification of suitable duties and in the provision of a supportive work environment [33].

Key Points for Managers

OHS hazards and risks exist, to varying degrees, in all occupational groups within healthcare. While overall responsibility and governance may reside with senior management, managers and supervisors play a critical role in both the prevention

Table 9.3 Key OHS considerations for managers

Legislative obligations & hospital policies
An understanding of the principles of OHS and Rehabilitation and Return to Work legislation in the jurisdiction
Working knowledge of the hospital OHS and Injury Management system
Hazard management
Knowledge of the tasks staff undertake, the hazards and risks associated with these tasks, and how they are controlled
Encourage the reporting of hazards, near misses, and minor incidents. They can provide an early-warning of future injuries and facilitate preventative strategies
Early reporting of injuries and illness can facilitate early intervention and improve worker outcomes
Data triangulation (the collation of information from sources including injury reports, communication with workers and direct observation) is a useful tool in the investigation of injury and illness trends
Any change to the work environment can affect existing control measures and may introduce new hazards. For example new equipment purchases must be assessed from the end-users perspective. This includes their suitability for intended use and any requirements for ongoing maintenance and repairs
Communication and support
As a multicultural society, hospital staff members and patients are likely to come from a range of different backgrounds. Managers need to foster a culture of respect for such diversity
Hospital staff demographics range widely as do staff attributes including skills, work experience, physical capacity and general health
The capacity of workers to undertake the tasks required of them must be greater than or equal to the work demands imposed
Good communication with staff, both formal and informal, is critical. Formal mechanisms can include the addition of OHS matters as a regular item on meeting agendas or scheduling meetings with a staff representative. Informal mechanisms can include general discussions during worksite safety inspections or during daily encounter
Psychosocial factors such as poor communication, unclear job expectations and workplace conflict can increase the likelihood of both psychological (stress) and physical (back pain) disorders
The protection of worker health can improve patient care. Many of the hazards faced by workers also affect patients (protection from infection, inadequate staffing levels etc.)
Model the behaviour and attitudes you would like your staff to adopt—they are watching what you do and say

and management of worker injuries and illnesses. Minimum knowledge should include the following key OHS considerations (Table 9.3):

Gaps and Future Directions

The development and application of nanotechnology is progressing rapidly. Along with a range of other industries this poses a new area of occupational risk for healthcare workers. Nanomaterials are those in which particle dimensions are between 1 and 100 nm—a size which is comparable to atoms and molecules. Their extremely small size allows them to circulate freely within the body by moving in and out of the circulatory system and cells [35]. This ability bestows benefits for therapeutic and diagnostic purposes. However, these benefits for patient care may also expose healthcare workers to new risks as gaps regarding the toxicity of nanomaterials remain [36]. The unintended exposure to nanomaterials by healthcare workers can occur via three pathways—(1) inhalation; (2) ingestion; (3) dermal (skin) penetration [37, 38].

While clinical healthcare workers who are involved in the preparation and administration of nanodrugs are most likely to be exposed non-clinical workers may also be at risk. Non-clinical exposure can occur in a variety of scenarios—during routine cleaning and maintenance activities in areas where nanodrugs are handled; the incidental handling of contaminated items; and during the clean-up of nanomaterial spills [37].

The potential health effects due to exposure can range from symptoms of contact dermatitis [39] to lung disorders, including asbestos-like effects [40].

This emerging area poses specific challenges to carrying out workplace risk assessments due to limitations in knowledge of the hazardous properties of nanomaterials and in the methods available to measure both emission and exposure levels. There are currently no specific guidelines for the prevention of OHS risks due to nanomaterials in the healthcare environment. However, the application of the principles of hazard identification, risk assessment, development of controls measures, review and evaluation remain relevant.

Summary

The complexity of work in the healthcare environment poses significant challenges in the management of OHS hazards and risks. While different hazards may be allocated to various categories the overarching framework for their management is consistent. A systematic approach to the identification of hazards; the assessment of risk; the development of control strategies; and review of their effectiveness are fundamental principles. Such an approach is particularly important when the outcomes of unexpected or uncontrolled risk exposure can range from minor injury to death. The challenge for managers in the healthcare environment is to balance the dual priorities associated with staff and patient safety.

References

1. World Health Organisation http://www.who.int/occupational_health/topics/hcworkers/en/. Accessed 2 Feb 2014
2. Victorian Auditor-General's Report (2013) Occupational health and safety risk in public hospitals. Victoria, Melbourne
3. European Agency for Safety and Health at Work (2013) Priorities for occupational safety and heatlh resarch in Europe: 2013–2020. Publications Office of the European Union, Luxembourg
4. United States Department of Labor. Strategic plan—fiscal years 2014–2018. http://www.dol.gov/_sec/stratplan/. Accessed 28 Jan 2014
5. Safe Work Australia. Australian work health and safety strategy 2012–2022. http://www.safeworkaustralia.gov.au/sites/swa/about/publications/pages/australian-work-health-and-safety-strategy-2012–2022. Accessed 28 Jan 2014
6. World Health Organisation (2001) Occupational health—a manual for primary health care workers. Regional Office for the Eastern Mediterranean, Cairo
7. Cross J. (2012) Risk. HaSPA (Health and Safety Professionals Alliance) The core body of knowledge for generalist OHS professionals. Safety Institute of Australia, Tullamarine
8. Safe Work Australia (2009) Work-related injuries in Australia, 2005–2006—health and community services industry. Barton, ACT, Australia
9. Ruschena L. (2012) Control: prevention and intervention. HaSPA (Health and Safety Professionals Alliance) The Core Body of Knowledge for Generalist OHS Professionals. Safety Institute of Australia, Tullamarine
10. HSC Advisory Committee on the Safety of Nuclear Installations (1993) ACSNI study group on human factors, third report—organising for safety: Health and Safety Executive. ISBN 9780717608652
11. Zohar D (2010) Thirty years of safety climate research: reflections and future directions. Accid Anal Prev 42:1517–1522
12. Woolf AD, Pfleger B (2003) Burden of major musculoskeletal conditions. Bull World Health Organ 81:646–656
13. Dawson AP, McLennan SN, Schiller SD, Jull GA, Hodges PW, Stewart S (2007) Interventions to prevent back pain and back injury in nurses: a systematic review. Occup Environ Med 64:642–650
14. Hignett S (2003) Intervention strategies to reduce musculoskeletal injuries associated with handling patients: a systematic review. Occup Environ Med 60:e6
15. Martimo KP, Verbeek J, Karppinen J et al (2008) Effect of training and lifting equipment for preventing back pain in lifting and handling: systematic review. BMJ 336:429–431
16. Amick B, Tullar JM, Brewer S, Irvine Q, Mahood L, Pompeii A, Wang D, Van Eerd D, Gimeno D, Evanoff B (2006) Interventions in health-care settings to protect musculoskeletal health: a systematic review. Institute for Work and Health, Toronto
17. Stewart SK, Rothmore PR, Doda DVD, Hiller JE, Mahmood MA, Pisaniello DL (2014) Musculoskeletal pain and discomfort and associated worker and organizational factors: a cross-sectional study. Work: J Prev, Assess Rehabil 48(2):261–271
18. Hoogendoorn WE, Van Poppel MNM, Bongers PM, Koes BW, Bouter LM, Hoogendoorn L (2000) Systematic review of psychosocial factors at work and private life as risk factors for back pain. Spine 25:2114–2125
19. Linton SJ, Warg LE (1993) Attributions (beliefs) and job satisfaction associated with back pain in an industrial setting. Percept Mot Skills 76:51–62
20. Williams RA, Pruitt SD, Doctor JN et al (1998) The contribution of job satisfaction to the transition from acute to chronic low back pain. Arch Phys Med Rehabil 79:366–374
21. Macfarlane GJ, Pallewatte N, Paudyal P et al (2009) Evaluation of work-related psychosocial factors and regional musculoskeletal pain: results from a EULAR Task Force. Ann Rheum Dis 68:885–891
22. Cox T, Griffiths A, Rial-Gonzales E (2000) Research on work-related stress. http://osha.europa.eu/en/publications/reports/203. Accessed 28 Feb 2014

23. Health and Safety Executive (2014) Violence at work—a guide for employers. 1996. http://www.hse.gov.uk/pubns/indg69.pdf. Accessed 28 Mar 2014
24. International Labor Office (2002) Framework guidelines for addressing workplace violence in the health sector. International Labor Office, Geneva
25. University of Iowa Injury Prevention Research Center (2001) Workplace violence: a report to the nation. http://www.public-health.uiowa.edu/iprc/resources/workplace-violence-report.pdf. Accessed 4 Feb 2014
26. McPhaul KM, Lipscomb JA (2004) Workplace violence in health care: recognized but not regulated. Online J Issues Nurs 9(3):7
27. Wilburn SQ, Eijkemans G (2004) Preventing needlestick injuries among healthcare workers: A WHO-ICN collaboration. Int J Occup Environ Health 10:451–456
28. Elder A, Paterson C (2006) Sharps injuries in UK health care: a review of injury rates, viral transmission and potential efficacy of safety devices. Occup Med 56:566–574
29. Clarke SP, Sloane DM, Aiken LH (2002) Effects of hospital staffing and organizational climate on needlestick injuries to nurses. Am J Public Health 92:1115–1119
30. Gershon RRM, Stone PW, Zeltser M, Faucett J, Macdavitt K, Chou SS (2007) Organizational climate and nurse health outcomes in the United States: a systematic review. Ind Health 45:622–636
31. Lang TA, Hodge M, Olson V, Romano PS, Kravitz RL (2004) Nurse-patient ratios: a systematic review on the effects of nurse staffing on patient, nurse employee, and hospital outcomes. J Nurs Adm 34:326–337
32. Black DC (2008) Working for a healthier tomorrow. TSO, Norwich
33. Australasian Faculty of Occupational & Environmental Medicine (2011) Realising the heath benefits of work—a position statement. https://www.racp.edu.au/page/policy-and-advocacy/occupational-and-environmental-medicine. Accessed 4 Feb 2014
34. Franche RL, Baril R, Shaw W, Nicholas M, Loisel P (2005) Workplace-based return-to-work interventions: optimizing the role of stakeholders in implementation and research. J Occup Rehabil 15:525–542
35. Lauterwasser C (2005) Small size that matter: opportunities and risks of nanotechnologies. http://www.oecd.org/dataoecd/32/1/44108334.pdf. Accessed 4 Feb 2014
36. European Agency for Safety and Heatlh at Work (2013) Nanomaterials in the healthcare sector: occupational risks and prevention. https://osha.europa.eu/en/publications/e-facts/e-fact-73-nanomaterials-in-the-healthcare-sector-occupational-risks-and-prevention/view. Accessed 4 Feb 2014
37. Murashov V (2009) Occupational exposure to nanomedical applications. Wiley Interdiscip Rev: Nanomed Nanobiotechnol 1(2):203–213
38. National Insitute for Occupational Safety and Heatlh (2009) Approaches to safe nanotechnology—managing the health and safety concerns associated with engineered nanomaterials: US Department of Health and Human Services, Center for Disease Control and Prevention, DHSS
39. Toyama T, Matsuda H, Ishida I et al (2008) A case of toxic epidermal necrolysis-like dermatitis evolving from contact dermatitis of the hands associated with exposure to dendrimers. Contact Dermatitis 59(2):122–123
40. Nanowerk (2012) Introduction to nanotechnology. http://www.nanowerk.com/nanotechnology/introduction/introduction_to_nanotechnology_1.php. Accessed 2 Mar 2014

Suggested Further Reading

41. Centres for Disease Control and Prevention. Workplace Violence Prevention for Nurses Online course. CDC Course No. WB1865—NIOSH Pub. No. 2013–155. http://www.cdc.gov/niosh/topics/violence/training_nurses.html. Accessed 10 Mar 2014
42. Loisel P, Anema J (2013) Handbook of work disability: prevention and management. Springer, New York (ISBN: 978-1-4614-6213-2 (Print) 978-1-4614-6214-9)

Chapter 10
Coping with Stress at Work

Christopher Griffin

> *Life is not a matter of having good cards, but of playing a poor hand well*
> —Robert Louis Stevenson

Abstract Stress in the workplace affects everyone at some stage in their lives. Stress in itself can be used to promote productivity. However, there is a bell shaped curve relationship with a point when passed, the stressful input imparts a negative impact upon performances. Individuals react differently to stress. Personality traits and gender influence both our response and adaptation to stress. In the healthcare industry, stress is recognised to emanate from both within as well as from peers, colleagues, superiors, patients and events. Identifying stress is of paramount importance to implement coping mechanisms. These mechanisms can be initiated by the employer or the employee. Group debriefings and regular individual appraisals are powerful tools for managers to use especially in the face of major disasters. Exercise/activities and humour are some of the common methods individuals use to reduce or prevent stress. There is no 'best' exercise or activity other than one chosen by the user for the satisfaction this will produce for them. Humour whether self induced or group derived is a cheap, fast and burgeoning area of stress manipulation. Recent attention has spread to dietary manipulation including the use of probiotics which show great promise in improving mental and physical well being.

Keywords Stress · Bullying · Workplace · Appraisal based coping · Avoidance coping · Distancing coping · Healthcare · Exercise · Laughter clubs · Probiotics · Anxiety · Depression · Individual response · Consultant rules · Personality · Samuel Schem · Hasyayoga · Hypothalamic pituitary axis

C. Griffin (✉)
Department of Maternal and Fetal Medicine, King Edward Memorial Hospital for Women, 374 Bagot Road, Subiaco, City of Perth, WA 6006, Australia
e-mail: christopher.griffin@health.wa.gov.au

School of Women's and Infants' Health, the University of Western Australia

© Springer International Publishing Switzerland 2015
S. Patole (ed.), *Management and Leadership – A Guide for Clinical Professionals,*
DOI 10.1007/978-3-319-11526-9_10

137

Key Points
- Stress can be both contagious and uncontrollable.
- Unhealthy stress can be modulated and ameliorated with correct understanding and commitment to change by all parties concerned.
- Personality is a major factor in how we react to stress.
- Diet, exercise, laughter and probiotics can reduce stress.

Stress is derived from the shortening of the word distress, denoting hardship or force exerted on a person for the purpose of compulsion. From the United Kingdom, the Health and Safety Executive's (HSE) formal definition of work related stress is: "The adverse reaction people have to excessive pressures or other types of demand placed on them at work." The HSE continue: Stress is not an illness—it is a state [1]. However, if stress becomes too excessive and prolonged, mental and physical illness may develop [2]. Studies have unequivocally shown that high stress levels reduce work efficiency, increase sickness leave, inculcate abnormal behaviour patterns and lead to a poor retention of staff. Similarly, outside of the work arena, high stress levels lead to addictive or dependent behaviour patterns, relationship issues, personal disease e.g. hypertension and overall a vastly reduced quality of life [2–6].

We all become stressed, some more frequently than others. Our lifestyles can become completely built around stress—living to work as we often hear rather than working to live.

> Stress is like spice—in the right proportion it enhances the flavor of a dish. Too little produces a bland, dull meal; too much may choke you.
> —Donald Tubesing

Stresses at Work

More working days are lost per year in the UK from stress related illnesses than any other singular medical illness or accident at work. Nearly 17 % of UK workers thought their job was stressful or very stressful (HSE). Performance at work is negatively related to levels of stress with some workers actually showing increased productivity in the phase before burnout. Increasing stress also increases abnormal behavioural patterns in employees such as theft, vandalism and the crossing of professional boundaries [7, 8].

Believe it or not, there is a reasonable chance that you will see more of your work colleagues in your life than other people outside of the work environment. We sleep and work for an average of 8 h each per working day and spend variable amounts of time travelling to and from work as well as preparing for and awakening from sleep.

Therefore it makes practical sense to have as good a working life as possible so as to positively influence the remainder of your life—unless you do only live to work. For members of the last mentioned group, ask yourself how long it will take for people to miss your professional input—you will be surprised how short this time scale is!

Depending upon circumstances, stress at work will affect us all. Acute events such as a major disaster, unexpected treatment complications, a drug error, personality clash, feeling of low self esteem and difficulty in meeting deadlines are just some of the precipitating factors for stress [9, 10]. These factors can develop both a stress reaction in ourselves as well as affecting the incidence of stress in individuals within our workplaces. Some issues appearing minor to one person will be major to another [2, 7].

An amusing anecdote was a patient hooked up to an intravenous saline infusion who was the centre of attention during a consultant ward round. During the bedside discussions I noticed the man becoming more and more agitated. I stopped the discussion and asked him what it was that was obviously bothering him. He replied that he was soon to die if we didn't stop the micro bubble of air coming down the IV giving set into his vein!

So what are the types of extrinsic stress that we can be exposed to at work?

The line manager or supervisor is reported to be the major cause of work place stress in some studies [11]. Comments such as *'they just don't know what it is like'* do have a sense of truth about them.

Major Frank Burns was the head of the MASH (mobile army surgical hospital) unit in the TV series around the time of the Korean war. He recognised the stress involved at the front line and his part to play—*"We all know it is brutal up there at the front, especially those of us at the rear"*.

Recognition that bosses can both initiate and attenuate stress is complicit in any organisation's culture for a harmonious and productive work environment. A supportive boss or supervisor has been shown to also reduce the incidence of post-traumatic stress disorder [11].

Almost all of us at some stage will feel irritated or angry with our fellow workers. This is one of the commonest effectors of stress. As such, this should be recognised as a normal everyday reaction and accepted by all concerned. However, a repetitive irritation and anger action directed towards someone when knowingly this will instigate such a response is victimisation or indeed bullying. Up to a third of all nurses have reported bullying [12].

There are numerous other sources of stress such as employees you have to manage, patients' attitudes particularly borderline personality disorders, natural consequences of a disease process—complications or death, media attention—front page news denigrating healthcare workers, deadlines for training, exams, research or writing papers, dealing with shift work. The list is not inclusive but shows that when you start examining your working lifestyle balance, there are many areas in which to look for changes. The following is a list of behavior patterns that is adapted from Simon Wein [13]. The list is neither exhaustive nor validated. However, like the main religions or philosophies of the world express a manner in which to live your life, this list is aimed at reducing or removing the origins of stress in the workplace.

Fifteen Rules that All Workers Should Aspire to Holding—Adapted from Wein [13]

1. Do not scream or raise your voice or show exasperation.
2. Do not despair openly BUT if you do state it is frustration within!
3. Do not express anger in front of staff.
4. Do not lie or bend the truth to suit your own ends.
5. Do not play favourites with patients or staff.
6. Always ask for help.
7. Do not override/belittle junior, equal level or senior staff in public.
8. Do not abuse patients or family.
9. Do speak to junior staff privately on at least a weekly basis and for 15 min minimum time preferably 30 min.
10. Always say "thank you".
11. Always show humility when praised and dutiful acceptance when corrected.
12. Always show objectivity in your appraisal of a situation.
13. Always forgive.
14. Always use your own mistakes to teach others and not theirs.
15. Create an atmosphere of respect around you and your colleagues.

I think all of these rules are self explanatory. The first 14 rules will most certainly influence rule 15!

An interesting exercise is to print a copy of this list and tick off each day when you accomplish or part accomplish one of the 15 points then repeat it after you have had a stressful day. Then place crosses against the items when you feel others have not adhered to the 15 points in question and reflect upon your findings. Objectivity is fundamental when seeking out sources of stress or prevention strategies.

Working shifts particularly night shifts on a regular or irregular basis leads to many negative life events including early onset cardiovascular disease and cancer [2]. Stress levels assessed in night shift workers compared to day shift workers are almost twice as high. Yet how many night shift workers say they work night as they are less stressful for them [2, 12].

The easiest way to avoid stressful situations is not to go to work! However, the easy option is only available as a last resort. So how do we cope with the purely extraneous influences upon our stress levels?

The first, second and third method is communication. A problem shared is a problem halved. Ensuring good communication channels with your work colleagues is imperative to enjoy a fruitful and healthy work life [12]. There are many people at work who you can approach, from your mentor to your union representative. If they are the source of distress and direct communication is not of help then you could seek help from the institutional departments of psychological medicine or pastoral care. These departments are there for you as much as they are there for the patients.

If you don't want to communicate then put yourself into the shoes of the person who is causing you the stress and envisage what view they are logically holding [14]. Although their view may appear illogical to you today, tomorrow it may appear very differently. Over the years I have thought over many stress induced events directed at me or around me or initiated by me. One association I have found is as follows; the highest level of stress induced in others originates from the person who probably has or is having a near major life event but cannot see how it this is affecting themselves or those around them who are not directly involved with the instigating life event [9]. The contagiousness of the stress from such individuals can be most debilitating to those around.

I once worked for an obsessive boss who always wanted to know who the person was who wrote in the patient notes as the level of identification in the institution was poor. Every day he would in some way or another make a comment about this. I could understand his frustration but despite discussing this he couldn't see a solution. Half of my solution to this was to personally buy a stamp with my details on it. The other half of the solution was to remember to use the stamp! The desired effect was obtained though and eventually the boss on seeing the solution to his own distress persuaded the hospital administration to purchase everyone a stamp. However, he soon found another obsession to fill the gap!

What is our response in the workplace to stress? [3]. This list is not exhaustive but is intended to highlight the common reactions we employ.

Anger and Resentment

> Resentment is like drinking a poison and then hoping that your enemy will die
> —Nelson Mandela

This quote probably sums up one of the most destructive self induced responses to stress. Anger and resentment within the workplace are two extremely negative reactions that unless objective reflection and appropriate action occur will eventually lead to a breakdown in working relations [15]. Both of these emotions can be linked to the pre morbid personality of the sufferer [8].

Anxiety and Depression

A third of all personnel within an emergency department are found to meet sub-clinical levels of anxiety and depression [16]. This fact is no surprise given the acute nature of the work involved as well as the odd major disaster turning up at work. Recognition of this and preparation of the staff for recognising the profound effects of dealing with unpredictable major work events reduces mental illness secondary to stress [2, 7, 10].

Incorrectly Lowered or Raised Self Esteem—The EGO

Self esteem is one of the most important tools that we use to operate at work—or indeed in our lives [17]. Recognition for our work is important to the development of our professional confidence. In an institution this is often a peer reviewed process. The process itself though can be extremely threatening to both the provider and user of the review process [4, 17]. Support from a colleague or representative at the time of a formal work review for either side of the table will help greatly to reduce the stress involved. However, bloated self recognition -bordering on egotistical behaviour—which can result from both peer and self reviewed performance is potentially an extremely stressful force that is often not recognised within the holder [7, 8].

A colleague confided in me this personal story. The woman in question had won a prestigious award at examination time. At the time she felt very proud but did not recognise the change in her behaviour from one of relative neutrality in opinion to one where she felt her opinion should always be proffered and reference to the award made as often as possible. She felt on reflection that she now had to practice to a new higher standard and that those around her had to be made aware of such a standard that was commensurate with the award. Upon fully reflecting this period of her life some years later, she felt that the life of those around her was made extremely stressful as their opinions did not matter to her as she had the formal recognition that she was now 'head of the pack'. This resulted in belittling behaviour of her colleagues as well as the false elevation of her self status to those around her—in her own words—*I must have been a nightmare to work with!*

When dealing with multiple professional status environments this power play is sadly only too common.

Signs and Symptoms of Stress

The physical symptoms of stress include; pounding heart, palpitations, a dry mouth, headaches, odd aches and pains, loss of appetite for food, reduced libido, altered menstruation pattern, weight changes, increased symptomatology of existing disease disorder, headaches, visual disturbances especially acuity and non specific viral type illnesses. This list is not exclusive and indeed changes from culture to culture [5, 7].

Signs of stress in colleagues include lack of concentration, reduced decision making skills, unable to perform task to the usual or expected levels, frustration at minor issues, deterioration in relationships at work, negative approach to work and personality changes [18]. Again, this list is not exclusive but it touches upon one of the main influences upon how individuals react to or cause stress—personality [19]. Not everyone is born a 'natural coper' or is able to reflect upon their actions and implications around them—in fact most of us need to be taught these skills.

How we Adapt to Reduce Stress

Men and women cope with stress differently. In a general population study involving 2816 people (ages: 18–65 years), 'women tended to score significantly higher than the men on the emotional and avoidance coping styles and lower on rational and detachment coping' [20]. In a study of nurses, no health complaints were attributed to stress as long as the individuals concerned had high active or constructive rather than passive coping abilities. Active coping strategies include problem solving whilst passive coping is waiting to see what happens or avoiding potential problem arenas. Emotional distancing coping strategies rather than detachment strategies produced less stress and burnout for nurses [16].

Mechanisms for coping with stress are necessary to build up personal resilience i.e. building up mechanisms in life that increase the ability to categorise, compartmentalise, appraise or remove stress [21].

Individuals as the noun defines are at will to cope with stress in as many different ways as possible.

Appraisal based coping strategies are our innate coping strategies to stress. Akin to removing our hand from a very hot object to protect ourselves, distancing is where we take ourselves away both physically and/or mentally from the stressful situation or stress originator e.g. avoiding people at work or being in the toilet when the emergency buzzer is pressed etc. [22, 23]. Most studies examining distancing coping have determined that it is the weakest and least successful method for coping with chronic stress. Similarly, detachment coping is a weak method though both detachment and distancing are important immediate responses. To overcome long term aspects of stress i.e. anxiety, depression and ill health, more complex mechanisms have to be used [22, 23].

Problem focused coping is a more advanced method of addressing longer term issues.

Both this method and emotion-focused coping have a large overlap in their functionality. Although a large part of each of these mechanisms can be exercised as an individual e.g. reflection, turning negatives into positives etc, the influence of the individual's personality may require some direction from an objective outside source e.g. a counselor [4, 5, 7, 12].

Activities that Are Most Commonly Used to Reduce Stress

Humour

In the 1980's virtually every newly qualified doctor in the western world read the House of God by Samuel Schem. The book chronicalised the life of a newly qualified North American intern. The stressful events of long working hours with no end in sight for the chronic medical and social problems was described in a very offbeat almost black humour style. However, the junior medical profession worldwide took to it as the bible of workplace survival. The humorous stories provided a recognition that the problems of the profession were worldwide. Unless you laughed with the evolving experience you would quickly start drowning in the stress of the working environment. This approach did not remove the importance of providing professional care in a most professional and compassionate manner but allowed one to put the current situation into perspective within one's life. The importance of the annual, often irreverent institutional revue cannot be underestimated in the positive manner in which it is delivered. However, the revue is a fine line between parody and persecution of individuals. Thus, the individuals being parodied must be prepared to [24, 25]. However, the obvious benefits of laughter has spawned a most intriguing new social interaction amongst people—laughter yoga or Hasyayoga. Initially founded in India in the 1990's, the concept of voluntary laughter leading to longer term spontaneous laughter outside of the sessions has lit the imagination of the public worldwide. Two small studies have examined this in patients and nursing students. Whilst these are not randomised controlled studies, they both showed an improvement in mood and quality of life coupled with a decrease in anxiety [26, 27].

Laughter is as powerful a tool as exercise and meditation in producing positive physiological changes in the body. Laughter whether forced or spontaneous reduces most systemic inflammatory markers, cortisol, blood sugar, pulse rate, blood pressure and increases endophorin release as well as altering gene expressions [28].

Exercise

Exercise allows us 'my time' to recover and increase our resilience to stress. Exercise also gives us a sense of completion and personal goal achievement which improves self confidence [29]. Hospitals have recognised this fact and there are increasing numbers of staff gym facilities. One of the commonest symptoms of stress is tiredness. Contrary to logical thought processes of stressed exercise [30].

Interestingly the brain is still a pliable organ in older age with regular [31] Stress has a negative influence upon the function of these areas of the brain probably via the action of the increased cortisol levels. Is one form of exercise better than another in reducing stress? How long should one exercise for? It is probably not important on the form of exercise but more about performing an exercise you enjoy. Long-term physical changes are best achieved with a daily regimen of 30 min. Again, some individuals will require more time some less but whatever your choice do not make your goals unattainable—aim for 20% of your goal and then expand your limits as you attain the goal. The feeling of failure will only negatively influence feelings of well-being and self worth.

Historically, claims for the psychological benefits of physical exercise had lacked scientific evidence. However, we now know that studies examining both long term and singular aerobic exercise interventions reduce the levels and incidence of anxiety and depression [29, 30] Furthermore, both the overall well-being of the individuals and the resilience of such people to stress are improved. The exact mechanism is pluripotential. One hypothesis is 'The hypothalamic–pituitary–adrenal axis (HPAA) response seems to be more specific to a psychosocial challenge incorporating ego involvement.' However, there are many factors which affect this system such as arginine vasopressin (AVP) and the circulating levels of available cortisol. Cortisol is also influenced by the sex hormones [32].

Diet, Probiotics and Stress

> Let food be thy medicine and medicine be thy food.
> - Hippocrates

Stress affects both our food intake and the microbiome of our bodies. Our microbiome (bacteria, fungi and viruses that live in our body) appears to be linked to our psychological/psychiatric well-being affecting anxiety and depression as well as the incidence of chronic migraines [33]. A randomised control trial using validated stress assessments show that ingesting probiotics (bacteria that are beneficial to us) reduces the biochemical response to stressful situations as well as improving the overall quality of life scoring [34]. The exact mechanisms behind these changes include a poorly defined neuro-enteric pathway, a reduction in systemic inflammation and an increase in serotonin and other central nervous system transmitters [33]. However, stress can potentially have a reverse negative affect upon the same good bacteria in our bodies [35]. This is an area of greatly increasing research with a very positive sounding future [36]. Of interest is that chewing gum reduces stress levels and improves work efficiency—so does foot tapping! [37].

Summary

Stress is something that professionals are exposed to on a daily basis but stress is transferrable from one person to another [38]. Our coping mechanisms to stress are complex but thankfully, in the vast majority of circumstances are complete. This chapter though skimming over the surface of a topic that has so much published data will hopefully aid you in reflecting, correctly apportioning and coping with the origins and results the of stress. In the words of Mahatma Gandhi: *'nobody can hurt me without my permission'*.

References

1. Health and Safety Executive: http://www.hse.gov.uk/statistics/causdis/stress/index.htm
2. Mcvicar A (2003) Workplace stress in nursing: a literature review. J Adv Nurs 44:633–642
3. Sterud T, Ekeberg O, Hem E (2006) Health status in the ambulance services: a systematic review. BMC Health Serv Res 6:82–92
4. Williamson AM (1994) Managing Stress in the Workplace. Int J Ind Ergonom 14:171–196
5. McGowan B (2001) Self-reported stress and its effects on nurses. Nurs Stand 15:33–38
6. Hader K, Broome M, West M, Nash M (2001) Factors influencing satisfaction and anticipated turnover for nurses in an academic medical center. J Nurs Adm 31:210–216
7. Stop stress at work: a guide for workers. ACTU (2000) ACTU–OHS Unit. 2000.
8. Bowling N, Eschleman K, Tetrick L (2010) Employee personality as a moderator of the relationships between work stressors and counterproductive work behavior. J Occ Health Psychol 15:91–103
9. Stordeur S, D'Hoore W, Vandenberghe C (2001) Leadership, organisational stress and emotional exhaustion among hospital nursing staff. J Adv Nurs 35:533–542
10. Kivimaki M, Elovainio M, Vahteera J (2000) Workplace bullying and sickness absence in hospital staff. Occup Environ Med 57:656–660
11. Shirey M, Mcdaniel A, Ebright P, Fisher M, Doebbeling B (2010) Understanding nurse manager stress and work complexity: factors that make a difference. JONA 40:82–91
12. Ball J, Pike G, Cuff C, Mellor-Clark J, Connell J (2002) RCN Working well survey, RCN online. http://www.rcn.org.uk/__data/assets/pdf_file/0011/78527/001595.pdf
13. Wein S (2013) Ten things a ward consultant should never (ever) do. Med J Aust 198:51
14. Morris M, Messal C, Meriac J (2013) Core self-evaluation and goal orientation: understanding work stress. Hum Resour Dev Stress Q 24:35–63
15. Wittenberg-lyles E, Demiris G, Parker Oliver D, Washington K, Burt S, Shaunfield, S (2012) Variances among informal hospice caregivers. Qual Health Res 22:1114–1125
16. de Boer J, Lok A, van't Verlaat E, Duivenvoorden H, Bakker A, Smit B (2011) Work-related critical incidents in hospital-based health care providers and the risk of post-traumatic stress symptoms, anxiety, and depression: a meta-analysis. Soc Sci Med 73:316–326
17. Edwards D, Burnard P, Bennett K, Hebden U (2010) Longitudinal study of stress and self-esteem in student nurses. Nurse Educ Today 30:78–84
18. Lee R, Lovell B, Brotheridge C (2010) Tenderness and Steadiness: relating job and interpersonal demands and resources with burnout and physical symptoms of stress in Canadian physicians. J Appl Soc Psychol 40:2319–2342
19. Brebner J (2001) Personality and stress coping. Personal Individ Differ 31:317–327
20. Matud M (2004) Gender differences in stress and coping styles. Personal Individ Differ 37:1401–1415
21. Travers C (2011) Unveiling a reflective diary methodology for exploring the lived experiences of stress and coping. J Vocat Behav 79:204–216
22. Kuo B (2013) Collectivism and coping: current theories, evidence, and measurements of collective coping. Int J Psychol 48:374–388
23. Beasley M, Thompson T, Davidson J (2003) Resilience in response to life stress: the effects of coping style and cognitive hardiness. Personal Individ Differ 34:77–95
24. Doosje S, De Goede M, Van Doornen L, Goldstein J (2010) Measurement of occupational humorous coping. Humor: Int J Humor Res 23:275–306
25. Wanzer M, Booth-butterfield M, Booth-butterfield S. (2005) "If we didn't use humor, we'd cry": humorous coping communication in health care settings. J Health Commun 10:105–125
26. Yazdani M, Esmaeilzadeh M, Pahlavanzadeh S, Khaledi F (2014). The effect of laughter Yoga on general health among nursing students. Iran J Nurs Midwifery Res 19:36–40
27. Dolgoff-Kaspar R, Baldwin A, Johnson M, Edling N, Sethi G (2012). Effect of laughter yoga on mood and heart rate variability in patients awaiting organ transplantation: a pilot study. Altern Ther Health Med 18:61–66

28. Hayashi T, Murakami K (2009) The effects of laughter on post-prandial glucose levels and gene expression in type 2 diabetic patients. Life Sci 85:185–187
29. Salmon P (2001) Effects of physical exercise on anxiety, depression, and sensitivity to stress: a unifying theory. Clin Psychol Rev 21:33–61
30. Yeung R (1996) The acute effects of exercise on mood state. J Psychosom Res 40:123–141
31. Erickson K, Leckie R, Weinstein A (2014) Physical activity, fitness, and gray matter volume. Neurobiol Aging pii: S0197-4580(14)00349-2 doi:10.1016/j.neurobiolaging. 2014.03.034. [Epub ahead of print]
32. McMorris T, Davranche K, Jones G, Hall B, Corbett J, Minter C (2009) Acute incremental exercise, performance of a central executive task, and sympathoadrenal system and hypothalamic-pituitary-adrenal axis activity. Int J Psychophysiol 73:334–340
33. Dinan T, Quigley E (2011) Probiotics in the treatment of depression: science or science fiction? Aust N Z J Psychiatry 45:1023–1025
34. Yang H, Zhao X, Tang S, Huang H (2014) Probiotics reduce psychological stress in patients before laryngeal cancer surgery. Asia-Pac J Clin Oncol. doi:10.1111/ajco.12120
35. Palma G, Collins S, Berick P, Verdu E (2014) The Microbiota-Gut-Brain axis in gastrointestinal disorders: stressed bugs, stressed brain or both? doi:10.1113/jphysiol.2014.273995
36. Sharkey K, Mawe G (2014) Neurohormonal signaling in the gastrointestinal tract: new frontiers. J Physiol 592:2923–2925
37. Smith A. Chaplin K, Wadsworth E (2012) Chewing gum, occupational stress, work performance and wellbeing. an intervention study. Appetite 58:1083–1086
38. Buchanan T, Preston S (2014) Stress leads to prosocial action in immediate need situations. Front Behav Neurosci 8:5

Suggested Further Reading on Stress Assessment and Management

39. NHS stress at work: http://www.nhs.uk/Conditions/stress-anxiety-depression/Pages/workplace-stress.aspx
40. NHS mood self assessment: http://www.nhs.uk/Conditions/stress-anxiety-depression/Pages/mood-self- assessment.aspx
41. American Institute of Stress: http://www.stress.org/self-assessment/
42. NIOSH Generic Job Stress Questionnaire: http://www.cdc.gov/niosh/topics/workorg/detail088.html

Chapter 11
The Nature of Conflict in Health-Care

Catherine Campbell and Corinne Reid

In the middle of difficulty lies opportunity
—J. A. Wheeler on Einstein (1979)

Abstract Conflict in health-care, at all levels of the organization is both common and expected. Providing care to patients presents unique challenges in an environmental context that is characterized by physical and emotional adversity, and especially for practitioners, persistent stress. This chapter discusses issues that are central to the nature of conflict encountered in health-care settings from a relational person-centered perspective. Conflict is viewed as non-linear and multi-determined. A conceptual overview of the common sources of conflict, and its impact, in a health care setting are discussed in terms of the patient-practitioner relationship as well as within multi-disciplinary teams. Understanding patient's responses to communication of illness as well as group dynamics within treating teams is critical to a fulsome understanding of the role conflict plays within these relationships. Principals of authenticity, empathy and unconditional positive regard from a person-centered perspective are presented as a guide for navigating these relationships toward resolution and growth when conflict inevitably arises.

Keywords Conflict at work · Conflict in multidisciplinary health · Patient and practitioner conflict · Conflict in adjustment to illness · Person-centered conflict resolution

C. Campbell (✉)
Neonatal Clinical Care Unit, King Edward Memorial Hospital, Level 1,
A Block 374 Bagot Rd, 6008 SUBIACO, Western Australia
e-mail: Catherine.Campbell@health.wa.gov.au

UWA Centre for Neonatal Research and Education, School of Paediatrics and Child Health,
University of Western Australia, GPO Box D184, 6840 PERTH, Western Australia

C. Reid
School of Psychology and Exercise Science, Murdoch University, Perth, WA, Australia

© Springer International Publishing Switzerland 2015
S. Patole (ed.), *Management and Leadership – A Guide for Clinical Professionals,*
DOI 10.1007/978-3-319-11526-9_11

Key Points

- Conflict in health care is common and expected.
- Conflict is a feature of highly skilled teams and necessary for growth.
- The nature of conflict is best understood along relational dimensions and is multi-causal.
- Conflict is influenced by our communication style, emotional experience (and expression), histories of conflict, values, interests/needs, knowledge and organizational culture.
- Openness in relationships offers the best prevention of, and facilitates an optimal response to, conflict. The relational qualities of being genuine, empathic and unconditional in our regard for others (patient and colleague) are the central features of successful conflict resolution.

Caring for patients presents unique challenges for hospital staff. There are few other occupations as emotionally charged, where critical decisions are made in the context of grief, stress and fatigue for patients, families, and their practitioners [1]. Moreover, optimal patient management relies upon the successful interplay between individuals, families and multidisciplinary groups. These inter-related systems are dynamic and complex. Conflict in health-care is both common and expected, occurring daily as differences in opinions are expressed about patient care, and as responsibilities change as patients recover [1]. Conflict also emerges during negotiations for finite financial and human resources to meet seemingly infinite need. This chapter discusses issues that are central to the nature of conflict encountered in health-care settings from a relational person-centered perspective, drawing upon the experience of working in a neonatal intensive care unit (NICU). The aim of this chapter is to prompt a reflective process in our reader. At the heart of all encounters with conflict is *reflective practice*. Reflection is a process of critically thinking about our experiences to make sense of events. Reflection occurs both during (reflection in action) and after the experience (reflection on action) [2].

Part 1: The Nature of Conflict

How we understand the role of conflict in interpersonal relationships will largely determine our approach to managing conflict [3]. While it is tempting to think about the 'root cause' in linear trends, conflict occurs along multiple and simultaneous cognitive, emotional and behavioural dimensions. Understanding how conflicted relationships and conflicted organizations emerge, and are maintained, is more predictably understood in terms of *circular causality* [4–6]. That is, there is not a single internal or external factor shaping the course of a conflicted interaction [7]. In multidisciplinary teams, opportunities for conflict are abundant! Conflict takes the form of: (i) interpersonal; (ii) within-group; and (iii) between-group differences. Each member of a team and each patient (and their family) come with individual differences in world-view, experiences and opinions that impact their decision-making and influences the attitudes they bring to their relationships. Health-care staff must also contend with expedient ministerial instructions for change; budget amendments; competition for scant human or physical resources, as well as more innocuous but persistent stressors such as personnel rotations and shift work [8, 9]. And those are just the challenges at work!

Not all conflict is unhelpful or problematic [10]. Conflict is necessary for growth and can positively impact development, including one's adjustment to illness or loss, professional development and team growth. In a health setting conflict is expressed at every level of the relational landscape, between patients and their practitioners, between practitioners of same and different disciplines; and between health-care and administrative teams. Conflict is often the catalyst that facilitates a point of contact between families and their practitioners as they work to clarify critical elements of care and decision-making. Moderate conflict, especially within highly skilled teams, can facilitate re-evaluation of practice protocols and stimulate new ideas for 'translational' research [11]. Thus, we encourage a departure from the idea of conflict as combative (or even competitive), and instead adopt a relational appreciation of the dynamics of conflict between individuals and between groups as necessary and welcomed.

When Conflict Occurs

Previous research has identified three common relationships most impacted by conflict in health-care provision: (i) practitioner-patient/patent's family conflict; (ii) between members of a treating team (intra-team conflict); and (iii) between different treating teams (inter-team conflict). Most conflict observed in our experience, can be understood through the lens of two relational ideas: First, how *difference* is experienced; and second, how *adjustment* (resolution) is facilitated in highly emotional circumstances. Understanding the common and predictable fault-lines that appear when conflict resolution is attempted in highly stressful circumstances will help practitioners navigate, prevent and manage conflict more effectively. For example, avoiding conflict is rarely successful, and often leads to an acute escalation ("blow-up"). On the other hand, seeking resolution to different perspectives by prioritizing persuasion, can inadvertently amplify hostility as each party attempts to explain and justify their position. Teams that are intolerant to different perspectives and actively encourage 'sameness' from their members, often see patients or team members forced to "choose" one opinion over the other. This is a particularly risky dynamic in the context of high-pressure circumstances where decisions have both immediate and long-term impact. Learning to manage conflict in an open and respectful way requires thinking carefully about the role it plays within our helping and working relationships. If we take the view that conflict is hostile and should be avoided, a *closed* response pattern will follow. On the other hand, if we accept that

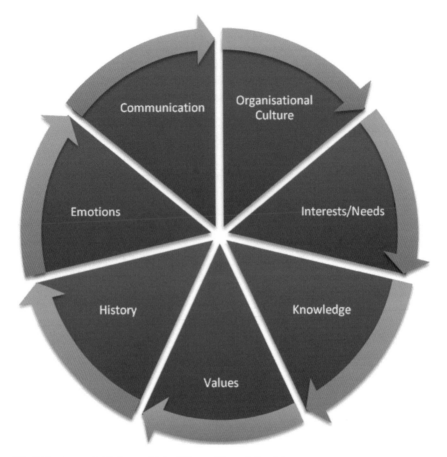

Fig. 11.1 Areas of risk for conflict within working relationships

conflict, however uncomfortable, is an opportunity for growth, learning and adjust-ment, an more *open* response pattern is possible.

Assessing Conflict

There are many models to understand the complex dynamics, assessment, and driv-ers of conflict [12]. Two models, 'The Circle of Conflict' [13], and the 'The Wheel of Conflict' [12] have been summarized to provide a conceptual outline of the inter-personal drivers in most conflict scenarios (Fig. 11.1).

1. **Communication**: Communicating about complex issues, especially when dis-tressed, is difficult. Many interpersonal, internal and external factors influence how well we communicate. Some examples include: language, ethnic culture, gender, age, social-status, education, organizational status, organizational culture.

Discomfort and common errors in our attempt to hold *critical conversations* often relate to inaccurate or incomplete understanding of the problem, stereotyping, differences in world-view, and premature foreclosure on solutions without a fulsome attempt to understand the problem. Communication requires effortful processing, especially in stressful situations that often tempt us with resignation to hopelessness or reaction.

2. **Emotions**: Understanding emotion is important because it both fuels conflict as well as being important in de-escalating conflict [12]. One of the challenges faces in resolving conflict is both understanding and tolerating the expression of difficult emotion. Expressing distress is important for the patient-practitioner relationship as well as for teams wrestling with the challenges of change. There is a narrow pathway between useful expression of difficult emotion and unhelpful polarization of relationships [12].

3. **History**: People bring their own complex history of experiences to the table when addressing conflict. The way we have successfully and unsuccessfully dealt with conflict in the (immediate and distant) past will present a powerful influence on the present. History is cautions us against seeing conflict in isolation.

4. **Values**: Conflict becomes more emotionally charged and intractable when it is influenced by differences in core beliefs or by a perception that values are being questioned [12]. Values can be so ingrained as to be 'invisible' without careful reflection and often present obstacles to acknowledging the perspective of others. Reflecting explicitly on values can assist people to become more open to different possible resolution pathways.

5. **Knowledge**: At the simplest level, discrepancies between how people understand a situation or the information needed to make a decision are common knowledge-based issues that drive conflict. Lack of necessary information, being overwhelmed by too much information or misunderstanding information leads to much conflict in patient-practitioner relationships. In teams, holding knowledge (or having expertise) but being excluded from decision-making processes also readily leads to conflict within teams.

6. **Interests/Needs**: Needs range from primary human survival needs to more latent interests. Misinterpreting needs or interests may lead us along unhelpful resolution pathways. For example, suggesting family counseling for a homeless parent and child is unlikely to be an effective resolution to primary problem driving relational conflict–instability of homelessness.

7. **Culture/Organizational structure**: The organizational structure and culture provide an important guiding framework for the expression of conflict within relationships and groups—does the culture allow or encourage conflict to be expressed? How is the expression of conflict tolerated? Is hostility permitted or is passivity prioritized? Issues related to available resources, decision-making authority and processes (power), time constraints, communication protocols, and physical settings can play central roles in conflict driving people towards competitive rather than cooperative positions. Group dynamics comprising organizational culture will be discussed later in this chapter. A series of questions, that will help in assessing the nature of conflict are summarized in Table 11.1 [7].

Table 11.1 Conflict assessment

1.	What is the emotion about?
2.	What is the person seeing, feeling or experiencing that I am not yet aware of?
3.	Are there aspects of the person's culture, ethnicity, gender, age etc. that might be helpful in explaining his/her unique experience?
4.	How do these things fit with what else I know about the person?
5.	Are there any distortions or exaggeration between the event and the person's experience of the event?
6.	What is the impact of this conflict on the person, their private relationships, their working relationship and other people around the conflict?
7.	How might I assist this person to become more aware of their role in this situation?
8.	Is this person representing any small group alignments that might be having a dynamic influence over this conflict?
9.	What is the contribution of the group's culture in this event?
10.	What are the options available for containing the distress of the conflict, and what must be carefully considered in avoiding further escalation?

Part 2: Conflict at Work

Conflict Between Patients and Practitioners

Patient-practitioner conflict is frequent in an intensive-care environment. For example it is reported that up to 78 % of parent/family-care teams face conflict at some point during the baby's NICU admission [10]. Poor communication with patients is common and conflict often arises in everyday decision-making. Learning to share difficult and often complex information is essential for hospital staff. However, too often the staff prioritize what to say (*content*) without understanding the relational process that safeguards the conversation (*interpersonal process*). Dorr Goold, Williams, Arnold [14] identified features of the patient, practitioner, and wider organization that contribute to common conflict scenarios (Table 11.2).

1. **Communicating Illness**: In health-care, conflict often results from people's attempts to cope with overwhelming stress [15]. Emotion-laden thinking ("hot cognition") and the 'social contagion' (or spread) of extreme negative emotion often precipitate conflict in the absence of any real differences in perspective between parties. We will discuss more about "hot cognition" later in this chapter. Understanding that conflict expressed through relationships is an indicator of distress is important for 'reading' the emotional landscape driving conflict and in providing an insight into possible resolution pathways. Resolution in such conflict scenarios is often synonymous with a person's psychological adjustment to illness.
2. **Understanding adjustment to illness**: Understanding some principals of psychological adjustment to adverse events is important to the resolution process

Table 11.2 Common features associated with conflict in intensive care medicine[a]

Family Features
Understanding complex medical information, adjusting to illness and making critical decisions is influenced by individual differences in
Longitudinal appraisal of the acute event (i.e. the current episode is usually a small part of a much longer story)
Information obtained from various sources—the media, internet, other practitioners, friends and relatives
Beliefs about causes, consequences and prognosis of the patient's condition
Psychological adjustment to receiving bad news, for example Emotional readiness to hear bad news and safe expression of strong negative emotion—guilt, shame, grief etc. Coping style—denial, "acopia", acute stress reaction may lead to attentional biases interpreting information (e.g. avoidance of or hyper-focus on less salient but controllable information; or positive/negative attributions to prognostication) Education and ability to understand complex medical information and hearing key messages without confusion Memory retention for bad ness is fraught often leading to repetition of bad news—while ignoring a person's tolerance for the repetition that may further drive defended responses and escalate conflict Differences in meaning of the language of illness (e.g. "death with dignity" or "he seems more alert today") Cultural/family beliefs as different from practitioner(s)—often lead to rumour and innuendo, which is grossly unfair to families honestly struggling with situation

Practitioner Features
Discomfort with prognostic uncertainty leading to hesitation or over-confident responses to treatment and counsel
Discomfort talking about death, serious injury, long-term disability and confronting 'medical failure' or 'medical impotence'
Underestimation of quality of life for their patient relative to patients and their families
Knowledge and skill deficits can catalyze conflict with families, including prognostic inconsistencies, lack of knowledge or experience to manage ethical, legal and policy factors
Limited interpersonal experience and training required for critical conversations
Fatigue, frustration, stressed, and otherwise beset with competing obligations

Organizational Features
Culture of health care to prioritize emergent decisions, technology and speedy discharges may increase emphasis on "high tech" interventions and the avoidance of time-consuming conferences with families
Training emphasis on procedural techniques
Economic pressure
Hospital policies at odds with family of patients (e.g. restricted visiting to control infection) and legislative obligations to write treatment orders (e.g. paperwork), legal ramifications for end-of-life treatments or management of serious injury

[a] Distilled from Dorr Goold et al. [14]

because it can play a critical role in emerging and escalating conflict. When we talk about a person's emotional adjustment to diagnosis, poor prognosis

Table 11.3 Acute distress and its expression in patients of the NICU

Underlying emotion	Headline message
Shock	*"I went home last night after the doctors round and just felt numb, I just feel nothing." (numbing, passivity)*
	"This is just plain ridiculous, you guys don't have a clue what you are doing. I don't care what any of you say. This is my baby and I will make the choice that's right for my baby. I am taking her home and none of you should get in my way." (rage)
Denial	*"Yes, of course I heard what the doctor said, I just think that it is really important for us to keep things as normal as possible, and going to work is what I would be doing at any other time." (obstructive, passive, angry)*
Avoidance	*"I want to be with her, but I just feel like I'm getting in the way. If you need me give me a call."*
Panic	*"I know the doctor said she would survive this treatment, but I just can't stop thinking about it, I look at her an all I see is the worse case scenario and then I can't control my crying and feel like my whole life is just one big mess"*

or loss what are we looking for? Certainly, there are critical periods in a person's adjustment to stress when the risk of conflict is higher. And, this can occur between the practitioner and patient, as well as between the members of a patient's family or members of the caring team as they strive to cope with their emotions. Understanding the relational dynamics of distress *and* adjustment may better prepare us for preventing conflict with patients. This is especially true when the expression of distress is overwhelming, uncomfortable or "prickly".

Briefly, it can be helpful to think about a person's current mental state along a continuum of positive adjustment, rather than pathology. Some people may be quicker, or slower to adjust to bad news. Struggling to accept bad news is simply an unfolding process toward a 'new normal' for that person (what does life look like after the death of a partner, or living with cancer or parenting a child with disabilities). Just as in other life changes, equilibrium must be disturbed before a 'new normal' (homeostasis) can be achieved. Learning to 'read' even the most intense or unusual expressions of distress in this way, may assist us in accurately identifying the issues driving conflict, and assist the patient to absorb information and accept support, to contain their fear.

From this relational perspective, it is important then to differentiate *expression of emotion* from the *meaning of the distress*. In this sense, interpersonal interactions can be thought of in terms of 'layers' of meaning [16, 17]. For example, a hostile expression of fear may carry a more surface level 'headline message' (sensational statements), while the underlying meaning is a person overwhelmed by fear. Responding to hostility will escalate conflict while responding to the underlying emotion will act as a container where fear is expressed safely. Table 11.3 summarizes the common ways people express distress in the immediacy of unexpected bad news and provides examples of 'headline messages' that often disguise underlying meaning.

3. **Culture**: Differences in cultural perspectives are another common source of conflict. Cultural differences may relate to ethnicity as well as different belief-systems or family arrangements. With rapidly growing cultural diversity it is inevitable that clashes in belief systems will impact not only relationships between practitioners and their patients, but also within health care teams. The predominant value of 'truth telling' and 'open disclosure' in Western medicine is not globally shared and often in philosophical conflict with how 'truth' is regarded by many cultures [18]. In some cultures, medical disclosure is conditional upon the patient's ability to 'tolerate' truth with minimal psychological 'damage' and often entrusted to a patient proxy. Autonomy in decision-making may not be similarly valued, as in Western cultures, and the influence of the patient's extended family may be instead prioritized. Awareness of cultural differences improves our ability to identify potential conflict and diminish or prevent its adverse impact.

Conflict Within and Between Multi-disciplinary Teams

Culture is an important factor influencing how teams organize themselves toward productivity. The cultural environment of teams contributes to conflict at work. The influence of culture on how team members adjust to conflict is largely a function of clear leadership about conflict in groups and the nurtured robustness to tolerate differences. When appraising conflict in teams, it is important to understand that the multi-directional dynamics of the group is greater than the sum of its individual members. When a group is destabilized by conflict, members will respond in predictable patterns as the group strives to achieve change (morphogenesis) or normality (homeostasis). Understanding group psychology helps to accurately appraise and resolve conflict.

1. **Team dynamics and circular causality**: The dynamics between two people finding ways of working (and relating) together are complex. At the simplest level, understanding a person's choice to work for a given organization will be tied to important meaning, values, history, emotions, knowledge, interests and needs. Along with their personal and professional goals, these factors influence how they relate to colleagues. Beyond the individual-level, the face-to-face working relationships within and between teams exponentially increases the potential for conflict [19]. Conflict events are usually multi-causal, multi-determined, and reciprocal rather than linear. While this may sound overwhelming, it also lends to multiple potential solutions to conflict.
2. **Group-size and stability**: The social impact of group composition and size powerfully influences team functioning [20]. Large and changing groups are at a greater risk of reduced individual commitment and interpersonal collaboration. Social loafing is more prominent, because members are able to be less visible in large groups and are less accountable in groups with changing membership. Certainly inactivity or passivity can be incredibly divisive, especially if inactivity is noticed in a large group and challenged publically. While

smaller groups of about five people provide the best mix of individual commitment and collaboration, smaller groups too carry the risk of conflict. They are at greater risk of under-evaluating performance and engaging in a slippery path toward self-justified ethics and choices. Small groups can suffer from being excessively conservative, or more radical in their decision-making as stability is prioritized over critical self-evaluation. Introduction of new members or role transitions can be poorly tolerated and sources of conflict emerge in 'in-group/out-group' dynamics that manifest from strong bonds or 'cliques'. Changing shift rosters in hospital settings create the potential for a permanently unstable team dynamic. While changing teams help promote transparency and accountability processes that protect the perpetuation of bad habits that emerge from over-familiarity, changing teams also run the risk of differences neither being acknowledged nor addressed. A comprehensive description of these group processes as potential sources of conflict is beyond the scope of this chapter. However, we emphasize the importance of appraising group dynamics when assessing conflict at work.

3. **Systemic defense**: Being aware of predictable systemic defenses is helpful in preventing escalation of low-dilemma conflict and providing insight into options for resolution. Health care settings are especially vulnerable to powerful systemic defenses because of the chronic exposure to extreme distress. Systems exposed to persistent stress can develop a "hardness" that feels intractable when attempting to resolve conflict [21]. There are several important dysfunctional patterns (Table 11.4) that emerge when a system is stressed and ripe for hostile conflict. Learning to read dynamics in groups is difficult, but identifying interaction styles, verbal and nonverbal, provides rich information about what defenses may be at play and/or how they are assisting people to cope with conflict. Behaviours to reflect on include:

- facial expressions;
- body posture;
- special positioning (seating at meetings);
- silence; and
- role assignment/assumptions.

4. **Exceptional teams**: A common feature of highly skilled teams is that they are comprised of practitioners with high levels of confidence in their individual expertise. In health, this is further accentuated by hierarchical and closed structures. But, this is not to say that conflicted teams cannot be exceptional. Success is rarely the outcome of conflict-free teams [22]. Exceptional teams not only tolerate conflict, but actively invite conflict through a process of engaging difference. The key to successful working groups is to build robustness in conflict management at the individual as well as group level. The outcome of conflict then becomes solidarity when group members share newly formed goals. Getting the right balance in collaborative working relationships is difficult and is tied to the developmental evolution of the working group. Appraising the developmental terrain and capacity for tolerating differences

Table 11.4 Common systemic defenses driving conflict in teams

Systemic Defense	Characteristics
Enmeshment	Occur when people feel threatened by an external source
	Manifest in tightly connected relationships in an attempt to ward off danger
	Enmeshed coping is inward focused and rejecting of external influence
	Relationships become covert in their loyalty and systems are resistant to new ideas, are conservative and often static
Disengaged	Characterized as individualistic and disconnected from the welfare, goals or activities of the group
	Manifest in non-attendance at meetings, non-participation in team discussions, and deliberate omission of important information
	Disengaged coping allows overt conflict to be avoided
	Relationships are mistrustful and secretive
Alignments	Characterized by stable coalitions between sub-groups within larger teams such as
	Diffusing stress between members of a sub-group by designating blame (scapegoating) to another team member
	Triangulation is when two opposing parties align against another
	Relationship appear sinister, are complex and all-encompassing of system-wide conflict
Passive-aggressive	Prominent during acute periods of change or chronic levels of systemic distress
	Characterized by hostility or resistance that is expressed covertly rather than directly
	Manifest in patterned and habitual negativism, inefficiency and forgetfulness
	Relationships 'hold' passive-tension often when teams are reach saturation of extreme negative emotion and there is no explicit avenue to reflect on its impact. Deeply intense or negative emotion cannot simply lie dormant and unattended [19]

among individual members is more difficult and beyond the scope of this chapter [22]. But, the core relational qualities required to build robust working relationships within multidisciplinary teams are the same as those required to build trusting and robust relationships between practitioner and patient when conflict arises.

5. **Power in relationship**: Conflict is particularly confronting when it involves or is perceived to involve the abuse of power. Just as with our patients, the power differentials within large hierarchical organizations often present considerable challenge in preventing and resolving conflict. Dual relationships at work are common and often seemingly invisible to parties until conflicted [23]. Much conflict between a subordinate and their senior, stems from poor understanding of the risk of dual relationships. Dual relationships involve a person of power holding two or more potentially conflicting roles that influence how they meet their responsibility to a junior staff member. Dual

relationships present a high degree of risk for intra-and-inter-team conflict, because they blur role expectations, risk competing responsibilities and impaired judgment [23]. Common examples of problematic dual relationships include: line managers responsible for employment conditions simultaneously acting as professional development mentors or providing professional supervision. Good organizational governance involves careful thought about the distribution of power and influence, structures and processes that facilitate accountable behaviour and clear guidelines for navigating or avoiding dual relationships. Indeed new employees should be carefully inducted into grievance process steps within their organization, usually produced to protect the organization from the impact of abuse to power.

6. **Dealing with uncomfortable feelings**: Another common source of conflict within working relationships involves people's capacity to deal with uncomfortable feelings [24]. Discomfort is an important emotional process for any learning. Learning how to use these feelings to draw the most from each professional development opportunity, rather than as a catalyst for conflict, is important, especially in supervisory relationships. To do this, it is necessary that we prioritize maintaining contact with one another (rather than avoiding/hiding) and adopting a respectful/positive position despite differences. Genuineness is critical when approaching conflict issues. Even in the context of strong disagreement, maintaining a relational openness and engagement will usually suffice to resolve conflict rather than escalate it, especially when there is mutual interest in maintaining a relationship with that person. More discussion about these relational ideas of openness, positive regard and authenticity (or being genuine) is provided next.

Part 3: Conflict Resolution

Resolving Conflict at the Level of Individual Relationships: A Way of Relating

Learning to navigate relationships is more helpful than concentrating on strategies to avoid or mediate conflict. The answer lies in the interpersonal space between people and is served well by person-centered practice. That is, all people have an inherent drive towards growth and positive adjustment but this drive can become stuck when significant life events challenge our sense of efficacy. For example, in a NICU, families face a crisis of self-efficacy—they are acutely disempowered in their role as new parents and often despairing about the wellbeing of their infant. The medical team members, who care for them at this time, are also facing chronic levels of stress, which can impact their coping. It is in this context that the family and practitioners come together. The person-centered model recognizes that in all life contexts, but especially those of high emotion and stress, significant change and resolution is possible when three necessary relational conditions are in place: establishment of genuine relationships; empathy; and unconditional positive regard. Both parties experience positive change when these processes are in place [25].

Genuine Relationships Being genuine is not as easy as it seems. Learning to be genuine is usually a gradual evolutionary process that matures along with the practitioners 'confidence to be herself' as she discards her professional façade and learns to respond transparently with her patients. In person-centered practice this is known as striving towards congruence [26]. The practitioner's contextual 'selves' (professional and personal) are congruent and translated into their interaction with patients [27, 28]. In other words, they are not "acting" a part. Distress and conflict are thus invited with warmth and genuine understanding of the dilemma faced even when there is a difference in view.

Empathy One of the central features of a helping relationship is *empathy*. That is, the ability to understand another persons' way of experiencing and perceiving their reality while putting aside our own world-view [29]. In an intensive care environment where tremendous challenges are faced daily, and the expression of intense and negative emotion is confronted regularly, it is paramount that our collegial relationships mirror the relational empathic qualities we strive to achieve with our patients. As in practitioner-patient relationships, collegial relationships are, as much as possible, threat-free, trusting, genuine and validating of a desire to collaborate as part of the team, while being understanding of the barriers to doing so.

Unconditional Positive Regard Unconditional positive regard is sometimes misconstrued as a requirement to be "nice" to our patients [29]. While kindness and respect is important to the helping relationship, this is not what the term unconditional positive regard refers to in person-centered practice. It refers to the practitioners' offer to accept their patient (or colleague) for whoever he/she is without conveying disapproval or idolization [29]. Relationships are characterized by attuned listening without unnecessary or forced interruption, judgment or direction (giving advice). In a conversation about medical options, for example, this could be conveyed as a process of 'guiding' the patient through information they need to make a decision, rather than, offering a recommendation.

Openness If relationships are genuine, empathic and positive in regard for one-another, then they move from being guarded to open. Being open to difference is an important step toward managing conflict. Being open also reflects respect for the input from other members of the group including the patient or family or other team members, and acknowledges that the whole group (or family) is stronger than any one individual in achieving resolution or helpful working relationships. Indeed taking a person-centered relational approach to health-care involves actively valuing relationships as bidirectional. Healthy systems, are not conflict-free, but instead undergo almost constant growth in the form of restructuring and are responsive to new circumstances. A governance structure for the management of conflict within teams and/or with our patients is summarized in Fig. 11.2.

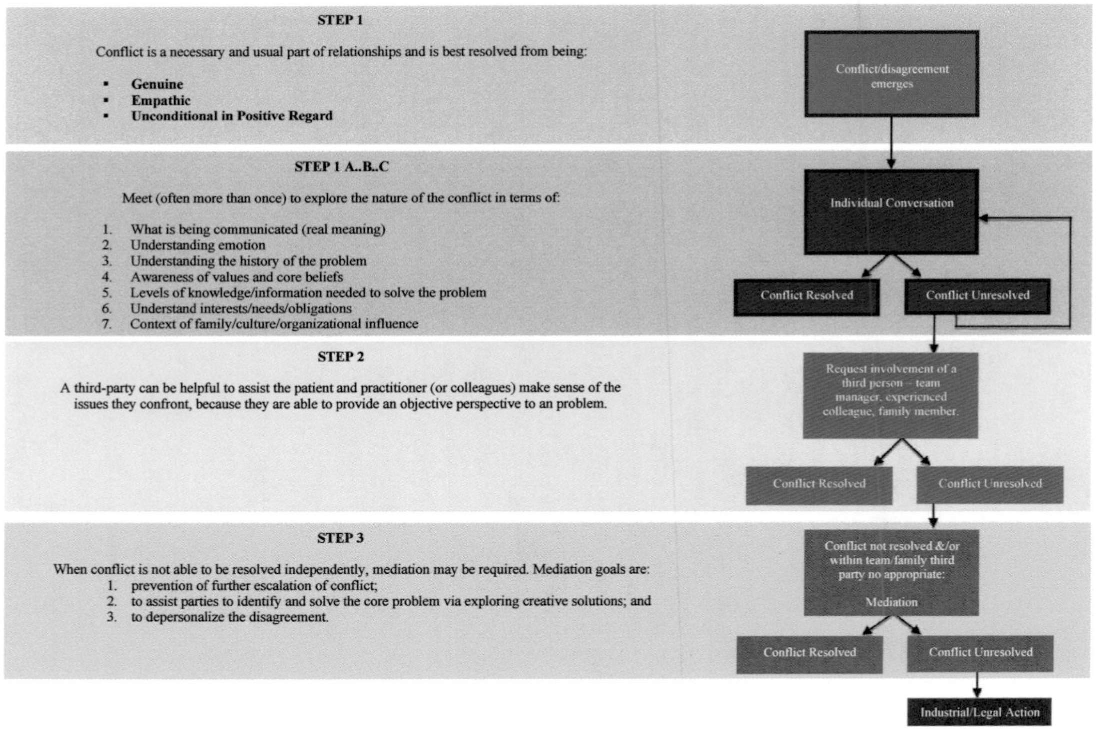
STEP 1
Conflict is a necessary and usual part of relationships and is best resolved from being:
▪ Genuine
▪ Empathic
▪ Unconditional in Positive Regard
STEP 1 A..B..C
Meet (often more than once) to explore the nature of the conflict in terms of:
1. What is being communicated (real meaning)
2. Understanding emotion
3. Understanding the history of the problem
4. Awareness of values and core beliefs
5. Levels of knowledge/information needed to solve the problem
6. Understand interests/needs/obligations
7. Context of family/culture/organizational influence
STEP 2
A third-party can be helpful to assist the patient and practitioner (or colleagues) make sense of the issues they confront, because they are able to provide an objective perspective to an problem.
STEP 3
When conflict is not able to be resolved independently, mediation may be required. Mediation goals are:
1. prevention of further escalation of conflict;
2. to assist parties to identify and solve the core problem via exploring creative solutions; and
3. to depersonalize the disagreement.
Conflict/disagreement emerges
Individual Conversation
Conflict Resolved
Conflict Unresolved
Request involvement of a third person – team manager, experienced colleague, family member.
Conflict Resolved
Conflict Unresolved
Conflict not resolved &/or within team/family third party no appropriate:
Mediation
Conflict Resolved
Conflict Unresolved
Industrial/Legal Action

Fig. 11.2 Conflict resolution decision making flow

Resolution of Hostile or Problematic Conflict: Mediation

When conflict is unavoidable and efforts toward resolution have been unsuccessful, careful management is required. Organizational psychology, business management, mediation and litigation law provide many strategic options for mediating conflict. For the work place, conflict resolution might involve formal mediation and in clinical practice, grievances are usually addressed by the customer service unit or clinical ethics committee. In the world of conflict mediation, resolution is about agreement upon an outcome to a dispute that is mutually acceptable by all parties [12]. However, resolution to serious conflict is rarely neat or comprehensive, and usually involves a iterative process of resolving narrow issues. It is important to understand that resolution is not that same as agreement, and mediation processes do not seek agreement on the essential elements/beliefs fueling the conflict, but agreement to a tolerable solution [12]. Broadly the objectives of mediation include: (1) prevention of further escalation of conflict; (2) assisting parties to identify and solve the core problem via exploring creative solutions; and (3) depersonalizing the disagreement.

Conclusion

Conflict in health settings is inevitable as people adjust to bad news and staff finds ways of managing chronic exposure to distress. Any organizational structure presents risks for conflict and no system is perfect. Together, these human and organizational circumstances create the perfect storm for multi-person, multi-level conflict. Yet, the difference between an exceptional team and a troubled one, is not the presence or absence of conflict potential, or *actual* conflict, but rather the lens through which such conflict is viewed, and the capacity of the system in enabling the healthy expression and resolution of conflict. Given its daily occurrence and its systemic impact, conflict is an important issue for hospital staff. A relational approach that prioritizes openness, authenticity and positive regard for one another, is the best prevention and defense against conflict escalation, as well as affording fertile opportunity for growth and adjustment.

References

1. Studdert DM, Burns JP, Mello MM, Puopolo AL, Truog RD, Brennan TA (2003) Nature of conflict in the care of pediatric intensive care patients with prolonged stay. Pediatrics 112:553–558
2. Lang M, Taylor A (2000) The making of a mediator. Jossey-Bass, San Fransico
3. Mayer B (2000) The dynamics of conflict resolution: a practitioner's guid. Jossey-Bass, San Fransico
4. Witherington DC (2011) Taking emergence seriously: the centrality of circular causality for dynamic systems approach to development. Hum Dev 54:66–92
5. Juarrero A (1999) Chapter 1: Introduction. Dynamics in action: Intentional behavior as a complex system. Cambridge: MIT Press, pp 1–11
6. Juarrero A (2009) Top-down causation and autonomy in complex systems. In: Murphy N, Ellis GER, O'Connor T (eds) Downward causation and the neurobiology of free will. Springer, Berlin, pp 83–102
7. Kottler JA, Englar-Carlson M (2010) Learning group leadership: An experiential approach, 2nd. ed. Sage Publications, California
8. Harrington J (2001) Health effects of shift work and extended hours of work. Occup Environ Med 58:68–72
9. Stansfeld S, Candy B (2006) Psychological work environment and mental health: a meta-analytic review. Scand J Work Env Hea 32(6):443–462
10. Back AL, Arnold RM (2005) Dealing with conflict in caring for the seriously ill. JAMA 293:1374–1381
11. Brown R (2000) Group processes. Blackwells, Oxford
12. Mayer B (2000) The dynamics of conflict resolution: a practitioners guide. Wiley, San Francisco
13. Moore C (2003) The mediation process. Jossey-Bass, San Fransico
14. Dorr Goold S, Williams B, Arnold RM (2000) Conflicts regarding decisions to limit treatment: a differential diagnosis. JAMA 283:909–914
15. Gillotti C, Applegate J (2000) Explaining illness as bad news: individual differences in explaining illness-related information. In: Whaley BB (ed) Explaining illness: research, theory, and strategies. Lawrence Erlbaum Associates Inc., Mahwah, pp 100–120
16. Finnegan R (2004) Communicating humans … but what does that mean? In: Barett S, Komaromy C, Robb M, Rogers A (eds) Communication relationshis and care: a reader. Routledge, New York, pp 7–13
17. White M (1986) Negative explanation, restraint, and double description: a template for family therapy. Fam Process 25:169–184
18. de Pentheny O'Kelly C, Urch C, Brown EA (2011) The impact of culture and religion on truth telling at the end of life. Nephrol Dial Transpl 26:3838–3842
19. McIlduff E, Coghlan D (2000) Reflections: understanding and contending with passive-aggressive behavior in teams and organizations. J Manage Psychol 15:716–736
20. Clegg S, Kornberger M, Pitsis T (2011) Managing teams and groups. In: Clegg S, Kornberger M, Pitsis T (eds) Managing and organisations: an introduction to theory and practice. Sage Publications, London
21. Lazarus RS (2000) Toward a better research on stress and coping. Am Psychol 55:665–673
22. Reid C, Stewart E, Thorne G (2004) Multidisciplinary sport science teams in elite sport: comprehensive servicing or conflict and confusion? Sport Psychol 18:204–217
23. O'Donovan A, Halford WK, Walters B (2011) Towards best practice supervision of clinical psychology trainees. Aust Psychol 46:101–112
24. Nellis AC, Hawkins KL, Redico MJ, Way SK (2011) Productive conflict in supervision. 2011 ACES Conference, 26–28 October 2011 Nashville Tennessee
25. Motschnig-Pitrik R, Barrett-Lennard GT (2010) Co-actualization: a new construct for understanding well-functioning relationships. J Humanist Psychol 50:374–398

26. Rogers C (1957) The necessary and sufficient conditions of therapeutic personality change. J Consult Psychol 21:95–103
27. Barrett-Lennard GT (2013) The relationship paradigm: human being beyond individualism. Palgrave Macmillan, Houndmills
28. Barrett-Lennard GT (2005) Relationship at the centre. Northwestern University, Whurr
29. Mearns D, Thorne B (2007) Person-centred counselling in action. Sage Publications, London

Chapter 12
Evidence Based Management

Ravi Madhavan and Ajay Niranjan

A wasteland of vocationalism that needed to be transformed into science-based professionalism
—Nobel Laureate Herbert Simon, on business education in the 1950s.

Abstract In their managerial roles, clinicians face the challenge of how to access, assess and deploy the most relevant and current management knowledge. This challenge is exacerbated by the fact that the management discipline is a relative latecomer to the evidence-based paradigm. Although the research-based model of business education can be traced back to the 1950's, the management discipline is still characterized by a multiplicity of theoretical perspectives, the lack of consensus on a hierarchy of evidence, and the lack of point-of-use tools that translate scientific results into protocols. As a result, popular claims based on anecdotal evidence often compete with rigorous empirical studies for the manager's attention. In the last decade, however, a small but growing evidence-based management (EBMgt) movement has taken shape. EBMgt's influence can be seen in the increasing numbers of meta-analyses, a greater interest in experimental studies, the newfound acceptance of replication studies, and practical approaches such as fact-based consulting. This chapter provides an overview of EBMgt along with a practical resource list of evidence-based sources in three key areas: managing people, managing process and systems, and managing strategy.

Keywords Evidence-based management · Managerial decision making · Managerial action · Managing people · Managing process and systems · Managing strategy · Leadership · Change management · Recruiting · Staffing · Influence · Quality improvement · Lean · Six Sigma · Innovation · Culture · Strategic planning · Diversification · Mergers & acquisitions · Decision supports

R. Madhavan (✉)
Katz Graduate School of Business, University of Pittsburgh, 208 Mervis Hall, Pittsburgh, PA 15260, USA
e-mail: rmadhavan@katz.pitt.edu

A. Niranjan
Department of Neurosurgery, University of Pittsburgh, Pittsburgh, USA

© Springer International Publishing Switzerland 2015   167
S. Patole (ed.), *Management and Leadership – A Guide for Clinical Professionals,*
DOI 10.1007/978-3-319-11526-9_12

Key Points

- The management discipline has built up a significant empirical research base, but a systematic approach linking practice to directly relevant evidence is less than a decade old.
- Systematic review techniques are gaining traction among management scholars, but the discipline still lacks point-of-use tools that translate research into concrete action guides.
- Influential studies in management span the entire hierarchy of evidence, ranging from opinion pieces through large-sample statistical analyses to systematic reviews.
- Given the relative nascency of EBMgt, research opportunities abound for clinicians- e.g., testing and developing point-of-use decision and process tools.
- An EBMgt resource list is provided for three key areas of management: managing people, managing process and systems, and managing strategy.

Whatever their specialty and role as medical professionals, most clinicians also have management responsibilities—such as recruiting and supervising staff who have the appropriate skills and experience; developing, implementing and upgrading safe work practices and systems; and ensuring the longer-term growth and sustainability of their practice or organization. The increasing popularity of graduate management programs for physicians attests to the widespread acceptance of this dual clinician-manager role, as well as to the need for systematic education in the art and science of management [1]. Used as they are to the well-established culture of evidence-based medicine, however, clinicians in their managerial roles often face the challenge of how to assess and deploy the most current and relevant management knowledge. In this chapter, we provide an overview of evidence-based management (EBMgt) for clinicians. EBMgt is defined as the systematic, evidence-informed practice of management such that the content and process of the manager's decisions and actions incorporate the most current scientific knowledge [2].

The chapter proceeds in four main sections. The first section traces the development and current state of EBMgt. The second section presents several exemplars of EBMgt most relevant to clinicians. The third section outlines possible future directions for EBMgt. The fourth and final section sketches key implications for clinicians.

EBMgt: The State of the Art

The management discipline is a relative latecomer to the evidence-based paradigm. The research-based model of business education, currently well established in business schools worldwide, can be traced back to the 1950's, when the Ford

Foundation became interested in enhancing management practices through improved professional education [3]. The resulting report, "Higher Education for Business" [4], along with a contemporaneous report funded by the Carnegie Foundation [5], kicked off an approach to management that was research-based, analytical, and founded in economics and other social sciences. In the decades since, management scholars have steadily accumulated systematic empirical evidence on many aspects of managerial work. Today, although business school curricula still contain a considerable volume of anecdotal knowledge and colorful stories, most observers would agree that management education is no longer the "wasteland of vocationalism" that Herbert Simon referred to [6]—see the Epigraph to this chapter. In fact, the current criticism is that management research may have swung to the other extreme—trading off practical relevance against academic rigor [7]. More to the point, the discipline is still characterized by a multiplicity of theoretical perspectives, the lack of consensus on a hierarchy of evidence, and the lack of point-of-use tools that translate scientific results into managerial protocols. Further, a distressing gap between research and education has been pointed out—only about a quarter of business program syllabi utilized scientific evidence in any form [8]. As a result, popular claims based on anecdotal evidence often out-compete rigorous scientific evidence when it comes to informing everyday management decisions and actions. On the whole, it remains true that managers tend to rely largely on personal knowledge and anecdotal evidence, including business books by celebrated leaders such as Jack Welch, rather than on systematic evidence about effective management practices. Yet, it is very difficult to learn from experience, and a lot of such presumed learning turns out to be wrong [9]. Two overarching factors have been pointed out as inhibiting widespread adoption of EBMgt: the tendency among scholars to overvalue novel findings and undervalue the accumulation of convergent findings, and the lack of systematic research syntheses [10]. In addition, a research culture fixated on esoteric theoretical questions rather than on questions of practical importance [11], evidence that is poorly indexed and hard to locate even where it exists [12], and managers who have not been trained in the direct use of evidence in decision making[13] have also been pointed out as barriers to EBMgt. Perhaps an even more fundamental issue has been that Null Hypothesis Significant Testing is the dominant approach to conducting research in management. Derived from, and consistent with, the falsification approach to theory testing—in which the focus is on assessing the fit between a theory and patterns in the data, rather than on effect sizes—this orientation has also been somewhat of a barrier to cumulative knowledge building in management [14].

In the last decade, however, a small but growing EBMgt movement has slowly taken hold among management scholars, although yet more slowly among practicing managers. Inspired by evidence-based medicine, Denise Rousseau, the then president of the Academy of Management, called for a concerted effort to close the prevailing "research-practice" gap [15]. Evidence-based practice requires more than scientific insight—it requires new research norms that encourage scholars to study problems with practical import, significant translation effort (e.g., building decision supports based on current evidence), technology-enabled access to the latest evidence, and a culture of incorporating systematic evidence into decision processes. References to EBMgt tend to use evidence in two senses -locally developed evidence that managers should rely on to make data-based decisions (evidence with a "little e") and cumulative scientific Evidence (with a "big E.")[15]-both are important. Jeff Pfeffer and Robert Sutton [16] laid out a parallel approach emphasizing evidence with the "little e," whereby managers could avoid poor decision making practices, such as casual benchmarking, by incorporating relevant data as well as research evidence. According to them, an EBM mindset has two critical components: the willingness to put aside individual belief and conventional wisdom, and a commitment to gather the facts necessary to make sound decisions as well as to stay current with new evidence.

Emerging from a series of meetings organized by Denise Rousseau in Pittsburgh ("the Evidence-Based Management Collaborative"), *The Oxford Handbook of Evidence-Based Management* [17] was published in 2011, representing an important milestone by summarizing the current state and challenges of EBMgt. The core of EBMgt consists of four fundamental activities in the daily exercise of managerial decision-making and actions [2]:

* Use of the best available scientific findings
* Gathering and analyzing systematic organizational data
* Use of critical, reflective judgment and decision aids so as to reduce bias and improve decision quality
* Consideration of ethical issues with respect to stakeholder impact.

Extending beyond a small band of EBMgt scholars, the movement's broader influence can be seen in the increasing numbers of meta-analyses in the discipline. The number of meta-analyses published in management journals climbed from 28 in the 1980s to 220 in the 1990s to 744 in the period 2000–2013 [18]. Of related interest is greater scholarly engagement with experimental studies, such as Bloom, et al.'s [19] field experiment on large Indian textile firms, which showed that the adoption of modern management practices raised productivity significantly and led to business growth. Inching away from the tradition of an excusive fascination with novel findings, there is also a newfound acceptance of replication studies—illustrated by the launch in 2014 of a new Academy of Management journal- *Academy of Management Discoveries*- dedicated to phenomenon-based (as against theory-driven) empirical research and replication studies [20] and to the *Strategic Management Journal* special issue focused on replication research [21]. Management scholars are also engaging in a robust discussion of appropriate methods, as illustrated by Geyskens et al.'s [22] review and evaluation of meta-analysis practices in management research and a recent debate about the continuing relevance of vote-counting (instead of meta-analysis) as a systematic review technique for some classes of questions in the field [23]. The traction seemingly gained by EBMgt on the research front finds its echo in the growing practical interest in fact-based decision making [24] and fact-based consulting [25]. The recent interest in business analytics and "big data" appears likely to boost the progress toward more fact-based decisions.

Exemplars of EBMgt

Against the background sketched above, we now turn to presenting an illustrative list of evidence-based sources in three key areas: managing people, managing process, and managing strategy. The broad discipline of Management has many subfields, often categorized as micro (organization behavior, human resource management, and others) and macro (strategy, organization theory, corporate governance, business ethics, and others). Although the boundaries between the sub-fields have always been porous, the field has now evolved to also include intersectional interest groups such as strategic human resource management, reflecting the intellectual appeal of a multi-disciplinary mindset as well as recognition of the need for integrated managerial approaches in a complex world. From the clinician's standpoint, however, it may be more helpful to think about *managing people* (drawing upon organization behavior and human resource management), *managing process and systems* (drawing upon organization theory and organization behavior as well as related areas such as operations management), and *managing strategy* (drawing upon strategy and business ethics). Managing people refers to the clinician-manager's responsibilities in the area of recruiting and supervising staff members who have the appropriate skills and experience. Managing process and systems refers to responsibilities in the area of developing, implementing and upgrading safe work practices and systems. Managing strategy refers to responsibilities in the area of ensuring the longer-term growth and sustainability of one's practice or organization. Within each area, we present three exemplar studies of possible interest to clinicians. We then conclude the section by briefly comparing and contrasting EBMgt in the micro and macro areas of management.

Managing People One EBMgt exemplar that may be familiar to readers of this chapter is from the widely known National Research Council report, "Keeping patients safe: Transforming the work environment of nurses"[26]. Chapter 4 of this report, "Transformational leadership and evidence-based management," marshals the evidence behind five keys management practices consistently associated with successful change initiatives and achievement of safety goals in and highly error-prone conditions (Table 12.1). A second exemplar, Gary Latham's "Becoming the evidence-based manager," [27] is designed to give the reader the essential information needed to become an evidence-based manager from the hiring stage to the retention stage of managing people. The book is structured around six evidence-based lessons (Table 12.1). Behind each lesson is a synthesis and translation of management research, resulting in practical guidelines for the manager who is concerned with people-related responsibilities. For example, Lesson One, "Use the right tools to hire high performing employees," discusses the following:

- What doesn't work—conversational questions such as "Tell me about yourself," asking different applicants different questions
- What works—the situational interview, patterned behavioral interviews, job simulations and realistic job previews

Table 12.1 Exemplars of EBMgt—managing people

Exemplar	Key ideas
National Research Council report [26]	Five best practices for successful change initiatives and safety programs
	Balancing the distinction between production efficiency and safety
	Creating and sustaining trust through the organization
	Actively managing the process of change
	Involving workers in decision-making
	Using knowledge management practices to create a learning organization
Latham's book [27]	Six lessons from the hiring stage to the retention stage
	Use the right tools to identify and hire high-performing employees Inspire your employees to effectively execute strategy
	Develop and train employees to create a high-performing team
	Motivate your employees to become high-performers
	Instill resiliency in the face of setbacks
	Coach, don't appraise, your employees to be high-performers
Cialdini's book [28]	Six key principles of persuasion
	Reciprocity—people tend to return a favor
	Commitment and consistency—once people commit to something, they are likely to follow through
	Social proof—people will do what do they see others doing
	Authority—people tend to obey authority figures
	Liking—people are more easily persuaded if they like you
	Scarcity—perceived scarcity will generate greater interest

- Specific, step-by-step guidance in implementing the above four tools
- Where to find supporting evidence attesting to the effectiveness of the tools.

A third exemplar, Robert Cialdini's "Influence: The psychology of persuasion," [28] compiles six principles underlying the art of persuasion (i.e., getting another person to agree to something), based on extensive empirical research and illustrated using practical examples (Table 12.1). As a relatively mature field that is over a century old, and with many scholars trained in psychology, a foundational discipline in which meta-analysis is well-established, this area of management is perhaps somewhat better developed from an EBMgt perspective [29], as illustrated by the availability not only of systematic review articles but also integrative books that explicitly translate research findings into practice guidelines [30, 31].

Managing Process and Systems Given the current interest among clinicians in managing quality, it is appropriate to feature an EBMgt exemplar from that field. Glasgow et al., [32] in their systematic review of Lean and Six Sigma methods, assessed their effectiveness in creating and sustaining improvements in the acute

Table 12.2 Exemplars of EBMgt—managing process and systems

Exemplar	Key ideas
Glasgow et al.'s systematic review of Lean and Six Sigma [32]	Systematic review of 47 articles that met inclusion criteria showed that Lean, Six Sigma, and Lean Sigma can be helpful as quality improvement approaches. However, the absence of rigorous evaluation and clear evidence of sustained improvement makes it difficult to judge their true impact
Damanpour's meta-analysis of innovation[33]	Statistically significant predictors of innovation across 23 studies
	Specialization
	Functional differentiation
	Professionalism
	Centralization
	Managerial attitude toward change
	Technical knowledge resources
	Administrative intensity
	Slack resources
	Type of organization and scope of innovation are more effective moderators than are the type of innovation and stage of adoption
Stahl and Voigt's meta-analysis of culture differences in M&A [34]	Meta-analysis of 46 studies showed that cultural differences between merging forms affect sociocultural integration, synergy realization, and shareholder value in different, and sometimes opposing ways. Degree of relatedness and the dimensions of cultural differences are significant moderators, as are study research design and sample characteristics

care setting. Their conclusion was that, although these methods have been implied in a wide range of settings, their true impact is difficult to judge, given the lack of rigorous evaluation—thus calling for further strengthening the evidence base. A second exemplar is Damanpour's meta-analysis [33] of the determinants and moderators of organizational innovation. This analysis showed that organizational determinants such as functional differentiation, professionalism, and managerial attitude towards change were significantly associated with innovation outcomes. A third exemplar is Stahl and Voigt's meta-analysis [34] of the relationship between cultural differences and performance in Mergers and Acquisitions (M&A). This meta-analysis of 46 studies suggested that cultural differences affect post merger integration and financial performance, although in nuanced ways that reflect antecedent conditions, research design, and sample characteristics. Table 12.2 provides some additional details for each exemplar.

Managing Strategy The three exemplars featured in this area deal with issues that are of central concern to strategists and top managers. The first deals with the effectiveness of strategic planning. Although the annual strategic planning cycle is a staple of modern management, various empirical studies over two decades had produced inconsistent results with respect to the relationship between strategic planning and firm performance. However, Miller and Cardinal's meta-analysis [35] confirmed the positive effect of strategic planning, and demonstrated that inconsistencies in prior research were primarily due to variations in methods. The second exemplar deals with the effectiveness of diversification strategies. When faced with growth constraints in current markets, many managers contemplate diversifying into related and sometimes unrelated segments. Yet, examples of both successful and unsuccessful diversification are in abundance, and the empirical base had produced divergent results. Palich et al. [36] brought clarity to this debate by showing that the relationship between diverse education and performance is curvilinear—moderate levels of diversification are associated with the highest performance. The third exemplar deals with the effectiveness of M&A transactions. In many industries, we tend to see periodic cycles of M&A activity. Yet, scholars in management as well as in finance debate how effective M&A actions are in enhancing firm performance. King, Dalton, Daily and Covin's meta-analysis [37] brought order out of this chaos by demonstrating that across studies, M&A transactions have at best a slightly negative impact act on performance. More important, they pointed out that unidentified variables may explain significant variance in post-acquisition performance, highlighting the need for additional theory development and changes to M&A research methods. Subsequent results, such as the finding that the bulk of negative impact is concentrated in large M&A deals, and that smaller deals tend to be more effective [38], have borne out their insights. Table 12.3 provides additional details for each exemplar.

Table 12.3 Exemplars of EBMgt—managing strategy

Exemplar	Key ideas
Miller and Cardinal's meta-analysis of strategic planning [35]	Meta-analysis of 26 studies showed that strategic planning positively influences from performance. Prior inconsistencies in the planning—performance linkage explained by methods factors
Palich et al.'s meta-analysis of diversification [36]	Meta-analysis of 55 studies showed that moderate levels of diversification yield higher levels of performance than either limited or extensive diversification. The conclusion is that performance increases as firms shift from single- business strategies to related diversification, but decreases as they change from related diversification to unrelated diversification. Variations in the operationalization of diversification and performance are key moderators of the relationship between diversification and performance
King et al.'s meta-analysis of M&A [37]	Meta-analysis of 93 empirical studies of the relationship between M&A activity and financial performance yielded robust results indicating that acquiring firms' performance does not positively change as a function of their acquisition activity, and is negatively affected to a modest extent. In other words, there was no evidence that acquisitions improve the financial performance of acquiring firms. Unidentified variables may explain significant variance in post-acquisition performance

EBMgt in Micro and Macro Areas It is worth noting that the maturity of EBMgt approaches is not uniform across all areas of management. The micro areas, anchored by organizational behavior, are perhaps the most mature and have yielded plenty of evidence-based principles to guide practice [29]. In contrast, the macro areas, such as strategy, are more recent and are characterized by an inherent focus on complex, multilevel, and unique problems—which in turn implies a significant role for research methods such as case studies and qualitative analysis [39]. Thus, even within management, different groups of scholars must continue to work on differentiated problem sets as they advance the EBMgt agenda.

What is in EBMgt's Future?

What are some of the next steps in the evolution of EBMgt? As EBMgt gains further traction, we see two main areas of emphasis. The first is to continue expanding the influence of EBMgt beyond its current base of committed scholars—for instance, recruiting more researchers to conduct systematic reviews of important questions, as well as encouraging the development of integrative books and articles that translate their results into concrete principles and managerial protocols. While there has been significant progress on the side of systematic reviews, translational work has lagged behind. This is at least partly due to the incentive structure in business schools, which tends to privilege the scholarship of discovery over the scholarship of synthesis [40]. A second related area of emphasis should be the development and testing of "point of use" tools such as decision support aids [41] and action checklists [42]. Unlike medicine, where numerous decision support aids such as patient care protocols, detailed handbooks of drug interactions, and online tools are available to practitioners, the management profession has very few, at least in the public domain[41]. In this regard, it is worth noting that scholarship in management has typically neglected the type of research in which competing protocols are tested against each other to assess their relative effectiveness. Encouraging scholars to move from concepts to concrete protocols and then to test their effectiveness in real managerial settings is a critical next step in the evolution of EBMgt.

Implications for Clinicians

Before we conclude, we would like to highlight a few implications of EBMgt for clinicians in two separate roles—as clinician-managers and as clinician-researchers. In their managerial roles, clinicians can certainly benefit from the EBMgt perspective, as well as from the output of EBMgt scholars. As a community already attuned to evidence-based practice, clinicians can function as "lead users" who can help to move EBMgt forward [43]. In this regard, Tables 12.4 and 12.5 may be

Table 12.4 A starter list of EBMgt resources

Type	Resources
Books	Rousseau DM, ed. *The Oxford Handbook of Evidence-Based Management*. Oxford University Press, New York, 2011
	Kovner AR, Fine DR, D-Aquila R. *Evidence-Based Management in Healthcare*. Health Administration Press, Chicago, 2009
Background on link between EBMgt and Evidence-based Medicine	Barends E, ten Have S, Huisman, F. Learning from other evidence-based practices: The case of medicine: In Rousseau DM, ed. *The Oxford Handbook of Evidence-Based Management*. Oxford University Press, New York, 2011; 25–52
Journals that occasionally publish EBMgt and related articles	*Academy of Management Discoveries* (new) *Academy of Management Learning and Education* *Academy of Management Perspectives* *Evidence & Policy: A Journal of Research, Debate and Practice*
Online resources	EBMgt discussion group, at https://groups.google.com/forum/#!forum/evidence-based-management, last accessed June 21, 2014 Center for Evidence-based Management, at http://www.cebma.org, last accessed June 21, 2014 The Campbell Collaboration, at http://www.campbellcollaboration.org/, last accessed June 21, 2014
Course syllabi	Instructor: Denise Rousseau, at http://www.heinz.cmu.edu/academic-resources/course-results/course-details/index.aspx?cid=397, last accessed June 21, 2014 Instructor: Anthony Kovner, at http://wagner.nyu.edu/courses/padm-gp.4113, last accessed June 21, 2014
Other leading management journals (empirical)	*Academy of Management Journal* *Administrative Science Quarterly* *Organization Science* *Strategic Management Journal*

Table 12.5 EBMgt for clinicians—A checklist

1. State the focal decision clearly—the concrete decision or action that you want to get right (e.g., whether to diversify or not, or how best to interview a job candidate)

2. Formally identify the "priors"—your own experience, guidance from experienced colleagues, popular books and articles, consultant input

3. Critically assess the evidence for and against those "priors"—query experience and learning by analogy, use the "ancestry method" to track down citations in publications. Use databases such as "Business Source Premier" to locate systematic reviews, any experimental studies, and other empirical studies directly relevant to the focal decision or action

4. Update the "priors" on the basis of your analysis of the evidence

5. Make the decision and/or implement action

6. Track how your decision/action worked out

helpful. Table 12.4 provides an initial list of learning and community resources that, along with the citations already included in this chapter, may be of use in a further exploration of EBMgt. Table 12.5 provides a suggested process checklist for implementing a personal EBMgt approach for managerial decisions and actions. Given its relative nascency, EBMgt lacks widely accepted models, such as the PICO approach for Critically Appraised Topics in medicine, for the formulation and critical appraisal of management questions. Thus, lead users of EBMgt can benefit from a well-honed personal process of clarifying and structuring the decision context, formally recognizing the initial subjective assessment (the "prior"), critically appraising the relevant evidence, and monitoring the outcome such that it informs the next decision.

In their research roles, clinicians can take advantage of EBMgt's nascency by contributing to its research base. The intersection of the healthcare setting and the managerial task set is a natural place to start. However, as EBMgt matures, management journals may also be open to studies of clinician-managers and their experiences with management practices. Among other possibilities, this suggests the promise of more collaborative research between clinicians and management scholars.

Conclusion

This chapter has provided an overview of EBMgt for clinicians, who, in their managerial roles, often find it difficult to access, assess and deploy the most relevant management knowledge. Given the nature of the field, popular claims based on anecdotal evidence often compete with rigorous studies for the manager's attention. Leveraging the growing appeal of EBMgt, we have sketched the evolution of EBMgt and highlighted exemplar studies in three areas of concern to clinicians— managing people, managing process and systems, and managing strategy—as well as provided some practical resources for a further exploration of EBMgt.

References

1. Russo F (22 July 2013) Doctors interested in MBAs are increasingly looking for traditional business programs, not healthcare-specific degrees. Kaiser Health News [Internet]. http://www.kaiserhealthnews.org/stories/2013/july/21/doctors-executive-mba.aspx. Accessed 21 June 2014
2. Rousseau DM (2011) Envisioning evidence-based management. In: Rousseau DM (ed) The Oxford handbook of evidence-based management. Oxford University Press, New York, pp 3–24
3. Zimmerman JL (2001) Can American business schools survive? Simon School of Business Working Paper FR 01-16, University of Rochester
4. Gordon RA, Howell JE (1959) Higher education for business. Columbia University Press, New York
5. Pierson FC (1959) The education of American businessmen: a study of university-college programs in business administration. McGraw-Hill, New York
6. Simon HA (1991) Models of my life. Basic Books, New York
7. The more things change (4 June 2009) The Economist [Internet]. http://www.economist.com/node/12762453. Accessed 21 June 2014
8. Charlier SD, Brown KG, Rynes SL (2011) Teaching evidence-based management in MBA programs: what evidence is there? Acad Manage Learn Educ 10:222–236
9. Pfeffer J (2011) Foreword. In: Rousseau DM (ed) The Oxford handbook of evidence-based management. Oxford University Press, New York, pp vii–x
10. Rousseau DM, Manning J, Denyer D (2008) Evidence in management and organizational science: assembling the field's full weight of scientific knowledge through syntheses. Acad Manage Ann 2:475–215
11. Axelsson R (1998) Towards an evidence based health care management. Int J Health Plann Manage 13:307–317
12. Walshe K, Rundall T (2001) Evidence-based management: From theory to practice in health care. Milbank Q 79:143–163
13. Kovner A, Elton J, Billings J (2000) Evidence-based management. Front Health Serv Manage 16:3–24
14. Carlson KD, Hatfield DE (2004) Strategic management research and the cumulative knowledge perspective. Res Methodol Strategy Manage 1:273–301
15. Rousseau DM (2006) Is there such a thing as "evidence-based management"? Acad Manage Rev 31:256–269
16. Pfeffer J, Sutton RI (2006) Hard facts: dangerous half-truths and total nonsense. Harvard Business School Press, Boston
17. Rousseau DM (ed) (2011) The Oxford handbook of evidence-based management. Oxford University Press, New York
18. Buckley PJ, Devinney TM, Tang RW (2013) Meta-analytic research in international business and international management. SSRN. http://dx.doi.org/10.2139/ssrn.2207505
19. Bloom N, Eifert B, Mahajan A, McKenzie D, Roberts J (2013) Does management matter? Evidence from India. Q J Econ 128:1–51
20. Academy of Management Discoveries. http://aom.org/amd/. Accessed 21 June 2014
21. Strategic Management Journal. http://smj.strategicmanagement.net/strategy_design.php. Accessed 21 June 2014
22. Geyskens I, Krishnan R, Steenkamp JEM, Cunha PV (2009) A review and evaluation of meta-analysis practices in management research. J Manage 35:393–419
23. Newbert SL, David RJ, Han S (2014) Rarely pure and never simple: assessing cumulative evidence in strategic management. Strateg Organ 12:142–154
24. Ayres I (2007) Super crunchers: why thinking-by-numbers is the new way to be smart. Bantam, New York

25. Buono AF (2009) Emerging trends and issues in management consulting: consulting as a janus-faced reality. IAP, Charlotte
26. National Research Council (2004) Transformational leadership and evidence-based management. In: National Research Council (ed) Keeping patients safe: transforming the work environment of nurses. The National Academies Press, Washington
27. Latham GP (2009) Becoming the evidence-based manager: making the science of management work for you. Davies-Black, Boston
28. Cialdini R (2006) Influence: the psychology of persuasion. Collins New York (revised)
29. Rousseau DM (2011) Organizational behavior's contribution to evidence-based management. In: Rousseau DM (ed) The Oxford handbook of evidence-based management. Oxford University Press, New York, pp 61–78
30. Locke EA (2009) The handbook of organizational behavior: indispensible knowledge for evidence-based management, 2nd edn. Wiley, New York
31. Luthans F (2011) Organizational behavior: an evidence-based approach. McGraw-Hill, New York
32. Glasgow JM, Scott-Caziewell, JR, Kaboli PJ (2010) Guiding inpatient quality improvement: a systematic review of lean and six sigma. Jt Comm J Qual Patient Saf 36:533–540
33. Damanpour F (1991) Organizational innovation: a meta-analysis of effects of determinants and moderators. Acad Manage J 34:555–590
34. Stahl GK, Voigt A (2008) Do cultural differences matter in mergers & acquisitions? A tentative model and examination. Organ Sci 19:160–176
35. Miller CC, Cardinal LB (1994) Strategic planning and firm performance: a synthesis of more than two decades of research. Acad Manage J 37:1649–1665
36. Palich LE, Cardinal LB, Miller CC (2000) Curvilinearity in the diversification-performance linkage: an examination of over three decades of research. Strateg Manage J 21:155–174
37. King DR, Dalton DR, Daily CM, Covin JG (2004) Meta-analyses of post-acquisition performance: indications of unidentified moderators. Strateg Manage J 25:187–200
38. Moeller SB, Schlingemann FP, Stulz RM (2005) Wealth destruction on a massive scale? A study of acquiring-firm returns in the recent merger wave. J Finance 60(2):757–782
39. Madhavan R, Mahoney JT (2011) Evidence-based management in "macro" areas: the case of strategic management. In: Rousseau DM (ed) The Oxford handbook of evidence-based management. Oxford University Press, New York, pp 79–91
40. Boyer EL (1997) Scholarship reconsidered: priorities of the professoriate. Jossey-Bass, San Francisco
41. Rousseau DM, McCarthy S (2007) Educating managers from an evidence-based perspective. Acad Manage Learn Educ 6:84–101
42. Gawande A (2011) The checklist manifesto: how to get things right. Picador, New York (reprint)
43. von Hippel E (1988) The sources of innovation. Oxford University Press, New York

Chapter 13
Clinical Handovers

Sachin Amin

Handovers, the serious business of transferring the professional responsibility and accountability

Abstract Handovers refer to transfer of information and responsibility from one health care team to another. This process is often unstructured and hence, prone to errors. Miscommunication between health care providers is a leading cause of adverse events. Review of medical malpractice claims found communication failure as an important contributing factor. Other high risk industries such as commercial aviation and oil and natural gas industry have reduced adverse events by standardizing handover process. These strategies could be adapted to improve medical handovers. Lack of standardization, formal training, supervision and communication problems are some of the barriers to effective handovers. Involvement of patients in handover process improves satisfaction and reduces errors. Computerized handover tools and mnemonics can be used to improve quality of handovers. Further research is necessary to study various strategies to improve medical handovers.

Keywords Handover · Sign out · Handoff · Resident physician · Nurses · Hospital · Healthcare · Medical errors · Mnemonics · SBAR · iSoBAR · I PASS · IPASS the BATON · Communication · Check lists · Patient safety · Malpractice · Joint commission · Simulation

S. Amin (✉)
Division of Neonatology, University of Illinois at Chicago,
840 S.Wood St.Suite 1256, Chicago, IL 60612, USA
e-mail: sachina@uic.edu

Neonatal Intensive Care Unit, Children's Hospital of University of Illinois,
Chicago, USA

© Springer International Publishing Switzerland 2015   181
S. Patole (ed.), *Management and Leadership – A Guide for Clinical Professionals,*
DOI 10.1007/978-3-319-11526-9_13

Key Points

- Handover process is often unstructured and the protocol for handover varies in the clinical setting.
- Communication errors between clinical teams is a major cause of adverse medical events
- Various regulatory agencies are stressing need for a standardized handover process
- Electronic and IT solutions are often helpful in increasing accuracy and efficiency of handovers
- Development of mnemonics has been helpful in handover process
- Efficacy of various handover solutions needs to be evaluated in a systematic manner

Effective communication is essential for patient care safety and quality. Miscommunication between health care providers is a leading cause of adverse events in various health care settings. The Joint Commission sentinel event statistics in the US suggests that communication errors contribute to a majority of reported sentinel events. Clinical handover refers to transfer of patient care from one health care provider to another. This could be a physician hand-off or between nurses and other auxiliary staff. In addition to exchange of health-related information, handover involves transfer of responsibility and accountability from one care giver to another [1]. Handovers between health care personnel are often unstructured, and therefore often lead to medical errors jeopardizing patient safety [2–7]. Errors in handovers can lead to adverse outcomes including delayed diagnosis, increased hospital length of stay, increased patient and health care provider dis-satisfaction and increased readmission rates [8].

According to Joint Commissions definition, hand-off communication refers to a standardized process in which information about patient/client/resident care is communicated in a consistent matter. Communication failures between health-care personnel accounts for over 60 % of sentinel events reported to the Joint Commission on Accreditation of Healthcare Organizations. Academic Hospitals are often staffed by physicians in training, who change shift more than once a day. Lack of experience and discontinuity of care adds to the risks of adverse medical outcomes.

Improving quality of medical handovers has become a priority for regulatory agencies across the globe. There has been keen interest in developing and implementing new strategies to improve handovers, thereby reducing medical errors.

Transfer of Information in other High Risk Industries

There is ample research in improving and standardizing hand-over process in other high risk industries such as aviation, NASA (National Aeronautic Space Administration), nuclear power plants, oil and natural gas industry and railways.

"Safety Management Systems" refers to systematic application of management processes to minimize hazards an organization/industry faces [9]. Oil and natural gas industry has effectively used this concept to minimize hazards. Commercial aviation industry has similarly adopted "Standards and Recommended Practices" to minimize accidents and adverse events in civil aviation. Healthcare organizations and researchers are increasingly looking at these industries to improve communication and teamwork between healthcare workers to minimize errors and improve healthcare outcomes.

One such method used in aviation industry is LOSA audits (Line Operations Safety Audit). This method uses observations made by expert observers in the cockpit during routine flights to record errors, threats to safety and behaviors used to prevent and manage errors. Thomas and Colleagues developed behavioural audit form to assess performance of providers during neonatal resuscitation. They modified existing LOSA aviation behavioural markers and applied them to neonatal resuscitation [10].

Malpractice Claims due to Communication Failures

Multiple studies have attributed hand-off failures as an important cause in malpractice lawsuits. In a retrospective review of 307 cases in the ambulatory setting, 20 % cases were due to improper hand-offs [11]. A review of 79 claims from emergency department revealed inadequate hand-offs responsible for 24 % of the cases [12]. Deficiencies in hand-outs were found to be responsible for 30 % of 74 cases in another review of malpractice cases from the emergency department [13]. Similar findings were repeated in a similar review of 90 malpractice cases in obstetrics and gynaecology, in which 31 % adverse events were attributable to communication errors [14]. In a review of 444 surgical malpractice claims, Greenberg et al. [15] identified 60 cases (13.5 %) with 81 communication breakdowns. Hand-off errors accounted for 43 % of the communication errors, a majority involved breakdown in communication between residents and consultants regarding critical events, and attending-attending sign-outs.

Change in Residents' Duty Hours

Restriction of duty hours for doctors in training has been a worldwide trend in recent years [16–18]. ACGME (Accreditation Council on Graduate Medical Education) mandated reduction in resident duty hours for all US programs in 2003. These changes were initiated in NY State in 1989 in view of adverse patient outcomes due to resident fatigue. This has led to increase in the number of handoffs during a patients hospital stay. ACGME established new set of guidelines regarding resident duty hours in 2011 [18]. In addition to recommendations regarding resident supervision and oversight, there was a new recommendation restricting maximum shift length for interns (first year residents) to 16 h. Night float system was introduced in response to these restrictions in resident duty hours. Residents on cross cover team have inadequate information about patient's clinical condition. They are not able to communicate effectively with the patients' families, and cause more harm by ordering un-necessary tests [19].

In a survey regarding perceived impact of duty hour regulations, US Paediatric program directors expressed concern reported negative impact on continuity of care, resident education, preparation for senior roles as well as diminished resident accountability [20]. In a similar survey of all program directors (549 of eligible 730 residency program directors belonging to internal medicine, paediatrics and general surgery), most of the respondents expressed concerns regarding negative impact of residency duty hours limitations on continuity of care (82 %) and handovers (88 %) [21]. Residents have expressed concerns regarding their education, experience and preparedness as a senior as a result of these rules [22].

In a longitudinal prospective cohort study involving 51 residency programs comparing interns before and after duty hours changes (2009/2010 and 2011), Sen et al. [23] reported that decrease in duty hours was not associated with increase in sleep hours or improvement in depressive symptoms. The percentage of interns who reported concern about making serious medical error increased from 19.9 to 23.3 % ($P = 0.0070$). In a survey of 464 US surgical residents, majority (57 %) residents reported that 16 hour duty restriction rule resulted in inadequate sign-outs, and affected patient care [24]. Most paediatric and neonatal intensivists (91.9 %) reported either no change or decrease in medical errors after instituting duty hour changes. According to this survey, increased frequency of hand-offs was believed to be an important cause of increased medical errors [25].

The European Working Time Directive (EWTD) has been implemented in European countries since 1998. It mandates reduction in working hours for physicians to 48 h a week. There have been difficulties in implementing these directives for residents in training. Change in rules required creative ways of implementing these rules including shift work. Most residents (71 %) reported no improvement in work-life. Shift work led to more handovers, causing fatigue and medical errors [17].

Though reduction in duty hours was meant to improve quality of work-life, reduce fatigue and improve education for residents, it has led to inadvertent consequences such as deterioration in communication due to multiple handovers contributing to increase in medical errors.

Stages of a Handover

Physician handovers occurs in various settings such as from emergency department to inpatient services, from wards to intensive care units and vice versa, from ambulatory settings to inpatient wards, from wards to nursing homes and so on. Various authors have tried to conceptualize the actual process of handovers. Lawrence et al.

collected data from interviews and questionnaires given to emergency room staff. They proposed five phases of handovers:

1. Anticipatory
2. Preparatory
3. Actual handover
4. Immediate post-handover
5. Post-handover

In anticipatory phase, outgoing physicians actively anticipate handover and wrap up clinical issues and pending clinical decisions from their shift. Preparatory phase involves actual gathering of pertinent information necessary for a handover. During handover process, there is exchange of information between outgoing team and the incoming team regarding vital information, clinical condition and treatment plans of the patients. The immediate post- handover phase provides opportunities to both the teams to complete vital pending tasks and focus on immediate urgent issues. Some strategies include seeing patients who are more unstable and need immediate intervention. In post -handover stage, the incoming team settles in and takes over the clinical management of the patients [8]. These stages can be adapted for various other settings such as intensive care units and inpatient wards.

Barriers to Handover

In a study from an Australian Public Hospital, Bomba and Prakash found that the handover process was unstructured, informal and error prone, with the majority of doctors noting that there was no standard or formal procedure for handover [26]. Many studies have confirmed that medical handovers tend to be idiosyncratic and erroneous. In many settings, there is no designated time or place allotted for handovers, with no formal requirement to attend one [27–29]. Handover process at three US academic centres was found to be unstructured and unstandardized. The burden of handovers fell primarily on interns with little or no formal training. Templates or checklists were rarely used in this process [30].

Horwitz and colleagues reported on handover process based on surveys from 202 US internal residency programs. There was a great variation in transfer systems among and within institutions: 55% did not consistently require both a written and an oral sign-out at transfers of care, 34% left sign-out to interns alone, and 59% had no means of informing nurses that a transfer had taken place. In addition, a majority (60%) of the programs did not provide any formal training in the form of lectures or workshops on sign-out skills [27]. Arora et al. [31] interviewed 26 interns after receiving sign-out from another intern using critical incident technique. Twenty five discrete critical incidents were reported by these interns. Two major themes that evolved from their analysis were content omissions (such as medications, active problems, pending tests) and failure prone communication processes (such as lack

Table 13.1 Barriers to effective handovers

A)	No standardization
	No written template
	No checklists
B)	Communication problems
	Omission
	No face-face discussions
C)	Time constraints
	Lack of allotted time
D)	Physical barriers
	Lack of assigned space
	Interruptions
	Noisy environment
E)	Staffing problems
	Overworked physicians (too many patients)
F)	Lack of training
	No formal lectures on handovers
	Lack of formal curriculum
G)	Lack of trainee supervision
	Senior physicians absent during handovers

of face to face handover). In a recent systematic review, Riesenberg et al. [19] have categorized handover barriers into major categories: communication barriers, lack of standard requirement/system, lack of training, missing information (omission), physical barriers, lack of time and difficulties due to complexity (Table 13.1).

Strategies to Improve Physician Handovers

In recent years there has been an increase in the awareness about importance of effective handovers to improve clinical outcomes and reduce medical errors. Various strategies can be employed to achieve this goal (Table 13.2).

Increased awareness about importance of handovers in improving patient safety can be achieved by education and involvement of the leadership team. Allotting designated time and place for a formal handover process is essential. Strategies towards standardization including written templates, handover cards, electronic tools, and information technology (IT) solutions improve consistency and accuracy of handovers. Senior physicians should be present to observe and guide handovers. Lastly, mnemonics are helpful as useful tools to improve the handover process.

Table 13.2 Strategies to improve physician handovers

A)	Training and education
	Development of curriculum
	Formal lectures
B)	Physical environment
	Allocation of time and space
	Minimize interruptions
C)	Standardization
	Written guidelines, templates
	Electronic (IT) solutions
	Mnemonics
D)	Communication
	Face to face handover
	Clarification
	Reconciliation
E)	Supervision by senior physicians
F)	Policy and regulatory requirements
	Residency training to incorporate handovers

Electronic Handover Solutions

Electronic systems can be utilized to improve the handover process.Existing medical record systems can be utilized for handover purposes [32]. Alternatively, stand-alone IT tools are available to aid the handover process [33, 34]. Use of a computerized handover tool has led to improved quality and completeness of physician handover, increased physician efficiency [35] and resulted in fewer adverse events [36]. Patient identifiers and medications are accurately extracted from medical record after implementation of a computerized handover tool [37]. A recent systematic review of interventions improving patient handovers by Arora et al. [38] reported that implementation of IT handover solutions was associated with an improvement in handover quality, healthcare team satisfaction and reduction in adverse events. However, though these electronic tools improve the accuracy of handover information, they do not influence the behavioural aspects of the handover process and may not improve communication between the health care providers [39].

Non-Electronic Handover Solutions

Various non-electronic solutions have been tried to improve quality of handovers. These could be hand-out templates, simulation techniques or mnemonics [1]. Lee et al. [40] used a standardized handover cards to facilitate handover process. Interns in the study group had fewer omissions in their handovers as compared to controls. Junior physicians can be trained using simulation techniques. Bhabra et al. [41] compared three handover styles over five consecutive handover cycles: oral only, oral with note taking, oral with written instructions using handover simulation scenarios performed by senior house officers. After five handover cycles, only 2.5 % of patient information was retained using the verbal-only handover method, 85.5 % was retained when using the verbal with note taking method and 99 % was retained when a printed hand-out containing all patient information was used.

Mnemonics

Mnemonics are increasingly becoming popular to facilitate handover process. Mnemonics aid health care staff in memorizing important steps in the handover process. Joint Commission has added "Implement a standardized approach to hand-off communications" to its National Patient Safety Goal in 2006. Mnemonics have evolved according to the needs of particular health care setting. SBAR has been, by far, most utilized and studied mnemonic in the literature. It can be used by physicians as well as nurses in diverse clinical settings It has been modified to suit a particular healthcare setting (i.e. SBARR, SBAR-T) [42]. Porteous et al. [43] reported on use of a similar mnemonic iSoBAR in Western Australia. They found that iSoBAR form and accompanying tool-kit was widely accepted in this region owing to extensive clinician involvement and leadership. Horwitz et al. [44] developed an oral handover curriculum for medical students and residents emphasizing a structured handover format with the help of mnemonic HANDOUT. The participants demonstrated statistically significant increase in perceived comfort with providing sign-out after the intervention. Strimmer et al. have recently reported on development of mnemonic I-PASS, which is currently being evaluated in a multi-centre study [45]. Some authors have cautioned that handoffs, especially in some settings like critical care, can be very complex. Catchy mnemonics may not be adequate to deal with the complexity and nuances of the process [42] (Table 13.3).

Nursing Handovers

Nursing hand-offs occur multiple times a day as nurses exchange information typically at the time of shift change [51]. Nurses seldom receive any formal training for this important aspect of patient care. Errors in nursing handoffs are an important contributing factor to adverse clinical events. Furthermore, nurses also share the legal liability in case of a malpractice suit resulting from an adverse clinical event due to improper hand-offs. Traditionally, nursing handovers fit into one of the following models:

Table 13.3 List of mnemonics used to facilitate handovers

Mnemonic	Description
ANTICipate [30]	A Administrative data
	N New information
	T Tasks
	I Illness
	C Contingency planning/code status
I PASS [45]	I Illness severity
	P Patient summary
	A Action list
	S Situation awareness and contingency planning
	S Synthesis by receiver
I PASS the BATON [46]	I Introduction: introduce yourself, your role
	P Patient: name, identifiers, age, sex, location
	A Assessment: chief complaint, vital signs, symptoms, diagnosis
	S Situation: current status, code status, recent changes, response to treatment
	S Safety concerns: critical lab values, allergies, alerts, socioeconomic status
	B Background: co-morbidities, previous episodes, family history
	A Actions: which were taken or required, providing brief rationale
	T Timing: level of urgency, explicit action and prioritization of actions
	O Ownership: who is responsible (e.g. nurse, doctor, team) including patient and family
	N Next: anticipated changes in condition or care
SBAR [46–49]	S Situation (identify the patient, why is the patient here)
	B Background (history, lab findings, test results)
	A Assessment (assessment of the course of care and patient condition)
	R Recommendation (recommendation for continuation of care)
iSoBAR [43, 50]	I Identify: introduce yourself and your patient
	S Situation: why are you calling? briefly state your problem
	O Observations: recent vital signs and clinical assessment
	B Background: pertinent information related to the patient
	A Agreed plan: what needs to happen? assessment of the situation
	R Read back: clarify and check for shared understanding
SHAREQ [46]	S Situation: describe the situation
	H History: medical history, allergies, home medications
	A Assessment: current medications intake, output, status
	R Recommendations: results, discharge planning
	Q Questions: opportunity to ask questions

Table 13.3 (continued)

Mnemonic	Description
SIGNOUT [44]	S Sick or DNR? (highlight sick or unstable patients, identify DNR/DNI patients)
	I Identifying data (name, age, gender, diagnosis)
	G General hospital course
	N New events of the day
	O Overall health status/clinical condition
	U Upcoming possibilities with plan, rationale
	T Tasks to complete

1. Verbal handovers (face-face)
2. Tape recorded handovers
3. Bedside handovers
4. Written handovers [52–54]

In a review of these handover styles, McKenna did not identify one style superior to another. The author recommended written guidelines for nursing handovers to improve consistency and clinical outcomes [52]. In an observational study comparing verbal, taped and bedside handovers, O'Connell and Penney identified strengths and weaknesses of each style. Verbal handovers provide an opportunity for the staff to debrief, and clarify information and are narrative in nature. However, verbal handovers run the risk of becoming too subjective and superfluous, omitting vital information. Tape-recorded handovers can be to the point and less time consuming. There is no opportunity to clarify information, education and debriefing. Bedside handovers provide opportunity to clarify information, reconcile medications and involve patients, fostering individualized care. These, however can be time consuming and prone to interruptions [55]. In a study comparing taped versus face to face nursing reports, taped reports were found to have more omissions (information left out during hand-off leading to increased inefficiency) and less incongruence (information relayed during a hand-off that differs from the medical record) than the latter [56].

Patients' Participation During Nursing Handovers

Nursing handover at the patient's bedside is an important component of patient-centred care. It provides an opportunity for the patients to participate in their care and encourages their active involvement in their health-care decisions. In a descriptive study from Australia, McMurray reported on ten patients' views about bedside nursing handovers. Most patients appreciated to be acknowledged as partners in their care, viewed it as an opportunity to correct mistakes and appreciated nurse-patient interaction [57]. Anderson et al. [58] reported on a shift in nursing policy at a US Hospital from a traditional handover towards a patient-centric bedside report. Several benefits were realized by patients as well as the health-care team. The patients' satisfaction improved significantly as they were better informed and felt involved in making their health-care decisions. This change in policy translated into several benefits including financial savings for the health care institution and increased satisfaction for the hospital nursing staff, patients and physicians.

Barriers to Effective Nursing Handovers

Communication problems including irrelevant information, lengthy reports, problems with recall, language barriers, inadequate communication between physician, and nursing teams account for majority barriers to effective nursing handovers. Other barriers include lack of standardization of hand-off process, lack of training, environmental issues such as too many interruptions, poor lighting, and human factors including inadequate staffing and overworked nurses [51].

Strategies to Improve Nursing Handovers

Various strategies can be implemented to improve nursing handovers. This should be one of the priorities of the administrative leadership. Standardization of the process helps minimize errors of omission and congruence. Nursing handovers should happen in a quiet environment, with adequate lighting and minimum interruptions. The handover should be objective, relevant and to the point. Combination of written or taped handover along with face to face communication is most effective in relaying a complete clinical picture between the nursing teams. Nursing handovers should provide an opportunity to debrief and reconcile management plans between nursing and physician teams.

Administrative Aspects of Medical Handovers

There are other important legal, administrative and educational aspects of medical handovers. In addition to transfer of medical information, handovers also mark the transfer of legal responsibility of the medical care to the receiving team [59]. As described earlier, a large proportion of medical malpractice claims are attributed to communication failure between health care personnel [60–66]. It is very important for the hospital administrative team to invest in the development of a standardized, streamlined, defined process to facilitate handovers. Presence of written handover policy is an important step towards reducing medical errors, thereby decreasing financial costs to the system due to medico-legal claims. Handover process provides an opportunity to the medical team to discuss clinical issues, exchange ideas about management, reconcile medication and laboratory investigations and clarify management issues. Bedside handovers provide patients an opportunity to participate and provide valuable information relevant to their care. Missing parts of clinical and social history can be clarified, thereby reducing the possibility of medical errors. Handovers also provide a platform for social interaction between health care team members, thus improving emotional support for physicians and nurses [67–70].

Future Research

Lack of systematic research focused on handoffs has been amply documented [19, 30]. Systematic research needs to be done to develop a standardized handover process which can be implemented across various clinical settings. Lessons can be learnt from other high risk industries like civil aviation and oil and natural gas industry to stream line communication and reduce adverse events. Effectiveness of various interventions needs to be studied systematically to streamline strategies to improve quality of medical handovers.

References

1. Raduma-Tomas MA, Flin R, Yule S, Williams D (2011) Doctors' handovers in hospitals: a literature review. BMJ Qual Saf 20:128–133
2. Apker J, Mallak LA, Gibson SC (2007) Communicating in the "gray zone": perceptions about emergency physician hospitalist handoffs and patient safety. Acad Emerg Med 14:884–894
3. Gandhi TK (2005) Fumbled handoffs: one dropped ball after another. Ann Intern Med 142:352–358
4. Horwitz LI, Moin T, Krumholz HM, Wang L, Bradley EH (2008) Consequences of inadequate sign-out for patient care. Arch Intern Med 168:1755–1760
5. Horwitz LI, Meredith T, Schuur JD, Shah NR, Kulkarni RG, Jenq GY (2009) Dropping the baton: a qualitative analysis of failures during the transition from emergency department to inpatient care. Ann Emerg Med 53:701–710 e704
6. Sutcliffe KM, Lewton E, Rosenthal MM (2004) Communication failures: an insidious contributor to medical mishaps. Acad Med 79:186–194
7. Wilson RM, Runciman WB, Gibberd RW, Harrison BT, Newby L, Hamilton JD (1995) The quality in Australian health care study. Med J Aust 163:458–471
8. Lawrence RH, Tomolo AM, Garlisi AP, Aron DC (2008) Conceptualizing handover strategies at change of shift in the emergency department: a grounded theory study. BMC Health Serv Res 8:256
9. Hudson P (2003) Applying the lessons of high risk industries to health care. Qual Saf Health Care 12:i7–12
10. Thomas EJ, Sexton JB, Helmreich RL (2004) Translating teamwork behaviours from aviation to healthcare: development of behavioural markers for neonatal resuscitation. Qual Saf Health Care 13:i57–64
11. Gandhi TK, Kachalia A, Thomas EJ et al (2006) Missed and delayed diagnoses in the ambulatory setting: a study of closed malpractice claims. Ann Intern Med 145:488–496
12. Kachalia A, Gandhi TK, Puopolo AL et al (2007) Missed and delayed diagnoses in the emergency department: a study of closed malpractice claims from 4 liability insurers. Ann Emerg Med 49:196–205
13. White AA, Wright SW, Blanco R et al (2004) Cause-and-effect analysis of risk management files to assess patient care in the emergency department. Acad Emerg Med 11:1035–1041
14. White AA, Pichert JW, Bledsoe SH, Irwin C, Entman SS (2005) Cause and effect analysis of closed claims in obstetrics and gynecology. Obstet Gynecol 105:1031–1038
15. Greenberg CC, Regenbogen SE, Studdert DM et al (2007) Patterns of communication breakdowns resulting in injury to surgical patients. J Am Coll Surg 204:533–540
16. Gough IR (2014) The significance of Good medical practice: a code of conduct for doctors in Australia. Med J Aust 200:148–149
17. Canter R (2011) Impact of reduced working time on surgical training in the United Kingdom and Ireland. Surgeon 9:S6–S7
18. Nasca TJ, Day SH, Amis ES Jr, Force ADHT (2010) The new recommendations on duty hours from the ACGME task force. N Engl J Med 363:e3
19. Riesenberg LA, Leitzsch J, Massucci JL, et al (2009) Residents' and attending physicians' handoffs: a systematic review of the literature. Acad Med 84:1775–1787
20. Drolet BC, Whittle SB, Khokhar MT, Fischer SA, Pallant A (2013) Approval and perceived impact of duty hour regulations: survey of pediatric program directors. Pediatrics 132:819–824
21. Drolet BC, Khokhar MT, Fischer SA (2013) The 2011 duty-hour requirements—a survey of residency program directors. N Engl J Med 368:694–697
22. Drolet BC, Spalluto LB, Fischer SA (2010) Residents' perspectives on ACGME regulation of supervision and duty hours—a national survey. N Engl J Med 363:e34

23. Sen S, Kranzler HR, Didwania AK et al (2013) Effects of the 2011 duty hour reforms on interns and their patients: a prospective longitudinal cohort study. JAMA Intern Med 173:657–662 (discussion 663)
24. Lee DY, Myers EA, Rehmani SS et al (2012) Surgical residents' perception of the 16-hour work day restriction: concern for negative impact on resident education and patient care. J Am Coll Surg 215:868–877
25. Typpo KV, Tcharmtchi MH, Thomas EJ, Kelly PA, Castillo LD, Singh H (2012) Impact of resident duty hour limits on safety in the intensive care unit: a national survey of pediatric and neonatal intensivists. Pediatr Crit Care Med 13:578–582.
26. Bomba DT, Prakash R (2005) A description of handover processes in an Australian public hospital. Austr Health Rev 29:68–79
27. Horwitz LI, Krumholz HM, Green ML, Huot SJ (2006) Transfers of patient care between house staff on internal medicine wards: a national survey. Arch Intern Med 166:1173–1177
28. Laxmisan A, Hakimzada F, Sayan OR, Green RA, Zhang J, Patel VL (2007) The multitasking clinician: decision-making and cognitive demand during and after team handoffs in emergency care. Int J Med Inform 76:801–811
29. McCann L, McHardy K, Child S (2007) Passing the buck: clinical handovers at a tertiary hospital. N Z Med J 120:U2778
30. Vidyarthi AR, Arora V, Schnipper JL, Wall SD, Wachter RM (2006) Managing discontinuity in academic medical centers: strategies for a safe and effective resident sign-out. J Hosp Med 1:257–266
31. Arora V, Johnson J, Lovinger D, Humphrey HJ, Meltzer DO (2005) Communication failures in patient sign-out and suggestions for improvement: a critical incident analysis. Qual Saf Health Care 14:401–407
32. Flemming D, Hubner U (2013) How to improve change of shift handovers and collaborative grounding and what role does the electronic patient record system play? Results of a systematic literature review. Int J Med Inform 82:580–592
33. Campion TR Jr, Denny JC, Weinberg ST, Lorenzi NM, Waitman LR (2007) Analysis of a computerized sign-out tool: identification of unanticipated uses and contradictory content. AMIA Annu Symp Proc 99–104
34. Palma JP, Sharek PJ, Longhurst CA (2011) Impact of electronic medical record integration of a handoff tool on sign-out in a newborn intensive care unit. J Perinatol 31:311–317
35. Van Eaton EG, Horvath KD, Lober WB, Rossini AJ, Pellegrini CA (2005) A randomized, controlled trial evaluating the impact of a computerized rounding and sign-out system on continuity of care and resident work hours. J Am Coll Surg 200:538–545
36. Petersen LA, Orav EJ, Teich JM, O'Neil AC, Brennan TA (1998) Using a computerized sign-out program to improve continuity of inpatient care and prevent adverse events. Jt Comm J Qual Improv 24:77–87
37. Flanagan ME, Patterson ES, Frankel RM, Doebbeling BN (2009) Evaluation of a physician informatics tool to improve patient handoffs. J Am Med Inform Assoc 16:509–515
38. Arora VM, Manjarrez E, Dressler DD, Basaviah P, Halasyamani L, Kripalani S (2009) Hospitalist handoffs: a systematic review and task force recommendations. J Hosp Med 4:433–440
39. Sharit J, McCane L, Thevenin DM, Barach P (2008) Examining links between sign-out reporting during shift changeovers and patient management risks. Risk Anal 28:969–981
40. Lee LH, Levine JA, Schultz HJ (1996) Utility of a standardized sign-out card for new medical interns. J Gen Intern Med 11:753–755
41. Bhabra G, Mackeith S, Monteiro P, Pothier DD (2007) An experimental comparison of handover methods. Ann R Coll Surg Engl 89:298–300
42. Riesenberg LA, Leitzsch J, Little BW (2009) Systematic review of handoff mnemonics literature. Am J Med Qual 24:196–204
43. Porteous JM, Stewart-Wynne EG, Connolly M, Crommelin PF (2009) iSoBAR—a concept and handover checklist: the National Clinical Handover Initiative. Med J Aust 190:S152–156

44. Horwitz LI, Moin T, Green ML (2007) Development and implementation of an oral sign-out skills curriculum. J Gen Intern Med 22:1470–1474
45. Starmer AJ, Spector ND, Srivastava R et al (2012) I-pass, a mnemonic to standardize verbal handoffs. Pediatrics 129:201–204
46. Sandlin D (2007) Improving patient safety by implementing a standardized and consistent approach to hand-off communication. J Perianesth Nurs 22:289–292
47. Narayan MC (2013) Using SBAR communications in efforts to prevent patient rehospitalizations. Home Healthc Nurse 31:504–515 (quiz 515–507)
48. Powell SK (2007) SBAR-it's not just another communication tool. Prof Case Manag 12:195–196
49. Haig KM, Sutton S, Whittington J (2006) SBAR: a shared mental model for improving communication between clinicians. Jt Comm J Qual Patient Saf 32:167–175
50. Yee KC, Wong MC, Turner P (2009) "HAND ME AN ISOBAR": a pilot study of an evidence-based approach to improving shift-to-shift clinical handover. Med J Aust 190:S121–124
51. Riesenberg LA, Leitzsch J, Cunningham JM (2010) Nursing handoffs: a systematic review of the literature. Am J Nurs 110:24–34 (quiz 35–26)
52. McKenna LG (1997) Improving the nursing handover report. Prof Nurse 12:637–639
53. Tucker A, Fox P (2014) Evaluating nursing handover: the REED model. Nurs Stand 28:44–48
54. Matthews A (1986) Patient-centred handovers. Nurs Times 82:47–48
55. O'Connell B, Penney W (2001) Challenging the handover ritual. Recommendations for research and practice. Collegian 8:14–18
56. Richard JA (1988) Congruence between intershift reports and patients' actual conditions. Image J Nurs Sch 20:4–6
57. McMurray A, Chaboyer W, Wallis M, Johnson J, Gehrke T (2011) Patients' perspectives of bedside nursing handover. Collegian 18:19–26
58. Anderson CD, Mangino RR (2006) Nurse shift report: who says you can't talk in front of the patient? Nurs Adm Q 30:112–122
59. Patterson ES, Wears RL (2010) Patient handoffs: standardized and reliable measurement tools remain elusive. Jt Comm J Qual Patient Saf 36:52–61
60. Rogers SO Jr, Gawande AA, Kwaan M et al (2006) Analysis of surgical errors in closed malpractice claims at 4 liability insurers. Surgery 140:25–33
61. Gawande AA, Zinner MJ, Studdert DM, Brennan TA (2003) Analysis of errors reported by surgeons at three teaching hospitals. Surgery 133:614–621
62. Studdert DM, Mello MM, Gawande AA et al (2006) Claims, errors, and compensation payments in medical malpractice litigation. N Engl J Med 354:2024–2033
63. Simpson KR, Knox GE (2003) Common areas of litigation related to care during labor and birth: recommendations to promote patient safety and decrease risk exposure. J Perinat Neonatal Nurs 17:110–125 (quiz 126–117)
64. Gandhi TK, Zuccotti G, Lee TH (2011) Incomplete care—on the trail of flaws in the system. N Engl J Med 365:486–488
65. Singh H, Thomas EJ, Petersen LA, Studdert DM (2007) Medical errors involving trainees: a study of closed malpractice claims from 5 insurers. Arch Intern Med 167:2030–2036
66. Poon EG, Kachalia A, Puopolo AL, Gandhi TK, Studdert DM (2012) Cognitive errors and logistical breakdowns contributing to missed and delayed diagnoses of breast and colorectal cancers: a process analysis of closed malpractice claims. J Gen Intern Med 27:1416–1423
67. Cohen MD, Hilligoss PB (2010) The published literature on handoffs in hospitals: deficiencies identified in an extensive review. Qual Saf Health Care 19:493–497
68. Kerr MP (2002) A qualitative study of shift handover practice and function from a sociotechnical perspective. J Adv Nurs 37:125–134
69. Evans AM, Pereira DA, Parker JM (2008) Discourses of anxiety in nursing practice: a psychoanalytic case study of the change-of-shift handover ritual. Nurs Inq 15:40–48
70. Strange F (1996) Handover: an ethnographic study of ritual in nursing practice. Intensive Crit Care Nurs 12:106–112

Chapter 14
The Educational Role of Senior Hospital Staff

Fiona Lake

> *Good teaching is more a giving of right questions than a giving of right answers.*
> —Josef Albers

Abstract Education is a key and enjoyable component of a senior staff's work, but for many in hospitals, competes with their clinical, research and administrative roles. The new challenge at the senior level, such as for doctors, nurses and allied health staff, are you take ultimate responsibility for patient care, so close clinical supervision and learner support is key. The supervisor needs to provide feedback and accurately assess, usually for multiple levels of learners and workers. In considering the educational program senior staff should establish, new research has focused in how we learn and become good. Learners move through multiple stages when developing competence but those displaying high levels of expertise are reflective, where they continue to actively review their performance with the aim of being even better. This is termed deliberate practice and is what we should aim to encourage in our learners, by providing them with clear outcomes, opportunities to practice and quality feedback. The learning cycle is a useful model to plan how a senior staff can facilitate learning in students, junior or specialist trainees and new staff. Phase 1 involves planning in terms of defining learning outcomes and teaching methods; Phase 2 involves facilitating learning, using a range of strategies and Phase 3 requires constructive and balanced feedback and assessment, which should allow learners to develop further. By using efficient strategies that integrate teaching and learning with clinical work, the educational role of senior staff should enhance clinical and other work and is more likely to ensure safe patient care and a highly effective workplace.

Keywords Teaching · Run · Senior staff · Educational role · Assessor · Learning cycle · Apprenticeship model · Competence · Reflective competence

F. Lake (✉)
University of Western Australia School of Medicine and Pharmacology, M503 SCGH Unit 35 Stirling Highway, Crawley, WA 6009, Australia
e-mail: Fiona.Lake@uwa.edu.au

Harry Perkins Institute of Medical Research, QEII Medical Centre, 6 Verdun Street, Nedlands, WA 6009, Australia

© Springer International Publishing Switzerland 2015
S. Patole (ed.), *Management and Leadership – A Guide for Clinical Professionals,*
DOI 10.1007/978-3-319-11526-9_14

· Communication skills · Professional skills · Facilitating Learning · Clinical teachers · Educational strategies · Supervision · Feedback · Assessment · Levels of Feedback · Performance · Clinical interaction

Key Points

1 Education integrates with clinical service and other hospital based work and involves overlapping roles of clinical supervision, workplace supervision, teaching, assessing and mentoring.
2 Phases in the implementation of any educational program involves firstly *planning*, secondly facilitating learning and finally, assessment of performance and provision of feedback.
3 During Planning, understanding outcomes expected of the learner and ensuring they fit with your workplace, including the clinical environment, is key.
4 A range of strategies should be used to facilitate learning, through involvement in clinical work, performance of discrete tasks, tutorials and self-directed learning.
5 Ensure feedback is frequent, balanced (what has been done well and what could be improved) and constructive (how to improve), but start by encouraging reflection (what do you think you did well? Could improve?).
6 Regularly ask yourself about how well you are fulfilling your role as an educator: What are you doing well and what could be improved?

By the time a health professional reaches their first senior job in a hospital, they will have been involved in "teaching" for many years, starting as a student teaching colleagues, subsequently teaching and supervising others, then at a senior level, being expected to giving comprehensive feedback and assess performance [1, 2]. Most people enjoyed this aspect of work more than other areas but, stressed by juggling busy workloads and passing their own exams, wondered if they could do better [3]. As a senior doctor, nurse, allied health professional or administrator, there are now different challenges to finding the time to be a good teacher, namely to become established in your own field and for many, to become a researcher, an effective leader and administrator and frequently, the desire to focus on one's personal life and family.

Skills of a good teacher, such as clear thinking, good communication and being approachable are important in all other aspects of work [3–5]. Teaching integrates with clinical care and administrative work and improves it. Having a good understanding as to what your learners need, setting aside a little time for preparation, having techniques that engage the learners, and strategies that use the clinical environment well, will allow you to integrate work and education in a manageable and enjoyable way [1, 2].

Unless you are an academic when it is expected you will take on additional educational responsibilities, such as curriculum development, course management or assessment, the preparation and delivery time for education for our students and trainees is limited and must fit in with the other duties of a clinician, researcher, administrator and leader. It is useful to consider changes in your educational role which occur when making the transition to a senior staff member. These changes are particular important in the health professions involved in patient care, as outlined below, but relevant in different ways with staff working in hospitals but not with direct patient contact. Three important changes are;

- For doctors and other health professionals, you are the person who is ultimately responsible for ensuring safe patient care. As much of the direct patient care is carried out by your junior staff or others you supervise, you must be able to accurately determine their competence level, supervise them closely and train them in deficient areas [6–8].
- The quality and extent of your teaching, supervision and feedback is likely to play a significant role in the learner's and new staff's success [7–9].
- Most important assessments or workplace performance reviews will fall to you and your decision to pass or fail students and trainees has the potential to have a big impact on career progression and/or the safety of our graduates. Your decision which may impact on a staff member continuing or not, but equally importantly, whether you have a good workplace with committed staff or not. Although you are only one of many who contribute to the decisions, training organisations and your workplace rely on you to make an informed judgment [8, 10, 11].

This Chapter will provide guidance on incorporating education into the role of senior staff in a hospital on a daily basis. Education not only applies to student or trainees who you are responsible for, but new staff, who similarly you need to train, provide feedback to and make judgments about performance, and with others, make decisions about continuing employment. Senior staff will be required to deal with a mix of learners from students to specialist trainees to new junior staff, with different needs. In this Chapter, approaches relevant for all levels are discussed and the term "learner" will be used, encompassing students through to specialist trainees and junior staff and new staff. Specific strategies relevant to particular level will highlight the learner group. The Chapter will show how by putting time in to plan how you will facilitate learning through various activities, and over time reflecting on how well it has worked and what can be improved, education can seamlessly blend with your other work and not feel like a time consuming burden.

Educational Role of Senior Staff

Educational roles expected of you as a staff member have been given a variety of names but include [12, 13]

- Clinical supervisor—providing appropriate support and guidance but ultimately, taking responsibility for patient care delivered by those you supervise, and supervision for non-patient care in administrative and leadership settings.

Fig. 14.1 Development of Competence

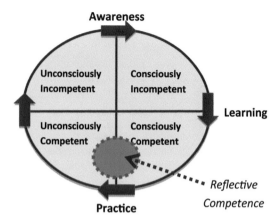

- Teacher—guiding learning and imparting knowledge using a range of methods.
- Assessor—providing feedback for development and/or assessment of performance.
- Mentor—providing personal and career guidance, using your knowledge and experience.

These roles overlap and are usually complementary. Conflicts between roles occasionally arise when you are trying to mentor or support a learner, in particular one who is struggling but also have to act as their assessor, risking biasing your judgment. In general however, they are seamless and all involve observing and interacting with the learner, providing knowledge or guidance, responding to needs, judging competence and providing feedback.

The apprenticeship model of clinical or other learning [14], occurring by gradual accumulation of knowledge and skills with learners being immersed in the environment and watching or practicing under supervision, defined the way health professionals learnt in the past, although many elements still form the basis of current learning. New thinking about how we can support our students and trainees to learn and improve has stemmed from studies of how people become really good at something, be it doctoring, playing a violin or running a race [13]. "Deliberate practice" is a term arising from this research studying experts; those not just good enough but performing at a high level, something we aspire to as health professionals as it translates to better patient care [15]. Ideally, it is what we would wish for in our learners. Research in the medical field and areas such as sport and music, show it's neither innate ability nor just practice that ensures high level performance, nor getting old *per se* explains decline. Rather, it is the way we practice that explains development of, or loss of, expertise [16].

During the development of competence, for example performing an operation, carrying out a clinical assessment or a new complex management task, learners move through a number of stages (Fig. 14.1) [17]. We start as incompetent, either **unconsciously incompetent (UI)**, when we are not aware of the knowledge or skills available to solve a problem, or **consciously incompetent (CI)** when you are

Fig. 14.2 Learning cycle. (Modified from Lake [2])

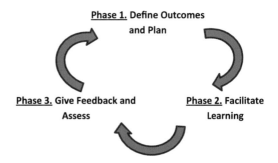

Phase 1. Define Outcomes and Plan

Phase 2. Facilitate Learning

Phase 3. Give Feedback and Assess

aware of what needs to be done but are not skilled as yet to do it. With learning and training we become **consciously competent (CC),** managing to do it if we concentrate hard. With practice we become **unconsciously competent (UC)**; seeming to leap to the answer without thinking, for example, picking the atypical and coming up with the rare diagnosis, knowing the process for accreditation of new staff, finding the clinical sign others missed, at ease breaking bad news.

Experts, recognised by colleagues for being at the top of their field, may appear to be unconsciously competent (UC), but develop their high level of performance by remaining conscious of their performance and reflect on what they have done, how well they did it and whether they should take a different approach next time. They do this when working in challenging cases or when an error was made, but even when there are no problems, they still ask "Could I have done this better?" The addition of a fifth stage, termed **"reflective competence"** to the standard model of developing competence reminds us we need to regularly slow down and review our competence, and it is through this we continue to improve and perform at a higher level [15, 16, 18].

The translation of these concepts to what kind of learning environment you establish is that by engendering a culture of reflection and reinforcing it through teaching, learners are much more likely to gain knowledge and skills and take responsibility for the learning themselves [19]. As the teacher, the following are important aspects of deliberate practice you are responsible for [20];

• *Define outcomes* (or use University or College set outcomes, or job description), which are important to focus on in your setting.
• Ensure learners have the *opportunity to repeat tasks and improve.*
• Provide learners with good *supervision and feedback.*

It is up to the learner to reflect on performance, remain motivated and put in the effort and plan so time is used optimally.

A simple approach to establishing the educational program for students, trainees or new health professionals based with you from a few weeks to many months, is shown in Fig.14.2 [2]. This similarly applies to new staff who have a probationary period and who are expected to come with skills and learn new ones. You start with understanding and then defining for your specific setting, the learning outcomes; secondly, you facilitate the learning experience; and finally, provide feedback aiming to help learners improve or assess to determine their competence. The rest of this Chapter will use this framework to explore each area in depth.

Phase 1: Defining Outcomes and Planning

Senior staff often think at the last moment about what they can teach and students are often asked "what do you want to learn about today" (not uncommonly leading to an awkward silence). We less often consider what a learner should leave the attachment knowing or be capable of doing, be it over 2 weeks or 12 months. As a teacher, you will receive the guidebooks for the clinical rotation, from the University for your students, the hospital for prevocational trainees and Colleges for specialist trainees, and job descriptions for new staff, outlining expected learning outcomes, learning activities and assessment or performance expected [21]. Often lengthy and complicated, these need to be turned into something manageable for yourself and useful for learners, which can provide guidance on a week to week basis but ensure comprehensive coverage on a term basis [21, 22].

Learning outcomes are explicit statements that refer to what a learner needs to know or be able to do at a given point in time.

Frequently based around *clinical competence* (knowledge and procedural skills), *communication* and *professional* skills, they are to guide the learning and are linked to assessment [21]. To tackle outcomes by aiming to tick each one off, makes for an impossible task for the teacher. The beauty of learning in the clinical environment is that multiple outcomes are fully integrated in activities or skills we use on a daily basis; such as talking to patients and colleagues, making a diagnosis or choosing a treatment. By encouraging activities that include multiple clinical, communication and professional outcomes, such as clerking patients, and then ensuring presentation to you and others is combined with discussion of a range of issues (not just the diagnosis), guidance to further learning and importantly provision of feedback on the learners performance, we can feel comfortable as to the breadth of learning. Ideally this is supplemented by highlighting difficult or complex topics in tutorials or grabbed moments during work.

Although as noted stated outcomes are often extensive and learning around a patient very integrated, so it is useful to personalise the outcomes and activities for your own setting, knowing what conditions are common, opportunities the practice provides, degree of supervision required and extent of risk if learners are unsupervised and your personal style. A suggested step by step approach to develop your own Plan is outlined below, with examples as to how outcomes can link to learning activities and how they may differ for a student or a senior trainee (Table 14.1).

1. Start with the Learning Outcomes
2. Choose outcomes covering areas which are a core part of your practice and therefore able to be met (Taking a history on inpatient ward; obtaining informed consent in a surgical day ward, assessing home safety, organising financial reports).
3. Highlight or add your own outcomes, by considering what is special about your environment that you think is important to learn (breaking bad news in an Oncology ward).
4. Relate the chosen learning outcomes to learning activities that are possible and manageable in your environment [1, 5, 23, 24]. Consider;

Table 14.1 Linking Outcomes and Learning Activities

Outcomes: what it is hoped is learnt	Learning activities: how they will go about learning
Clinical competence—SURGICAL WARD	
Physiotherapy student *Take a history, perform an examination and formulate a post-operative mobilisation plan for a patient undergoing abdominal surgery*	Clerk patients, write in notes, present to supervisor Ensure they seek out common scenarios (emergency and elective surgery, elderly)
Vocational medical trainee *Manage an acutely deteriorating patient in the inter-operative period*	Simulation training Observation and discussion during assisting with increased responsibility matching competence
Communication—PAEDIATRIC EMERGENCY DEPARTMENT	
Medical student *Obtain informed consent for a common minor procedures (such as IV cannulation)*	You role model with student observation and reflection Practice under supervision Role play
Trainee administrative officer *Demonstrate effective verbal communication skills and styles with hospital staff*	Role modelling and observation with discussion during supervised placement, with increasing responsibility matching competence Seek feedback from other staff on performance
Professionalism—GENERAL MEDICAL TEAM	
Nursing student *Describe and explain the principles of multi-disciplinary care*	Role modelling, student observation, reflection and discussion Attachment to another professional and reflection on observations Required attendance at weekly multidisciplinary meeting
Vocational trainee *Recognise, display and discuss ethical behaviour in clinical practice*	Discussion around critical incidents Discussion on specific scenarios (referrals, treatment decisions in incompetent patients)

  a. Who else can teach, supervise and give feedback? (share the load, involve other professions).
  b. What resources are on hand to assist learning (e.g. on-line, simulation).
  c. What activities will you organise? (tutorials, case reviews, learning on ward rounds or in theatre).
  d. How can they learn by themselves? (Set guidelines for using unallocated time).

5. Consider when you will observe and give feedback.
6. Do you need to assess for competence? (As set by Universities, Hospitals and Colleges) [11].
7. Make all this explicit to the trainee/student at an orientation meeting.

The key principles behind well written outcomes, are that they are *SAM*;

Specific Worded clearly so they know what is to be achieved ("take a history") and at what level ("patients with common conditions").

Achievable How long will it take to reach the set standard (is the term long enough)? Are there sufficient cases and opportunity to practise? Do they have the basic skills to tackle the outcomes (passed basic surgical skills course prior to attempting an appendectomy)?

Measurable The learner (through reflection) and you (by assessing) can determine if competence has been reached (i.e. 80 % of cannula in first time).

Even with extensive experience and learning, gaps may still be significant. These need to be identified, through regular review of the outcomes by both the learners and supervisor and supervisor reflection on whether performance is matching the expected outcomes for that learner.

Phase 2: Facilitating Learning: Providing Opportunities to Repeat Tasks and Improve

Familiarity with expected outcomes provides you with the guidance as to what needs to be learnt. The previous section also touched on how learning can be encouraged, for example through learners interacting with patients and discussion encourages reflection on important topics. However, when it is busy, things often fall apart. For students, the complaint is often they feel in the way, and have no real role. Under stress, junior or new staff tend to focus on tasks and or mainly learn how to survive. Therefore you need a range of strategies to ensure learner engagement which will push learners out of their comfort zone, while allowing you to cope with the workload and still provide safe patient care [1, 3, 5, 23, 24, 25]. Much has been written about this area, including frameworks for couching a teaching session [25]. Important tips are to avoid trying to cover too much, ensuring the topic and questions are pitched at the correct level and, use questions to explore what learners do NOT understand (rather than reinforcing what they do know) [25, 26, 27] and provide guidance at the end to what further reading they should do or resources they should look at. Table 14.2 provides a range of practical ideas for different settings.

Being the senior staff member responsible for multiple students and trainees, from different levels can be difficult and risks one of the groups of learners receiving teaching pitched too high, too low or receiving too little from the Consultant. Strategies to overcome this are;

- Planning—be very familiar with outcomes for each group and discuss expectations for each group at an orientation meeting.
- Use the higher levels to teach the lower levels and if needed give them guidance as regards topics or teaching methods. Being able to teach is often an outcome expected from trainees, so ensure you gather feedback as to how well they teach and offer support if required.
- Ensure you set some time aside to meet with each group.

Table 14.2 Educational strategies for clinical teachers

Setting	Opportunities
Ward rounds	Evidence shows patients like being involved in teaching and learning as long as they are asked permission, treated with respect, have their answers questions. They are a good source of feedback for learners
	Make the student write in the patient notes and provide feedback on their efforts
	Allocate each patient depending on their problem and who knows them to someone (you, junior medical staff, student) and that person should lead the patient interaction (greetings, introductions, questions, examination, explanations). Check understanding before entering and let students know you are there as a backup. Afterwards, all provide feedback on the interaction (ensure your performance is also critiqued). Students are terrified but love the experience and sometimes are better than the doctors! Valuable learning points, in particular around communication and professional behaviour, are often raised for the doctors
	Involve everyone in discussion around the problems, diagnosis or management by getting those more senior to answer student's questions. Rather than ask Learners questions (which tends to test what they do know), ask what they do *not* understand about a case [25]
	Teaching moments—on each patient grab a few minutes to reinforce a specific point, check understanding and recommend further reading *(Avoid trying to cover too much)*
	Use SNAPPS, [26, 27] show to increase clinical reasoning, as a guide to the interaction around a patient's problem;
	Learner *S*ummarises history and exam
	*N*arrows the problem list and differential
	*A*nalyses the problem
	Learner (not teacher) *P*robes about areas not understood
	Together *P*lan care
	Teacher *S*ummarise and recommend follow up reading *(Not when you are frantically busy)*
Patient interactions: bedside tutorials or consultations	To save you time, get the students to find cases, ask permission and ensure availability [19]
	For students, ensure patients come not just from your specialty area but cover broad range of areas
	For trainees and junior doctors, don't just discuss the patient problem; ensure you give feedback on the learners performance [8]
	Be flexible—grab opportunities to change the learning topic, such as when a patient says they know they are dying
Group tutorials	Never teach on something that can easily be found in a text book. Focus on complex problems, difficult to understand areas, or provide practice for learners (analysing cases, investigations)
	Make the learners do the preparation. If they run the session, give them feedback on their teaching or facilitation skills

Table 14.2 (continued)

Setting	Opportunities
Procedural skills and theatre	Again, ensure you provide feedback on a trainee's performance—technical, communication, teamwork—and do not just discuss the patient's problem [8]
	Use the 4 step approach to teach skills, shown to be more efficient than the usual watch and try [28, 29, 30]
	Step 1: Teacher demonstrates, usual speed, no commentary
	Step 2: Teacher demonstrates while describing steps
	Step 3: Teacher demonstrates while learner describes steps
	Step 4: Learner demonstrates while learner describes steps
	Modify the 4 step approach according to the task
	Use simulation, on-line resources to replace steps
	Do over a number of sessions (e.g. central line insertion)
Outpatients	Avoid students sitting and watching—give them a specific area to watch (how did I break bad news; what diagnoses did I explore through the questions) and discuss reflections later [1, 5]
	Make senior students see patients and dictate letters Provide a framework for writing letters. Then review students, junior doctor and specialist trainee's letters and either meet, or remotely (via email) give feedback. These provide invaluable insights into whether they understood patients problems, are diligent in correcting letters and whether they took advice on how a letter should be written
Office setting	Make it clear your role is as a supervisor which is to help them learn, to provide feedback with the aim of optimising performance and to support them. Note should be a two way process and you welcome questions
	Get new staff member or trainee to articulate their approach to a task or if necessary, you articulate your approach step by step
	Do not presume they know something. Rather than "You know how to, don't you?" Say "Are you comfortable doing?"

Increasingly we will find ourselves teaching students or graduates from multiple professions in interprofessional settings [31]. Interprofessional education is about learning "with, from and about" another profession. Often the biggest challenge is knowing what outcomes are relevant for each profession. Professional and communication outcomes overlap significantly in the health professions, therefore may offer good topics for review. Additionally, by drawing on the knowledge and skills of the learners, or asking for reflection from differing perspectives, you can facilitate the teaching "from" and "about".

Phase 3: Supervision, Feedback and Assessment

Supervision involves interacting—observing, listening, questioning, instructing, advising—with students, junior staff and new staff to determine their strengths and weaknesses, allowing you to be confident about what they can safely do independently and what needs ongoing supervision [7, 8, 12, 13].

In some areas (Emergency Department), you and your colleagues will work closely with students and trainees, so will be able to judge performance with some accuracy. In other areas, such as surgical rotations, and office based work, when you are only present for ward rounds or emergencies, otherwise spending time in theatre, or off at meetings, you may have little interaction with students or junior staff and you will need to rely on the feedback from others (doctors, nurses) as to performance.

In the third phase of the learning cycle, feedback is the most important activity to understand and perform well [8, 32, 33], as it is through feedback your trainee and students will learn, will learn to make accurate judgments about their own performance and make you more comfortable they are progressing to an independent practitioner [7, 8, 34], or indeed if your feedback is not heeded, that you are dealing with a problem.

To provide feedback, you need to make a judgment about performance, be it a small area (knowing the causes of chest pain) or comprehensive component (adequate overall performance over a number of weeks, ability to organize and implement a complex project) [10, 11, 32, 33]. The purpose is to help learners understand strengths and weaknesses and direct future learning, so during the rotation, you can feel comfortable they can safely work at the expected level without extensive input from you. From the learner's viewpoint, in the end they wish to be deemed competent and move to the next level of training. Assessment is an extension of feedback and will not be covered here other than to say, like feedback, assessment requires making a judgment about someone's performance as set out in the assessment set by the medical school for students or College for vocational trainees (e.g. Mini-CEX (a short clinical encounter); an end of term assessment; a long case discussion) [10, 33] or simple observation of performance. Unlike simple feedback which is aimed to help someone improve, assessment contributes to a decision as to whether that learner can progress.

Feedback should be [8, 34];

- *Frequent:* informally on a daily basis (how well they assessed or interacted with a patient) and more formally, as regular comprehensive feedback during the attachment or at set time since commencing work.
- *Balanced* and includes *learner reflection*: Ask "What did you think you did well?" then you say what you thought they did well; Ask "What could you think you could improve?" and you say what could be improved.
- *Detailed:* As outlined in Table, detailed enough to use the feedback to change practice [34].
- *Constructive:* They and you develop plans to address areas to improve.

Table 14.3 Levels of Feedback for Performance during a clinical interaction [8, 9, 12, 13, 32–34]

Assessment of a new patient with chest pain			
Little use very useful			
Feedback	Personal, lacks useful detail	Detailed and specific	Detailed, can be extrapolated to other situations
Good Performer	"Excellent job, you should come and work with us!"	"Well done, you presented the history succinctly, I agree with the diagnosis of angina and the differential of reflux."	"The presentation was succinct and important you had a range of well supported differentials. Would this differ if the patient was 80 rather than 60?"
Poor performer	"That was no good and needs to be much better for your level of training."	"Your presentation was long winded and poorly organized so the importance of pain was not clear. Based on the history, shouldn't reflux be in the differential?"	"On presenting a patient problem, what are the key components you need to communicate, and in general how long should that take? How many differential diagnoses do you think you should consider?"

Some other important strategies are to seek information from multiple sources (nurses, allied health and administrative and other staff) and be a role model after an interaction by you reflecting out loud or seeking feedback from the learners on what you could improve. Feedback should be given, in particular to trainees you are responsible for, on a regular occasion which is planned, for which you have gathered comments from colleagues, when you sit down and comprehensively review all aspects of work (clinical, communication, professionalism) and develop a learning plan or agreement as to areas they need to improve, how you can help and when you will next meet.

Some find it easier to provide poor performers with feedback, as there is much to talk about, whereas they cannot find anything to say to the excellent trainee who is eager to be even better. Others find it hard because they do not like to have to say people are not performing. By ensuring feedback is balanced and the above strategies used, giving feedback becomes easier

The biggest complaint from learners or new staff regarding feedback is it is not sufficiently detailed to be useful [34]. Table 14.3 outlines three levels of feedback, in terms of impact and ability to apply the information beyond the specific case. The commonest feedback given is in the form of broad comments, in particular focused on the personal, which has minimal impact on learners. This can be improved by providing detail as to what was done well or could be improved or by stepping beyond the content and focusing on processes, as outlined in Table 14.3 for a clinical encounter.

The ideal health professional is a reflective one and that concept is incorporated in many descriptions as to what is expected of a "good" doctor, nurse and so forth. However research shows we are poor judges of our own performance. However, learners can do better, firstly through practice and secondly by comparing one's self-assessment with an "experts" assessment [18, 35, 36]. For your learners, this is feedback from you, the senior, more experienced staff member or by you drawing attention to the gold standard and making it available at the time the task is finished, so the learners can compare their performance with the gold standard [35, 36].

As a member of senior staff, therefore, it is important

- You encourage reflection but also provide quality feedback so they can compare their judgment.
- You have on hand guidelines, framework or videos, showing the standard of expected performance you can direct learners to.

Feedback closes the learning cycle by allowing the learners (and you) understand the strengths and weaknesses of each person and based on this, what areas (or outcomes) they should focus on in the future. This should lead to a revision of their learning and your teaching/supervision strategies and ongoing learning.

The final closure if the learning cycle is for you to reflect on who well you have performed as an educator and supervisor. By asking yourself at the end of each session, day or week how well you have done and how you could improve, keeps your performance evolving. Other important sources of feedback are the learners themselves, gathered both anonymously, with a written survey, or by asking the learners what they found useful and what should be improved. These simple measures should keep you interested and the educational experience of the learners at the highest level.

Summary

The educational role of senior staff working in hospital settings integrates well with clinical work, and research, administrative and leadership tasks and if done well, can improve patient outcomes, work productivity and satisfaction. Investment of a relatively minor amount of time planning the outcomes and experiences can provide a framework which should be useful for years. Research would suggest the area we do least well is in the provision of feedback. Although initial work highlighted the amount of feedback, current work has focused on the quality of feedback and this would be a useful area for all new Consultants to consider. By establishing feedback as a core component of clinical supervision, and ensuring it is of high quality, we are likely to establish an environment seen to focus on excellence and continuing learning. Ongoing reflection on your part and review of feedback from the learners should ensure your educational program remains relevant and helpful into the future.

References

1. Spencer J (2003) ABC of learning and teaching in medicine: learning and teaching in the clinical environment. Br Med J 326:591–594
2. Lake FR (2004) Teaching on the run tips: doctors as teachers. Med J Aust 180:415–416
3. Locke KA, Bates CK, Karani R, Chheda SG (2013) A review of the medical education literature for graduate medical education teachers. J Grad Med Educ 5:211–218
4. Jochemsen-van der Leeuw R, van Dijk N, van Etten-Jamaludin FS, Wieringa-de Waard M (2013) The attributes of the clinical trainer as a role model: a systematic review. Acad Med 88:26–34
5. Hesketh EA, Bagnall G, Buckley EG, et al (2001) A framework for developing excellence as a clinical educator. Med Educ 35:555–64
6. Irby DM, Papadakis M (2001) Does good clinical teaching really make a difference? Am J Med 110:231–232
7. Forsyth KD (2009) Critical importance of effective supervision in postgraduate medical education. Med J Aust 191:196–197
8. Chur A, McLean S (2006) On being a supervisor: the importance of feedback and how to give it. Psychiatry 14:67–71
9. Paice E, Moss F, Heard S, Winder B, McManus IC (2002) The relationship between pre-registration house officers and their consultants. Med Educ 36:26–34
10. Epstein RM (2007) Assessment in medical education. N Engl J Med 356:387–396
11. Rethans JJ, Norcini JJ, Baron-Maldonado M, Blackmore D, Jolly BC, LaDuca T (2002) The relationship between competence and performance: implications for assessing practice performance. Med Educ 36:901–909
12. Kilminster S, Grant J, Jolly B (2007) AMEE guide no. 27: effective educational and clinical supervision. Med Teach 292–319
13. Kilminster S, Jolly BC (2000) Effective supervision in clinical practice settings: a literature review. Med Educ 34:827–840
14. Sheehan D, Bagg W, de Beer W, Child S, Hazell W, Rudland J, Wilkinson TJ (2010) The good apprentice in medical education. N Z Med J 123:89–96
15. Ericsson KA, Charness N (2004) Deliberate practice and the acquisition and maintenance of expert performance in medicine and related domains. Acad Med 79:70–81
16. Ericsson KA (2004) Deliberate practice and the acquisition and maintenance of expert performance in medicine and related domains. Acad Med 79:70–81
17. Peyton JWR (1998) The learning cycle. In: JWR Peyton (ed) Teaching and learning in medical practice. Manticore Europe Ltd, Rickmansworth, 13–19
18. Sargeant J, Armson H, Chesluk B, et al (2010) The processes and dimensions of informed self-assessment: a conceptual model. Acad Med 85:1212–1220
19. Beckman TJ, Lee MC (2009) Proposal for a collaborative approach to clinical teaching. Mayo Clin Proc 84:339–344
20. Schuwirth L, van der Vleuten CPM (2006) Challenges for educationalists. BMJ 333:544–6
21. The Australian aurriculum framework for junior doctors (2012). http://curriculum.cpmec.org.au/. Accessed 30 Apr 2014
22. Harden RM (2002) Learning outcomes and instructional objectives: is there a difference? Med Teach 24:151–155
23. Meggison D (1996) Planned and emergent learning: consequences for development. Manage Learn 27:411–428
24. Swanwick T (2005) Informal learning in postgraduate medical education: from cognitivism to 'culturism'. Med Educ 39:859–865
25. Lake FR, Vickery AW, Ryan G (2005) Teaching on the run tips 7: using questions. Med J Aust 182:126–127
26. Wolpaw T, Papp KK, Bordage G (2009) Using SNAPPS to facilitate the expression of clinical reasoning and uncertainties: a randomized controlled trial. Acad Med 84:517–524

27. Wolpaw TM, Wolpaw DR, Papp KK (2003) SNAPPS: a learner-centered model for outpatient education. Acad Med 78:893–898

28. Barelli A, Scapigliati A (2010) The four-stage approach to teaching skills: the end of a dogma? Resuscitation 81:1607–1608

29. Krautter M, Weyrich P, Schultz J, Buss SJ, Maatouk I, Junger J, Nikendei C (2011) Effects of Peyton's four step approach on objective measures in technical skills training: a controlled trial. Teach Learn Med 23:244–250

30. Lund F, Schultz J, Maatouk I, Krautter M, Moltner A, Werner A, et al (2012) Effectiveness of IV cannulation skills laboratory training and its transfer into clinical practice: a randomized, controlled trial. PLoS One 7:e32831

31. Thistlethwaite J (2012) Interprofessional education: a review of context, learning and the research agenda. Med Educ 46:58–70

32. Homboe E, Sherbino J, Long D, Swing S, Frank J (2010) The role of assessment in competency-based medical education. Med Teach 32:676–682

33. Norcini JJ (2003) ABC of learning and teaching in medicine: work based assessment. Br Med J 326:753–755

34. Hattie J, Timperley H (2007) The power of feedback. Rev Educat Res 77(1):81–112

35. Koole S, Dornan T, Aper L, et al (2011) Factors confounding the assessment of reflection: a critical review. BMC Med Educ 11:104

36. Sargeant J (2012) How external performance standards inform self-assessment. Med Teach 34:267–268

Chapter 15
Mentoring

Deepika Wagh and Sanjay Patole

> *If I have seen it further it is by standing on the shoulders of giants*
> —Isaac Newton

Abstract Mentoring is a planned pairing of a more experienced person with a lesser skilled individual for the purpose of achieving mutually agreed outcomes. It is a partnership in which both individuals share in a growth process and the personal development of one another. This dyad relationship is highly complex and has different phases. Good mentors with qualities of openness, humility, commitment, patience, and receptive learning, can help young physicians attain their goal efficiently and progress in career while maintaining confidentiality. Mentorship plays a significant role in the personal and professional development of academic leaders in medicine. Systematic reviews of mentorship studies have shown that mentorship not only influences career choice and academic development but also improves research productivity. Mentoring helps produce great leaders in an organisation. Organizations are using mentoring programs as a way to retain and recruit talent. This chapter reviews the qualities of a mentor, mentoring techniques and provides suggestions for choosing an appropriate mentor, and ideas for creating a supportive mentoring environment.

Keywords Mentor · Mentoring · Mentorship · Mentor attributes · Professional development · Mentee · Mentoring relationships · Academic medicine · Supervision · Training · Fellowship · Mentor attributes · Leadership

D. Wagh (✉) · S. Patole
Department of Neonatal Paediatrics, King Edward Memorial Hospital for Women, 374 Bagot Road, Subiaco, WA 6008, Australia

Princess Margaret Hospital, Perth, WA, Australia
e-mail: deepika.wagh@health.wa.gov.au

S. Patole
Centre for Neonatal Research and Education, University of Western Australia, Perth, Australia

© Springer International Publishing Switzerland 2015
S. Patole (ed.), *Management and Leadership – A Guide for Clinical Professionals,*
DOI 10.1007/978-3-319-11526-9_15

Key Points

- Mentoring is the process by which an expert person facilitates learning in the mentee through the arrangement of specific learning experiences.
- Mentoring is a valuable relationship based upon reciprocal trust and respect, by either an informal association or a formal agreement.
- Mentoring has been shown to improve productivity, goal clarity and the sense of belonging.
- The process of mentoring compared to supervision and managing is an everlasting and obligatory relationship.
- Mentoring can be a rewarding experience not only for the mentor and mentee but also for the organization. It contributes to a positive organizational climate and promotes a more clear understanding of professional responsibilities and expectations.

Mentoring is a planned pairing of a more experienced person with a lesser skilled individual for the purpose of achieving mutually agreed outcomes [1, 2]. It is a partnership in which both individuals share in a growth process and the personal development of one another [3, 4]. The above quote by Isaac Newton is a clear example of mentoring in action. We can learn in a variety of different ways including by experience, reflection or modeling. However, when we follow the footsteps of those who have gone before us we can progress rapidly towards our goals as narrated by Sir Isaac Newton.

The concept of mentoring originated in ancient Greek mythology around 1200 B.C. When Odysseus left for the Trojan War, he entrusted his household and son Telemachus, in the care of the noble Mentor Athena, the Greek goddess of wisdom [5, 6]. Athena acted as an advisor to the young Telemachus, helping him overcome challenging obstacles. Historical records show that skills, culture, and values in preparation for manhood were learned in this paired relationship.

There are varied definitions of mentorship including the following:

- A relationship that may vary along a continuum from informal/short-term to formal/long-term in which faculty with useful experience, knowledge, skills, and/or wisdom offers advice, information, guidance, support or opportunity to another faculty member or student for that individual's professional development [7].
- An alliance of two people that creates a space for dialogue that results in reflection, action and learning for both [8].
- Mentoring is the process by which an expert person facilitates learning in the mentee through the arrangement of specific learning experiences [8, 9].

Mentoring relationships are believed to be important in the career development of many professional fields including medicine, business, education, and law [2].

More and more businesses are embracing mentoring as a tool for professional development. Organizations are witnessing dramatic improvements in efficiency, productivity, and transfer of institutional knowledge and leadership skills from one generation to the other after adopting mentorship programs [8].

Why Is Mentoring Essential?

Organizations today are constantly striving for cost effective ways to improve the work performance of their employees. Mentoring can be a powerful and affordable strategy that contributes immensely to staff performance and personal development, but its potential value is often not acknowledged [8]. Mentoring is much more than coaching and counselling. It not only complements the training but also provides better understanding of the qualitative and subjective parts of our job such as handling frustration, disappointment and giving constructive criticism [10]. It is a responsibility we owe to the institution. It is essential that one gives back to the organization, the development of people who can be part of and carry on the culture, so that future generations of people who work could maintain the same mood, atmosphere and positive organizational culture that exists today [10]. Mentoring helps individuals become great managers and leaders of tomorrow. Organizations are using mentoring programs as a way to secure and recruit talent to fertilise it further.

Mentoring relations could be either informal associations wherein a mentee learns by observation or by formal agreements where there is a to and fro transfer of experience and perspective. Be it formal or informal, the ultimate goal of mentoring is to provide career advice as well as both professional and personal enrichment. One often comes across examples of mentoring schemes during formal periods of training, preparation for vocational or professional qualifications, and induction of new employees, to help staff members consider objectively their medium and long term development aspirations, and to prepare senior members for their next posts [11]. Mentoring schemes are used as part of the staff development processes at universities and colleges of higher education, and within schools to foster development of gifted pupils. They are also adopted in social and sporting activities to help new entrants in getting acquainted with the organisation, its culture, and develop new skills [11].

Qualities of a Good Mentor

A mentor is someone who has been there, done that, learned from experience and is willing to share. Mentoring is first and foremost a teacher/student relationship. Effective mentors should possess a wide variety of qualities to facilitate a positive mentor-mentee relationship.

Mentors must be compatible on a personal level, listen actively, be able to identify potential strengths in their mentees and assist mentees in ascertaining and reaching their goals.

Melanson identified some core qualities of a successful mentor based on his observation of military and civilian mentors [12]. He stated that an ideal mentor should be approachable, empathetic so that he or she can feel, understand and appreciate the fears and desires of the mentee, be reflective and able to refine lessons learnt from their career. The ideal mentor should be very patient and should be given an opportunity to demonstrate new skills and achieve new endeavour [13]. Honesty and loyalty to the mentee in giving critical feedback in a caring manner is a must according to Melanson. Mentors should be authentic and value ongoing learning and growth. Finally, mentor commitment is the key to a successful mentoring relationship [12].

Sambunjak has reported a systematic review of the characteristics of mentoring [14]. There were six studies that reported the desired qualities of a mentor. These were classified as pertaining to the mentor's personality, interpersonal abilities and professional status. Good mentors should be honest and sincere, patient, understanding, non-judgemental, reliable in their dealings with mentees, be able to listen actively, accessible, be able to identify potential strengths in their mentees, compatible in terms of practice style, vision and personality and have a well established position within the academic community [14].

Roles and Responsibilities of a Mentor

Darling reported on a study that explored the different roles of a mentor. One of the most significant outcomes of the study was the identification of the characteristics of mentors that enable learning [15, 16]. Characteristics that are most desirable for a mentor to possess include acting as a professional role model, being supportive of and involved in a trainee's progress, serving as a trusted evaluator of the mentee and being a leader in their field. Mentors who have these traits may have greater success in attracting and training mentees [17]. It is essential that mentors also provide both positive and negative feedback in a way which enhances further learning, invest an appropriate amount of time in the mentee, impart their own knowledge and experience, provide guidance in career planning, stimulate mentees to more critical thinking and explore issues more deeply and always be willing to provide opportunities to the mentee [15, 16].

Sambunjak's systematic review revealed six studies, which explored the role of good mentors and how they interacted with their mentees [14]. Some of the actions were aimed at academic growth of mentees while others were targeted toward personal growth. From this review, they concluded that there was an increasing level of privacy and intimacy from the institutional to the personal side. On the institutional side, mentors were seen to improve mentees' visibility and connections within the academic environment. On the personal side, mentors provided moral support, vision-building, goal setting, self reflection and created a safe environment for expression of thoughts and feelings [14].

> **Box 1: Tips for Mentors**
> - Be approachable and open minded
> - Act as a role model
> - Show concern, compassion and empathy
> - Provide moral support
> - Be enthusiastic and invest appropriate time in mentee
> - Possess good communication skills including listening skills
> - Offer constructive feedback
> - Be confidential
> - Nurture mentoring relationship

Qualities of a Mentee

Not everyone makes a good mentee; however, those who are effective often share similar characteristics [18]. Good mentees find their own mentors; associate with them; learn from their guidance, wisdom, support and benefit from the global experience. Melanson identified some qualities in the junior officers in the army medical department who according to him would benefit the most from mentoring [19]. The recognized qualities of effective mentees according to him are those who have a deep rooted drive and initiative for learning, are eager to take personal charge of their mentoring, confidential in all matters, are careful risk takers, learn from their mistakes and failures, enthusiastic, open-minded and receptive to feedback and coaching and improvise from mistakes. Commitment according to him is the key to the mentoring relationship and by becoming mentors themselves the mentee would gratify and reciprocate the obligation [19].

Roles and Responsibilities of a Mentee

The mentee has an equal if not a greater charge in a mentor–mentee relationship [20]. The mentee should initiate the mentoring relationship, articulate goals and objectives, identify strengths and weaknesses, listen attentively, be patient, demonstrate willingness to work as a team player, be willing to learn and take risks, have a positive attitude, use constructive feedback, share enthusiasm for growth and success, willing to accept challenges, nurture mentoring relationship, recognize and accept limitations of the relationship [18]. The Mentee should affirm and speak on behalf of the mentor's role exhibiting and picturing the mentor as a 'developer of people' publicly acclaiming the credit to the mentor for useful ideas. They should flourish with the mentor's emotional support and friendship and have admiration and respect for the mentor as appropriate [21].

Box 2: Tips for Mentees

- Initiate mentoring relationship
- Determine their own strengths and weakness
- Willing to learn and take risks
- Accept challenges
- Listen attentively
- Recognise and accept limitations of the mentoring relationship

Mentoring Vs Supervision

Supervision and mentoring are often used synonymously. Mentoring is a power free, two-way mutually beneficial learning situation where the mentor provides advice, shares knowledge and experiences, and will usually have a longer term and more strategic focus on the mentoree's development [22]. A supervisor, on the other hand, has an authoritative power with short-term targets to reinforce or change skills specific for the task. Supervision implies critical watching and directing without the warmth that is implied in mentoring [3, 22]. The most successful mentoring programs are those, which have the full and continued support of the supervisors outside the mentor relationship. A real measure of success is when these supervisors volunteer to be mentors in the next mentoring program [23].

Mentoring Vs Managing

Both mentoring and managing can be used synonymously and this could be within or beyond an organisation depending on the varied purposes, processes and benefits for both. The relationships of the mentoree with the mentor and the manager could be varied. The mentor–mentee relationship is life long and career supportive as the former implants the ingredients in the latter who reaps it often in his/her career, creating a psychological and social bonding among themselves. It also acts as a long-term return on the investment done by the mentor on the mentee. It is a mutually beneficial exchange, enhancing personal and professional growth, aiming and striving to evaluate the effectiveness 'to do the right things'. On the other hand, the relationship of the manager and mentee is a job supportive relation as long as both are with the organisation, leading to work related performance. This could result in a short-term return and also on the one way transfer of skills within the job related perspective. This relationship emphasises and streamlines on efficiency to 'do things right' [21].

Evolution of the Mentoring Relationship

Mentoring relationships progress through predictable phases that often build on one another [24]. After the selection and approval of the mentor and the matching process have occurred, the next step in the mentoring process involves the preparation and implementation of the key phases by the mentor. Understanding of the phases, and awareness that there may be overlaps between the phases sequence is key to successful mentoring relationships [25].

Clutterback described the phases of the mentoring process as rapport building, direction setting, making progress and moving on [25]. In the first phase, it is essential for the mentor and the mentee to establish a good rapport with each other wherein both openly share their willingness to exchange views, values, goals and expected outcomes. They agree upon a way of working together, identify and plan resources and set up future meetings to review these on an ongoing basis. Goals for mentoring could be agreed in the initial or second meeting. The mentor should help the mentee clarify their focus, goals, set objectives, identify priority work and set appropriate actions to achieve them. It is in this stage that there will be more listening, sharing and confiding in each other. In the third phase of making progress, both the mentor and the mentee should use each other's expertise and facilitate reflective learning and professional networking. At this meeting, they should review the progress and reflect on the successes since the last meeting along with identification of new issues. This helps achieve a two-way feedback between the mentor and mentee. It is here where new challenges are presented and achieved. In the concluding stage of the mentoring relationship, the mentor and mentee review what has been achieved, discuss moving forward and allow the relationship to end with a plan for future communication and accountability [26].

In summary, in the four stages the mentor and the mentee acquaint themselves, ascertain aims and objectives accomplish those goals and cease their relationship. The progression from one stage to the next depends on the successful resolution of the previous stage [26].

Monitoring Success of the Mentoring Relationship

The relationship that mentors share with their mentees is expected to significantly affect the success of mentoring interventions [27]. A successful mentoring relationship requires a two-way flow of compassion and recognition in an environment that allows the relationship to develop [6]. Mentoring relationships should follow the rules of professional etiquette. Both the mentor and mentee should have expectations that run parallel to each other [6, 28, 29]. A mentoring relationship would be ravaged if there is failure to support each other, unsettled conflicts, boundary violations and failure to respect each other's goals [6]. The most important measure of successful mentoring is the success of the mentee. Mentors who do not devote time and resources will be unable to have a lucrative mentoring relationship [5].

A study by Goldner et al. examined the association between relationship qualities and mentee functioning in children [27]. They concluded that qualities like closeness, dependency and unrealistic expectations for the continuation and deepening of the relationship, beyond the planned period, were positively associated with the children's social and academic adjustment, and contributed to perceived academic competence, social support and wellbeing [27].

For a successful relation the mentor and mentee should discuss the following- if goals initially stated by the mentee were achieved, if goals were redefined during the mentoring relationship and if these new goals were met, what other outcomes were achieved during the relationship, was organisational knowledge increased, were problem-solving skills enhanced, what professional and personal gains were made by mentee and mentor, what aspects of the mentoring relationship they appreciated and the aspects of mentoring they found challenging [30]. In a nursing education faculty study conducted by Hodges, the use of learning contracts, formulation of ground rules, use of information in handbooks and discussion of the expectations of the mentor and mentee were found to be helpful in preventing or counteracting problems in the mentoring relationship [31].

Formal mentorship training of senior health care professionals has been found to result in a more successful mentor–mentee relationship[1, 31–34]. Mentors trained in strong academic environment and culture, are found to be better mentors even without formal mentorship training [1]. There is a lot of published data to date showing increasing mentee satisfaction and productivity from institutions, which had a formal mentoring programme in place [1, 35, 36].

Speed Mentoring

Speed mentoring is a new concept designed after speed dating. The format provides an opportunity to seek professional guidance from and network with other professionals from diverse backgrounds with the goal of finding a potential mentor. Speed mentoring is not mentoring. It is only a more time efficient way for people to meet potential mentors to determine if they could fit for a longer term. The mentors and mentees meet for only a few minutes and then rotate to another mentor/mentee immediately afterwards. By providing a structured method for mentees to pursue their own mentoring relationships during a fast-paced event, speed mentoring allays many of the disadvantages of formal mentoring programmes [37]. Women have reported speed mentoring to be particularly helpful as it helped save time by cutting short the initial phase of a developing relationship and determining the match suitability from the beginning.

In a pilot study conducted by Cook et al. to evaluate a speed mentoring program in which mentees spent time with multiple mentors with a view to develop and evaluate a speed mentoring program for the juniors, they concluded that although the speed mentoring event did not stimulate a durable mentor–mentee relationship, they were able to achieve other educational objectives and that this low cost brief intervention to facilitate mentoring relationships merited further attention [7].

Benefits of Mentoring

Benefits to Mentors

Several studies have shown a positive impact on the mentor by the mentoring relationship. It created opportunities for experienced professionals to strengthen their knowledge base and improve communication skills. In a study assessing the benefits of mentorship, Lafleur et al. have reported that several mentors were reading more literature related to their practice and developed personally and professionally along with improvements in managing conflicting roles and responsibilities after participating in a mentorship program [38]. This study also showed that being a mentor also provided intrinsic satisfaction by helping an emerging professional develop to their potential.

Being a mentor enhances the leadership, teaching and coaching skills of mentors and encourages them to become more reflective practitioners. It promotes the professional recognition of mentors for their commitment to developing the talents of new professionals and promotes development of new support groups within and across institutions [18].

Benefits to Mentees

Mentoring programmes are designed primarily for the benefit of the mentees. Mentees gain crucial perception beyond their own education and experience. Mentorship promotes development of a supporting, professional relationship that nurtures guidance during the mentee's development. It increases the self-confidence of a new professional as he/she becomes familiar with a new role, increased responsibilities, or a new organizational culture. Mentees are challenged to go further, take risks, set new goals and achieve at a higher personal and/or professional standard by reflecting on their individual needs. Mentoring provides a forum to seek advice on balancing new responsibilities provides role modeling for professional leadership and facilitates the development of stronger interpersonal skills [18, 39]. Mentees gain confidence and plan their career more strategically with an increasing job satisfaction [39, 40]. Mentees match a new professional with an experienced professional in the field and promote networking and visibility [41].

Benefits to the Organization

The benefits of mentoring to the organization can be incredible and invaluable. The mentoring process itself can be a very positive experience and valuable addition to the institution [39]. It contributes to a positive organizational climate and promotes a more clear understanding of professional responsibilities and expectations. It may increase employee satisfaction and retention by reducing a new employee's sense of isolation. Facilitating integration of new staff through a coordinated mentoring process was perceived as a good business sense [20]. Mentorship results in improved employee job performance, contributes to faster learning curves and results in a better trained staff. It reflects an investment in employee development and could increase employee commitment and loyalty [18].

Mentoring in Medicine

Mentorship is often quoted as a key component of successful academic career development and has been studied in several disciplines of medicine [1, 42–48]. A qualitative study by Jackson et al. revealed lack of mentoring as the most important factor behind delaying career progress [42, 49]. Many studies have shown that influential and sustained mentorship enhances research activity and a researcher's career [50]. A systematic review of mentorship studies involving medical students and physicians showed that mentorship not only influenced career choice and academic development but also improved research productivity [51]. Many previous studies have shown that institutions can also develop formal mentoring programmes to improve research productivity [14, 52, 53].

Physicians by virtue of their training and profession have to be leaders. It is with these leadership like qualities that they are able to share a vision, coach other team members, focus on perfection and train their junior members to become effective leaders [54]. The growth and development of younger colleagues is a positive factor of reward for the mentor's growth, maturity and legacy [4]. Thus, mentoring is beneficial to produce great leaders in an organization.

A study from a surgical training unit in Ireland showed that mentorship and satisfaction with allocated rotations had a positive influence on trainee satisfaction and trainees were then more content in surgical training [55]. A systematic review in surgical training also showed that developing formal programs can help overcome several barriers and build an effective mentor–mentee relationship for training quality surgeons [56]. Results from a study in nursing education also support mentoring programmes in their respective field to provide a caring and supportive environment, enhance recruitment and promote retention of the newly hired in the future [57]. A study to assess neonatal fellows' satisfaction with their training and the role of mentorship showed 75 % of the respondents to be satisfied with their training and the presence of a mentor to correlate with being prepared for academic practice (p =0.013) and plans to enter academic practice (p =0.031) [45]. Correlation between mentorship and completion of the research requirement showed a trend (p =0.09). Fellows who had a mentor were found to be more prepared for academic practice and were more likely to be satisfied with their fellowship training. Thus mentorship was found to play an important role in neonatal training programs [45].

Implementing a Formal Mentoring Program

A successful mentoring program depends on more factors other than just finding some mentors and mentees. The following is a suggested framework for developing a mentoring program [8, 58]:

1. **Assess institutional needs**

    a. Assess current beliefs to training and professional development
    b. Assess the organizational need for mentoring
    c. Agree on purpose, target group and mentoring options

2. **Set mentoring objectives**
3. **Program design**

    a. Promote program
    b. Advertise information about the mentoring program
    c. Design orientation and training program
    d. Select participants
    e. Match partners
    f. Skills development
    g. Provide ongoing support
    h. Evaluation and measurement of outcomes

4. **Orientation and training**

    a. Establish a rapport amongst colleagues
    b. Defining roles and responsibilities
    c. Establish protocols
    d. Provide skills training via workshops, workbooks etc
    e. Implement a scheme for a personal development plan

5. **Pilot the program**
6. **Evaluate to measure the results and improvise improvements**
7. **Introduce the program on a larger scale**

Summary

Mentoring relationship has been a time- honoured practice in medicine and has gained prime importance, initiating a lot a research in diverse settings such as business, education and nursing. Mentoring in academic medicine is a complex phenomenon. The mentors help mentees to flourish in the challenging environment of academic medicine by offering them emotional and moral support, working to build their personal and professional abilities. Successful mentoring requires both commitment and interpersonal skills of the mentor and mentee and also a facilitating environment of the organization. In business, mentoring relationships are associated with positive career outcomes at a younger age and greater career satisfaction.

Mentoring is currently faced with a lot of barriers including time constraints and lack of qualified mentors. Despite consensus that mentorship is a critical determinant of career success, many academic health centres do not provide formal training for their mentors. It is prudent that every organisation enhances the environment by providing recognition for mentoring, develop programs to facilitate the initiation of mentoring relationships and provide resources to assist mentors and mentees in their roles. Mentoring, despite being one of the most important functions in medicine still continues to lobby for greater appreciation. Strengthening the quality of a mentoring relationship will help bring a better tomorrow for the future generation of medical academics.

Responsibilities gravitate to the person who can shoulder them
—Elbert Hubbart

References

1. Cohen JG, Sherman AE, Kiet TK, Kapp DS, Osann K, Chen LM et al (2012) Characteristics of success in mentoring and research productivity-a case-control study of academic centers. Gynecol Oncol 125:8–13
2. Bray L, Nettleton P (2007) Assessor or mentor? Role confusion in professional education. Nurse Educ Today 27:848–855
3. Chong SA (2009) Mentoring: are we doing it right? Ann Acad Med Singapore 38:643–64
4. Coddington CC, Satin AJ (2008) Mentorship: discovering a key to the future. Fertil Steril 90:1571–1573
5. Holmes DR Jr, Hodgson PK, Simari RD, Nishimura RA (2010) Mentoring: making the transition from mentee to mentor. Circulation 121:336–340
6. Marks MB, Goldstein R (2005) The mentoring triad: mentee, mentor, and environment. J Rheumatol 32:216–218
7. Cook DA, Bahn RS, Menaker R (2010) Speed mentoring: an innovative method to facilitate mentoring relationships. Med Teach 32:692–694
8. Rolfe-Flett A (2002) Mentoring in Australia: a practical guide. Pearson Education, Australia
9. Tovey MD (1999) Mentoring in the workplace: a guide for mentors and managers. Prentice Hall, Sydney
10. Why Mentoring is important, Advertising Educational Foundation. http://www.aef.com/industry/careers/memos/8021. Accessed 7 Oct 2014
11. David Kay RH (2009) A practical guide to mentoring: how to help others achieve their goals. How to Books Ltd., Oxford
12. Melanson MA (2013) Qualities of the ideal mentor. Army Medical Department Journal July-Sept; 47–51
13. Fawcett DL (2002) Mentoring-what it is and how to make it work. AORN J 75:950–954
14. Sambunjak D, Straus SE, Marusic A (2010) A systematic review of qualitative research on the meaning and characteristics of mentoring in academic medicine. J Gen Intern Med 25:72–78
15. Darling LA (1984) What do nurses want in a mentor? J Nurs Adm 14:42–44
16. Gopee N (2008) Mentoring and supervision in Healthcare. Sage publications, London
17. Ripley E, Markowitz M, Nichols-Casebolt A, Williams L, Macrina F (2012) Training NIH K award recipients: the role of the mentor. Clin Transl Sci 5:386–393
18. Mentoring essentials for IDP supervisors and mentors (Nov 2012), American Institute of Architects, Intern Development Programme. 1–14. www.aia.org/mentorship
19. Melanson MA (2009) Qualities of the ideal protege. US Army Med Dep J 2009:44–46
20. Greene MT, Puetzer M (2002) The value of mentoring: a strategic approach to retention and recruitment. J Nurs Care Qual 17:63–70
21. Mellish L (2001) Appreciative mentoring: Mellish and Associates. Mellish & Associates, Maleny
22. Davis LL, Little MS, Thornton WL (1997) The art and angst of the mentoring relationship. Acad psychiatry 21:61–71
23. The Growth Connection Articles (1999–2012) The role of the mentor versus the supervisor. http://www.growthconnect.com.au/articles. Accessed 7 Oct 2014
24. Caine RM (1994) Empowering nurses through mentoring. Medsurg Nurs 3:59–61
25. Clutterbuck D (2001) Everyone needs a mentor. CIPD, London
26. Baylor University, Stages of a mentoring relationship. Community Mentoring for Adolescent Development Trainer's manual: 56–62. Accessed 7 Oct 2014
27. Goldner L, Mayseless O (2009) The quality of mentoring relationships and mentoring success. J Youth Adolesc 38:1339–50
28. Gordon FS (2002) Mentoring: how to develop successful mentoring behaviors. 3rd edn. Crisp, Menlo Park
29. Mentoring tips, The Mentoring group. http://www.mentoringgroup.com. Accessed 7 Oct 2014

30. Monash University Strategies for creating successful mentoring relationships. Monash Alumni-Student Mentoring Programme. Accessed 7 Oct 2014
31. Hodges B (2009) Factors that can influence mentorship relationships. Paediatr Nurs 21:32–35
32. Johnson MO, Subak LL, Brown JS, Lee KA, Feldman MD (2010) An innovative program to train health sciences researchers to be effective clinical and translational research mentors. Acad Med 85:484–489
33. Kupfer DJ, Hyman SE, Schatzberg AF, Pincus HA, Reynolds CF 3rd (2002) Recruiting and retaining future generations of physician scientists in mental health. Arch Gen Psychiatry 59:657–660
34. Feldman MD, Huang L, Guglielmo BJ, Jordan R, Kahn J, Creasman JM et al (2009) Training the next generation of research mentors: the University of California, San Francisco, Clinical & Translational Science Institute Mentor Development Program. Clin Transl Sci 2:216–221
35. Levy AS, Pyke-Grimm KA, Lee DA, Palla SL, Naranjo A, Saulnier Sholler G et al (2013) Mentoring in pediatric oncology: a report from the Children's oncology Group Young Investigator Committee. J Pediatr Hematol Oncol 35:456–461
36. Wingard DL, Garman KA, Reznik V (2004) Facilitating faculty success: outcomes and cost benefit of the UCSD National Center of Leadership in Academic Medicine. Acad Med 79:9–11
37. A Speed Mentoring Toolkit, University of Kentucky, Women's forum. www.uky.edu/PCW/Speed Mentoring Toolkit. Accessed 7 Oct 2014
38. Lafleur AK, White BJ (2010) Appreciating mentorship: the benefits of being a mentor. Prof Case Manag 15:305–311 (quiz 312–313)
39. Hisaw T, Comello RJ (2009) Mentoring for the next generation of new managers. Radiol Manage 31:34–37 (quiz 38–39)
40. Roch GR (1979) Much ado about mentors. Harv Bus Rev 57:14–20
41. LGPro Mentoring Programme The Benefits of Mentoring. http://www.lgpromentoring.com.au/benefits of mentoring. Accessed 7 Oct 2014
42. Holliday EB, Jagsi R, Thomas CR Jr, Wilson LD, Fuller CD (2014) Standing on the shoulders of giants: results from the Radiation Oncology Academic Development and Mentorship Assessment Project (ROADMAP). Int J Radiat Oncol Biol Phys 88:18–24
43. Steiner JF, Lanphear BP, Curtis P, Vu KO (2002) Indicators of early research productivity among primary care fellows. J Gen Intern Med 17:845–851
44. Steiner JF, Curtis P, Lanphear BP, Vu KO, Main DS (2004) Assessing the role of influential mentors in the research development of primary care fellows. Acad Med 79:865–872
45. Pearlman SA, Leef KH, Sciscione AC (2004) Factors that affect satisfaction with neonatal-perinatal fellowship training. Am J Perinatol 21:371–375
46. Hoffman MS, Bodurka DC (2009) Surgical education and training program development for gynecologic oncology: American perspective. Gynecol Oncol 114:47–51
47. Sciscione AC, Colmorgen GH, D'Alton ME (1998) Factors affecting fellowship satisfaction, thesis completion, and career direction among maternal-fetal medicine fellows. Obstet Gynecol 91:1023–1026
48. Mrazek DA, Shapiro T, Pincus HA (1991) Current status of research activity in American child and adolescent psychiatry: II. A developmental analysis by age cohorts. J Am Acad Child Adolesc Psychiatry 30:1003–1008
49. Jackson VA, Palepu A, Szalacha L, Caswell C, Carr PL, Inui T (2003) "Having the right chemistry": a qualitative study of mentoring in academic medicine. Acad Med 78:328–334
50. Kjeldsen K (2006) A proficient mentor is a must when starting up with research. Exp Clin Cardiol 11:243–245
51. Sambunjak D, Straus SE, Marusic A (2006) Mentoring in academic medicine: a systematic review. JAMA 296:1103–1115
52. Keyser DJ, Lakoski JM, Lara-Cinisomo S, Schultz DJ, Williams VL, Zellers DF et al (2008) Advancing institutional efforts to support research mentorship: a conceptual framework and self-assessment tool. Acad Med 833:217–225
53. Levinson W, Kaufman K, Clark B, Tolle SW (1991) Mentors and role models for women in academic medicine. West J Med 154:423–426

54. Woo KT (2007) Physician leadership. Singapore Med J 48:1069–1073
55. O'Sullivan KE, Byrne JS, Walsh TN (2013) Basic surgical training in Ireland: the impact of operative experience, training program allocation and mentorship on trainee satisfaction. Ir J Med Sci 182:687–692
56. Entezami P, Franzblau LE, Chung KC (2012) Mentorship in surgical training: a systematic review. Hand (NY) 7:30–36
57. Sawatzky JA, Enns CL (2009) A mentoring needs assessment: validating mentorship in nursing education. J Prof Nurs 25:145–150
58. Lacey K (1999) Making mentoring happen: a simple and effective guide to implementing a successful mentoring program. Business & Professional Pub. Pty Ltd., Warriewood

Chapter 16
Expert or Impostor—Understanding the Role of the Expert Witness

Denise Bowen

*A good medical expert must serve but one client, and that client
should be truth*
—Erle Stanley Gardner

Abstract Medical staff are often required to undertake the difficult journey starting with the subpoena and ending with the testimony in the courtroom as an expert. The information they provide to the judges and the juries is expected to be factual, comprehensive, unbiased, and up to date. To give effective expert testimony, medical staff must recognize the basic differences in the culture between the legal and medical world. They need to understand and follow the basic rules for preparing and providing the evidence in the courtroom, and be aware of the fact that such an undertaking may have significant personal, professional and financial implications for the parties involved. In order to prepare a professional report the medical experts need to develop report writing skills to compliment their clinical knowledge and expertise. Considering that the front line staff in any health care providing organisation is not formally trained to handle the responsibility of testifying as an expert, the journey from the subpoena to the testimony in the courtroom can be very stressful. This chapter provides an overview of the role of the expert in legal matters and the substantial responsibilities that are undertaken in preparing a legal report and giving expert evidence in the court.

Keywords Clinical practice · Clinical records · Legal request · Jurisdiction · Negligence claims · Court guidelines · Important considerations · Code of conduct · Clarification · Reference material · Confidentiality · Public sector standards · Evidence in chief · Cross examination · Re-examination Conflict of interest · Giving evidence · Tips · Errors · Media

D. Bowen (✉)
Mediation & Legal Support Services, Women & Newborn Health Service, KEM Hospital
for Women, 374 Bagot road, Subiaco, City of Perth, WA 6008, Australia
e-mail: denise.bowen@health.wa.gov.au

© Springer International Publishing Switzerland 2015
S. Patole (ed.), *Management and Leadership – A Guide for Clinical Professionals,*
DOI 10.1007/978-3-319-11526-9_16

Key Points

1. It is not advisable to prepare an expert report in an area of practice that is outside of your current scope of practice
2. There is a code of conduct for experts when preparing a report for legal proceedings specific to each area of law
3. The testimony of a medical expert must be within the limits of science
4. There is no substitute for thorough preparation and practice under the guidance of the hospital's legal advisors
5. Don't be overconfident, remember that for every expert there is an equal and opposite expert

The complexity of medical care has increased significantly following the technological advances over last few decades. The long strenuous shifts together with the reliance on complex technology often make it difficult for medical staff to provide that special human touch in the management of patients, and to support their family members. Gaps in communication, written or verbal, are also not infrequent. It is therefore not surprising that the risk of errors, conflict, complaints, and litigations is high under such situations. The purpose of this chapter is to provide some guidance about what is involved in being an expert witness in a legal matter. Essentially the clinician will either be asked to prepare a clinical report or discharge summary where he/she has had direct involvement in the care of the patient/client or requested to prepare a report in an expert capacity commenting on the clinical care provided by another clinician or team of clinicians. Legally and clinically variation in practice does not always mean a breach in the expected standard of care given to a patient.

It is generally recognised that clinical expertise develops over time and exposure to different learning opportunities and is continuous. Specialisation by its nature focuses learning in a particular area and of necessity reduces exposure to other specialised areas of practice. Whilst general clinical knowledge continues to grow throughout a clinician's working career and is required to enable a clinician to recognise that *something is not right and requires further examination* it does not necessarily make them an expert in all fields.

With these factors in mind it is important to remember that 'hindsight' does make diagnosis and treatment planning much easier but it is not available up front to clinical staff. When preparing an expert report, it is essential to assess the standard of care from the position of the clinical staff at the time of providing care and work forward from first contact rather than working backwards from a known diagnosis (Checklist 1). Developing a working chronology ensures all aspects of clinical care are considered when preparing an expert report.

Checklist 1: Clinical Practice Review

Clinical records demonstrate:

- Clinical staff with up-to-date knowledge and skills
- Appropriate physical examination of the patient with well documented findings.
- A documented treatment plan
- Proper instructions for ongoing clinical tests
- Complete record of patient observations and medications
- Regular medical review with adjustments to treatment plan as necessary
- Results from pathology and radiologic examination reviewed and care adjusted accordingly
- Evidence of communication across the clinical team
- Series of provisional diagnoses in a complex patient leading to a final diagnosis
- Post-operative complications from a surgical procedure emerging over a number of days.

Initial Legal Request

The initial contact from a lawyer may be verbal or written and is made to establish if you would be prepared to provide an expert opinion in relation to clinical care in a particular legal matter. This first contact usually provides limited information about the nature of the report and if you agree, the contact will be followed up with a more detailed written legal request. The follow up letter should set out clearly the details of the case including whom the lawyer is acting for and who the parties to the matter are. Careful consideration should be given to the information contained in this letter (Checklist 2). The lawyer will set out their case and provide an overview of the situation. Details about clinical care and allegations of poor care may be made in the letter. The request may direct you to specific issues related to the patient care. Attached to the letter of request should be the relevant clinical records for the particular case. It is essential that you are provided with all of the relevant clinical records to enable you to fully inform yourself of the clinical facts and prepare your report. In addition to patient records there may also be a copy of expert reports previously prepared by other clinicians. If you require additional clinical records and information relating to the patient before you commit to do the report you need to advise the lawyer and request that the information is made available to you. Copies of relevant clinical guidelines and policies may also be necessary to assess the standard of care requirements relevant at the time of the incident.

Take particular note of the date of the initial incident that you are being asked to comment on as the legal position requires that the standard of practice is to be assessed as at the time of the incident and not current practice. For example if you are being asked to prepare a report about care given to a baby at the time of birth note the date of birth. If the date of birth is 1 January 1999, then the relevant standard of practice is what was in place in 1998–1999, including the equipment in use at that time. Additional references may also be required in order to support your opinion on the standard of care that was relevant in 1999.

As a rule do not use abbreviations as these can vary from health service to health service depending on location and type of services offered. It is important to ensure the report provides a plain language interpretation of the clinical condition and care provided as it cannot be assumed that the lawyers and the court have clinical training. Your opinion needs to be formed after careful review of all available documents and clinical records relevant at the time of the incident. As an expert you need to be able to clearly articulate how you reached your opinion and what facts were relied upon to support your view. Clear reference to dates and clinical documents containing the facts that support your opinion is required.

Checklist 2: Important Considerations

- Who is requesting the report?
- Are they lawyers representing the plaintiff (party taking legal action against another) in a medical negligence claim; or
- Are they lawyers for the Defendant (party defending themselves against a negligence claim); or
- Is it a person representing themselves in a legal claim;
- Does the legal action involve the place where you work;
- Does the legal action involve clinicians that you know;
- Do you have any concerns around possible conflict of interest; and
- Do you have any reservations about doing the report now that you have reviewed the detailed request and clinical records?

If after considering all of the information you decide that you do not wish to proceed in preparing the report then notify the lawyer/person who made the request and return the file of documents as quickly as possible. If you agree to do the report it is important that the report is done as promptly as possible. If you have unexpected delays in getting the report completed then you need to advise the lawyer as there are court defined deadlines that have to be meet and delays in receiving an expert report may require court proceedings to be adjourned off until the report is available.

Remember expert reports are relied on in determining the course of the legal proceedings so it is essential that the every report is done in a careful and considered manner. As an expert you have a duty to the court to provide an expert opinion that is unbiased and fairly assesses the facts of the case. The lawyer should provide you with a copy of the 'Duties of an Expert' relevant to the court where the proceedings are being conducted. Professional credibility and integrity can come into play when different experts hold different views on the clinical care provided in a particular case. If your clinical views are challenged ensure you remain focussed on the facts and place reliance on clinical evidence to support your views.

What Jurisdiction is the Report for?

Just as health care is divided into different areas of expertise so is the law with different courts responsible for different types of proceedings (Checklist 3). The focus of the expert clinical report will differ according to the type of legal proceedings in progress. There are key areas where an expert report may be requested and each has specific requirements for information. It is important for a clinician preparing an expert report to be aware of their legal obligations to the court and the jurisdiction that they are working in to ensure their report covers the necessary information. Most courts have a website that provides detailed information to the public about the court and their work. This is a reliable source if you require some additional information about the court system and the legal process within that court before you prepare a report.

Checklist 3: Different Reports for Different Courts

- Medical negligence claims are managed through the District Court under the civil proceedings list. The key legislation covering this area is the Civil Liabilities Act (2002) Western Australia.
- Criminal matters such as assault, child abuse or sexual assault are managed under the Criminal Code through the Magistrates District and Supreme Court depending on the seriousness of the offence.
- The Children's Court deals with matters related to children less than 18 years including child offences as well as child protection proceedings.
- The primary role of the Family Court is to deal with issues around family breakdown and protecting the best interests of the child. The Family Court also considers applications for 'special treatment approvals' for children with conditions such as gender identity disorder.
- An additional protection for children and mentally impaired is provided through the Supreme Court in circumstances where there is a dispute about treatment between the health service and the patient/parents. This is heard under the parens patraie jurisdiction of the Supreme Court.
- Guardianship applications in Western Australia go through the State Administrative Tribunal and require expert medical reports to assist the Tribunal in making a guardianship decision.

- Workers compensation cases are initially progressed through the workers compensation tribunal but may move into the civil courts if a common law claim is pursued. Expert reports will be required for these proceedings.
- Injuries sustained as a result of a motor vehicle accident or criminal injuries also require expert reports to determine the extent of injuries and the amount of compensation that should be paid.
- In addition the Coroner's Court is responsible for examining all of the sudden unexpected deaths that occur in Western Australia and again this court relies on expert clinical information in making a determination around the cause of death.

The Role of the Expert in Negligence Claims

During the course of legal proceedings independent expert reports are an important source of information for the parties involved in litigation. These expert reports are essential in assessing the merits of the legal claim and risk exposure to determine if a negotiated settlement should be progressed or the matter taken to trial. The author of a report where the matter proceeds to trial will be called to give evidence in the court in relation to the opinion they have provided about various aspects of care and recovery.

In medical negligence claims an independent expert report is initially sourced by the lawyer representing a person contemplating commencing legal proceedings. Due to the substantial legal costs involved in taking legal action the opinion of the initial expert becomes vital in determining whether or not to proceed with a legal claim. If the independent expert assesses the facts of the case and determines that the clinical standard of practice was appropriate for the time and nature of the case then it is unlikely that the claim will proceed.

It is not uncommon however for lawyers to seek more than one report in order to find a clinical expert that supports the allegations of negligence and then to rely on that information to set out the plaintiff's claim. Once a supportive report is obtained then the plaintiff lawyer will issue a Writ and Statement of Claim in relation to alleged medical negligence. These documents will be served on the health service or clinician (defendant) named on the Writ. On receipt of a Writ the health service/ clinician needs to notify their insurer of the claim so a defence lawyer can be appointed. The lawyer representing the defendant/s will review the available health documents to establish the facts of the case along with any documents or expert reports provided by the plaintiff. Following discussion with the defendant/s to clarify the clinical and legal issues arising from the claim an independent expert report will be sought on behalf of the defendant/s. The decision about whether or not to defend a legal claim or to negotiate a settlement is contingent on expert evidence and whether the facts of the case indicate there has been a breach in the expected standard of care. At each step of the negligence pathway expert reports are vitally important in the management decisions related to the claim.

Relevant Expertise

Before agreeing to prepare an expert report the clinician needs to carefully assess whether or not they hold the requisite knowledge, skills and experience to be considered an expert in their field. In any legal matter there are usually a number of experts who prepare reports. If the matter progresses to trial each expert will be cross examined on the content of their report. A well written report will ensure the clinician is able to support their opinion with fact and provide appropriate assistance to the court. The clinician should provide an up to date curriculum vitae so that their professional training and expertise is evident to those assessing the qualifications of the report writer. Current clinical practice in the field is held in high regard and is considered necessary in most cases where a clinical report is required. It is not advisable to prepare an expert report in an area of practice that is outside of your current scope of practice.

Court Guidelines on Being an Expert

All clinicians asked to prepare an expert report need to be aware that there is a code of conduct for experts who are preparing a report for legal proceedings specific to each area of law. It is a legal practice requirement that lawyers seeking an expert report provide a copy of the relevant court guidelines to the expert when they request the report. All experts are required to acknowledge that they have been provided with these guidelines and that they have prepared their report in accordance with the court guidelines.

Seeking Clarification of the Request

It is essential the clinician asked to provide an expert report has a clear understanding of the request. Sometimes the letter of instruction from the lawyer requesting an expert report is poorly written and the information the lawyer is seeking is unclear or doesn't fit with the available clinical information. Legal misinterpretation of the available clinical information can occur. In such circumstances it is essential that there is clarification of the request before the clinician agrees to write a report. Remember in most cases an expert report will be circulated and assessed by other lawyers and clinicians involved in the management of the legal matter. Basing an opinion on misinformation can lead to professional criticism and is ultimately unhelpful in resolving a legal dispute. Once a report is prepared should new information become available the clinician who wrote the expert report will be asked to comment on whether the new information alters their opinion of the matter. The clinician should be honest—if the information does influence the clinical facts and leads them to a different view then the clinician should say so and state the reasons why their opinion has altered.

Requesting Additional Information

In some cases the expert witness is only provided with part of the clinical records by the lawyer and this can impact on the clinicians ability to undertake a professional assessment of the standard of care given to the patient. If this occurs then additional documents should be requested from the lawyer. This becomes particularly important if there are missing documents such as CTG traces, pathology reports or radiology information. The professional credibility of the expert can be called into question when a report commenting on clinical care is based on limited information. If the lawyer is unable to provide all of the essential documents the clinician should carefully consider whether or not they are in a position to provide a detailed expert report and ensure that any resulting limitations are noted on their report.

Essential Reference Material

All references used in preparing an expert report will need to be properly acknowledged and a copy of the material provided with the final report. The use of appropriate references in the preparation of a report is expected. Clinician 'opinion only' comments unsupported by evidence of established professional standards, research and professional journal publication's, hold little weight in legal proceedings. In every legal case there will be a number of expert reports and opinions that form part of the evidence to be considered in assessing the merits of the legal claim.

Confidentiality

Maintaining appropriate patient confidentiality must always be a consideration when dealing with confidential health records and information. The lawyer seeking an expert report is either working on behalf of a client taking legal action in which case they have obtained consent from their client to assess their health information; or the lawyer is working for the client who is defending a legal action, in which case there is implied consent as the party has the right to defend themselves. Under the legal requirements for discovery of information the defending party has a right of access to all relevant information on which the claim is based. Any documents provided to a clinician in order to prepare an expert report should be carefully stored and either returned or destroyed at the end of the legal action to limit the opportunity for unauthorised disclosure of clinical information.

Conflict of Interest Issues

If the clinical expert becomes aware of a potential conflict of interest they should immediately discuss their concerns with the lawyer who has requested the report. If the conflict of interest is significant then it may be necessary to withdraw from giving an opinion. Be aware that in certain circumstances a complaint to the governing professional body can be made if the person affected by the report believes there has been a professional breach. Whilst an expert witness cannot be sued for defamation by providing an expert report to the court, a complaint to the relevant professional practice board is a separate legal matter and is governed by different legislation.

Public Sector Standards

Clinical staff working in the public sector are required to work in accordance with the prescribed Public Sector Standards governing the public health services in Western Australia. Public servants are not permitted to profit from their paid employment. This means that clinical staff cannot independently raise accounts for the provision of reports related to public patients of the health service outside of the salaried pay agreement. In certain circumstances the health service can raise an account for services rendered and reimburse the clinician through the normal pay system. It is important to clarify the arrangements for payment up front to avoid a potential breach of standards.

Checklist 4: Common Errors Made by Experts

- Failing to make the proper enquires in relation to the clinical records to ensure all relevant documents have been provided.
- Not being provided with a copy of the relevant code of conduct for expert witnesses for the relevant court and not requesting this prior to agreeing to do a report.
- Failure to support clinical opinion with factual evidence from the clinical record and/or relevant clinical guidelines and research.
- Adopting a bias in preparing the reporting according to who is seeking the report rather than as a professional report to assist the court.
- Developing a fixed position even when additional facts and information becomes known that may require further consideration and adjustment of opinion.
- Providing an expert opinion outside of the clinician's area of expertise.

Additional Tips for Giving Evidence in the Court

1. Be prepared

Prior to giving evidence in court the expert needs to have read their report/s and be able to answer questions about their opinion and how it was formed. As an expert it is essential that all relevant documents have been reviewed along with other expert reports provided during the course of the legal proceedings. The expert should work closely with the lawyer who has engaged them to ensure they understand the nature of the claim and the legal process of giving evidence in the court. Legal counsel will usually meet with the expert to go through their evidence prior to the trial. The lawyer managing the claim and legal counsel are generally different people. Legal counsel or barristers specialise in presenting matters in the court.

2. Understanding the legal process

Depending on the court there will be at least two legal counsellors and a judge. Each party to a legal claim has the right to be represented in the court. Legal counsel will introduce witnesses called by the party they are representing (*evidence in chief*). At the end of giving evidence the witness will be cross examined by the legal counsel representing other parties to the legal action (*cross examination*). Once cross examination is completed the original legal counsel is able to re-examine the witness to clarify any issues that may have arisen during cross examination (*re-examination*).

An expert witness will be asked questions about the expert report previously prepared for the proceedings and their professional opinion about the relevant clinical issues. It is essential that the expert listen carefully to the questions being asked or the proposition being put to them. If the expert considers the questions to be unclear they should seek clarification from the legal counsel before responding. In some case the legal counsel may put a proposition to the expert in relation to the case that is not in line with their clinical knowledge and/or opinion—if this occurs the expert can say they disagree with the proposal put forward. Equally, if a proposal is put forward by legal counsel that is reasonable and may offer a different clinical view the expert can state that this is an alternative view. On occasions the judge may ask the expert questions directly. If the judge does ask a question the expert should answer these questions as completely as possible. Part of being an expert witness is to ensure that clinical comments are kept to the experts established area of expertise.

3. Dealing with media

A clinical experts involved in giving evidence in court may be approached by the media to comment about the evidence they have given. It is best for the expert to avoid discussing their evidence with the media as the case is still in progress and any comments they make may be taken out of context. A decisive 'no comment' is usually sufficient to stop media reporters. It should be noted however this will not stop the media from taking photos and publishing their own comments about evidence that the reporters have heard in the court. Media reporting will vary in content according to the way in which the reporter has interpreted the evidence given in the court. In general the court system is Western Australia open to the public unless there is a court order restricting access or publication of certain information. In Western Australia the public health system has a designated public relations area that manages all media enquiries and media information releases on behalf of health services. Unless authorised individual public health employees should not comment to the media on legal matters.

Summary

Obtaining an expert report for legal purposes is an important and critical component of any legal matter that may have significant personal, professional and financial implications for the parties involved. In order to prepare a professional report the expert needs to develop report writing skills to compliment clinical knowledge and expertise. The preparation of an expert report requires a substantial commitment of time and careful consideration of the clinical facts of the case along with review of the relevant clinical guidelines and available research findings. A clinician should not agree to do an expert report unless they have the relevant clinical expertise and the time available to properly prepare the report. Inappropriate report writing can be subject to professional practice review if a complaint is made to the relevant professional practice board. A clinician preparing an expert report needs to apply the same professional integrity to the function as would be applied in any other clinical practice area. This chapter has provided an overview of the role of the expert in legal matters and the substantial responsibilities that are undertaken in preparing a legal report and giving expert evidence in the court.

Recommended Reading

Arenson KJ, Bagaris M (2002) Understanding evidence, Ch 11. Lexis Nexis Butterworths, Australia

Clarke A (2003) Negligence—a practical learning approach. Lexis Nexis Butterworths, Australia

Curthoys J, Kendall C (2006) Advocacy—an introduction. Lexis Nexis Butterworths, Australia

Donn SM (2005) Medical liability, risk management, and the quality of health care. Semin Fetal Neonatal Med 10:3–9

Expert Evidence District Court of Western Australia, Circular to Practitioners CIV 2007/2. Date of Issue: 3 August 2007

Madden B, McIlwraith J (2013) Australian medical liablity, 2nd edn. Lexis Nexis Butterworths, Australia

McNicol SB, Mortimer D (2001) Evidence, 2nd edn. Ch 19. Butterworths, Australia

Medical Protection Society Guide to Writing Expert Reports (2014) http://www.mps.org.UK

United Medical Protection (2003) Medico-legal handbook—a guide to legal issues in medical practice. Big Box Publishing Pty Ltd, NSW

Chapter 17
How to Dress at Work

Rajkishore Nayak, Rajiv Padhye and Lijing Wang

clothes make the man

Abstract In addition to the thinking and decision making ability, the other distinguishing feature between humans and animals is the wearing of clothes. The initial judgement of a person can be made from the clothing of the person. One's clothing choices, grooming, personality and body language play a crucial role for successful work life. It is well documented that the way one is dressed plays a vital role for a successful career in today's workplace. Factors such as garment style, garment fit, nature of job and guidelines for dress code are important considerations while selecting the appropriate outfit for a particular job. Grooming is essential for both men and women for a successful career. A suitable clothing selection for a particular job is influenced by the job requirements, colour, design, fit and comfort. Special clothing is needed for the people working in healthcare, fire fighting, defence and other similar areas to protect from various types of threats. Hence, selection of appropriate clothing is essential both for success, personal safety and wellness.

Keywords Clothing style · Successful career · Garment fit · Garment comfort · Job interview · Grooming · Personality and clothing · Clothing and emotion · Dress code · Garment colour · Garment design · Warm colours · Cool colours · Neutral colours · Clothing requirements · Clothing for healthcare people · Hospital acquired infections · Type of job · Protective clothing

R. Padhye (✉)
School of Fashion and Textiles, RMIT University, Building: 512, Level: 1, Room: 11A,
Brunswick, Melbourne, Australia
e-mail: rajiv.padhye@rmit.edu.au

R. Nayak · R. Padhye · L. Wang
School of Fashion and Textiles, RMIT University, Melbourne, Australia

© Springer International Publishing Switzerland 2015
S. Patole (ed.), *Management and Leadership – A Guide for Clinical Professionals,*
DOI 10.1007/978-3-319-11526-9_17

Key Messages

1. The way one is dressed plays a vital role for a successful career in today's workplace.
2. Several factors such as garment style, garment fit, nature of job and rules for dress code are involved while selecting the appropriate outfit for a particular job. In addition, grooming and the individuality/personality accentuate the clothing.
3. The selection of appropriate clothing often depends on the nature of the job. Special personal protective clothing is necessary for jobs such as fire fighting, police, ambulance, defence personnel and various other specialty occupations.
4. The way the doctors and nurses dress and address their patients is likely to influence the development of the relationship between them.
5. It is important to know that health care worker's attire and accessories are potential source of hospital acquired infections and should be cared for.

It is well documented that the way one is dressed plays a vital role for a successful career in today's workplace [1–3]. The appearance of a person translates to the performance. One's clothing choices, grooming, personality and body language play a crucial role for a successful work life. While selecting clothes, one should get a sense what the office likes and which cloth would suit appropriately in that environment. The way one dresses and acts, determines what people think about the person. The clothes one wears talk about the personality quietly. To wear the best outfit, one first needs to know all about self. The best appearance always needs careful attention to the clothing and personal grooming. One should be dressed in a well-groomed and non-distracting fashion.

One's inner feelings are often reflected outside by the clothing and action. If one expects positive response from others, then he or she must be well-dressed, well-groomed and act positively. Appropriate clothing helps in boosting the confidence. It was established that the people dressed with doctor's lab coats achieved higher scoring on attention related tasks than those who had not [4, 5]. A survey of business leaders published in 2012 by the Centre of Professional Excellence at York College (Pennsylvania) showed that two-thirds mentioned that image makes a major impact, when progress in the career is considered [6].

Major Factors for an Appropriate Dress

Several factors such as garment style, garment fit, nature of job and rules for dress code are involved while selecting the appropriate outfit for a particular job. In addition, grooming and the individuality or personality accentuates the clothing. These factors are discussed in the following sections.

Garment Style

The style of a garment is a unique feature. Different garment styles express variety of expressions [7, 8]. Styles create an impression which reflects the outlook of the times. The garments can be classified in styles such as casual, formal, unisex, sophisticated and business wear. One specific style of clothing may not be suitable for people of different personalities. Hence, one should be aware to match the clothing with the personality. For example an extrovert is well matched with bright coloured and attention grabbing clothing. However, bold coloured and body revealing clothing is not appropriate for a shy and reserved personality.

Garment Fit

One should select clothing based on personal preferences [9]. However, it should be always remembered that very tight or very loose clothing may not provide a good appearance [10, 11]. An oversized-clothing makes a thin person to appear thinner. Snugly fitted clothing reveals body irregularities by emphasizing body contours. This can be minimised by using clothing with proper fit and texture, which does not follow the body contours. One should wear clothes that fit appropriately and should try to be dressed at par with the colleagues. Too small or too large clothing should be avoided. If the pants can not be pulled in smoothly in the leg, it bunches around the thighs and can not close the buttons/other fasteners, it means the pants are too small. If one can not pull the sleeve smoothly over the arms or can not bend the arm easily and the buttons can not reach to the button holes, the shirt is too small. In addition, if the gaps between the buttons of a shirt reveal the inner clothing, the shirt is too small. Similarly, the outfit should have proper fit without being baggy or floppy [12]. If necessary, the hems of the trousers and sleeves of the shirts should be shortened. If wearing glasses, one should make sure the glasses fit properly and are not sliding down the nose. A pair of glasses with loose fitting becomes distracting. It is a general fact that the sweaters, blazers or jackets should cover the clothing worn underneath; vest length should meet or extend over the pants; collars should not be baggy and the sleeves should be of right length.

Nature of Job and Clothing

The selection of appropriate clothing often depends on the nature of the job. Special personal protective clothing is necessary for jobs such as fire fighting, police, ambulance officers, defence personnel and various other specialty occupations. Each department should provide guidelines for the selection and use of appropriate personal protective clothing and equipment.

If working in a company where the job involves getting dirty, one may have more leeway in clothing selection. If the job includes customer interaction with casual style suits, a change of clothes around or something to add is ideal. Wearing a blazer or sport coat (for women) and a necktie (for men) to a basic shirt will supplement the outfit. Women should consider their body types while selecting the clothing for best fit. If uniforms or work wears are in force, one should emphasize perfect fit, neat and cleanliness of the dress. Ties should be worn while representing the company in exhibitions or conferences or important consumer meetings. They should be knotted firmly, not loosely around the shirt collar. If someone has tattoos, they should be covered at work. Covering the tattoos is almost a definite during hospital job interviews.

Dress Codes

Most organisations, including the health sector, have dress codes, which should be followed. Selecting the dress at work as per the institutional guidelines is important. The dress codes relate to identification, professional appearance, safety and hygiene. However, many companies are flexible on the dress codes. In these circumstances, casual dress can be worn on Fridays or the days when there is no special events or meetings. However, formal dress is mandatory for meetings and discussion with customers. As casual wear is becoming more popular in the modern workplace, often it could be challenging to select the outfit for a right appearance. Observing the clothing style of others especially the boss(es) is very essential while selecting the appropriate outfit. The clothing standards may be more relaxed in some occasions, however a good clothing selection and good grooming is always the standard [13]. Career and etiquette experts can be consulted to get better ideas on these. Fulfilling the employer's requirements needs planning and a set of new habits, which can help in the career success.

Dress Code During a Job Interview

During a job interview, the potential employers seek the person who can represent the values of their organisation in addition to the necessary skill and qualification [14]. During the job interview, the appearance decides whether one will fit in with the company's culture or not [15]. The way one is dressed, reveals a lots of information about self. Therefore, it is essential to make a good first impression with the interviewer [16]. A planned outfit is essential for getting selected in the interviews. The first impression created with the employer can not be altered. Hence, one should pay attention to all little details from head to toe during the interview process. In addition to the clothing, the way that one acts, communicates and stands, affects the performance. Hence, it is essential to always think positively and look good to boost self-confidence. A positive thinking indicates a high confidence level and maintaining a positive attitude indicates commitment to the job.

Dress Code in Workplace

Once selected, the person is expected to represent the company's culture. During the first few days in a job, one can watch the clothing patterns of colleagues and boss, and develop ideas on the dressing styles. If it is difficult, the person can discuss with someone who is easily approachable and has a good understanding on the clothing. To the customers, the employees are the company. Hence, the clothing style affects the relation of the company with the costumers. As a member of an organisation, one should reflect the values of the company. It is essential to self-analyse with the question "Will my clothes and appearance be matching with the events such as meeting with the boss or head?" One should always start the work fresh and neat and never let down the personal appearance.

A regular personal assessment of clothing is essential to show professionalism at the work place. The clothing and accessories should also be updated regularly to match the current fashion trend. Adding two/three clothing items every season is a good habit for keeping in line with the fashion trend. Similarly, new shoes can be added to the existing or the old shoes can be refurbished. A smiling face shows positive appearance and good feeling to co-workers. One should maintain a balanced diet plan and consult to the doctor when necessary for a healthy appearance.

Grooming

Selection of the right outfit is not the sole thing for a successful career. For a complete professional look, personal grooming and accessories are also equally important. Grooming is the way of caring for ourselves. It is the way we represent our hair, nails, skin and face. The physical attractiveness of a person can not be created, it can only be improved. Well-grooming includes styled hair, healthy skin and manicured nails, which help to improve the personality. Perfumes, mouthwashes, hairspray, deodorants are all essential parts of grooming. Grooming and the use of matched, clean and ironed clothes are always better.

Men: Men should trim the hairs in the nose, ear and neck. The nails should be short and clean. They should brush and floss the teeth daily [17]. The belt and shoes should match the selected outfit and the shoes should be well polished. The most conservative shoe styles include black/brown colour leather shoes with cap toe and wingtip designs [18]. The shirts should preferably be light coloured either plain or with stripes (horizontal/vertical) in light colours. Suitable shirt colours include white, off-white, cream, beige, pale and light yellow for office jobs. The long-sleeved shirts should always be buttoned at the cuffs and never rolled up. Plain shirt should be used with check or stripe trousers, whereas light colour shirts should be used with the complementary dark trousers. The trousers should be long enough to cover the leg but not too lengthy which fold over the shoes. Safari suits must be avoided. The socks should complement the suit and white or sport socks should be avoided. The tie should complement the suit and ties with huge patterns or cartoons should be avoided. The front end of the tie should touch the tip of the belt, whereas the back end should be properly tucked in. While not wearing a tie, the two collar buttons may be left undone, but buttoning them into the button holes is a good practice.

Women: The hair style selected by women should be neat, conservative and preferably off the face. Shocking or unusual hair colours such as blue, green and red should be avoided in office jobs. Furthermore, hair sprays and gels with strong odour should be avoided. Women should keep the nails clean and they should be trimmed or sculpted. The use of unusual or shocking nail colours should also be avoided. In business meetings nail art and nail jewels should be avoided. The makeup should be simple and appropriate. Wearing no makeup at all is as bad as wearing too much makeup [18]. The jewellery and other accessories should be carefully selected. The earrings should be small, simple and dangle above the earlobe. The jewellery worn should not be noisy (such as metal bangles or bracelets) and too large. Wearing no jewellery at all is better than wearing too much of them. All business women should wear at least a nice and conservative wrist watch. The breath should be fresh and clean so that there is no odour from the mouth. If the breath is smelly, a dentist should be consulted. Frequent gargling with mouthwash especially after eating is recommended. This also applies to working men. While selecting cologne, body sprays and deodorants with fresh and tingling smells should be selected and heavy smells should be avoided.

Clothing and Personality

Clothing also affects the degree of personal attractiveness, behavioural and physical [19]. The smartest people are the people with the most attractiveness. The attractive persons are expected to have better jobs and lead a happier life. People discount the worth of a person who is poorly dressed. The personality continually changes with the age and experience. The evidence of changing the clothing style with age is well documented in history [20, 21]. However, the modern clothing does not make any difference between the old and the young. The clothing we wear is often related to the communities and cultures we belong [22]. However, it is essential to look into the work culture while selecting clothing for work to avoid others identifying you as being different. Table 17.1 indicates the personality indications from different types of clothing. The clothing used by a person for adornment also reveals the emotions and feelings in addition to the personality [23, 24]. A range of emotions and feelings can be associated with the type of clothing as discussed in Table 17.2.

Things to be Avoided

There are certain things to be avoided people of both sexes, while working or selecting the right outfit for a work. The inner side of the handbag should be kept tidy,

Table 17.1 Personality indications from clothing styles [25]

Clothing features	Personality indications
People who emphasize comfort	Have a secure sense of identity
A person who uses old and out dated clothes	Personality indicates rigidity and inflexibility
Tight and uncomfortable clothing	Indicates tension, anxiety and inferiority
Loose and comfortable clothing	Well relate to others and comfortable about self. Cooperative, optimistic and adaptable
Choose to wear brighter clothing	If somebody is sad and feel to wear neutral or dark colour
Wear blue-green clothing	If someone want to make a positive impression
If someone avoids fashion	It indicates the person has much more things to be done rather than worrying about the clothes
People who select dark colours such as black or brown	Indicates they are depressed
Women with plain pumps and sandals	They want to understated and unobtrusive

Table 17.2 Clothing choice and emotions [25]

Emotion or feeling	Clothing choice
Happiness	Bright colour, fun-fashioned
Sadness	Sombre hue, body concealing
Youthfulness	The prevailing vogue for the teenage
Sophistication	Severe, understated, cosmopolitan
Sexuality	Body revealing
Superiority	High fashion, expensive, jewellery, club insignia, use of expensive symbols
Inferiority	Inappropriate, sleazy, worn or too perfect

especially if it has no zipper, which can attract others to have a glimpse from time to time. The use of too strong cologne or perfume should be avoided. A watch should be carefully selected, as the watch is the most common accessory drawing attention on both men and women. One should use socks with an appropriate length and try to avoid ankle socks with slacks. When crossing the legs and the pants slightly lift up, no skin should be visible. The use of excessive jewellery should be avoided. Wearing multiple necklaces, rings or bracelets can create a negative appearance. Wearing of dangling or multiple earrings should also be avoided. The use of body piercing paraphernalia such as nose rings, eyebrow and lip rings should also be kept to a minimum. Selection of an appropriate hair cut style is very essential as not every cut is going to look good on every person. If one wears non-ironed and wrinkled clothing and goes to work with untidy hair, people perceive that the person is careless. One should try to avoid: colours such as green or red, ripped jeans or skin fit T-shirts, shirts showing chest, sports cloths with emblems or large designer labels. Women should avoid contrasting undergarments under light tops.

Selection of Dress for Work

The selection of clothing depends on the type of job, clothing requirements, regulations, safety level and cultural influences. Employees in some organisations use the prescribed dress code (colour, design and style) as per the work wear policies. However, in many institutions people are free to select their clothing to express themselves. It is very hard today to predict the occupation of people from their clothes due to flexibility of clothing in many occupations. However, it is easy to identify certain types of work (such as a lawyer) if uniforms are used. In many occupations, the clothing is influenced by the current fashion trend, in spite of reflecting one's individual choices. Unless restricted, today's working men and women are not limited to the narrow range of dresses. A wide range of clothing differing in colour, design and style are available for them.

Clothing Selection Criteria

The selection of clothing depends primarily on the type work in the office. In addition, the body type, the appropriateness of colour and design, climatic conditions and other functional requirements are taken into consideration [26–28]. Clothing affects one's way of thinking. It has been shown that ladies dressed in a masculine manner during a job interview are more likely to be hired [29]. A study revealed that a teacher with formal cloth is perceived as more intelligent than the teacher with casual dress. In this study it was also reported that clothes can reveal one's employment, ambitions, emotions and spending habits. The research explained how psychology affects clothing choice and the ways to overcome key psychological issues related to clothing selection.

Improper clothing can not only prohibit us from doing our job properly but also change our perception by others at work. The physical appearance of a person plays an important role in the selection of the clothing. One should analyse their own features objectively in order to select the right clothing to enhance the assets and camouflage the problems. The appropriate clothing selection and body postures affect the degree of liking and attraction of a person. The following section highlights the criteria for appropriate clothing selection.

Influence of Colour

Colour is the first and most important element to which consumers/clients respond while selecting clothing [30, 31]. Colour expresses the language, reflects the personality and portrays the emotions [32, 33]. People relate personality to colour, usually either selecting or rejecting clothing because of its colour appeal. Colour affects personality because it causes emotional responses, and colour selection is based on events in lives and culture. Each person has colour liking and disliking. Clothing colours can reveal the ease or seriousness of a person [34]. The first impression of a person is influenced by the clothing colours and the style of dressing.

Table 17.3 Different colours and their suitability for various clothing types

Colour type	Expressions	Suitability for outfit type
Warm: red, yellow and orange	These colours are associated with fire and sun, and they are stimulating, aggressive and lively. Red is exciting, fiery and dangerous. It indicates valentine, love and romance. Yellow is bright, sunny, cheerful, friendly and optimistic. Intense orange is irritating and overpowering	Red: sportswear and eveningwear. Yellow: often difficult colour to wear and used for retro-reflective clothing and some other purposes. Orange: difficult colour to wear like yellow and limited to active wear and retroreflective clothing
Cool: blue, green and purple	These colours are associated with the sky and the sea and are refreshing and represent coolness. Blue suggests quiet, restful and reserved. Green is the most refreshing colour, indicating peace, rest and quiet	Blue: used in very high (pale blue) or very low (navy blue) values in clothing. Navy blue is one of the most popular clothing colours for spring or summer line. Green: least preferred for dresses, popular for interior design. Purple: sparingly used for women's clothing
Neutral: white, black, gray, beige, tan and brown	These colours present a pleasing background for the wearer without competing for attention. White is associated with purity and cleanliness for which doctors and nurses have traditionally worn it. Also as white reflects light, it is considered to be cool for summer wear. In western culture black is considered to be associated with death and villains. However, it is a sophisticated and important fashion colour	Neutrals are part of every season's fashion picture. White: outfit for doctors and nurses, and summer wear. Black: used in isolation or combination with other colours for many clothing

Colour can be classified as warm, cool and neutral [35, 36]. Red, yellow and orange are considered as warm; blue, green and purple are known as cool; and white, black, gray, beige, tan and brown are neutral colours. These colours create different impressions and are suitable for specific outfit as described in Table 17.3.

While selecting suitable colours for clothing, the skin, hair and eye colours should be taken into consideration [37]. Furthermore, colours should be selected according to the season, occasion, climatic conditions and type of the garment. Although, there is no governing rule for selection of colours, the colour combinations should be judiciously selected to make harmony and enhance the personality [31, 33]. There is no limit to the kinds and varieties of colour combinations. Colours create illusions, for example a garment in one colour creates the illusion of height. Warm, light or bright colours advance visually, making a design seems large; whereas cool, dark colours recede causing the figure to look small and slender. The contrasts in tone and contrasts in chroma are frequently used to disguise figure problems. Certain individual colours or colour combinations are more pleasing to some people. Each person need to experiment with various colour combinations by considering both physical and psychological self and establishing most harmonising colour combinations.

Influence of Design

The arrangement of lines, patterns, colour and texture is known as the design. Lines are an important element of design, which determine the direction of visual interest in dress. Straight lines indicate crispness and curved lines imply buoyancy. Lines have the power to create moods and feeling. Vertical lines indicate upright, majestic figures and stability. Horizontal lines are like lines at rest and they suggest repose, quiet and calmness. Soft curving lines express grace. Diagonal lines imply powerful movement and vitality, and indicate the feeling of movement. Zigzag lines create excitement but are often disconcerting.

Line should be properly interpreted for each figure type [38]. Long, unbroken vertical lines are most effective in adding height. The longer and stronger the line, the more effective it is. Vertical lines can be further strengthened by accentuating them with contrasting trimmings or buttons. The eye judges any measurement of length or width in relation to other measurements in the same composition. Longer skirts make the wearer appear taller and slimmer simply because their length is greater than their width [39]. Horizontal lines widen the figure i.e. they add bulk or mass to the figure. A contrasting belt on a dress cuts the average figure in to two, creating two chunky portions instead of one long and thin shape. The use of illusion is important in men's wear. Generally, men want to look taller and stronger. Therefore, throughout history manufacturers of men's clothing have tended to increase men's stature with vertical lines in jackets and trousers with built-up shoulders.

Functional Requirements

Functional requirements are an important issue in deciding what we wear at work. There are varieties of tasks such as fire fighting, military, chemical and biological industry, where the protective clothing must be used for personal protection [40–42]. For example in biological industry the hazards are mainly caused by the microorganisms or contamination [43]. In hospitals, exposure to hazardous bacteria and viruses from contaminated blood, bodily fluids or other similar objects can lead to the risks related to the biological hazards. In some instances the airborne pathogens may cause potential threat. The protective clothing used for chemical protection is mainly used for dermal exposure and lowering the risk of injury or illness. In addition to the required level of protection, the protective clothing should be comfortable to wear, should not restrict body movement and should be easy to produce commercially.

Comfort and Fit

While selecting clothing, in addition to the style and design, comfort and fit are also important parameters to be considered [44]. One should avoid using uncomfortable clothes, as it overrides the professionalism of an outfit. Everyone should have specific clothing items which are not only pleasant but also comfortable. In addition, fit is also an essential criteria for the selection of clothing. Perfect fit provides good appearance, physical comfort and self-confidence. The clothing should fit properly while seating, working, standing and bending. Clothing with improper fit can never be attractive. One should always check the clothing fit both in motion and stand still.

Clothing for Doctors and Nurses

The ways that the doctors and nurses dress and address their patients are likely to influence the development of the relationship between them [45–49]. The patients are also psychologically affected by the ways of clothing of the physicians [47]. In many hospitals, the surgery staff are differentiated from the patient care and other supportive staff by the use of different colour codes [50]. In some instances they can be custom made with cartoon characters or cheerful prints for children's hospitals, veterinary offices or paediatricians.

The types of clothing used by physicians affect patient's confidence. It was observed in a study that the professional attire inspired the most confidence on patients [51]. The confidence level of patients improved significantly with the professional clinical attire compared to the casual or scrub outfit. In another study the trust and confidence of patients was found to be significantly associated with physician's preference for professional dress [52]. The respondents were significantly more willing to share their social, sexual and psychological problems with the physician who were professionally dressed. The importance of female physicians' dress appeared to be significantly higher than the male physicians' dress.

It was observed that the resident physician's attire makes a difference to the patients [46]. The comfort level of patients and their perceptions of physician's (both male and female) competence were the highest in response to images of physicians dressed in scrubs with a white coat and least for casual dress. Similarly, patients expressed a preference for doctors wearing name tags, white coats and short hair but disapproved of clogs, jeans, trainers and earrings [53].

Physician Accessories and Hospital Acquired Infections

Feldman et al. studied colonisation of purses of 13 women doctors working in a hospital and of 14 non-health care women who had not visited a hospital in previous six months (controls) [54]. Their results showed that 9/13 doctors' purses were colonized with bacteria compared with 2/14 of controls [54]. Gopinath et al. assessed bacterial colonization rates among randomly selected pagers and stethoscopes [55]. They reported that 15 (25%) pagers and 11 (27.5%) stethoscopes were contaminated, with no significant difference in the colonization rates between shared and personal pagers [55]. Abuannadi et al. reported that bacteria commonly colonize in neckties and avoiding neckties may help in preventing nosocomial infections [56]. Lopez et al. reported significantly higher bacterial counts from ties that were rarely, if ever, cleaned than from shirts that were washed every two days or more frequently [57]. Weber et al. reported that an unsecured tie resulted in greater transmission of pathogens, but the sleeve length did not affect transmission rate [58]. Kotsanas et al. reported that identity badges and lanyards worn by health care workers may be contaminated with pathogens [58]. Wearing uniform at work, even if short sleeved, and newly laundered, may not reduce the risk of colonisation of physician's attire [59]. Wiener-Well et al. reported that up to 60% of hospital staff's uniforms were colonized with potentially pathogens [60]. Burden et al. showed that bacterial contamination occurs within hours after donning newly laundered short-sleeved uniforms [61]. After 8 h of wear, no difference was observed in the degree of contamination of uniforms compared with the infrequently laundered white coats. Thus their data did not support discarding long-sleeved white coats for short-sleeved uniforms changed daily [61]. Dancer et al. point out that it is not clear whether colonisation of physician attire and/or accessories actually increases the risk of hospital acquired infections [62]. Overall, the current evidence indicate that physician's attire and accessories are potential source of hospital acquired infections [63]. It is recommended that they should not be worn when leaving the hospital.

Summary

The first impression of a person can be made from the clothing of the person. The attractiveness and appropriateness of clothing affect the managerial abilities, credibility, task performance and perceptions of competence and intelligence. The positive psychological effects of wearing an appropriate outfit in a workplace are experienced by many people. An appropriate outfit elicits positive comments and compliments from others, which can boost the morale. On contrary, inappropriate clothing in a job can generate negative evaluations and reactions from others, which can undermine self-confidence. An appropriate dress at work not only helps in creating an image of professionalism and discipline, but also helps in motivating and communicating with colleagues at work. The perception of clothing depends on the person making the judgement. Generally, people wearing similar dresses are approving of each other; however, they are critical for those dressing differently. Higher is the difference, the harsher is the criticism. There are several studies supporting the old adage 'clothes make the man'.

References

1. Stebbins S (2012) [cited 2013 10 December] How to dress for success. http://www.realsimple. com/beauty-fashion/clothing/dress-for-success-00100000087310/. Accessed 29 Nov 2013
2. Behling DU, Williams EA (1991) Influence of dress on perception of intelligence and expectations of scholastic achievement. Cloth Text Res J 9:1–7
3. Blustein D (2006) The psychology of working: a new perspective for career development, counseling, and public policy. Routledge, New York
4. Adam H, Galinsky AD (2012) Enclothed cognition. J Exp Soc Psychol 48:918–925
5. O'Neal GS, Lapitsky M (1991) Effects of clothing as nonverbal communication on credibility of the message source. Cloth Text Res J 9:28–34
6. Smith J. (2013) [cited 2014 10 January] Dressing for sucess. http://misscareer.org.nz/ dressing-for-success/. Accessed 29 Nov 2013
7. Paek SL (1986) Effect of garment style on the perception of personal traits. Cloth Text Res J 5:10–16
8. Hamid PN (1968) Style of dress as a perceptual cue in impression formation. Percept Mot Sk 26:904–906
9. Raunio AM (1982) Favorite clothes—a look at individuals' experience of clothing. Research Report No. 16. Clothing and its Social, Psychological, Cultural and Environmental Aspects 179–94
10. Brockman HL (1965) The theory of fashion design. Wiley, New York
11. McJimsey HT (1973) Art and fashion in clothing selection. Iowa State University Press, Ames
12. Fan J, Yu W, Hunter L (2004) Clothing appearance and fit: science and technology. CRC Press, Boca Raton
13. Getting the cloth you need (2013) http://urbanext.illinois.edu/dress/08-job-success-04casual. cfm. Accessed 29 Nov 2013
14. Harris MB et al (1983) Clothing: communication, compliance, and choice. J Appl Soc Psychol 13:88–97
15. Forsythe S, Drake MF, Cox CE (1985) Influence of applicant's dress on interviewer's selection decisions. J Appl Psychol 70:374
16. Rucker M, Taber D, Harrison A (1981) The effect of clothing variation on first impressions of female job applicants: what to wear when. Social Behav Personal Int J 9:53–64
17. Personal grooming tips for men (2013) [cited 2014 15 December] http://management-studyguide.com/personal-grooming-tips-for-men.htm. Accessed 29 Nov 2013
18. Personal grooming & clothing—men & women (2013) [cited 2013 12 December] http:// www.citehr.com/54403-personal-grooming-clothing-men-women.html. Accessed 29 Nov 2013
19. Eagly AH et al (1991) What is beautiful is good, but…. A meta-analytic review of research on the physical attractiveness stereotype. Psychol Bull 110:109
20. Richards ML (1981) The clothing preferences and problems of elderly female consumers. Gerontol 21:263–267
21. Klepp IG, Storm-Mathisen A (2005) Reading fashion as age: teenage girls' and grown women's accounts of clothing as body and social status. Fash Theory J Dress, Body Cult 9:323–342
22. Hsu HJ, Burns LD (2002) Clothing evaluative criteria: a cross-national comparison of Taiwanese and United States consumers. Cloth Text Res J 20:246–252
23. Kwon YH (1994) Feeling toward one's clothing and self-perception of emotion, sociability, and work competency. J Soc Behav Personal 9:129–139
24. Colls R (2004) 'Looking alright, feeling alright': emotions, sizing and the geographies of women's experiences of clothing consumption. Soc Cult Geogr 5:583–596
25. Kefgen M, Touchie-Specht P (1971) Individuality in clothing selection and personal appearance: a guide for the consumer. Macmillan, New York

26. Cassill NL, Drake MF (1987) Apparel selection criteria related to female consumers' lifestyle. Cloth Text Res J 6:20–28
27. Donaldson G, Rintamäki HJ, Näyhä S (2001) Outdoor clothing: its relationship to geography, climate, behaviour and cold-related mortality in Europe. Int J Biometeorol 45:45–51
28. Gupta D (2011) Design and engineering of functional clothing. Indian J Fibre Text Res. 36:327
29. Forsythe SM (1988) Effect of clothing masculinity on perceptions of managerial traits: Does gender of the perceiver make a difference? Cloth Text Res J 6:10–16
30. Radeloff DJ (1990) Role of color in perception of attractiveness. Percept Mot Sk 71:151–160
31. Radeloff DJ (1991) Psychological types, color attributes, and color preferences of clothing, textiles, and design students. Cloth Text Res J 9:59–67
32. Valdez P, Mehrabian A (1994) Effects of color on emotions. J Exp Psychol 123:394
33. Lind C (1993) Psychology of color: similarities between abstract and clothing color preferences. Cloth Text Res J 12:57–65
34. Eysenck HJ (1947) Dimensions of personality, vol 5. Transaction, New Brunswick
35. Ou LC et al (2004) A study of colour emotion and colour preference. Part I: colour emotions for single colours. Color Res Appl 29:232–240
36. Nayak R, Mahish S (2006) Colour psychology and perception. Asian Dyer 3(2):61–66
37. Hsiao SW, Chiu FY, Hsu HY (2008) A computer-assisted colour selection system based on aesthetic measure for colour harmony and fuzzy logic theory. Color Res Appl 33:411–423
38. Raes B (2011) Slim your body with fashion optical illusion. http://www.bridgetteraes.com/2011/11/03/slim-your-body-with-these-fashion-optical-illusions/. Accessed 29 Nov 2013
39. Thompson P, Mikellidou K (2011) Applying the Helmholtz illusion to fashion: horizontal stripes won't make you look fatter. i-Percept 2:69
40. Krueger GP (2001) Psychological and performance effects of chemical-biological protective clothing and equipment. Mil Med 166:41–43
41. Scott RA (2005) Textiles for protection. Woodhead, Cambridge
42. Horrocks AR, Anand SC (2000) Handbook of technical textiles. Woodhead, Cambridge
43. Schreuder-Gibson HL et al (2003) Chemical and biological protection and detection in fabrics for protective clothing. MRS Bull 28:574–578
44. Daters CM (1990) Importance of clothing and self-esteem among adolescents. Cloth Text Res J 8:45–50
45. Gherardi G et al (2009) Are we dressed to impress? A descriptive survey assessing patients' preference of doctors' attire in the hospital setting. Clin Med 9:519–524
46. Cha A et al (2004) Resident physician attire: does it make a difference to our patients? Am J Obstet Gynecol 190:1484–1488
47. Palazzo S, Hocken D (2010) Patients' perspectives on how doctors dress. J Hosp Infect 74:30–34
48. Bond L et al (2010) Patients' perceptions of doctors' clothing: should we really be 'bare below the elbow'? J Laryngol Otol 124:963–966
49. Brase GL, Richmond J (2004) The white–coat effect: physician attire and perceived authority, friendliness, and attractiveness. J Appl Soc Psychol 34:2469–2481
50. Suprun N, Vlasenko V, Ostrovetchkhaya Y (2003) Some aspects of medical clothing manufacturing. Int J Cloth Sci Technol 15:224–230
51. Budny AM et al (2006) The physician's attire and its influence on patient confidence. J Am Podiatr Med Assoc 96:132–138
52. Rehman SU et al (2005) What to wear today? Effect of doctor's attire on the trust and confidence of patients. Am J Med 118:1279–1286
53. Hennessy N, Harrison D, Aitkenhead A (1993) The effect of the anaesthetist's attire on patient attitudes. Anaesthesia 48:219–222
54. Feldman J, Feldman J, Feldman M (2012) Women doctors' purses as an unrecognized fomite. Del Med J 84:277–280

55. Gopinath KG, Stanley S, Mathai E, Chandy GM (2011) Pagers and stethoscopes as vehicles of potential nosocomial pathogens in a tertiary care hospital in a developing country. Trop Doct 41:43–45
56. Abuannadi M, O'Keefe JH, Brewer J (2010) Neckties for physicians: yes? no? maybe? Mo Med 107:366–367
57. Lopez PJ, Ron O, Parthasarathy P, Soothill J, Spitz L (2009) Bacterial counts from hospital doctors' ties are higher than those from shirts. Am J Infect Control 37:79–80
58. Weber RL, Khan PD, Fader RC, Weber RA (2012) Prospective study on the effect of shirt sleeves and ties on the transmission of bacteria to patients. J Hosp Infect 80:252–254
59. Kotsanas D, Scott C, Gillespie EE, Korman TM, Stuart RL (2008) What's hanging around your neck? Pathogenic bacteria on identity badges and lanyards. Med J Aust 188:5–8
60. Wiener-Well Y, Galuty M, Rudensky B, Schlesinger Y, Attias D, Yinnon AM (2011) Nursing and physician attire as possible source of nosocomial infections. Am J Infect Control 39:555–559
61. Burden M, Cervantes L, Weed D, Keniston A, Price CS, Albert RK (2011) Newly cleaned physician uniforms and infrequently washed white coats have similar rates of bacterial contamination after an 8-hour workday: a randomized controlled trial. J Hosp Med 6:177–182
62. Dancer SJ (2013) Put your ties back on: scruffy doctors damage our reputation and indicate a decline in hygiene. BMJ 346:f3211
63. Pandey A, Asthana AK, Tiwari R, Kumar L, Das A, Madan M (2010) Physician accessories: doctor, what you carry is every patient's worry? Indian J Pathol Microbiol 53:711–713

Chapter 18
Managing Ethically Complex Issues in Critically Ill Patients—A Neonatal Perspective

Paul Byrne and Brendan Leier

> *The secret in caring for the patient is to care about the patient*
> —Francis W. Peabody MD 1925

Abstract Ethically complex issues are commonly encountered in critically ill patients in intensive care units and usually relate to disagreements about care in such high risk situations. Because the clinical course is often uncertain and unpredictable, serious disagreements about the plan and priorities of care occur. This is presented simplistically as a conflict between the (surrogate) autonomy of the family members and the physician (health care professional) authority, in promoting the *patient's best interests*. The ethical issues emerge only when discussion includes broader concerns about morbidity, mortality, and meaning to family and the hospital staff. We review the theoretical ethical basis of decision-making in such situations in the context of neonatal intensive care units and recommend that the physician focuses on the professional role of *advocate* for the infant's best interests. Reflective conversations with family, including openness about uncertainty and willingness to re-evaluate care plans, are essential to maintain trust. This mediation approach supports different moral views in an atmosphere of mutual respect. Expert ethics assistance early on in high risk cases is recommended. We suggest that this be provided by an ethics consulting service readily available to the staff for optimizing care and preventing the development of crises.

Keywords Neonate · Ethics · Intensive care · Perinatal · Best interests · Clinical ethicist · Theory · Ethical basis · Models of ethics · Family centered · Extreme prematurity · Severe encephalopathy · Hypoplastic left heart · Congenital anomalies · Prognostic points · Complex cases · Decision making

P. Byrne (✉)
Stollery Children's Hospital, John Dossetor Health Ethics Centre, University of Alberta,
5–16 University Terrace, Edmonton, AB, T6G 2T4, Canada
e-mail: Paul.Byrne@albertahealthservices.ca

B. Leier
Stollery Children's Hospitals & Mazankowski Alberta Heart Institute, John Dossetor Health Ethics Centre, University of Alberta, Edmonton, Canada

© Springer International Publishing Switzerland 2015
S. Patole (ed.), *Management and Leadership – A Guide for Clinical Professionals,*
DOI 10.1007/978-3-319-11526-9_18

257

Key Points

1. Ethically complex issues are common in intensive care units and relate to clearly identifiable groups of patients
2. These problems can be anticipated before crises occur
3. Early involvement of an ethics consultation service will more likely prevent crises
4. Ethics education will enhance staff understanding of underlying issues
5. Institutional and health care professional's support is essential for success of an ethics consultation service

Management of ethically complex issues in critically ill patients is a difficult and stressful issue for the clinical (e.g. doctors, nurses) as well as non-clinical (e.g. hospital administration, legal support services, ethics committee members) staff in a hospital. Considering the potential for conflict and the stress on the families of such patients, the risk of litigations is high in such situation. Needless to say without formal training, the process of decision making for such patients is difficult for the front line staff, especially those who are inexperienced. We provide the perspective from neonatal intensive care in the management of ethically complex cases.

The progress and expansion of the neonatal intensive care unit (NICU) over the past five decades has been dramatic. Neonatal intensive care units are now an integral part of high-risk perinatal regional centers. The availability of neonatal expertise in decision-making extends from prenatal and intrapartum consultation to ongoing neonatal care for weeks and months after birth [1, 2]. The improvement in survival and in long term outcome of high-risk infants has been remarkable such that the majority of deaths occur after limitation or withdrawal of life supporting treatment (LST) [2–6]. This positive outcome for the vast majority of NICU graduates has contributed to an expectation that all infants admitted to NICU will survive and have a normal outcome long term. Death in NICU is now very unusual even among three clearly identifiable high-risk groups of infants; the extremely preterm, those with severe life-threatening congenital anomalies, and severely encephalopathic infants. Most ethically complex issues in the NICU relate to problems concerning the care of infants from these three high risk groups [6–10].

Despite dramatically improved outcomes for neonates in NICU, there remains a small percentage of infants for whom survival is fraught with serious life-threatening complications, both acutely and long term. Whenever this degree of increased risk can be identified prenatally, as in the case of multiple congenital anomalies, threatened extremely premature labour, severe intrauterine growth restriction or indications of chronic foetal distress, discussion with the family about the appropriate course of action can begin before birth [1, 6, 10–12]. Unfortunately in many cases clear identification and prediction of risk may not be possible prenatally. In addition in cases where predictions have been made prenatally, the clinical situation may change suddenly during pregnancy, intrapartum or in the NICU. This element of *clinical uncertainty* is always present in complex cases in NICU and makes clinical and ethical decision-making over time very difficult. It is this element of clinical uncertainty, allied with failure of the infant to respond as expected to LST, that contributes to the ethically complex situations most frequently encountered in the NICU [13–15].This chapter will focus on how to deal with these situations from a clinical ethics perspective and use them to illustrate how beneficial a clinical ethics service can be to the infants, families and staff in perinatal care and specifically in the NICU.

Case Based Clinical Ethics

We describe case examples to illustrate what we see as common causes of ethical complexity in NICU. Although the examples are hypothetical they represent situations that we encounter and are discussed in the neonatal ethics literature [2, 7–10, 16–18]. We identify "Prognostic Points" (PPs) to show how case based discussions flow in practice. While disagreement about medical evidence quality concerning these PPs likely exists, we see health care professionals (HCPs) using these PPs to discuss risks and benefits of treatments, goals of care, and end of life decisions. As such the PPs act as starting points for broader discussion if the course deteriorates and disagreements develop. Theoretical models of ethical analysis go beyond clinical parameters, but in NICU ethical concerns usually begin with disagreements about medical facts.

Case Examples

1. **Extreme Prematurity**
   A 43 year old mother G4 P0 is in labour at 25/52 with a twin gestation. Severe foetal distress is detected and an emergency C. Section is undertaken. There is only time for brief NICU prenatal consultation explaining each infant's appearance, estimated birth weight, and treatments required after birth. Twin A is born with apnoea, requires resuscitation, and responds well. Birth weight (BW) 680 g. Apgars 2, 8 at 1, 5 min. She develops respiratory distress, hypotension and hypoglycaemia, which respond to treatment. By day 7 she is on feeds, and clinically stable. Cranial ultrasound shows bilateral intraventricular haemorrhage (IVH) with ventricular dilatation. On day 12 she is diagnosed with necrotizing enterocolitis (NEC) with perforation.
   Twin B was stillborn.

Prognostic Points
Good: Easy resuscitation, clinically stable.

Bad: Foetal distress, emergency c-section, gestation 25 weeks, ? bilateral IVH plus dilated ventricles, and NEC with perforation.

2. Severe Encephalopathy

A 26 year old mother G3P2 with gestational diabetes is admitted at term in labour. Towards the end of labour she develops a large haemorrhage. Delivery is precipitous and the full term male infant requires resuscitation including endotracheal intubation, ventilation, CPR and IV epinephrine. BW 3600 g, Apgars are 1, 2, and 8 at 1, 5, 10 min. A large retroplacental clot is noted. The infant is ventilated, requires inotrope support, and develops systemic hypotension, pulmonary hypertension, and acute renal failure. He receives a blood transfusion for anaemia. He is treated with total body cooling for hypoxic ischaemic encephalopathy (HIE). Electroencephalography (EEG) shows multifocal seizures and a burst suppression pattern consistent with moderate to severe HIE. On day 3 brain MRI shows widespread oedema and bilateral cortical ischemic injury. He remains on ventilator support and has irregular spontaneous breathing. Systemic hypotension, pulmonary hypertension and renal failure have resolved. He is on maintenance anticonvulsant therapy with no clinical seizures. He remains NPO and on total parenteral nutrition.

Prognostic Points

Good: Acute (not chronic) hypoxic-ischaemic insult, Responded well to resuscitation, Transient multi—organ dysfunction resolved.

Bad: Large antepartum haemorrhage, moderate to severe HIE, abnormal MRI day 3 suggestive of bilateral cortical ischaemic injury, serious EEG abnormality.

3. Major Congenital Anomalies

A 36 year old mother G2P1 delivers at term with prenatal diagnosis of severe intrauterine growth restriction (IUGR), foetal anomalies including congenital heart disease, single kidney, absent corpus callosum. Amniocentesis 46 XY. Vaginal birth, BW 1820 g. Apgars 6, 9 at 1, 5 min. Infant develops persistent cyanosis and tachypnoea, He is intubated, ventilated, started on prostaglandin infusion. Echocardiography reveals pulmonary atresia, hypoplastic right ventricle, small left ventricle. Investigations reveal single right kidney, vertebral abnormalities, and esophageal atresia. Cranial ultrasound confirms absent corpus callosum.

Prognostic Points

Good: Vigorous at birth, clinically stable, chromosomes normal.

Bad: Multiple serious congenital anomalies, severe IUGR.

These "paradigm cases" are familiar and many neonatologists reading the brief descriptions will already have decided on a plan. This ability to rapidly process information is important in ICU especially with emergencies but is prone to error and subject to cognitive biases which contribute to clinical error [19]. One such bias in NICU is of selectively applying population data to individuals [20]. This data based approach ignores the fact that each infant and family is a more complex social unit than suggested by statistics of birth weight, gestational age, diagnosis, etc. requiring careful consideration [6, 11, 21–23]. In perinatology failure to examine this broader family and cultural context early on, will likely result in later conflict [11, 13, 20–22].

Handling Complex Cases

High risk perinatal care involves decision-making over hours, days, weeks, months for infants and families. Initially quality of care is consistent with expectations but when the course remains critical over days and weeks, opinions begin to differ. This is consistent with new information leading to better understanding of the complexity involved. Crucially it also relates to expectations being not realised beyond immediate medical parameters [12, 17, 21, 24]. Questions and differing opinions give way to doubts about the care plan's validity. Often a round of "novel" invasive higher risk treatments, are tried as part of LST While this may be dramatically life-saving, a "clinical status quo", is more often maintained with slow deterioration unless LST limitation or withdrawal is considered [2–6, 18, 25]. A delayed family awareness of disagreements leads to further confusion, stress and anxiety. The trusting relationship usually existing between family and NICU HCPs becomes eroded as the infant deteriorates and the care plan remains officially unquestioned.

Most ethically complex situations do not develop suddenly. They evolve as a worsening clinical scenario often due to our ability to support life long after the possibility of cure. Keeping family informed is recognized as an essential to shared decision-making, in keeping with the principles of consent and the philosophy of family centered care [6, 26–28]. This 'informing' may only occur as statistical estimates of survival. Consideration of any broader meaning may be neglected [6, 22, 28–30]. The ability of physicians to undertake such discussion varies and it may be relegated to junior HCPs or overlooked entirely [31]. Misunderstanding is common due to jargon, and the "wrong words" [31, 32]. The family's loss of trust may manifest as emotional instability, unrelenting questioning, and confrontations with staff. At such times NICU staff must strive to restore trust by utilizing mediation techniques and expertise. A key step is to enquire if the family can identify somebody they wish to include in discussions such as a. previously trusted HCP, friend, relative, cultural or religious community member.

Despite a prolonged critical course discussion of death may be avoided until the infant is moribund. The ensuing discussion frequently focuses on worsening statistics about survival and of serious disability. What is required in such cases before crises occur is an ongoing reflective process by HCPs and family, which includes self-reflection. For HCPs this is difficult as it introduces personal and professional beliefs that traditionally do not get expressed or explored. Such considerations delve beyond the usual risk–benefit calculus with which HCPs feel comfortable. However, reflection and openness to clinical and ethical uncertainty, is in keeping with a shared model of decision-making [1, 2, 26, 27]. Acknowledgement of clinical uncertainty goes contrary to the science-technology medical paradigm of neonatology being a speciality paternalistically devoted to saving fragile infants [33]. This reflective process may not be encouraged as it flies in the face of the traditional paternalistic culture and recently described patterns of patient directed treatment [34]. Refusal of physicians to re-evaluate treatment plans remains a serious example of cognitive bias [19].

Unavoidable changes in HCPs introduce many individuals with different opinions regarding the care. Any loss of trust by family may bear strongly on the quality of care. The infant's care needs may recede as a battle rages for the "right answer" to medical complications. An enormous professional effort is required to remain engaged with family when mutual respect is strained to breaking point [36]. While ethics expertise may help differing opinions and values to be expressed, understood and respected, it may be too late to be effective in the above scenario. Ideally ethics consultation assists with understanding the ethical basis of the current problems and how to resolve them [35–37]. It is early on in these situations (well recognized by HCPs), that ethics consultation is likely to help. In NICU when treatments considered effective no longer work a shift occurs away from choices supported by medical evidence, to novel or experimental approaches usually without ethical input. Such choices require assessment of complex probabilities of risk, and of beliefs and values about meaning, beyond clinical data. At a minimum, discussion of the family's understanding of risk, and values and beliefs is required. The potential conflict between the infant's interests and other interests, (including family and HCPs) requires examination [14, 22, 35]. The ethical substitute decision-making standard requires that the focus be exclusively on "infant best interests" [1, 2, 6, 9, 22, 33, 35]. In complex cases this approach is simplistic ignoring both difficulties in defining best interest and of legitimate competing moral interests. While frequently described as conflict between parental autonomy and professional authority, the reality is more nuanced and complex [1, 3, 6, 12–14, 18, 21, 23, 25, 38, 39].

The needs of the NICU infants, families and staff for ethical clarity about complex issues will be similar across many variations in national and international practice. Ethical dilemmas rooted in the complex clinical details of high-risk perinatology constitute the majority of situations requiring ethics consultations. Discussion of the extremely premature infant, the infant with severe encephalopathy, or the infant with multiple severe congenital anomalies, all require a cultivated atmosphere of trust, respect for different opinions, and knowledge about the ethical issues underlying these dilemmas. In this situation families and staff will likely experience the benefit of ethical clarity provided by a clinical ethicist. While a clear answer will not always be possible (otherwise an ethics consult is unlikely to be needed in the first place), the consultation process should be directed towards helping family and care providers at least in seeing the ethical issues and possible solutions more clearly.

Theory and the Ethical Basis of Decision-Making in NICU

Western medicine has a clear moral guideline from the Hippocratic tradition as a reminder that medical practice is eudaemonistic, that is, a reflective activity focused on clinical and moral excellence. Although modern health ethics focuses on "patient rights" and "family-centered" care, and various court jurisdictions influence medical decision-making, the physician's fiduciary duty remains as advocate for patients above all other obligations [35–37, 40]. We emphasize this because today the physician's role is no longer "voice of authority" but one of many voices, inside a care-team, institution, region, etc [26, 27, 36–39]. This decentralization of decision-making is reflected in health ethics teaching approaches *sub specie aeternitatis* that is, from an "objective" rather than embedded perspective [27, 32, 35–37, 41]. This perspective supposes that a single correct course of action can be reached on principles, i.e., "what is the right thing to do" as opposed to, "what is right for a *physician to do in this situation*". Rather than suggesting general frameworks or algorithms, we offer a conceptual discussion of ethical themes faced by physicians. We do not provide an algorithm about good ethical decisions because most dilemmas demonstrate conflict between the principles which ethics algorithms propose (e.g. patient autonomy vs beneficence), and because such principles draw clinicians into "objective" analysis [27, 35–37]. This "objective reflection" is thinking we discourage in the neonatologist. Clinical neonatology is practiced in a world of significant unresolved philosophical issues; e.g. who determines, and what constitutes treatments offered in the best interest of infants? [1, 2, 6, 9, 12, 22, 33, 36, 38, 39] Given this, the primary ethical task of the neonatologist *as advocate* is reflection on key issues and one's role in relation to them.

Medical ethics has shifted from a paternalistic to patient-centered account with respect for patient autonomy as central [27, 35–37]. Legislation and common law support this and describe the rights of patients to participate in medical decisions [26, 27, 35–37]. The tool assuring patient autonomy (patient consent) is the *de facto* conceptual standard in Western medicine. Despite differences between the (old) paternal and (new) patient autonomy paradigms, they are similar in that *both reduce to a standard of best interest*. Paternalism involves an expert (physician) making recommendations about medical risks versus benefits from the medical view alone with information flowing from physician to patient. The patient autonomy paradigm is based on empirical psychological observations that individuals use factors, beyond medical data, to make decisions (about health). This psychometric risk paradigm describes how individuals make decisions, especially under uncertainty (a characterization of most medical decision) [42]. These factors include psychological traits, beliefs, hopes, fears, cultural background, etc. that are profoundly subjective and undeterminable to clinicians. The patient autonomy paradigm casts decision-making as bi-directional dialogue between medical expert and patient. Information moves between physician and patient for consensual decisions. The right of a competent patient to be the final arbiter up to, and including, the ability to refuse LST is established. The significance of legal cases affirming this right is that justification extends beyond medical efficacy. Legal examples include affirmation of the rights of members of Jehovah's Witness community to refuse whole blood products for themselves [43]. When patients are no longer competent, surrogate decisions are guided by the known or expressed interests of the patient [35–37]. In the absence of prior wishes, a *best interest standard* is used. In NICU decision-making and the relationship between physician, patient, and surrogate (hereon parent) is complex in two ways: (1) neonates cannot (and never could) express, values, beliefs, wishes, etc. (2) neonates do not possess psychological characteristics that have subjective variability in preference, capacity, personality, etc., to justify significant inter—patient variation in LST.

Parents, however have unique preferences based on the aforementioned psychometric variables [21, 22, 38, 39, 42]. One set of parents might find inclusion of a severely disabled child consistent with family well-being, another set may not. If LST will likely result in such a child, do parents have the right to accept or refuse LST? The first legal and ethical question for the neonatologist is: what form does limiting the surrogate medical decisions take in NICU? (i.e., legislation, policy, "standard of care", etc) Limitation of parental rights presents difficulties if it is unclear what precedent exists [2–6, 13, 16, 25, 33, 35, 36, 38, 39]. The neonatologist must understand limits concerning responsibilities, rights, and degrees to which parental choice may diverge from medical advice.

A strong legal paternalistic presence remains in Western democracies, expressed as *parens patriae* [35–38, 44]. This concept describes the state's duty where parents or guardians are not fulfilling responsibilities to children. While a competent adult Jehovah's Witness has the right to refuse whole-blood products this does not confer the right to refuse such for a child, even as the child's legal guardian. For parents and NICU staff it may come as a shock that parental choice may be over-ruled by *parens patriae*. If the neonatologist judges that a treatment or procedure is in an infant's best interest, the fiduciary responsibility is to proceed with it. In cases of disagreement, this advocacy is exercised locally via ethics consultation, legal process or involvement of government child-welfare agency. Just as protection involves the State's utilization of *parens patriae,* the physician's role is as *patient advocate* not as moral arbiter. In this way the NICU team is not seen to be forcing treatment but supporting infant's best interests.

Establishing consensus on the philosophical—ethical concept of pediatric best interest is exceptionally difficult. Even if NICU physicians cannot come to a philosophical conclusion, the reflective process is essential to effective advocacy and to promote understanding of the complex moral dilemmas that the advancement of neonatal medicine has created.

The difficulty with the pediatric best interest standard comes from tension between two moral and legal traditions: The Western Liberal rights tradition which protects the rights of individual autonomous, rational agents [45], and the Natural Law or Proportionality tradition, which derives normative claims from empirical psychology, sociology, etc. assessing decisions on *proportionate benefit or burden* [46]. The former supports the freedom of rational agents to make decisions and of the State to ensure equal treatment of minors through *parens patriae.* The latter eschews legal and philosophical abstraction in favour of empirical criteria assessing benefits and burdens. To illustrate this tension, we might imagine an infant born with a prenatal diagnosis of hypoplastic left heart syndrome (HLHS). Forty years ago HLHS was fatal, yet currently complex staged corrective surgery or transplantation has high success rates. In terms of medical best interest, the outcome for infants with HLHS is extraordinary with remarkable survival stories today [47]. Similarly infants born at 23/52 weeks 40 years ago had a 100% mortality whereas today significant survival rates are reported [8, 11, 13, 14, 17]. These examples reflect ongoing debate as to whether parents of such infants should ever have the right to refuse LST and as to what constitutes valid criteria for parental decision-making? [1, 2, 5, 6, 8, 9, 12, 13, 16, 17, 23, 25, 33, 38, 39]

As the burden of having a 23/52 week baby or a baby with HLHS is borne differently by families, does such burden on a family ever qualify as a criterion for medical decision-making? While neonatologists familiar with family-centered care may imagine how it's principles would extend into ethical and legal aspects of practice this is mistaken as family-centered care is an organizational philosophy that institutions should be designed and operated to facilitate the needs of children and families [28, 48]. From the Western Liberal rights perspective, *Parens Patriae* ensures that child health cannot be compromised by family burdens. Proportionality perspectives argue that burden must be justified and offset by the benefit to the patient and in some moral traditions family burden is a consideration [49]. In NICU practice only in exceptional circumstances where burden to both infant and family is deemed excessive would a broader perspective beyond medical best interest be ethically or legally condoned [36, 38, 49].

Models of Ethics Consult Service in NICU

Our bias is that the individual clinical ethicist, appropriately educated and most importantly who has had clinical training and exposure in a variety of settings, is the best model for successful clinical ethics consultation in NICU [36, 37, 50]. In our view the ethicist, in addition to undertaking and documenting the case analysis, should make suggestions about care choices in every case consultation. This is in keeping with HCP and family expectations of other professional consultations in clinical care. Case analysis should include a full medical review of the course to date, clarification of details and concerns with HCPs and family, identification of the underling ethical issues, and recommendations to resolve the problems. Detailed theoretical ethical-philosophical analysis of the issues underlying the case without addressing specific concerns will likely not be helpful and may even frustrate those involved with the infant's care by its detached perspective. Similarly, overly prescriptive consultation, especially when it strays into medical and nursing details of care, can be counterproductive. The ethicist as clarifier of the moral issues involved, as mediator, as educator, is what we see as being the most important role in practice [36, 37, 50]. Over time this approach, within a culture of institutional support, will establish the clinical ethics service as an essential service in support of optimal care for infants and families in NICU. In addition, the incorporation of the ethicist into the day to day operations of the NICU, will provide educational benefits and support to all staff far beyond the specific consultations. This ongoing education should enhance the ability of all staff members to consider the ethical aspects of care inherent in everything that they do within the NICU [36, 40, 51]. Hand in hand with case consultation and review there should be ongoing education of NICU staff by members of the ethics service so as to develop a degree of ethical competence among staff. Regular involvement of the ethicist in clinical and educational rounds in NICU will facilitate the understanding that ethics is essential to good care for all infants and help to avoid the attitude that ethics is only required when there is major conflict.

There are well described models of how a clinical ethics service can be provided to NICU, who provides ethics services and how a clinical ethics service can be established and incorporated into the workings of a tertiary care center [36, 50]. Published descriptions range from a solo clinical ethicist, an ethics committee a blending of both, association with pastoral care, physicians or nurses with special ethics training, PhD philosophers, and lawyers. Expected functions of a clinical ethics service include consultation, mediation, education, an expectation for recommendations about care, policy review and development, clinical ethics research, etc. Clearly the potential for any ethics service to undertake these functions depends on the resources available and the level of institutional support and commitment. We believe that the most essential requirement for a successful clinical ethics service is that it must have strong support from the administration, and from the front line HCPs, especially the physicians, nurses, and allied health professionals that it serves directly. Without explicit promotion and support among HCPs and families, the influence of the ethics service will be marginal at best. To be successful a clinical ethics service must be seen as an essential part of the provision of the highest quality clinical care in perinatology—NICU rather than an optional add-on component. Serious limitation of effectiveness of an ethics service results from lack of support within the organization, from lack of training and expertise of ethicists, and from the difficulty in changing the physician/nurse culture to accept an "outsider's" input

Summary

Hospital staff commonly encounter ethically complex issues in caring for critically ill patients. The ethical complexity relates to the uncertainty of clinical care, major changes in course and likely outcome compared to predictions, and consequent disagreement about priorities in the ongoing plan of care of such patients. Rarely does the broader meaning for staff and family of what is happening to these patient get adequate discussion. We recommend that the staff remain focused on the traditional fiduciary based role of advocate for the patient's best interests as well as taking into account the welfare of the family. While recognizing that this concept of advocacy for patient's best interests is complex in theory and practice, it remains valid for physicians as their focus of care. We recommend involvement of an expert ethics consultation service routinely to assist in identifying the moral issues in complex cases before crises and conflicts arise and to promote ethics as essential to optimal care of patients and their families.

Acknowledgments We thank Carol Nahorniak for manuscript preparation and editorial assistance; and Patrizia Dambrosio in manuscript preparation.

References

1. Nuffield Council on Bioethics (2014) Critical care decisions in fetal and neonatal medicine: ethical issues. England, United Kingdom. http://nuffieldbioethics.org/wp-content/uploads/2014/07/CCD-web-version-22-June-07-updated.pdf. Accessed 21 Oct 2014
2. Cuttini M, The EURONIC Study Group (2001) The European Union collaborative project on ethical decision making in Neonatal Intensive Care (EURONJC): findings from 11 countries. J Clin Ethics 12:290–296
3. Ryan AC, Byrne P, Kuhn S, Tyebkhan J (1993) No resuscitation and withdrawal of therapy in a neonatal and a pediatric intensive care unit in Canada. J Pediatr 123:534–538
4. Fontana MS, Farrell C, Gauvin F, Lacroix J, Janvier A (2013) Modes of death in pediatrics: differences in the ethical approach in neonatal and pediatric patients. J Pediatr 162:1107–1111
5. Verhagen EAA, Janvier A, Leuthner SR, Andrews B, Lagatta J, Bos AF et al (2009) Categorizing neonatal deaths: a cross-cultural study in the United States, Canada, and the Netherlands. J Pediatr 156:33–37
6. McHaffie H, Cuttini M, Brölz-Voit LR, Mousty R, Duguet AM, Wennergren B, Benciolini P (1999) Withholding/withdrawing treatment from neonates: legislation and official guidelines across Europe. J Med Ethics 25:440–446
7. Wilkinson D, Thiele P, Watkins A, De Crespigny L (2012) Fatally flawed? A review and ethical analysis of lethal congenital malformations. BJOG 119:1302–1308
8. Lantos JD, Meadow W. (2009) Variation in treatment of infants born at the borderline of viability. Pediatrics 123:1588–1590
9. Janvier A, Watkins A (2013) Medical interventions for children with trisomy 13 and trisomy 18: what is the value of a short disabled life? Acta Paediatrica 102:1112–1117
10. Breeze AC, Lees CC, Kumar A, Missfelder-Lobos HH, Murdoch EM (2006) Palliative care for prenatally diagnosed lethal fetal abnormalities. Arch Dis Child Fetal Neonatal Ed 92:F56–F58
11. Partridge JC, Martinez AM, Nishida H et al (2005) International comparison of care for very low birth weight infants parents' perceptions of counseling and decision-making. Pediatrics 116:e263–e271
12. Jefferies AL, Kirpalani HM, (2012) Canadian paediatric society, fetus and newborn committee. Management and counseling for anticipated extremely preterm birth. Paediatr Child Health 17:443–444
13. Pignotti MS, Donzelli G (2007) Perinatal care at the threshold of viability: an international comparison of practical guidelines for the treatment of extremely preterm births. Pediatrics 121:e193–e198
14. Janvier A, Barrington KJ, Aziz K, Lantos J (2008) Ethics ain't easy: do we need simple rules for complicated ethical decisions? Acta Paediatr 97:402–406
15. Lee SK, McMillan DD, Ohlsson A et al (2000) Variations in practice and outcomes in the Canadian NICU network: 1996–1997. Pediatrics 106:1070–1079
16. Sauve RS, Robertson C, Etches P, Byrne PJ, Dayer-Zamora V (1998) Before viability: a geographically based outcome study of infants weighing 500 grams or less at birth. Pediatrics 101:438–445
17. Tyson JE, Parikh NA, Langer J, Green C, Higgins RD (2008) National institute of child health and human development neonatal research network. Intensive care for extreme prematurity moving beyond gestational age. N Engl J Med 358:1672–1681
18. Meadow W, Lagatta J, Andrews B et al (2008) Just in time: ethical implications of serial predications of death and morbidity for ventilated premature infants. Pediatrics 121:732–740
19. Croskerry P (2003) The importance of cognitive errors in diagnosis and strategies to minimize them. Acad Med 78:775–780
20. Haward MF, Murphy RO, Lorenz JM (2008) Message framing and perinatal decisions. Pediatrics 122:109–118
21. Hammerman C, Kornbluth E, Lavie 0, Zadka P, Adboulafia Y, Eidelman Al (1997) Decision-making in the critically ill neonate: cultural background versus individual life experiences. J Med Ethics 23:164–169

22. Marcello K, Lampron K, Stefano JL, Barrington KJ, Mackley AB, Janvier A (2011) Who's best interest? The influence of family characteristics on perinatal decision-making. Pediatrics 127:e934–e939
23. Paris JJ, Graham N, Schreiber MD, Goodwin M (2006) Has the emphasis on autonomy gone too far: insights from Dostoevsky on parental decision making in the NICU. Camb Q of Healthc Ethics 15:147–151
24. Berwick D (2009) What 'patient-centered' should mean: confessions of an extremist. Health Affairs—Web Exclusive. Project HOPE—The People-to-People Health Foundation Inc.
25. Bell EF (2007) American academy of pediatrics committee on fetus and newborn; non-initiation or withdrawal of intensive care for high-risk newborns. Pediatrics 119:401–403
26. Hall D, Prochazka A, Fink A (2012) Informed consent for clinical treatment. CMAJ 184:533–540
27. Beauchamp TL, Walters L (2003) The 'four principles' approach. In: Gillon R (ed) Principles of health care ethics. Wiley, New York, pp 3–12
28. Arango P (2011) Family centered care. Acad Pediatr 11:97–99
29. Nicholas D, Hendson L, Reis M (2014) Connection versus disconnection: examining culturally competent care in the neonatal intensive care unit. Soc Work Health Care 53:135–155
30. Berger TM (2010) Decisions in the Gray Zone: evidence-based or culture-based? J Pediatr 156:7–9
31. Pantilat S (2009) Communicating with seriously ill patients: better words to say. JAMA 201:1279–1281
32. Buckman R, Tulsky J, Rodin G (2011) Empathic responses in clinical practice: intuition or tuition? CMAJ 183:569–571
33. Silverman W (2005) Russian roulette in the delivery room. Pediatrics 115:192–193
34. Detsky J, Zlotnik SR (2013) Incentives to increase patient satisfaction: are we doing more harm than good? CMAJ 185:1999–2000
35. Johnson AR, Siegler M, Winslade WJ (1998) Clinical ethics, 4th edn. McGraw-Hill, New York
36. McKneally M, Singer P (2001) Bioethics for clinicians: 25. Teaching bioethics in the clinical setting. CMAJ 164:1163–1167
37. Jordan MC (1998) Ethics manual. 4th edn. American College of Physicians. Ann Intern Med 128:576–594
38. Paris JJ, Schreiber M, Elias-Jones A (2005) Resuscitation of the preterm infant against parental wishes. Arch Dis Child Fetal Neonatal Ed 90:F208–F210
39. Harrison H (2008) The offer they can't refuse: parents and perinatal treatment decisions. Semin Fetal Neonatal Med 13:329–334
40. Lyren A, Ford P (2007) Special considerations for clinical ethics consultation in pediatrics: pediatric care provider as advocate. Clinl Pediatr 46:771–776
41. Saint Thomas Aquinas. Summa Theologica
42. Slovic P, Baruch F, Lichtenstein S (1982) Why study risk perception? Risk Anal 2:83–93
43. Malette vs. Shulman. Ontario court of appeal no. 29–88, March 30, 1990
44. E. (Mrs.) v. Eve. (1986) 2 S.C.R. 388
45. Zwolinski M (2013) Libertarianism. Internet encyclopedia of philosophy. Accessed 2 Nov 2013
46. Hermeren G (2012) The principle of proportionality revisited: interpretations and applications. Med Health Care Philos 15:373–382
47. Batton B (2010) Healing hearts. JAMA 304:1303–1304
48. http//www.ipfcc.org
49. Kaveny C (2002) Conjoined twins and catholic moral analysis: extraordinary means and casuistically consistency Kennedy Inst Ethics J 12:115–140
50. MacRae S, Chidwick P, Berry S, Secker B, Hébert P, Zlotnik Shaul R, Faith K, Singer PA (2005) Clinical bioethics integration, sustainability, and accountability: the Hub and Spokes strategy. JME 31:256–261
51. Chochinov HM (2007) Dignity and the essence of medicine: the A, B, C, and D of dignity conserving care. BMJ 335:184–187

Chapter 19
Communicating Bad News in the Health Care Organization

Olachi J. Mezu-Ndubuisi

> *The most important thing about communication is hearing what is not being said*
> —Peter Drucker

Abstract Communication is the dynamic exchange of information or news either verbally or non-verbally, which can have a profound emotional impact on both the receiver and the deliverer of news, especially if bad news is delivered badly. In the health care industry, communication occurs daily between medical and non-medical staff working to provide efficient and compassionate patient care. Despite the constant need for physicians and other health care professionals to communicate bad news to patients, there is poor emphasis on formal training in effective communication in the training curriculum. There is also a paucity of evidence-based literature on how to have difficult conversations in the work place or how to break bad news to a patient. This chapter reviews a multi-faceted approach to effective communication, and proposes helpful, practical strategies to effective communication in the workplace and during patient care. Efficient communication requires adequate preparation, true self-knowledge and responsibility, consideration and good listening skills from both parties, genuine display of empathy and compassion, conveying positive, hopeful messages during the conversation, individualized information to the specific situation and person, appropriate control of emotions, and efficient plans for support and follow-up after the conversation.

Keywords Bad News · Communication · Compassion · Conflict management · Difficult conversations · Disclosure · Ethics · End of life · Formal communication training · Individualized disclosure · Hope · Healing · Health care organization · Managing oneself · Medical communication · Non-verbal communication · Palliative care · Physician-patient communication · Verbal communication · Words

O. J. Mezu-Ndubuisi (✉)
Departments of Pediatrics and Ophthalmology, School of Medicine and Public Health, University of Wisconsin, 600 Highland Avenue, Clinical Sciences Center—H4/431, Madison, WI 53792, USA
e-mail: olachimezu@pediatrics.wisc.edu

Key Messages

- Effective verbal and non-verbal communication is a vital part of daily interactions in the health care industry between medical, non-medical staff and patients.
- Delivery of bad news should be hopeful, positive and compassionate and individualized based on each unique circumstance and need.
- Bad news delivered ineffectively has profound and long-lasting negative effects on both the deliverer and receiver of bad news.
- Bad news can be communicated peacefully and effectively with specific considerations before, during and after delivery using the "PEACES" technique: (Preparation, Environment, Audience, Compassionate Conversation, Emotional Expression, and Support).
- Effective communication of bad news is a skill that can be learned through disciplined self-knowledge, structured practice, and non-judgmental evaluation.

History and Principles of Communication

Communication is defined as "eliciting", "imparting" or "making known information [1]. Bad news is defined as any information that elicits an undesirable negative emotion from the receiver and may also cause anxiety to the deliverer.

There is power in the use of "words" in communication. The "word" is a basic form of communication, yet is universally and historically viewed as omnipotent, dynamic, and even divine. In the biblical account of creation, life came to being from the power of words, when God said into the void, "Let there be light!" [2]— words that immediately replace the "formless void" with structure, banishing the deep darkness, and there was light [3]. Words can result in peace or strife. The Quran says *"... when you speak, observe justice"* [4]. The Bhagavad Gita, the 700–verse Hindu scripture of philosophical conversations proclaims peace and hope [5]. Words once spoken cannot be recalled, thus their potential for good or for evil is formidable, and uttered words take on a life and power of their own, in themselves and over all else [3].

Communicating Bad News in the Healthcare Setting

Life in organizations is punctuated by bad news [6]. The health care industry is the bee hive of challenging day to day communications between medical and non-medical professionals with diverse interpersonal skills working towards a common goal—delivery of efficient and compassionate patient care. Like in all organizations, bad news in health care includes negative performance feedback, [7] customer service failures, [8] refusal of requests, [9] downsizing, [10] employee layoffs or termination, [11] frequent errors in communications, and systems failure affect global functioning. Effective communication is a necessary core value for health care professionals [12]. Conflicts arise in organizational relationships when expectations are not aligned, and people expect others to be mind-readers.

Communicating Bad News

Communication involves the exchange of verbal and nonverbal messages between individuals. Verbal communication includes traditional face to face meetings, and the new age modes of electronic communication like phone calls, video conferencing, teleconferencing, and voice mails. Non-verbal communication includes emails, instant messaging, blogs, text messages, and the traditional letter writing or memos. Sussman and Sproul in their study comparing modes of news delivery noted that participants were more honest, accurate and satisfied when delivering bad news using computer-mediated communication than telephone or face-to-face communication [13]. Barriers to proper communication include inadequate communication skills, conflicting assumptions, different interpretations of the meanings of words (semantics), emotions, poor listening habits, insufficient feedback, and different interpretations of nonverbal cues [14]. The greatest inhibition to effective communication is one's ego.

Tips (Before Communicating Bad News)
- **Prepare yourself:** Gather your facts and information through objective and reliable means, and know the nature or demeanor of the person you will be communicating with.
- **Prepare the other party:** Psychological preparation or advance warning increases a sense of predictability of the bad news, [6] and can help individuals cope with negative emotions due to the impending bad news [15].
- **Build a relationship:** Trust and respect between the deliverer and the receiver of bad news reduces anxiety for both parties. If there is no prior relationship, the deliverer has to build this relationship early in the conversation.

Tips (During Communication of Bad News)
- **Location and Audience:** A serene and private ambience sets the tone of the conversation. Determine the appropriate audience for the conversation, whether private or key persons involved in case.
- **Have a true conversation:** A true conversation is not monotonous but solicits input or feedback from the receiver. A neutral or light opening statement may help break the ice. Non-verbal cues like posture, demeanor, eye contact, facial expressions, and body language may be more important than verbal cues. Use clear, precise and simplified term, and pause at serious junctures to enable the listener assimilate the news. Steven Covey, the management expert in his seven habits proposes that one should "begin with the end in mind," by determining what the desired outcome would be prior to having a difficult conversation [16].
- **Be simple and sensitive:** Communication should be polite, simple and to the point. Sensitivity to cultural, religious, language or socio-economic differences is crucial.

- **One minute rule:** Wait a minute before sending emotional or angry communication; which though valid at the moment to the sender, may be inappropriate when clarity is attained.
- **Always maintain a positive outlook:** This reduces the trauma of the news and helps the listener accept the news with hope. Use, what I call the "good 3A's" technique in breaking bad news: Acknowledge, Apologize, and Advise. Do not use the "bad 3A's": Avoid, Admonish, Attack.
- **Keep a record or document serious conversations:** Managers create a "paper trail" in the form of reports and documents, [17] As objective evidence about a situation that may lead to bad news [18, 19]. In the clinical setting, medical record documentation helps to keep the medical team abreast of care plans.

Tips (After Communicating Bad News)

- **Be a good listener:** Stone et al notes that difficulty listening during a conversation is from people mentally trying to decipher what really happened, how they or the other party is feeling, and wondering about their identity or what the others are saying about them [20]? Management expert and philosopher, Peter Drucker, famously said "the most important thing about communication is hearing what is not being said" [14].
- **Be prepared for emotions:** Despite a myriad of emotions expressed by the receiver of bad news, such as shock, fear, anger, denial, tears, silence, frustration, apathy or unexpected joy, the deliverer's daunting task is to maintain composure and empathy in validation of the receiver's feelings.
- **Show support and follow-up appropriately:** Respectfully find out the receiver's understanding of what was discussed and present any options to help them adjust to the new situation or move on from it.

Difficult Conversations in the Work Place

- **Use positive messages or statements:** People in management positions have the unpleasant tasks of giving performance evaluations and conveying news of inadequacy or unmet expectations to their sub-ordinates. Employing sensitivity and tact in difficult conversations yields positive reinforcement and mitigates the negative effect of the bad news.
- **Avoid premature judgments:** Premature punitive decisions based on unsubstantiated allegations are a common error in judgment by supervisors when evaluating colleagues, employees, or trainees. A supervisor should not join the bandwagon to admonish or reprimand employees, but rather serve as mediator to enhance understanding, encourage dialogue or reduce conflict. Evaluations should be based on objective evidence and not merely subjective reports. To avoid perception of personal bias, knowledge of personal crisis in an employee's life should never be used in a punitive way. Offer support to staff transitioning back to work. Address any valid concerns gently with the employee, giving suggestions for improvement before re-evaluating.

- **Manage conflicts appropriately:** Conflict management is important for effective functioning of an organization. Address conflicts at the appropriate level first. Escalating conflicts to higher management prematurely may make issues more difficult to control or resolve, [15] or create a hostile work environment. Five popular management strategies are competition, accommodation, avoidance, compromise and collaboration [16]. Competition entails overpowering the opposition during conflict of values or perspectives. Accommodation maintains a good working relationship by validating others' concerns. Avoidance evades conflict in matters of non-urgent importance. Compromise occurs when parties find a mutually acceptable solution is ideal. Fisher and Ury use "principled negotiation" tactic in conflict management, which involves looking for mutual gains when interests conflict based on fair standards [17]. There are two sides to every story, so seek to understand the other person's perspective and acknowledge their feelings before delivering your bad news.
- **Manage yourself:** Self-evaluation and feedback are keys to effective communication. Ericsson illustrates that becoming a good communicator can be learned with commitment and deliberate practice [18]. The sense of responsibility and feedback assessment that comes with managing oneself is vital to personal success and working well in an organization [19]. This feedback process begins with a deeper self-knowledge, and is so elaborately simplified by St. Ignatius of Loyola in his famous contemplative meditations "*Spiritual Exercises*" written in the fifteenth century after a period of self-discovery, discipline, and discernment [20]. It is human nature to expect others to change, but in reality one can only control or change oneself, which can have a profound influence on others [21].
- **Know yourself:** Awareness of one's personality promotes self-evaluation leading to personal responsibility in communication. I have observed three personality types in communication: silent, aggressive or defensive (SAD) communicators. *Silent communicators* may be silent-avoiders who evade uncomfortable conversations; or silent-narcissistic, feeling that certain situations are not worth their time; or silent-proactive, good listeners who carefully analyze information before communicating effectively. *Aggressive communicators* use very intense verbal and nonverbal attitudes and are easily offended. Some people are silent avoiders to prevent tendencies toward aggressive or defensive communication. *Defensive communicators* may not initiate the communication but usually have a rebuttal that is ineffective and unpleasant, though well-intentioned.

Practical Reflections on Difficult Conversations in the Workplace

Reflection #1 The scenario that comes to my mind is a nurse manager that I had to let go due to downsizing and reorganizing of the leadership team. The decision was not easy; I needed to make a decision that was best for the entire division. The skill set needed for the new, larger role was more strategic and I felt the individual was not a good match for that role. I acknowledged her abilities and leadership over the length of her career—giving examples where she shined as a leader. I apologized that I would have to be the person to change her life in a dramatic way, but restated why I needed to make a leadership change. I allowed her time to ask questions, which I answered honestly and gave her time with the HR representative who would discuss her severance options. **-Kathy Kostrivas, RNC, MBA, Asst. VP Women's Services, Meriter Hospital, Madison, WI.**

Reflection #2 Though difficult in large corporations, an employer vicariously stands in loco parentis vis a vis his employee. They are like one family. While I was the chairman of a corporation, an otherwise dutiful, hardworking and loyal employee suddenly starts missing work two or three times in a week and often comes late on other days or leaves early because of tiredness. He apparently had serious medical issues, and could not afford to lose his job with children to support, and a wife whose job could not sustain the family. His frequent absence was injurious to daily operations. As Chairman, I was constrained to invite the employee and his wife to my office for some discussions. After expressing my understanding of their challenges, I granted the employee fully paid leave until he resolved his medical problems with a promise he will be re-engaged when he recovers. They went home happy and relieved. Unfortunately the employee died within two months and the family was very grateful that the company gave him that consideration. **-Dr. S. Okechukwu Mezu, Imo State, Nigeria.**

Breaking Bad News to Patients and Their Families

Physician-Patient Communication: Bad news in clinical care is defined as "any news that drastically and negatively alters the patient's view or expectation of her or his future," [22, 23] or "news that results in a cognitive, behavioral, or emotional deficit in the person receiving the news that persists for some time after the news is received" [24]. Breaking bad news can be stressful and have a long-lasting impact on both the physician and the patient [1, 25]. Recipients remember for a long time details of the news they received, especially if delivered in an uncaring and insensitive manner; [26, 27] and physicians report anxiety for days after delivering bad news [25]. Thorne et al elaborately categorized communication mishaps between healthcare professionals and their patients into three categories, namely *occasional misses*, *systemic misunderstandings*, and *repeat offenders* [28]. **Occasional misses** are where the doctor, though well-meaning, is unable to effectively communicate news, but the patient is forgiving understanding human fallibility. **Systemic misunderstandings** occur when physicians are seen as aloof, brutally frank or emotionally distant, more concerned about liability and professionalism than empathy. **Repeat offenders** are physicians that totally lack insight or interest in proper communication, and seem unwilling or unable to convey basic courtesy, compassion, or respect [28].

Table 19.1 Evidence-based guidelines on how to break bad news

Ask-Tell-Ask Tool [33]	Involves asking what the patient understands (Ask) before telling the news (Tell) and then evaluating what the patient understood (Ask) from the information provided
ABCDE *mnemonic* [52]	Proposes *A*dvance preparation, *B*uild a therapeutic environment/ relationship, *C*ommunicate well, *D*eal with patient and family reactions, *E*ncourage and validate emotions
SPIKES *protocol* [53]	Considers "*S*etting," "*P*erception," "*I*nvitation," "*K*nowledge," "*E*xploration," and "*S*ummary/strategy" during delivering bad news to patients
Nondisclosure, Full Disclosure and Individualized Models [54]	*Nondisclosure* assumes the patient needs to be protected from bad news and physician decides what information to provide. *Full disclosure* upholding the patient's right to full information gives too much detail causing negative emotional experiences. *Individualized disclosure* model believes that people have different coping methods and desires for information and so tailors it to the patient's needs

Evidence-based Guidelines: Despite the increased interest in the physician-patient relationship, there remains a paucity of evidence-based guidelines in literature or a clear set of norms about the best way to break bad news—a few are listed in Table 19.1.

Individualize the Bad News: According to Hippocrates, when communicating, one should "*give necessary orders with cheerfulness and serenity, revealing nothing of the patient's future or present condition*" [29]. This norm has shifted historically in the physician-patient interaction to increased effort to open, honest and full disclosure. Some patients may not like full disclosure of their illness, and physicians are challenged with individualizing the bad news delivery based on the patients' needs and desires [30]. Though more time consuming, the individualized disclosure model is a more effective way of giving clinical information [31].

Hope and Healing In Medical Communication: Healing is making a patient feel better or helping them peacefully accept their diagnosis and prognosis through the preservation of hope and a positive outlook, no matter the gravity of the news. Healing is the wellness of not just the body, but the mind, attitudes and soul. Hope is the prerogative of every patient and should not be taken away [32]. Good communication is more than being a "warm and caring" physician, but the ability to effectively assess patient's understanding, elicit care values and preferences, and encourage participation [33]. Patients appreciate honesty, but also positive, supportive and hopeful statements not merely listing worst case scenarios [34]. Doctors by aligning themselves to their patients can learn to respect and respond to the patient's sense of hope, even though not fully sharing it [23]. "Nothing can be done" statements should be replaced with "everything will be done" attitudes by adopting a cultural shift away from singular, curative biomedicine to seeking resources that help patients embrace living "as well as you can for as long as you can" [35].

Full Disclosure is Vital in Medical Communication: Evading medical disclosure and shifting responsibility can foster negative feelings in patients or families. Saying "I'm sorry," is not an acceptance of guilt or responsibility—it is merely a sharing of empathy and validation of the suffering person's emotions. Hospitals have now established a risk management task force to investigate medical errors or mistakes, and make full disclosure to the families, which has improved accountability of medical staff, patient satisfaction, and reduced medico-legal liability.

Practical Reflections on Breaking Bad News in a Clinical Setting

Reflection # 1 When breaking bad news to a patient, it is important to strike the right balance between providing information and overwhelming a patient with details, by tailoring information to the individual situation. Physicians sometimes feel an obligation to complete a predetermined script and mentally check off boxes as each piece of information is provided. This can leave patients feeling overwhelmed and confused. It is important to realize that many details may need to be repeated later after the initial shock has worn off. The most important aspects of the initial encounter are to make sure the patient feels supported and that there's a clear plan and direction about what the immediate next steps will be, whether it is further testing, hospitalization, or other treatments and when the next contact with the provider will be. **-Amy L Fothergill, MD, Internal Medicine, Associated Physicians, Madison, WI.**

Reflection # 2 Historically, some medical professionals, especially doctors, are seen as aloof, abrupt and lacking empathy. Below are simple ways one can break bad news to patients:

- **Know your patient:** Know a little bit about your patient, especially if they need family around when receiving the news. When possible, break the news in private.
- Your **body language** speaks volumes before you break the news. Maintain a vibe that says, 'I am here for you'.
- **Maintain eye contact** while talking; and sit at the same level so as not to be formidable.
- **Breaking the news:** Be direct, but compassionate. You can say "we did everything we could", concerning loss of a patient. If a hospice patient, you can remind them that it was a peaceful death.
- **Absorption:** Give patients a few moments to understand and assimilate what you have just said.
- **Scientific data:** Some patients would like to see proof of illness—lab results, imaging studies, or treatment options. You could say that "This is obviously a lot to take in now, but I would like you to know that there are some options that we can talk about…" You could have a specialist to provide more information or invite the patient to get a second opinion, if doubtful.

- **Knick Knack:** Have tissue ready at all times. Be calm and collected, enunciate properly, and speak slowly. Always know where the exit is—although this has not been my experience, some patients have been known to be violent, so know when to go for help. **-Ngozi Mezu-Patel, MD Infectious Diseases, Kent General Hospital, Dover, Delaware.**

Reflection 3 It is easy to tell your patients that you see their perspective, but going through the motions of having heard yourself what you have just told them can really open your eyes. It was not until I tried to schedule my life as a dialysis patient that I realized what I had been telling my patients. To integrate 4 hour treatments three times a week opened my eyes to the independence, travel, work, privacy and freedom that were at stake. I now ask my patients about the rest of their lives and what is most important for them. This lets them know that they are seen as more than a disease, and that we are working with them to make their lives work, not just their kidneys. **-R. Allan Jhagroo MD, Division of Nephrology, University of Wisconsin, Madison.**

Communicating News About Serious Illness, End of Life or Palliative Care

Respect Spirituality in End of Life Communication: Death comes to all, yet the fore-warning in medical illness does not seem to allay the fear, shock or uncertainties about prognosis, extent of suffering, and end of life decisions. The best antidote for patients' uncertainties is effective communication [36]. Discussing death may be difficult for physicians due to a sense of personal failure, fear of how the family will react, or personal insecurities about mortality. For clinicians to be thorough and compassionate, their care must extend beyond the physical realm to the spiritual [37, 38]. Some patients want to discuss beliefs about the soul after death with their health care providers [39, 40]. Always offer patients spiritual care according to their religious affiliation, [41] as spiritual beliefs vary with each religious sect. Regardless of religious inclinations or lack thereof, there is a universal belief in love and compassion shared by all human beings, especially when in need of healing of physical or emotional pain.

To Speak or Not to Speak: Sometimes, words are unnecessary in times of grief or delivery of bad news; and a presence, quiet empathy, tears, touch or a hug is equally effective. People express grief in various ways, like apathy, anger, denial, sadness, or a smile. This individual right of expression should be respected, not judged. Understanding and compassion is all patients and families need from their health care providers.

Withdrawal of Life Support is Not a Withdrawal of Care: It can be extremely difficult for families of patients in the intensive care unit (ICU) to cope emotionally as they transition from thinking there may be a cure to, the next time, facing palliative care or imminent death [36, 42]. Although a physician has no obligation to provide futile care, patient care continues compassionately through helping the family cope with the loss. "*Do not resuscitate orders*" must be clear and unambiguous. Withdrawal life support should be done after open and honest discussions with the family and medical team. Health care professionals should provide the highest quality of terminal and palliative care for dying babies just as in adults [43]. Respecting families' end of life wishes, allowing them at the bedside during terminal procedures, providing time to gather other loved ones for support, and compassionate care of the patient and family help bring closure, peace and acceptance to the grieving family, and reassure them that "everything was done".

Ethics of Communication in Perinatal and Neonatal Care: With advances in neonatal and obstetric care, premature infants are surviving at younger gestational ages, bringing a unique set of clinical, moral and ethical challenges. Extremely premature infants have severe neurodevelopmental disability, [44] including cognitive deficits, hearing loss, cerebral palsy, and blindness that can affect them up to adolescence [45] and beyond. The ethical principles of autonomy, beneficence, non-maleficence, and justice, [46] apply to fetuses or infants facing a life-limiting diagnosis as well as their mothers. Caring for infants in neonatal intensive care units requires extraordinary sensitivity, extreme responsibility, and heroic compassion [47]. Physicians should present facts in an honest and unbiased way, avoiding grossly grim or falsely optimistic information. Find out what the family knows, before giving information in simple language devoid of excessive medical jargon, remaining supportive of the family's decision. Parents and medical staff are both advocates in considering the 'best interest' of the child. In complex ethical situations or when conflicts arise between parents' and physicians' desires for the child, a referral should be made to the hospital ethics committee for a formal consensus. Good palliative care entails a systematic multidisciplinary coordination of services to avoid communication breakdowns, [48–50] provide direction for clinicians and appropriate follow-up [51].

-Practical Reflections on Breaking Bad News in Special Situations

Reflection # 1 In a difficult conversation, like when asked by the obstetrics team to counsel a mother at high risk of delivering a premature infant, I first try to understand the medical situation and concerns from the referring physician and the mother's nurse. With the mother, I identify myself and my first question is, "what is your understanding of how things are going?" If there's a good understanding, I focus on high risk areas, clarify the baby's needs, provide relevant statistics on outcomes, and answer any specific questions. When providing information, I try to comment on the likelihood of survival, which is where the greatest fear lies—will my baby survive? If this fear can be allayed, then she more likely will remember the rest of the conversation. I find out if she knows whether the baby is a boy or a girl and the baby's name, as I want our discussion to be about an individual, not simply statistics. I like to end the conversation by asking if she plans to breast feed, giving her the responsibility of asking the nurses for help with pumping after birth. This gives her some control, reinforcing my perspectives of a longer term outcome, and let her know this is something important that only she alone can do to help her baby. **-De-Ann M. Pillers, MD, PhD, Professor and Chief of Neonatology, Department of Pediatrics, University of Wisconsin-Madison.**

Reflection # 2 There is no one good way of breaking bad news to a patient. What is important is the physician-patient relationship. A long term relationship does not necessarily make it easier to speak the bad news, but adds a different atmosphere to the room. At the moment of delivering the news, it is important that the physician stay with the patient and not run off or send in a chaplain. It also helps if family members are present when the news is delivered, in recognition that the news is not just for the individual, but is a family affair. Obviously, there are several levels of bad news and not everything needs to be stated at once. We have to face ourselves as well when we deliver bad news to others. A patient by definition is one who suffers and waits. It is our task to suffer and wait with them in a vicarious and empathic manner. **-Anthony O'Connell, Psy.D., Dip. Psa, Licensed Clinical Psychologist, Chicago, IL.**

Reflection # 3 To the deliverer of bad news, it can be an emotional, regrettable and overwhelming experience. To the recipient, that moment, whether absorbed with a calm, stoic demeanor, uncontrollable tears or more dramatic gestures, changes their life forever. I am very aware of that moment which is irreplaceable. They typically can sense the doom that looms ahead but harbor a slight hope that there might be an alternative. I usually have the loved ones meet in a quiet room, and pastoral services available if needed. I always ask if someone can be with them as bad news can sometimes be better braced by two or more rather than one. "I am so sorry to have to tell you…" I let them know that they did not suffer as that is very comforting to loved ones. I inform them that we did all we could, and I offer a hand, a shoulder, or a hug—whatever they may need. It is a difficult and heart breaking time for both ends, but their journey ahead can only be tougher than mine. **-Ure L. Mezu-Chukwu, MD, Cardiology-Electrophysiology, Georgia.**

Summary

Effective communication using hopeful, positive and compassionate methods is vital to the overall success of the hospital organization. Bad news can be communicated with the **"PEACES" (Preparation, Environment, Audience, Compassionate Conversation, Emotional Expression, and Support)** technique that incorporates effective skills and attitudes, which I believe, emphasizes the hopeful peace both parties should feel after the effective communication, rather than the dreaded pieces of hopelessness after poor communication (Table 19.2).

Table 19.2 Delivering bad news in peaces

Preparation	Advance preparation for both the deliverer and the receiver of bad news is crucial
Environment	Deliver news in quiet, private, and peaceful environment
Audience	Have the appropriate audience for the news.
Compassion	Ensure a compassionate conversation with good listening skills, empathy
Expression	Anticipate and respect expression of emotions from receiver
Support	Indicate and show your support and willingness to follow-up

The art of proper communication, like any craft, requires skills acquisition and training by observing, practicing, sometimes failing and re-learning till mastered, and evaluation of the completed task. Everyone in their lifetime has the privilege of wearing two hats: one of authority in delivering bad news and the other of dependence in receiving bad news. An emotion common to both parties is HOPE—hope for empathy, respect, understanding, acceptance, and a non-judgmental attitude; yet, deliverers of bad news tend to forget the feelings of dependence of being receivers of bad news. A peaceful communication should always be the goal when delivering news, because bad news delivered peacefully reduces the likelihood that bad news will be received badly.

References

1. Dias L, Chabner BA, Lynch TJ Jr, Penson RT (2003) Breaking bad news: a patient's perspective. Oncologist 8:587–596
2. The Bible (1982) The Holy Bible—New King James Version. Thomas Nelson, Nashville
3. Mezu RU (2004) The power of the word (Nommo) in social change in homage to my people. Black Academy, Pikesville, MD: 128–48.
4. Quran T (2012) The Quran. IB publisher, Hicksville
5. Zaehner RC (1996) Hindu scriptures. Goddall, D (Ed). University of California Press, CA.
6. Bies R (2013) Delivery of bad news in organizations: a framework for analysis. J Manage 39:136–162
7. Ilgen D, Davis C (2000) Bearing bad news: reactions to negative performance feedback. Appl Psychology 49:550–565
8. Michel S, Bowen D, Johnston R (2009) Why service recovery fails: tensions among customer, employee, and process perspectives. J Ser Manage 20:253–273
9. Izraeli DM, Jick TD (1986) The art of saying no: linking power to culture. Organ Stud 7:171–192
10. Cascio WF (1993) Downsizing: what do we know? What have we learned? Acad Manage Exec 7:95–104
11. Bennett N, Martin, CL, Bies RJ, Brockner J (1995) Coping with a layoff: a longitudinal study of victims. J Manage 21:1025–1040
12. Schofield NG, Creed F (2008) Communication skills of health-care professionals working in oncology: can they be improved? Eur J Oncol Nurs 12:4–13
13. Sussman SW, Sproull L (1999) Straight talk: delivering bad news through electronic communication. Inf Syst Res 10:150–166
14. Drucker PF (1993) Communication skills: "The most important thing in communication is hearing what isn't said." Management Now 24–47.
15. Lemieux-Charles L (1994) Physicians in healthcare management: managing conflict through negotiation. Can Med J 151:1129–1132
16. Thomas KW (1976) Conflict and conflict management. In: Dunnette MD (ed) Handbook of industrial and organizational psychology. Rand McNally, Chicago, pp 889–935
17. Fisher R, Ury W (1981) Getting to yes: negotiating agreement without giving, 1st ed. Penguin Books, New York.
18. Ericsson K, Anders P, Michael J et al (July-August 2007) The making of an expert. Harv Bus Rev 115–121.
19. Drucker P (2005) Managing oneself (HBR classic). Harva Bus Rev.
20. Ignatius St (2002) The spiritual exercises of St. Ignatious of Loyola. Random House, Toronto
21. Thornby D (2006) Beginning the journey to skilled communication. AACN Adv Crit Care 17:266–271
22. Buckman R (1984) Breaking bad news: why is it still so difficult?. BMJ (Clin Res Ed) 288:1597–1599.
23. Back AL, Arnold RM, Tulsky JA, Baile WF, Fryer-Edwards KA (2003) Teaching communication skills to medical oncology fellows. J Clin Oncol 21:2433–2436
24. Ptacek JT, Eberhardt TL (1996) Breaking bad news. A review of the literature. JAMA 276:496–502
25. Ptacek JT, Ptacek JJ, Ellison NM (2001) "I'm sorry to tell you..." physicians' reports of breaking bad news. J Behav Med 24:205–217
26. Maguire P (1998) Breaking bad news. Eur J Surg Oncol 24:188–191
27. Fallowfield L (1993) Giving sad and bad news. The Lancet 341:476–478
28. Thorne S, Oliffe JL, Stajduhar KI, Valerie Oglov BSW, Kim-Sing C, Hislop TG (2013) Poor communication in cancer care. Cancer Nurs 36:445
29. Hippocrates. Decorum X (1923) Hippocrates with an English translation. Heinemann, London

30. VandeKieft GK (2001) Breaking bad news. Am Fam Physician 64:1975–1978
31. Girgis A, Sanson-Fisher RW (1995) Breaking bad news: consensus guidelines for medical practitioners. J Clin Oncol 13:2449–2456
32. Mezu-Ndubuisi O. (2009) Tips for parents to help survive the journey before, during and after the NICU and improve interaction with NICU staff. http://wwwobiolarosefoundationorg/nicu-survival-tips-for-parents/. Accessed 3 Feb 2014
33. Schell JO, Arnold RM (2012) NephroTalk: communication tools to enhance patient-centered care. Semin Dial 25:611–616
34. Informing Families Project (2007) Informing families of their child's disability. http://wwwinformingfamiliesie/evidence-based-good-practice/sensitive-and-empathetic-communication252html. Accessed 3 Feb 2014
35. Kagan SH (2009) Nothing can be done-a reply to thoughtless prognostic declarations. Geriartr Nurs 30:424–425
36. Kirchhoff KT, Walker L, Hutton A, Spuhler V, Cole BV, Clemmer T (2002) The vortex: families' experiences with death in the intensive care unit. Am J Crit Care 11:200–209
37. Perkins HS, Cortez JD, Hazuda HP (2012) Diversity of patients' beliefs about the soul after death and their importance in end-of-life care. South Med J 105:266–272
38. Daaleman TP, VandeCreek L (2000) Placing religion and spirituality in end-of-life care. JAMA 284:2514–2517
39. Anandarajah G, Hight E (2001) Spirituality and medical practice: using the HOPE questions as a practical tool for spiritual assessment. Am Fam Physician 63:81–89
40. Balboni TA, Vanderwerker LC, Block SD et al (2007) Religiousness and spiritual support among advanced cancer patients and associations with end-of-life treatment preferences and quality of life. J Clin Oncol 25:555–560
41. Barnes S, Gardiner C, Gott M et al (2012) Enhancing patient-professional communication about end-of-life issues in life-limiting conditions: a critical review of the literature. J Pain Symptom Manage 44(6):866–879
42. McAdam JL, Puntillo K (2009) Symptoms experienced by family members of patients in intensive care units. Am J Crit Care 18:200–209; quiz 10
43. Wyatt J (2004) Neonatal ethics. CMF files 27.
44. Tyson JE, Parikh NA, Langer J, Green C, Higgins RD (2008) Intensive care for extreme prematurity-moving beyond gestational age. N Engl J Med 358:1672–1681
45. Hack M, Fanaroff AA (2000) Outcomes of children of extremely low birthweight and gestational age in the 1990s. Semin Neonatol 5:89–106
46. Purdy IB, Wadhwani RT (2006) Embracing bioethics in neonatal intensive care, part II: case histories in neonatal ethics. Neonatal Netw 25:43–53
47. Wanzer S, Federman DD, Adelstein SJ et al (1989) The physician's responsibility towards hopelessly ill patients. N Engl J Med 320:844–849
48. Wool C (2013) State of the science on perinatal palliative care. J Obstet Gynecol Neonatal Nurs 42:372–382
49. Chitty LS, Barnes CA, Berry C (1996) Continuing with pregnancy after a diagnosis of lethal abnormality: experience of five couples and recommendations for management. BMJ 313:478–480
50. Miquel-Verges F, Woods SL, Aucott SW, Boss RD, Sulpar LJ, Donohue PK (2009) Prenatal consultation with a neonatologist for congenital anomalies: parental perceptions. Pediatrics 124:e573–e579
51. Côté-Arsenault D, Denney-Koelsch E (2011) 'My baby is a person': parents' experiences with life-threatening prenatal diagnosis. J Palliat Med 13:1–7
52. Rabow M, McPhee SJ (1999) Beyond breaking bad news: how to help patients who suffer. West J Med 171:260–263
53. Baile WF, Buckman R, Lenzi R, Glober G, Beale EA, Kudelka AP (2000) SPIKES-A six-step protocol for delivering bad news: application to the patient with cancer. Oncologist 5:302–311
54. Donovan K (1990) Breaking bad news. In: Sanson-Fisher R, ed. Interactional skills: doctor/patient relationship. University of New Castle, Newcastle

Chapter 20
Managing Grief and its Consequences at the Workplace

Robert Anderson and Marie-Louise Collins

> *Everyone can master a grief but he that has it*
> —Much Ado About Nothing

Abstract Grief is a normal and personal response to loss that all will inevitably experience at some or various points of life. With increasing emphasis on clinical leadership, clinicians (e.g. doctors, nurses) are expected to handle more and more responsibilities including grief. Clinicians confront and/or experience grief on a scale more intense and more frequently than people may normally encounter in life outside a hospital. Historically doctors and nurses are not well equipped for providing skilled grief management, leadership and support. The failure to observe and address this reality may therefore pose a significant risk to the staff member, the grieving person and the organisation. It is thus incumbent upon management to develop a capacity for responding appropriately when this turbulence descends within the workplace. This chapter attempts to contextualise grief and its consequences within the dynamic of the clinical setting. It highlights the importance of recognising the personal but subtle formative shaping through the grief experiences of both the grieving person and the carer or manager; and summarises some core understandings of grief and loss. It is suggested that good grief management within the clinical context, is both a necessity for organisational risk management and for staff care, with potential to enhance the quality or spirit of the workplace.

Keywords Grief · Complicated · Counselling · Unresolved · Management · Loss · Supporting colleague · Assessment · Response · Bereavement · Tips for health care professionals · Gender · Tolerance of differences

R. Anderson (✉)
Department of Pastoral Care Services, Women & Newborn Health Service, King Edward Hospital for Women, 374 Bagot Road, Subiaco, 6008 City of Perth, WA, Australia
e-mail: robert.anderson@health.wa.gov.au

M.-L. Collins
Department of Pastoral Care Services, Women & Newborn Health Service, King Edward Hospital for Women & Child & Adolescent Health, Service Princess Margaret Hospital for Children Perth, WA, Australia

R. Anderson · M.-L. Collins
Child & Adolescent Health Service, Princess Margaret Hospital for Children, Perth, WA, Australia

© Springer International Publishing Switzerland 2015
S. Patole (ed.), *Management and Leadership – A Guide for Clinical Professionals,*
DOI 10.1007/978-3-319-11526-9_20

Key Points

- Grief is a normal and personal response to loss. People in grief seek and require the sense of belonging and support from peers.
- Grief has much to do with loosening of attachment. It is a process of transition that the clinical leadership needs to understand and tolerate.
- Compassion and development of a healthy resilient and flexible work environment is critical and central to grief care.
- Understanding the relational complexity of role diffusion when moving from management to care of a staff member in grief is important.
- Management should be aware that loss experience(s) may predispose staff to put clients, colleagues and/or themselves at risk, and should take necessary steps to protect them.
- Early recognition of the signs and symptoms is essential for effective management of grief and its consequences.

With increasing emphasis on clinical leadership, health care workers including medical staff, managers, and supervisors are expected to handle more and more responsibilities including grief. They also confront and/or experience grief on a scale more intense and more frequently than people may normally encounter in life outside a hospital. Historically doctors and nurses are not well equipped for providing skilled grief management, leadership and support. The failure to acknowledge and address this issue poses a significant risk to the staff member, the grieving person and the organisation. Effective leadership in the context of grief lies in the awareness, management and/or enablement of processes associated with loss and grief. This chapter briefly discusses the contemporary understanding of grief and its consequences, and suggests guidelines for its effective management at the workplace.

Grief and Loss

Grief may be defined as a response to loss. It is part of a normal process of adjustment to change. A grief response may range from being mild and transient to being intense and prolonged. Loss experiences can accumulate without being fully integrated and unresolved grief may contribute to a response which is seemingly more intense than warranted for a situation.

Grieving is as normal as it is complex. Loss is the shadow side of attachment, the deeper the attachment the greater the loss. Deep attachment however may not necessarily be a 'healthy' or life-giving attachment. It is an exhausting individual journey with no short-cuts. It is a road littered with potholes; a terrain sometimes never travelled before or at least a road less travelled [1]. It involves physical, emotional, psychological and social dimensions of living. Grieving is not a condition to be fixed but an unwelcome journey requiring companions along the way. These companions can be sometimes physically present, other times absent but not disconnected. The most important thing is not to add further regrets or resentments for the person to carry along this difficult road. The task is to provide road maps and nourishment for this journey. This is best achieved by empowering the bereaved person to recognise and mobilise their inner resources and the supports we can place at their disposal.

"If you touch one thing with deep awareness, you touch everything"
—Thich Nhat Hanh [2].

Thich Nhat Hanh speaks of the "Ocean of Peace" within each of us; he distinguishes between "the wave" and "the water" within the ocean. He speaks of the wave as a metaphor of the historical lived experience that each of us are in between being born and dying. The world of waves is the world of ups and downs, hopes and dreams and fears, success and failures, friendships and betrayals, attachment and loss. It is the world informed by the current and received historical context be that familial, cultural, or academic.

Loss will threaten equilibrium in our lives. Grief and loss is usually experienced as a time of intensity. Emotions are often intense and can range widely. It is a time for re-evaluating many things. Freud described grief as an attachment that has been lost and mourning as detachment from one who is loved. Since his initial work other theorists describe grief as stages [3], predictable, identifiable phases [4] to be experienced; and understood as descriptive rather than prescriptive, or a dynamic process of tasks to be achieved [5]. Building upon Freud's earlier work, Bowlby has further explored attachment theory [6] but from a very different perspective. More recently the challenging work of Klass and Silverman [7] has drawn considerable consensus amongst practitioners for their construct of developing successful readjustment to loss through maintaining a continuing bond with the deceased.

Whatever the understandings behind our knowledge of the experience of grief it is always a profoundly personal, a unique and individual experience, and it is always the result of a reflective process. Living the turgid experience that loss causes is, while generic to being human, a universal experience.

Loss usually involves a transition process. The disequilibrium tends to engineer a shift in attachment to beliefs, work practices, relationships, and ways of experiencing the world. The workplace manager and/or colleague is confronted with the task of supporting a staff member going through such a transition while ensuring that risks to staff and patients and case management are minimised.

Understanding the Experience of Grief

Grief is about the human response or reaction to loss, often described as the objective state of having lost someone or something precious. There are many varied experiences of grief not related to death such as loss of a job, role or income; loss of youth, a limb or organ, hopes, dreams, reproductive capacity, identity or body image to name a few.

Bereavement is a term used for the objective state of the individual when the loss is a relational loss through the death of someone close whereas *mourning* describes the outward behaviour and symptoms of someone who has experienced loss. Mourning is a process sometimes culturally defined through cultural or religious practises.

Understanding grief is an evolving study not dissimilar to our evolving understanding of what constitutes biological death. Parkes [8] points out that in recent times more attention has been paid to the context in which grief arises and in particular the nature of the attachments that precede and influence the grief experience. Moving from the traditional concepts based in the psychoanalytical tradition of Freud, various researchers notably Kubler Ross, Parkes, and Bowlby have understood grief as a process of identifiable or recognisable stages/phases aiming for resolution. Resolution is achieved when the grieving individual has emotionally detached from what has been lost and has made new attachments. More recent understandings such as those of Worden [9] who aligns more closely with the early work of Freud define the mourning process as a system of tasks. A significant feature in his more recent work fits with the concepts of Klass, Silverman and others who speak of continuing bonds with the dead, "We now know that people do not decathlete from the dead but find ways to develop 'continuing bonds' with the deceased" [10]. This is an important feature of understanding and very useful in the clinical setting. Klass and Silverman suggest that in understanding the mourning process and supporting the grieving person the essential focus is not about detachment or letting go of the memories of the dead but of continuing bonds with the dead. They suggest that when a person dies the relationship does not die but continues in a different way, a re-location of the relationship. This understanding especially supports recent developed practise surrounding the death of a baby or a child where memory-making such as foot/hand prints, lock of hair; photos and rituals engage symbolically to focus upon the integration of the physical absence through actively supporting the ongoing connections or continuing bonds with the deceased. The use of outward symbols and specific language contribute to keeping the person alive in memory while enabling the grieving person[s] to pick up the threads of life again.

The role of Personal Experiences

Whenever we meet another at depth, especially in the helping relationship, we do not come in a vacuum as a value-free blank canvas. We come with our own lifestory, values, beliefs, assumptions, prejudices and ways of coping with life's pain or grief and unconscious or forgotten learning. If, for example, I have grown up in an emotional desert, deprived of deep nurture, of touch, hugs and affirmation and if my sense of wellbeing derives from being compliant with the needs of others above my own, when meeting a bereaved person my deep seated internal conditioning, unless well understood will most likely become the lens through which the other person's story and pain is filtered. This lens is at least potentially irrelevant, more likely a hindrance, possibly a danger to the wellbeing of the other.

> It is all too easy when listening to some story or issue to transfer our own meanings and emotions onto it, rather than to allow the truth to surface…. If people are not in touch with who they are and what they think important then it is difficult to see how that can know another (Palmer 1088). Their sense and appreciation of others and the issues they face will be clouded and cluttered with debris (2008, 20) [11].

When working with the grieving the greatest gift we bring is, as Kelly says, our reflexive self. this is the self I have reflected upon and with whom I have learned to relate gently and with compassion.

Sitting alongside the grief stricken there are no magic words to offer. There is no script to read, no prayer, no ritual or repository of wisdom that will lessen the pain of neither that moment nor the hours, days, weeks and years that will follow for that person whose life has intrinsically and explicitly changed. When establishing a supporting relationship in the context of another's grief the following three criteria are essential.

1. A realistic self knowledge: One's own vulnerabilities, life grief's and losses, fragilities and emotionally wounding experiences will be confronted from time to time, sometimes unrecognised until the moment. A realistic assessment of ones strengths and limitations, ones own narrative of social and familial conditioning and philosophy of life that includes the inevitability of death is an invaluable strength that will avoid transference of another's pain or unhealthy self expectations.
2. Understanding role differentiation, relational shifts and impact upon the interpersonal dynamics of the environment that such support of a bereaved staff member may require or initiate.
3. Some basic knowledge about the phenomenon of grief in order to appropriately respond and build a level of competence and comfort for working with the bereaved.

Supporting a Grieving Colleague

Health care workers may particularly find it difficult to support a grieving colleague or the patient's family members as they are trained in science and/or administration yet grief support is essentially a relational skill. Not having a tangible, immediate and effective "cure" may incur a feeling of frustration, helplessness or of having failed. The inability and undesirability of making a person feel better or happier may invoke feelings of powerlessness contrary to the aims of the medical profession. The grieving person's family may likewise have expectations that the doctor or nurse is the expert and will "cure" or quickly resolve the family member's grief. Consequently the person's family may expect that the medical staff's intervention will also resolve their anxiety and emotional pain felt in relation to their loved one. Healthcare professionals are often ill-equipped to manage such expectations and some emerging research is currently focussing on the vulnerability and suffering of health care professionals.

We come with self-inflicted pains
Of broken trust and chosen wrong,
Half free, half bound by inner chains [12]

When a colleague or staff member indicates by a certain manner that all is not well (e.g. a change in behaviour, work capacity or ethic), a tentative approach is usually necessary to negotiate the pain barrier and establish trust. It does not matter whether that barrier is of self-inflicted pain, broken trust, chosen wrong or any other cause; the truth is that we all carry a protective shield which needs to be negotiated.

To establish rapport means that we are attempting to connect with the other's desire for relationship and core of peace while containing the emotional swirl of current pain. A primary task of the one seeking to exercise empathy is to contain their own personal dissonance and quieten themselves. This may require the exercise of assigning immediate work concerns and personal worries/ excitements to an internal place where they will not be forgotten but can reside such that the colleague who is hurting can have full, unbiased, non-judgemental attention.

The one who may respond to the offer of personal hospitality will discern whether or not the offer is safe and trustworthy. This is a very important process for it is a decision which will relate to the present moment; it will be taken in the context of the culture of the employing institution and in the context of a pre-existing relationship. In any institution there needs to be a balance between maintaining a position of power and authority within the structure and exposing one's personal vulnerability.

An encounter grounded in empathy will require the exercise of courage by both parties. To engage personal concerns in the workplace introduces another dimension of potential concern or conflict. It is important for each party to discuss the impact of an expression of current concern on each person and how it resonates with the way the workplace operates. This is a vital negotiation to undertake as the risk of real and/or experienced betrayal is potentially extremely damaging.

Risk management is multi-focussed and involves keeping patients/clients safe, maintaining workflow, protecting self as supervisor/colleague and protecting the one who is experiencing loss. Retention of role and working within its boundaries even while exercising empathy is important for safety. A supervisory role that needs to alternate between administrative and technical concerns and empathic engagement is dependent upon clarity around role for safety. The one seeking to establish empathy must be very clear as to why they wish to do this and would need to disclose this to the staff member occupying a junior position. For example: *"I observe that in the first three months of your placement you have been very enthusiastic and your work of high quality particularly in regards to (very explicit); in the last fortnight I notice a drop in your enthusiasm and when (explicit incident) happened and I am wondering if there is something here in the workplace that is contributing to this apparent change or if you have private concerns that may be impacting your work.*"

It is probably most useful to be able to negotiate how the workplace can accommodate with some flexibility the needs of a staff member who is engaging a process of loss. In summary, line management versus a humble desire for the wellbeing of a work colleague.

Tips for Health Care Professionals, Managers, Supervisors

Health care professionals are not expected to be experts in the field of grief care but they must have the basic knowledge and confidence as to what is appropriate grief care for those who are experiencing significant loss. Historically the medical/paramedical teaching institutions have viewed loss and grief education as an area for specialists such as psychologists and chaplains. A recent review of health profession courses (6 universities in Australia) requiring grief education has reported that only one course provided a unit dedicated to grief and loss [13]. The consequences of this being many health care professionals andmanagers feel inadequate to support those who are grieving [14]. Unless managers are equipped to alter a clinical culture that assumes grief care to be a specialist area of chaplains, social workers or psychologists staff stress will be increased through feelings of inadequacy when working with families experiencing the death or potential death of a patient. Subsequently they will not be empowered to adequately support patients, their families and importantly their colleagues experiencing grief [15].

Grief is a normal response to loss and bereavement is the lived experience of a loss. It is important to normalise grief and unless specific complications exist the essential task is to support what is occurring.

When working alongside people who are grieving we also bring our own experiences of loss and grief. These experiences or patterns may not necessarily be of healthy grieving. The relationship may therefore include theirs and our own morbidity. Recognition of the boundary between our own inner fears of incompetency, personal identity and professional identity becomes very important. It is not unusual for a grieving person to inadvertently remind the carer of someone familiar in their own experience, either through personal mannerisms, visual presentation, tone of voice, language or gestures. This can be quite off-putting and require careful self assessment of responses, reminding oneself that this person is not the person of ones previous experience and not to transfer the feelings associated with the uncomfortable of similarity into a basis of response.

Assessment Grieving is complex, it includes physical, spiritual, emotional and social dimensions. Assessment includes aspects such as what is this grief about; what or who has been lost or what language or descriptors are being used to describe it? Is there a religious or symbolic language used and what is its focus? Has the person had any previous losses? Who are the key persons involved; does the person have a strong, weak or non existent social support; what internal resources does the person demonstrate? What does this indicate for the focus of care? What body language is observed, and what might this suggest? If there are others present, what are they saying about the deceased or the person being supported or the relational dynamics occurring?

Response It is critical not to have a pre-conceived expectation of how the person[s] will act. It is more likely that a staff member will be withdrawn or teary even distraught at times. The initial breaking of bad news may exert a very wide range of response. This may initially be physical such as shouting, screaming or hitting a wall. This can be very disconcerting, even confrontational but discern whether the aggression is directed towards yourself or an inanimate object. According to Kast [16] referring to Parkes and Bowlby [17] anger follows a break out of numbness and corresponds to the personality of the mourner and is accompanied with corresponding phases of deep dejection. In addition it seems to be channelled either towards doctors or to relatives who are perceived not to have done the right thing. This explains a not unusual experience when working with the grieving in the clinical context. When confronted with an angry response only intervene or react to it if the person, you or others are at risk. Remember that grief is a very dynamic process containing a very broad range of feelings, often conflicting. Acknowledge the contradictory nature of the experience including those of denial, anger, shock, blame or sadness. Don't seek to give explanations or answers but affirm the normality of this. Remember the experience is both continual and a continuum in which people will move up and down. Some may withdraw and become isolated. While it is quite appropriate for people to want to withdraw and be alone in their grief, becoming isolated is not healthy. This is where a colleague, friend or manager, observing this may look for an appropriate way to circumvent it. Others lacking self confidence and social or personal supports may become overly dependant. While encouraging people to ask for what they want is useful and recognises their own strength, it requires careful management of boundaries by emphasising and practising carefully defined lines of support.

Gender and Tolerance of Difference Male and female relationships are complex and sometimes severely tested through a loss experience. Gender differences in grieving are well documented [18] but differences also exist through the maturity of the relationship. Relationships that are tolerant of difference are usually less brittle, less disengaged, more fluid and consequently more resilient. These will cope better than those relationships with less tolerance of difference. For many couples the experience or integration of grief follows very different patterns that can in part be described as opposite experiences. For example she needs to talk about the loss, continually go over it, try to recall every little detail while he may feel uncomfortable about this and want to look forwards and not backwards. In the clinical environment a female staff member may be feeling very isolated and lonely in her grief due to her internalising or processing the experience very differently to her partner. He may be also feeling very isolated in his workplace due to a lack of recognition that he has submerged his grief in order to support his partner through taking on a protector role. He could also be embarrassed to express his feelings, often fearing that he may not be able to control his tears. Men may tend to grieve alone, are often uncomfortable expressing their pain to their partner but may do so with a woman with whom there is no relationship except possibly a working relationship.

In order to work effectively with the grieving, health professionals need not only an adequate knowledge base and skill level, but also the ability to recognise the limits of ones comfort zone, and give the unspoken message, a commitment, to the bereaved that right now I do not want to be anywhere else than here to support you as a colleague.

Complicated Grief or Complicated Lives?

It has been said that there is no such thing as complicated grief, only complicated people! Clinical experience and the evidence leave little doubt about the truth of the proposition that much psychiatric illness is an expression of pathological mourning.

In order to understand attributes of complicated or abnormal grief, chronic sorrow or delayed grief it is important to clarify what is understood as normal grief. Worden [19] categorises normal grief under four general categories, feelings, physical sensations, cognition and behaviours. Complicated grief is more difficult to define and the literature does not show consensus. It is reasonable to define normal or functional grief being raw, intense and varied in response especially in the initial period, but no single response or behaviour lasts. The carer is thus required to have very broad boundaries of acceptance of a variety of behaviours especially in the initial phase. Complicated or abnormal grief is different in that a person becomes stuck and beliefs or behaviours persist instead of being transient. It may present as being boundless and overwhelming with no predictable end, a self perception of overwhelming sadness representing life's disappointments and fears. It is mostly cyclic, sometimes intensifying progressively over time and can be triggered by internal or external stimuli. Factors of past history, previous losses, life circumstances, attachment as investment in the meanings of the loss such as loss of a pregnancy or of person who has died may trigger these reactions. Psychologically unhealthy religious beliefs, domestic violence, substance abuse or cultural complexities may contribute to complicated grief. Specialised and prolonged treatment may be required to avoid deeper or ongoing damage, family breakup or psychological or psychiatric illness when a person becomes stuck in their experience. The essential task of most health professionals and managers is to be able to recognise complicated grief and provide the resources for the person to address it.

Key Points to Remember When Working With the Bereaved

1. Listen deeply, develop empathy, ask questions, don't assume anything, or say that you know what the other is enduring, that is unless you have been in their shoes, even then be careful not to overshadow the conversation with your own experience.
2. Wherever possible be prepared to provide a continuity of care over a long period of time. Grief is more like a journey than a moment or particular time.
3. Do not try to give existential answers or a rational reason for what has occurred, most times it is unreasonable and does not make sense and may not fit with the presumed pattern of life or notions of justice or fairness. Put differently, do not deny what has occurred.
4. There is no urgency, if necessary slow it down, for the grieving person it may be that things are going too fast, there is no urgency. You will make mistakes or sometimes say the wrong thing. While the bereaved are usually very emotionally brittle especially in the early days or weeks of bereavement they will forgive you if they also experience your care, warmth and empathy. In the words of Shakespeare *"Everyone can master a grief but he that has it"*. *(Much Ado About Nothing)*

Summary

Providing good grief care at the workplace is not easy for clinicians and managers who are trained and steeped either either within the scientific world of medicine or administration. The challenge is twofold. Firstly to enter the relational world of human dynamics and through this to develop best practise bereavement care for staff members. The imperative for undertaking this will in part be a strategy of risk management or harm prevention so that a grieving or distressed staff member does not put the patient, themselves or the organisation at risk; the second imperative will be a change in the organisational culture towards the provision of a more flexible, assured, professional and appropriately compassionate workplace. Providing a flexible and negotiated structure while allowing a colleague to transition through their experience of loss and grief involves taking a different type of risk. It requires a management approach based on trust, compassion and on the ability to negotiate different working parameters. The internal horizons of either party will shift and decisions may be made that involve separation. The rewards will be in terms of risk reduction, loyalty, re-investment in the workplace and/or profession. The culture of the workplace will be challenged towards change if a compassionate approach to loss is consciously engaged. We believe that such a change may be more a necessity than an option.

References

1. Scott Peck M (1978) The road less travelled. Touchstone, New York
2. Thich Nhat Hanh Maintaining emotional wellbeing in the intensive care unit: A grounded theory study from the perspective of experienced nurses. Siffleet, J. Unpublished Masters Thesis Curtin University 2011
3. Kubler Ross E (1969) On death and dying, MacMillan, New York (Parkes M Bereavement: studies of grief in adult life. Pelican, London 1978)
4. Rando T (1993) How to go on living when someone you love dies. Lexington Books, Lexington
5. Worden WJ (2009) Grief counselling and grief therapy—a handbook for the mental health practitioner. 4th edn. Springer, New York
6. Bowlby J (1983) Attachment and loss, vol. 1, 2nd edn. Basic Books, New York
7. Klass D, Silverman PR, Nickman SL (1996) Continuing bonds: New understandings of grief (Death education, aging and health care). Routledge, New York
8. Parkes CM (2002) Grief: lessons from the past, visions for the future. Death Stud 26:367–85
9. Worden WJ (2009) Grief counselling and grief therapy—a handbook for the mental health practitioner, 4th edn. Springer, New York
10. Klass D, Silverman PR, Nickman SL Worden WJ. (2009) Grief counselling and grief therapy, a handbook for the mental health practitioner, 4th edn. Springer, New York, pp 39–56
11. Palmer 1998 The courage to Teach: Exploring the Inner Landscape of a Teachers Life. San Fransisco: CA: Jossey-Bass in Kelly E (2012) Personhood and presence, self as a resource for spiritual and pastoral care. T & T Clark Int, New York p7
12. Wren B (2005), p 484 [Contemporary hymn writer] in Kelly E (2012) Personhood and presence, self as a resource for spiritual and pastoral care. T & T Clark Int, New York
13. Breen LJ, Fernandez M, O'Connor M, Pember AJ (2012–2013)The preparation of graduate health professionals for working with bereaved clients: an Australian perspective. Omega (Westport) 66:313–32
14. Charles-Edwards D (2009) Empowering people at work in the face of death and bereavement. Death Stud 33:420–36.
15. Dunkel J, Eisendrath S (1986) Families in the intensive care unit: their effect on staff. Ann Emerg Med 15:54–57
16. Kast Verena (1988) A time to mourn, growing through the grief process. Diamon Verlag, Switzerland (Am Klosterplatz, CH-8840 Einsiedeln)
17. Bowlby J (1980) Loss, sadness and depression. Hogarth Press, London
18. Overbeck B She cries, he sighs. Publications for transition loss and change. TLC Group. Griefnet Library, PO Box 28551 Dallas TX 75228
19. Worden WJ Grief counselling and grief therapy. A Handbook for the mental health practitioner, 3rd edn. p 35–39

Index